SARA AND ELEANOR

Also by Jan Pottker

Janet and Jackie:

The Story of a Mother and Her Daughter,

Jacqueline Kennedy Onassis

SARA AND

ELEANOR

The Story of Sara Delano Roosevelt
and Her Daughter-in-Law,
Eleanor Roosevelt

JAN POTTKER

ST. MARTIN'S PRESS
NEW YORK

To my younger daughter,

Carrie Gene Pottker-Fishel

www.stmartins.com

Design by Kathryn Parise

LIBRARY OF CONGRESS CATALOGING-IN-PUBLICATION DATA

Pottker, Janice.
    Sara and Eleanor : the story of Sara Delano Roosevelt and her daughter-in-law, Eleanor Roosevelt / Jan Pottker.—1st U.S. ed.
        p. cm.
    Includes bibliographical references (p. 347) and index (p. 395).
    ISBN 0-312-30340-8
    1. Roosevelt, Sara Delano, 1854–1941.   2. Mothers of presidents—United States—Biography.   3. Mothers of presidents—United States—Family relationships.   4. Mothers-in-law—United States—Biography.   5. Roosevelt, Eleanor, 1884–1962.   6. Presidents' spouses—United States—Biography. 7. Presidents' spouses—United States—Family relationships.   8. Daughters-in-law—United States—Biography.   I. Title.

E807.1.R56P67 2004
973.9'092—dc22
[B]

                                                            2003058792

First Edition: March 2004

10   9   8   7   6   5   4   3   2   1

CONTENTS

PROLOGUE

Perhaps the pivotal image of the twentieth century is that of Franklin Delano Roosevelt on December 8, 1941. He is signing the declaration of war against Japan, having just talked to the nation and to the larger world about the events of December 7, a date that would live in infamy.

The president is wearing a black band of mourning on his left arm. The black band was not originally donned in honor of those lost at Pearl Harbor; he has been in mourning for his mother, Sara Delano Roosevelt, who died three months earlier.

The misinterpreted mourning band is symbolic of the unacknowledged role Sara Delano Roosevelt played in the lives of her son and her daughter-in-law, Eleanor. Though she was the couple's greatest influence, Sara's full story has never been told, despite the myriad books and best-selling biographies of Eleanor and Franklin Delano Roosevelt.

This seminal figure—Sara Delano Roosevelt—has been swept aside: ignored, dismissed, and criticized. We think we know Eleanor's story, the one about the shy, awkward colt who marries the good-looking, confident young man. She and her husband work tirelessly during the next decades—he leading the nation out of its most devastating depression and securing freedom during the world war, and she veering a little to his left by making civil rights, humanism, and world peace her mission.

However, this story needs an antagonist, and in the tale that its tellers have wrought, that role has been played for nearly half a century by Sara. She is the woman we think we know: the one who tightly holds the family's purse strings, the one who tells her son and his wife what to do and how to do it, the one who makes Eleanor weep in despair, the one who would have kept her son out of politics—he, who restored our nation to prosperity and kept it safe from the horrors in Europe. Moreover, as the folk tale goes, Sara would have kept Eleanor at home and away from the causes that drew her into the world, thus washing away many of the social justice gains of the past half-century.

Virtually all recent accounts of Sara Delano Roosevelt vilify her. It was not always so: during Sara's lifetime she was praised and admired to the point of being revered by an entire nation. From the 1920s, when her son became a public figure, through the 1940s—even past her death and that of her son—Sara was one of America's most beloved women. It was not until the 1950s that her image took a sharp turn. Then, as her great-granddaughter Eleanor Roosevelt (Ellie) Seagraves has said, "All she has been given in return for all she did is a reputation of an ogre. It is unfair."

Perhaps some of the disdain heaped on Sara has been due to a bias against women of her time and class. Her great-grandson Curtis Roosevelt pointed out that "unquestionably, Sara Delano Roosevelt did represent a class background. She had all those things in place. Eleanor Roosevelt was very much against the class system."

The two women's relationship spanned a rift in American social history: the old order versus the new, the changing role of women in family and society, the evolving treatment of religious and racial minorities, and the breaking down of class distinctions. Eleanor led the charge into the modern world, and contrary to what has been reported, Sara at times was right behind—or sometimes ahead of—her. Those differences that they did have mirrored the shifting tides in their world.

It was typically Eleanor who urged Franklin to be a catalyst for change. But it was Sara who had given Franklin the supreme self-confidence (that she, too, possessed in abundance) to guide and lead and to implement the ideas he thought important, no matter how loud the criticism. It was his and Sara's glorious courage that spread throughout the nation when optimism was what was needed. Sara's granddaughter Anna Roosevelt Halsted has bluntly said of her grandmother's position in the Depression-era nation: "She helped save it. I don't think anyone's given credit to Granny—the credit she really is due."

Sara played an additional part in this story: her solid values and firm grounding in tradition gave Americans—especially Franklin's greatest critics, those among the 40 percent who opposed him in his first presidential election—the reassurance that Franklin would not go too far. Why else did Franklin insist on having Sara at his side during his first Fireside Chat? Sara's constant presence in Franklin's life calmed fears and tempered upper- and middle-class opposition to Franklin's new programs. At the same time, she served as a cautionary brake on both Eleanor and Franklin as they raced ahead to fix what they felt was wrong.

The same strength and self-confidence that Sara had inculcated in Franklin, she imbued in Eleanor through example. Although Eleanor's determination was in large part forged through her own character, Eleanor was constantly in the presence of two strong personalities, her husband's and her mother-in-law's. Sara was Eleanor's greatest female influence from her marriage at age twenty to her emergence as a public figure when she became First Lady at forty-nine. With Sara as a nearly constant presence, Eleanor became more tenacious as she grew older. By middle age, Eleanor was no longer the shy wallflower she had been when she first entered Sara's world; rather, she persisted in spite of the most voracious criticism faced by any First Lady, displaying the same resolve as her husband did regardless of national faultfinding.

This is the story that no one knows. What lingers in our minds is the image of an overbearing and dominating mother-in-law who reduced the nation's beloved Eleanor to tears. What we remember are the sanctioned histories such as the biased film shown at Sara's own Campobello Island that refers to her governing her son with "smothering dictatorial love." Nor did it help that Eleanor reinterpreted her own life after Sara's and Franklin's deaths, presenting a picture of her early marriage that her own letters and diaries do not substantiate. In fact, Eleanor's early writings firmly contradict her later portrait of the daughter-and-mother-in-law relationship.

Still, any statements of Eleanor's that are critical of Sara have been picked up, copied, reiterated, and regurgitated by Eleanor's writer friends and biographers. As Eleanor's son Elliott Roosevelt stated, "Joe Lash and most of the other biographers whom I have read have missed the boat completely on Mother. Completely." Although these writers give a quick nod to Sara's foundational role in shaping Franklin's character, they ignore Sara's unwavering support of Eleanor in her critical years as a young wife and mother. Rather than criticizing Franklin's inability to brace up his shaky wife—and, perhaps, his lack of interest in doing so—it is Sara who gets the heat. In this period, Eleanor treasured Sara as her surrogate mother and drew strength from her, strength that Eleanor eventually used to surpass her mother-in-law's accomplishments and, indeed, the achievements of all other American women of her generation. Here is the real story of the relationship between Sara Delano Roosevelt and her daughter-in-law, Eleanor Roosevelt.

I

"French by Ancestry, Dutch by Birth, and English by Association"

Much of what Sara Delano Roosevelt would come to stand for was determined long before she was born. Her lineage could be traced back to the old Huguenot, Puritan, and Pilgrim settlers, and both her family and that of her husband, James Roosevelt, were firmly rooted in America's history. In Sara's case, her blue blood derived from those who sailed to this new land to escape religious persecution.

Well before Sara Delano's birth in 1854, two great Hudson River families—the Delanos and the Roosevelts—had established themselves on opposite sides of the river. Sara's family, the Delanos, was on the west. There were no mysterious antecedents in this stock. The Delanos were the descendants of Philippe de Lannoy, a Dutchman of French Protestant ancestry: a Huguenot whose prosperous parents—Jean and Marie Mahieu de Lannoy—had left Lille, France, to escape Catholic persecution. About 1600 the de Lannoys arrived in Leyden, Holland.

Philippe was born in Leyden in 1602. His mother was a friend to neighboring Puritans who had, in 1609, similarly left their homeland—in this case, England—to escape religious oppression. In fact, Marie, whose husband died when Philippe was a toddler, had established twelve houses in Leyden for religious refugees, primarily English. One family she sheltered was the Mullinses, whose daughter Priscilla was celebrated in Longfellow's poem "The Courtship of Miles Standish" 250 years later.

However, even in the relative safety of Holland, the Puritans feared that Dutch culture would subsume their children and that their sons would be plucked away to fight in a Dutch war against Spain. As a result, William Bradford, a friend of the de Lannoys, organized his fellow Puritans (including the Mullins family) to depart Leyden for the New World on the ship *Mayflower*. They set sail for Virginia but in 1620 landed instead in Plymouth, in what would become Massachusetts.

The adventure of the new colony appealed to the teenage Philippe. Envying those who had sailed on the *Mayflower*, within the year Philippe cast his lot with the Pilgrims by leaving Holland for America. His ship was the *Fortune*, the first vessel to arrive in Plymouth Colony since the successful trip of the *Mayflower* eleven months earlier.

Plymouth records cite the first words the *Fortune* voyagers heard in the New World in 1621. "Sail, ho!" shouted the sentry from his post on Fort Hill. Captain Miles Standish was standing ready: fearing "buccaneers— French, Spanish or Turks," he aimed cannon and musket volleys at the *Fortune*, which, in keeping with her name, survived the firepower long enough to declare herself friend. Amidst this hostile tumult, nineteen-year-old Philippe arrived in the New World—the first French Huguenot to step on American soil.

Friendly fire was not all that the *Fortune* passengers had to fear. The Indian chief Canonicus quickly learned of the ship's arrival; his gift to the thirty-five new settlers was a prophetic bundle of arrows tied in snakeskin. William Bradford, now governor of Plymouth Colony, returned this omen of war—but only after restuffing the snakeskin with bullets and powder.

Soon after Philippe's arrival, Priscilla Mullins wrote back to Holland, "I were glad indeed to see all my friends of the house of de la Noye coming hither in the next ship." Philippe moved into the residence of his uncle, Francis Cooke, and his cousin, John Cooke, who had arrived on the *Mayflower*. He received one acre of land from the colony and then, as legend has it, sought the hand of the much-desired Priscilla. He was allegedly spurned on the very same day that she turned down a proposal from Captain Miles Standish that was delivered by John Alden—the man she loved—and "said, in a tremulous voice, 'Why don't you speak for yourself, John?'" the episode later celebrated by Longfellow's poem.

Philippe was as much a part of the Pilgrim community as any Englishman but formally asked for admission in 1633. After proving "himself to be come of such parents as were in full communion with the French [Protestant] churches," he was admitted first to the church of Plymouth and then to that of Duxbury, Massachusetts. Philippe was, as descendant Jonathan DeLeno said, "French by ancestry, Dutch by birth, and English by association."

In 1634 he married Hester Dewsbury in the bucolic Duxbury church. However, the peaceful church scene belied the dangers of the surrounding land. Three years after his marriage, Philippe—now Major de Lannoy—fought in the Pequot War of 1636–38, the colonial land's first skirmish between the Pequot Indians of Connecticut and the Puritans. He served under Captain Standish. For his service, Philippe was rewarded with forty acres of land that happened to abut the farm of John and Priscilla Alden.

Philippe also served the colony as a surveyor. A record of the era calls him "a man of much respectability"; other listings detail his conscientious tax payments and jury duty. After the death of his wife, Hester, Philippe married the widow Mary Pontus Glass, who years earlier had been chosen by Governor Bradford to preside as hostess at the first Thanksgiving dinner.

Philippe had four daughters and five sons by his two wives. The second generation of de Lannoys compressed their surname to Delano. The first son to bear the new family name was Philip Jr. (Note also the anglicized spelling of his given name.)

Philippe's second son, Thomas, would grow up to marry Mary Alden, Priscilla's daughter, in the nation's first recorded shotgun wedding. According to Plymouth Colony court records of October 30, 1667, Thomas was fined ten pounds "for having carnall copulation with his now wife before marriage." The judge who meted out punishment was none other than John Alden, Thomas's father-in-law and neighbor. After Thomas paid his fine, the couple, with their newborn son, moved straightaway to West Duxbury.

The other sons of Philippe were John, Samuel (who married the granddaughter of Captain Miles Standish), and Jonathan (a colonial army lieutenant). The girls were Mary, Hester, Jane, and Deborah. They were becoming New Englanders, and like their father, Philippe—who died in 1681 at the venerable age of seventy-nine—their interest in European affairs centered on how those affairs affected the colonies.

Of Philippe's nine children, Jonathan Delano—not the "carnall" Thomas—is the son to whom Sara traced her ancestry. Jonathan was born in Duxbury in 1647 or 1648. His father was among the thirty-four colonists who, in 1652, purchased Dartmouth (in what is now Massachusetts) from the Wampanoag sachem Massasoit and his son Wamsutta. (Dartmouth originally comprised what is now Fairhaven, New Bedford, Westport, and Acushnet in Massachusetts, and part of Tiverton, in Rhode Island.) Philippe gave his share of eight hundred acres to Jonathan, who married Mercy Warren in 1678. She was the granddaughter of the *Mayflower* passenger

Richard Warren, who had left the ship, as it approached the New World, on a small boat to select the landing place, which he named Plymouth Rock.

Jonathan and Mercy lived in perilous times. King Philip's War had cost the young colony nearly a thousand lives, and the French and their Indian allies had left in their wake thirteen destroyed towns. After this devastation, Jonathan Delano was one of eighteen colonists and twenty-two allied Indians who banded together successfully to slay the Wampanoag chief called King Philip and defeat his troops. In 1689 Jonathan was rewarded with the rank of lieutenant and was elected a deputy from Dartmouth to Plymouth Court.

He also held the titles of surveyor, constable, and selectman. He and Mercy had thirteen children, nine of whom survived childhood. (One of their sons would be the great-great-grandfather of Ulysses S. Grant.) In 1704 Mercy Warren Delano gave birth to a son named after Jonathan's errant brother Thomas. When the younger Thomas was twenty-three, he married Jean Peckham.

Thomas and Jean's son Ephraim was born in Dartmouth in 1733. Ephraim was the fourth generation of Delanos in America and the first of several generations of seafaring Delanos, an inevitable consequence of being born near the ocean. Ephraim purchased part of the waterfront tract of what became the village of Fairhaven, a southeastern Massachusetts coastal town along Buzzards Bay, across the Acushnet River from the New Bedford seaport. Captain Ephraim Delano married twenty-one-year-old Elizabeth Cushman in 1760. Their families had known one another for more than 150 years: Elizabeth's great-great-grandfather Robert Cushman had been a Puritan neighbor of Philippe de Lannoy's parents in Holland. Before the Puritans had emigrated to the New World, they had sent Robert Cushman to obtain from the Virginia Company a land grant that would also convey toleration for their religion. After Cushman's successful mission, he selected the ship *Mayflower* for their voyage. He was ill when she set sail and stayed behind in charge of the Puritans who remained in Leyden. He sailed a year later on the *Fortune* with Philippe de Lannoy.

Captain Ephraim left the sea to serve as a private in the Revolutionary War. In 1779 his son Warren was born in a house on Main Street in Fairhaven. Warren, a fifth-generation American, was the first Delano born after independence. Warren went to sea in 1797, shipping out on a freighter around the Horn to China at age eighteen.

In 1808, at twenty-nine, Warren Delano married Deborah Church of *Mayflower* lineage, whose father and grandfather were both sea captains. Within six years the couple had three children—Warren Jr., Sara's father, was born in 1809; Frederick, in 1811; and Franklin, after whom Sara's son would be named, was born in 1813. Edward (Ned) was born in 1817. Warren Sr. was part owner of more than half a dozen ships, but he lost two of them—one in Newfoundland and the other in Bermuda—when the British seized them in the War of 1812. In fact, he himself was held on a British prison ship for a short time during the war.

Warren's concerns lay more directly with the safety of his family. During the British war against the new nation, he and his wife accurately anticipated a shelling of Fairhaven's harbor from the British raider *Nimrod* in Buzzards Bay. They drove their children (with the infant Franklin lying in a chaise with runners) to a boat leaving for an Acushnet farmhouse miles away. So many others had brought their children to this house for sanctuary that the floors were covered with slumbering children. The toddlers slept one to a stair step, and all remained safe that night.

The war had left the country's maritime trade in upheaval by the time Warren's father, Ephraim, died in 1815 at age eighty-two. Nevertheless, Warren reopened the family's profitable routes to the Orient, traveling to the Macao port of call (a Portuguese colony) in the Canton region of China. Moreover, his other seafaring ventures, primarily whaling, brought the Delanos enough wealth to support comfortably a family that grew to four daughters and four sons.

After the death of his wife, Deborah, Warren Sr. remarried Eliza Adams Parker, the widow of a navy captain, in 1828. Because wealth for wealth's sake was never the aim of any Delano, Warren retired once he felt he had comfortably established himself, spending his remaining decades in Fairhaven enjoying the company of his second wife and his family. With Eliza by his side, he would drive his two-wheeled one-horse chaise for short jaunts to nearby aunts and uncles, sisters and brothers, and daughters and sons. His world became the safe harbor of the family circle.

These ancestors of Sara Delano Roosevelt—the paternal line from Philippe de la Noye down six generations to her grandfather Warren Sr.—were men of strong character, tenacity, and courage, with wives their equal in spirit. All raised large families and lived unusually long lives. Three generations of men preceding Sara had ties to the sea. Each generation became richer than the one before.

Yet Sara's illustrious ancestry through the Delano line was capped by her maternal lineage, which represented 234 years of American history, beginning with the *Mayflower* passengers. In fact, Sara descended from both the last living woman and the last living man among the *Mayflower's* passengers.

Her kin included the rebellious religious leader Anne Hutchinson, who was excommunicated and banished from Massachusetts Colony in 1637 for unorthodox Puritan doctrine. Sara's maternal ancestors also included the only judge to free an accused witch in the Plymouth Colony Court and two deputies who voted against executing Quakers. Other Delano relatives founded Virginia, Plymouth, and Rhode Island colonies.

Many of the women, as well as the men, were long-lived, an unusual circumstance for women before the twentieth century. Of one female from whom Sara descended, it was said at her death in 1693 at age ninety that she "Haveing lived a Godly life Came to her Grave as a shok of Corn fully Ripe." Sara's progenitors were nearly all connected in some manner to their spouses: if not by ancestry, then by history. Having rebelled once by leaving their native countries of England and France to seek religious freedom, they now settled into stations of respect and social position.

2

On the West Bank of the
Hudson River Lived the Delanos

Sara's father, Warren Jr., was born in Fairhaven, east of the Acushnet River, in 1809. As a boy, he spent summers on the west bank of the river, lazing in the sun on the New Bedford wharves, watching clipper ships and whalers come into port. On Sundays his family worshipped at the Washington Street Christian Church, which was mainly Unitarian. (Now it is Unitarian Memorial Church.) During the school year, he attended Fairhaven Academy, graduating in 1824 at age fifteen. He later accompanied his father to the opening of the Erie Canal in Albany. On this first trip up the Hudson River, he was transfixed by the valley's beauty. He swore to strike out from New England to build his own estate on the Hudson.

Soon he was apprenticed to a Boston merchant banking and shipping firm, working in the counting room. After a few years, when he was nineteen, he moved to New York to work for a mercantile business. He first put out to sea in 1833, leaving from the anchorage in Fairhaven known, then and now, as the Delano Wharf. He traded on both coasts of South America before sailing for the Pacific Islands and then to China, which he reached in 1834. His father, Warren Sr., had built what is known as the Delano Homestead at 39 Walnut Street in Fairhaven in 1832. This house looked its part as the family's gathering place for a hundred years. The de Lannoy coat of arms hung over its front door, and as the years passed, the attic became stuffed with old ships' logs and ivory figures carved by whaling men.

In Canton, China, Warren Jr. took the place of Samuel H. Russell in the Boston tea-exporting firm of Russell, Sturgis and Company (later Russell and Company) so that Mr. Russell could return home to Middletown, Connecticut, for a visit. Warren Delano remained in China for nine years, working as a commission merchant for tea and opium, eventually becoming chief of operations for Macao, Canton, and Hong Kong.

For 150 years, tea and silk had been the most profitable commodities for the Americans and the British. When the English found they did not have enough export goods to balance what they were importing from China, they brought in tons of opium that the British East India Company had harvested in India, a country under British control. By bringing the high-quality, reddish-brown addictive drug into China, they could make a fortune and use their hard currency to buy yet more tea. The opium trade devastated China with more than 12 million drug addicts. (At the same time, Queen Victoria made the trade and consumption of opium illegal in England.) The opium trade—although illegal in China by 1836—presented more financial opportunity than did tea and silk, despite the occasional crackdown by the Canton government. In 1838 a mob of some eight thousand angry Chinese stormed the Russell factories, with Warren caught inside. Only the intervention of Houqua, an honorary title for the Chinese agent Wu Ping-chien who handled most of the U.S. trade—and who was most likely bribed by the Americans—stopped the mayhem when he alerted the local militia.

The next year war broke out between China and Britain after a Chinese official destroyed $6 million of East India Company opium intended to keep its workers docile. The years that Warren was active in the opium trade coincided with the Opium Wars (1839–42 and 1856–60). Warren's brother Edward (Ned) was also in China working for Russell and visited opium dens in Singapore: "One man was prostrate under its effects—pale, cadaverous, death-like. . . ."

By 1839, despite the opium skirmishes, Warren had helped build Russell into a veritable empire through trading opium. Consequently, he was named senior partner. The aim of all the partners was to gain a "competence" of $100,000 ($2 million today) before returning home. Warren had gained several competences by the time he returned to New York briefly in 1843.

Warren was thirty-three years old and already a rich man. Turning his six-month stay to advantage, he married Catherine Robbins Lyman, the daughter of a Massachusetts supreme court judge, in Northampton on

November 1, 1843. Catherine's lineage was interwoven with Warren's; together, the couple represented thirteen family lines that began on the *Mayflower* voyage more than two hundred years earlier. Two of her ancestors had fought at the Battle of Lexington; one had been lieutenant governor of Massachusetts; and another, speaker of that state's House of Representatives. The Lymans were rich in ideas, if not in money. As a child, Catherine saw her parents entertain such men of letters and politics as Ralph Waldo Emerson, Daniel Webster, and President John Quincy Adams. Nevertheless, even in this company Warren shone, with his future mother-in-law declaring that there could "be nothing but pleasure in his society."

Catherine was only eighteen: a beauty whose skin was pale but delicately colored, whose eyes were dark and curved like a doe's, and who had a kind disposition. The popular artist William West painted dual wedding portraits of the couple. In contrast to Catherine's soft visage, Warren's appearance is sturdy, with wavy dark hair, side-whiskers, prominent chin, and beaked nose. Later he would acquire a walrus mustache.

The couple sailed for China immediately after their wedding, with Macao as their destination. (China eventually lost the Opium Wars. It ceded Hong Kong to the British and allowed foreigners immunity from Chinese law when importing opium into Canton and Shanghai, among other cities—thus continuing the opium traffic and its destructive impact on the Chinese.) Catherine wrote her cousin: "I knew you would be glad to hear of my determination to go to China. I feel it is my duty to go, but I do feel sad to think of the long separation from all my kind friends. I can not in the least realize that I am going so far away, and I hope I shall have courage at the last."

The voyage was uneventful, aside from its grueling length of 104 days. They headed toward the province of Kwangtung. Their home, located on Macao's bay, was sixty-five miles from Canton and was named Arrowdale. Again, the arrow symbolism proved prophetic. The blows struck in quick succession: Arrowdale burned to the ground and the couple's first daughter, Susan, born in 1844, lived only two years. Catherine took the death badly, acting "queer" and frightening Warren into thinking she might take her own life. She calmed during her second pregnancy; the next child, born in 1846, was named Louise, after Warren's cousin. When baby Louise was two, she became "very ill with a long attack of dysentery and was never really well again," the family remembered.

After three years in China, Warren had accumulated so much money that he and Catherine returned to New York City in 1846 to become members of the new leisure class, a life imitating that of European aristocracy. Warren was thirty-seven years old and expected that his only business would lie in investing his own fortune. The couple established themselves for the winter at 39 Lafayette Place (now Street), a few blocks northeast of today's City Hall, where they rented a house in the grandly named La Grange Terrace. The building, dubbed Colonnade Row, was a unique edifice that presented a single long front with twenty-eight two-story marble Greek columns running its length. Porches with wrought-iron rails were set behind the fluted columns, and the building was divided into nine five-story family dwellings. It was grand both outside and in: it had a striking staircase and marble mantels, and its interior doors were mahogany, flanged with sterling silver hinges. (Four of the houses stand today.)

Coming and going during the winter months, the Delanos might bump into Washington Irving, who was a frequent visitor to a Colonnade Row neighbor, as the writer preferred to winter as a Manhattan houseguest rather than remain isolated at his cottage up the Hudson River in Tarrytown. Charles Dickens visited, and also living in the row were the in-laws of President John Tyler.

Three doors up from Warren and Catherine resided Franklin Delano, Warren's brother, the boy who had been carried in a chaise to safety from the French and Indians. Franklin was twice blessed by luck: he was thought one of the handsomest men in New York society and, perhaps as a result, had made a stunning marriage to Laura Astor, whose grandfather was John Jacob Astor, the richest man in the United States. Immediately upon his fortunate union to a wife worth $5 million (nearly $100 million today), Franklin Delano retired from the commerce of shipbuilding. The couple's Colonnade Row house was a gift from the bride's venerable grandfather, who lived next to the Warren Delanos, at 37 Lafayette Place.

Across the street from Warren and Catherine were Franklin's father-in-law, William Backhouse Astor, and Franklin's young nephew, Willie. In 1848, two years after the Delanos moved into Colonnade Row, John Jacob Astor died and donated $400,000 and his property next to the William Backhouse Astors to establish a reference library in New York City. The Astor Library building (now the Joseph Papp Public Theater) was later consolidated with other private libraries to form the New York Public Library. Everywhere a Delano turned on Lafayette Place, there was a relative within shouting distance. (Not that any of them were prone to yelling.)

Their church was the progressive All Souls, an early Unitarian church founded on Chambers Street in 1819 with the belief that the Bible must be interpreted by reason. Its members would include the great novelist Herman Melville, the poet William Cullen Bryant, and the engraver Nathaniel Currier (although not his business partner, Ives). This church would not have been of interest to parochial or small-minded worshippers; by their membership, the Delanos showed their progressive leanings and liberal thought.

Warren's firm, Russell and Company, asked him to come out of retirement briefly to head the Hong Kong office. Russell was by now the most influential American house in the Far East. Warren felt obligated to go, and made a solo trip to China. He and Catherine had already decided that their growing brood of children should live in a more bucolic environment than Manhattan. Remembering his trip up the Hudson twenty-two years earlier, Warren found a Hudson River rental, where the family lived for a few summers. After his return from China, Catherine gave birth to three children in their Hudson River retreat: Deborah, called Dora, was born at only three pounds in 1847; Anna (Annie), in 1849; and Warren III, who died in infancy, in 1851.

That year, Warren looked to purchase an estate and found a fruit farm on the west bank of the Hudson River at Danskammer Point, on the bluffs two miles above Newburgh. It was easily accessible from Manhattan by the Hudson River Railroad; the trip was completed on the east bank up to Poughkeepsie, where a ferry operated. The Hudson is an unusual river: calm, restrained, and rarely reaching flood stage. It is part river and part estuary, due to its linkage with the Atlantic Ocean. Although the river is placid, its history is deep: the Hudson was the first river on the continent to be explored by Europeans, its steamships were the first to be successful, and its banks gave rise to the country's first prosperous railroad.

Warren named his estate Algonac, a word he derived from an Algonquin term meaning "hill and river." He hired the building and landscape architect Andrew Jackson Downing, who was responsible for the White House and Capitol grounds, to enlarge the house to forty rooms. Downing made sure that the building's expansion took every advantage of the natural scenery. The family moved into Algonac, an imposing brown and buff mansion with wide lawns high above the water, in 1852. A visitor entering the brick and stucco dwelling with deep verandas and overhanging eaves would find himself in an entry hall nineteen feet square. The drawing room measured eighteen by twenty-seven feet, the parlor sixteen by twenty, and the kitchen sixteen by twenty-one. Although the furniture was typical Victorian rosewood, Catherine accented the interior with Oriental art, Chinese porcelains, and two enormous Buddhist temple bells, making Algonac's decor unusually cosmopolitan for a Hudson River estate.

The curving staircase was an imitation of one Warren had admired in Paris. In the lower hall, hidden beneath the stairs, was a bathroom, a modern amenity for the time. Each bedroom included a tin tub, which servants would place in front of the fireplace on a bath rug and fill with water from cans brought from the kitchen—one with hot water, the other cold. The dining room was placed on the west side so the Delanos and their guests might catch the sun setting behind the mountains. A portrait by Thomas Sully of Catherine's younger sister, Susan Lyman Lesley, hung in the library, along with the wedding portraits of Catherine and Warren. A painting of the Chinese merchant Houqua was placed in a position of honor in the parlor.

Outside, the long house sat on sixty acres. The area immediately surrounding it was cultivated with gardens and walks. The house was sited on a curve in the Hudson, and the family would sit and watch the currents in the river's bend. Or they could sit in the back and gaze at the fir-clad mountains. Far beyond the house were the barns and stables, which held a dozen horses. The cottages of the coachman and gardener stood there, too.

Inside the house, there were a French and a German governess, a nurse, a cook, and a few maids. And then there were the odd auxiliary staff, occasionally dismissed by Warren as noted in his diary: "Discharged the boy, Wm. Gale, for good-for-nothingness."

(These Victorian times could be harsh on servants, especially the women. A few months after the Delanos engaged a young cook, Kate, their new coachman ran away. Soon after, Warren wrote in his diary: "Kate has been deceived." Later, Kate went to "attend to a matter of great importance" at St. Gabriel's Church. Apparently, things did not work out well, for shortly afterward Warren wrote of the departure of "our slut of a cook." Both the cook and the coachman had transgressed, but poor Kate paid the price.)

For all this large household and its staff of ten, Algonac was merely the Delanos' winter home. In summer, they moved their household to the senior Delanos' Homestead, the thirty-room house in Fairhaven, Massachusetts, with the Delano siblings and their families, cementing their already close affinity and ensuring that their children—the Delano cousins—would always regard one another as the closest of friends. Dora remembered the family as "united," caring most for one another. The family regarded the house itself as their shrine. Hoping Fairhaven would be his permanent resting place, Warren bought land, had it designated Riverside Cemetery, and gave it to the town, reserving a choice spot for the Delanos' mausoleum and future grave plots. Warren hired Richard Morris Hunt, later renowned as the architect of three Newport mansions, including The Breakers, to design the stately Delano crypt.

In 1852 Warren and Catherine had a second son. This one lived, and the couple bestowed on him the same patronymic as their last male infant: Warren Delano III.

On September 21, 1854, their seventh child, Sara Delano, was born and named after Warren's maiden sister, Sarah Delano. (The family originally named her Sarah, but dropped the *h* from her name so she wouldn't be confused with her aunt in correspondence.) There was quiet joy in the household. The first thought was to make her middle name Phillipa, in reference to the first American Delano. "I think well of leaving out of her name Phillipa," wrote her father, "plain Sarah Delano is decidedly better."

In this same year, the U.S. Mint opened in San Francisco to turn prospectors' gold into coins, *Walden* was published by Henry David Thoreau; a new contraption called an elevator was publicly demonstrated to men and women who screamed in fear as Elisha Otis plunged earthward; the doctrine of papal infallibility was announced by the Vatican; and, on the very day of Sara's birth, in Springfield, Illinois, a young lawyer named Abe Lincoln was writing a four-hour speech against slavery to use in a debate with Stephen A. Douglas.

America was now the world symbol of expansionary boldness. It triumphed over the seas, marched west across the forests and prairies, and cut iron pathways with railroad tracks toward the Pacific. And so Sara became the child of an era that was optimistic and self-confident. When she was just a day old, her four elder siblings crept into their mother's room to catch a glimpse of the sleeping newborn. Just as they came close, infant Sara yawned and raised her little arms, fists clenched, above her head. She was enshrined in their hearts forever.

However, Sara would not remain the family's baby. Philippe de la Noye Delano, doubly named after the founder of the American line of Delanos, was born in 1857. Despite his grand-sounding name, he was unceremoniously dubbed Phil.

Warren, now a millionaire, continued to spend his time managing the fortune he had made in the shipping trade. He invested in real estate in Manhattan, in coal mines near Johnstown, Pennsylvania, and in copper mines in Maryland and Tennessee. As a result, there is a town of Delano, Pennsylvania, as well as a Delano, Tennessee. (There are also three other Delano hamlets farther west, but these were named after other Delano men.)

Summers in Fairhaven were not sufficient time together for the friendship between Warren and Franklin, so Warren's brother built his own turreted home, Steen Valletje, across the river and seventeen miles north of Algonac, at Rhinebeck-on-the-Hudson. The land on which Steen Valetje was built had been carved out of Laura's father's upriver property, Ferncliff. (Franklin and Laura also had a European house, Sunflower, in Monte Carlo.) Sara and her four siblings enjoyed many visits from their childless uncle Frank and aunt Laura, who always arrived with a gift for each one.

Other aunts and uncles also indulged the children. One Christmas gift from Uncle Ned was a bark-roofed cottage with two rooms and a five-sided porch, where the children played on those rainy days called by Catherine "lovely drizzle droozle days." On sunny days, Sara and her siblings weeded the garden for a few pennies or groomed the ponies and donkey.

Some relatives actually moved into Algonac. They included Warren's unmarried brother Edward (Uncle Ned) and sister Sarah, which explains why little Sara was soon being called Sallie within the family. Moreover, before the birth of Katherine, or Kassie, in 1860, Warren's cousin Nancy F. Church arrived for "a long visit." She became the children's first teacher and promptly converted the breakfast room into a schoolroom. The children called her Nannie.

This family was a patriarchy, with Warren firmly at the helm. His wife always deferred to her husband, even in the smallest matter. Sara revered her father and remembered her mother, Catherine, as "very angelic." She was "almost too good, and never could deny us anything. And she never disciplined anything in her life!"

When little Sara was three, her father's prosperity was shattered by the crash of 1857: the wealth he had accumulated in China was gone. In addition, his ships were piling up losses rather than profits. Sara's brother later wrote: "The terrible panic of 1857 left him *flat*. If he tried to sell, he could get nothing for his holdings. He clenched his teeth and made up his mind that whatever else he did he would *not* sell."

The family was devastated when they were finally forced to put Algonac up for sale. "My father lost almost everything," Sara remembered, "and when he tried to sell our house, he found almost all prospective buyers in the same plight." The Delano estate was saved by default. Warren gave up the Colonnade Row house in Manhattan, but times were still difficult. His brother Ned wrote in his diary that Warren "is looking as well as before the disaster to his fortunes and says he feels tolerably well and has a better appetite."

At the time, the children knew nothing of their parents' worries. In this era, as Sara pointed out decades later, children were purposely kept "tranquil and unmarked by adult emotion."

To recoup his wealth, Warren, now fifty years old, returned to China by himself in 1859. He traveled to Hong Kong, which had replaced Canton as China's center of trade. Catherine was pregnant with their ninth child. Sara adored her father and felt dreadfully lonely without him. As a small consolation, she soaked foreign stamps off his letters and began a stamp collection.

Warren's brothers were skeptical about his China plans. Edward wrote:

"Warren has various projects, mostly impractical, one of which is to go to China to do business for five years and return with a fortune." As it turned out, Warren's plan was completely sound.

With war approaching, opium would again be Warren's salvation. The drug would be needed by tens of thousands of wounded soldiers as an analgesic, and Warren's task was to provide it to the Medical Bureau of the U.S. War Department. The Delano and, later, Roosevelt families have always stressed its humanitarian value—but thousands of wounded on both sides would turn addict and find any way to purchase the drug, imported at great profit by Warren. And much of it found its way into Chinese opium dens. The British bested the Americans in the opium trade, but virtually all the American export companies took part. In addition, the first families in America were engaged in importing opium: the Lows, the Perkinses, the Peabodys, and, of course, the family who owned Warren's firm, the Russells. The only important American firm that refused to do business in opium was owned by Quakers.

Earlier, Warren defended his business in a letter to his brothers: "I do not pretend to justify the prosecution of the opium trade in a moral and philanthropic point of view, but as a merchant I insist that it has been a fair, honorable and legitimate trade; and to say the worst of it, liable to no further or weightier objections than in the importation of wines, Brandies & spirits into the United States, England, & c."

The Union army was thankful for the painkiller. Although family lore has it that a grateful President Lincoln asked Warren to draw up the first federal trade agreement with China, there is no proof of any such request. Yet Warren was a Republican: one of his often-quoted remarks was "I will not say all Democrats are horse thieves, but it does seem that all horse thieves are Democrats." Warren and his Dutchess County friends would sit on the veranda at Algonac in their white linen suits and talk politics. Of course, he supported the Union—perhaps more than he did Abraham Lincoln himself, sometimes questioning whether Lincoln was up to the task. He wrote his brother Franklin on this issue, insisting as well that there must be "just laws for the Colored as well as the White man."

The money to be made from opium—and Warren's subsequent loneliness in China—led to the greatest adventure of Sara's life, one that she would later pass down as nautical lore to her own son, Franklin. On June 25, 1862—just as the Seven Days battles began in Virginia—Sara, at age seven, would be sailing twenty thousand miles to China with her mother and six siblings to join their father.

3

❦

"My Orderly Little Life"

Catherine, with the assistance of Warren's New York agents, carefully prepared for the voyage to China. Algonac was rented—to relatives, of course. The family was to sail on Warren's square-rigged clipper ship the *Surprise*, which was famous for her speed. It was built in 1850 and ran 183 feet overall with a beam of close to 39 feet. The voyage was occasion for a major family celebration: a steam tugboat crammed with Delanos moved in company with the *Surprise* out of New York Harbor while the high-spirited relatives waved, fired off guns, and cheered. This trip was one of contrast: it presented the danger of any sea voyage from New York to China, sailing down the North and South Atlantic, around the Cape of Good Hope, and up the Indian Ocean to the South China Sea. Yet it was also a microcosm of Victorian family life, cozy and secure.

Preparing to embark with thirty-seven-year-old Catherine were her seven children, ranging in age from sixteen to two. Starting with the eldest, they were Louise, Dora, Annie, Warren III, Sara, Philippe, and Katherine (Kassie). The last Delano to be born at Algonac was Kassie, who was known as "the posthumous child" because she was born after Warren had left for China. They were all blonds, but as they grew older their hair would darken to brown. Cousin Nannie accompanied Catherine, as did a maidservant and a nurse for the baby. Warren had secured the vessel solely for his family: there were no other passengers. "I was naturally completely thrilled at the dramatic change in my orderly little life. To go to China!" Sara remembered.

Forget what you know about putting to sea. The experience of Sara and her family was entirely different. First, food provisions could be kept cold only as long as the ice lasted, so Sara's fellow passengers included chickens, pigs, geese, and turkeys, all secured in pens. (Although the manifest did not list a cow, Sara remembered there being one on board, and family journals indicate that they had milk at meals.) After they set sail, it seemed as if the family was living on a farm, not a ship, with sheep baaing and hens clucking.

Propriety demanded living quarters that resembled the best of houses, albeit smaller. The *Surprise* had a parlor with a fireplace, a dining room with a large table, and bedrooms. The furniture was not sleek or built-in, as it is on ships today; it was bulky and large, for the point was to show your status by having the same appointments as at home. There were Oriental rugs, plush sofas, bookcases lined with the novels of James Fenimore Cooper and Nathaniel Hawthorne, and tall highboys—even an upright piano so the children could continue their music lessons. Dining was scarcely different at sea than at Algonac, with linen tablecloths and napkins. One slight difference was that the Delanos' meals were served on the highest-quality ironstone rather than on bone china.

A brass rail ran along the walls of the living quarters, not for decoration but for safety. In heavy seas, the ship's captain, Charles A. Ranlett Jr., would hurry sailors into the family's private rooms to anchor the furniture to the railing with coils of thick line. To secure the dining-room table in the room's center, the men screwed hooks into the floorboards and lashed the heavy piece tightly. Catherine and the children would quickly wrap wall paintings, lamps, clocks, and knickknacks and pack them in wooden sea chests. As the ship pitched and rolled, everything was either tied down or stowed in trunks. In winter, lifelines were strung around the poop deck and stayed there for the duration of icy weather.

Sara, rather than being frightened, thought life on the perilous sea was a great adventure. In fact, she was far less bothered by the terrible seasickness that overtook her siblings in the first weeks of the journey, although once her mother wrote in her journal that "it took Sallie until noon to get dressed." The only food the others could keep down was congé, a gruel of rice and water. Sixteen-year-old Louise dropped to a dangerously low weight. Once the children had acquired their sea legs, when the *Surprise* rode the rough waves Sara and her siblings slid back and forth on the floor, laughing as they tumbled into one another. During gales, they wanted to peek out the portholes to watch the water crash against the glass, but Catherine held them back, fearing a wave might shatter even its thickness. Luckily, the ship did not broach and the children never knew the terror of being on a ship that had rolled onto its side.

"Our lives were regulated just as they had been at home," remembered Sara. Calm days included school lessons with Nannie and games on deck: playing catch with beanbags (balls would bounce overboard), tag, foot-races, hide-and-seek—a cubbyhole by the masthead was a favorite spot—and any other childhood sport normally played on land. The children, especially Phil, would try to catch seabirds that flew onto the deck.

During warm and sunny weeks, the sailors spread an awning out over the deckhouse to protect the Delanos from the heat, which reached 126 degrees on deck. The crew shouted if they caught a child climbing the rigging, as the lofty heights were strictly off-limits. When a seaman fell from the bow at night—and was rescued by a rope "hoved in a twinkling" by the captain, Catherine wrote—the children learned the real danger of which they had been warned. But the sailors would craft makeshift swings from ropes, and Sara could sway back and forth, looking out over a vast ocean.

When another ship was sighted, everyone ran on deck to wave while the crews exchanged greetings with signaling flags. If one were heading back to the United States, the *Surprise* would send a small boat out with mail. Once, spotting a ship, Captain Ranlett feared it was a privateer, but it passed by without incident. He noted in his journal that "C.D. was perfectly cool and not at all frightened."

Soon the Delano children learned the meaning of the signaling flags and would stand on different sides of the ship, signaling one another in their new language. They picked up rollicking sea chanteys from the sailors, songs that Sara would remember all her life. The sailmaker in his loft taught them to tie knots and lured them with "wonderful tales of the sea, of Sweden and of Norway," Sara said. The carpenter carved them wooden toys. At night, the ship's captain taught the children the basics of celestial navigation, and they learned to identify stars and planets.

In rainy weather, there was always a child willing to play "Bonnie Doone" on the piano, taffy pulls in the galley, and marshmallows heated on tongs in the parlor fireplace. Sara would organize her stamp collection, rich with postage from China. The adults played whist and cribbage, as well as such word games as Proverbs and Consequences, and read aloud to the children from *Springles,* a novella written by a Fairhaven cousin, to while away the long hours. Rainy days at least meant fresh water rather than salt water for bathing: what luxury! Still, heavy rain trickled into the family's living quarters, and "there was a perfect Niagara Falls off the poop deck," wrote Catherine.

They celebrated birthdays—on September 21, 1862, Sara shared her eighth with Captain Ranlett's twenty-ninth*—with roast goose, boiled ham, corn, peas, tomatoes, rice, champagne, tea, frosted cakes, and tarts. On holidays, decorations went up on schedule. At noon on the Fourth of July, with all flags flying, the *Surprise* fired thirteen guns, meant to represent the original states. The men "spliced the main brace," which, Warren III wrote with disappointment, meant "only taking a glass of whiskey." However, the captain, Catherine, and cousin Nannie shared champagne before eating ice cream (the ship's ice lasted all the way to Cape Hope) and cake. At night there were rockets and firecrackers, and the family enjoyed "a poetical effusion" before singing "The Star-Spangled Banner" and "Yankee Doodle."

Every Sunday the Delanos attended church services presided over by the captain. They often prayed for the success of the Union army, now well into its second year of battle against the Confederacy. The pace of their lives, whether on the Sabbath or a weekday, was set by Catherine's example. Sara's brother later reminisced: "She never worried, and was neither excited nor bored. It was her job, and it was all in the day's work."

On October 31, 1862, four months and six days after last setting foot on land, Catherine and her children sighted the Hong Kong harbor. The small craft that met the ship was commanded by Warren—"tall, slight, and keen, dressed in white linen, with his side whiskers and mustache," remembered Sara—who joyfully transferred to the *Surprise* and shed his usual reserve to greet his family and take them to Rose Hill, their home eighty-five miles down the Pearl River from Canton. The sailing family, isolated from news, unhappily learned that the Confederates had outmaneuvered Union general George B. McClellan in the Seven Days battles that had begun as they sailed from New York.

Nevertheless, this blow to the Union could not blunt the family's joy at being together. They were carried in a cavalcade of sedan chairs to Rose Hill, where the family was to live secluded from the Chinese except for those hired to serve them. Their property was walled; their lives were insular. There was good reason to keep a distance. Catherine remembered her first trip to Canton, when shouts of "Fanqui" (*Fan-kue*) or "foreign devils" greeted her. Besides the mere fact of their being outsiders, the family's role

---

*Other sources give his age as twenty-six, but the *Surprise*'s log places him at twenty-eight when the ship sailed.

in the opium trade created hostility. In fact, Warren forbade the children to learn Chinese specifically to keep them from understanding insulting words.

So after what Sara called an "incredibly exciting" voyage on the open sea, the women and children stayed becalmed within Rose Hill, and only Warren was able to come and go freely. Rose Hill was appointed with English furniture punctuated by Chinese touches. Over the dining-room table hung a *punkah*, or large muslin panel that moved the stagnant air by ropes operated by a servant standing behind a screen. (A few of the English estates in the area had a *punkah* in each bedroom, operated while the residents slept, but the Delanos felt this was extravagant.) Although Sara found the exotic blossoms and palms of the compound splendid, she disliked the new restrictions and found her daily routine "monotonous," despite its opulence.

Sara's lessons continued, and she drew sailing boats on an old accounting book that had been used to keep track of the chests of opium leaving on Warren's ships. There were occasional outings, though: the entire family went to the horse races, where they sat in the Russell and Company stand, but only the elder girls were allowed to attend balls with Catherine. Sara envied their freedom. Warren owned a tempting stable of horses, yet the girls could not leave the grounds without an escort. Their ten-year-old brother, Warren, was allowed out, though, and he would ride on his beloved pony to the Chinese racetrack to watch the horses being trained. Of course, the girls' unhappiness was compounded by the humiliation of being driven in a small barouche around the grounds by their little brother handling the reins of his donkey, Blackberry. Once, they all went to dine with Houqua. The children thought the food exotic and would have left their meal untouched if their parents hadn't already impressed upon them the importance of pleasing their host. Sara was awestruck by his "magnificent china and silver," but their hostess's bound feet, "scarcely three inches long," shook Dora.

Catherine was too gentle to punish the children when it was necessary, so that task was left to Warren. "Father spanked some of the children," Sara remembered, "but I was never spanked. I was probably so canny that I never let him know that I was naughty. We were not afraid of him, but if we were quarreling or doing what we shouldn't in the room in which he was writing, he would say, 'What's that? Tut, tut,' and we immediately stopped."

In September 1863 Catherine added the infant Frederick to the family. Within hours of the boy's birth, Warren brought him to be admired by his associates at Russell and Company. A daughter was born in 1864, named Laura Franklin Delano after Aunt Laura Astor Delano and Uncle Franklin. She would be the youngest child. Catherine's brood now numbered nine, not counting the two children lost in infancy. However, Phil was at risk: he had fallen seriously ill with diphtheria, which resulted in a prolonged high fever and, later, frequent seizures.

The distance between the Delanos in China and those in the United States guaranteed a voluminous correspondence, although the letters were two months stale by the time they were received. The Delanos were savers and collectors all, so these missives were lovingly preserved. Most families did not go to such great lengths to keep their correspondence, but the confident Delanos foresaw their prominence and noted the most trivial matters in their letters, journals, and diaries. Nothing that affected a Delano could be unimportant.

Although the Delanos lived in the midst of other American and British traders—there were nearly 6,700 foreigners in China, representing close to four hundred firms—they distrusted the British because they were southern sympathizers, calling them "hated neighbors." Sara used her generous quiet time to stitch muslin shirts for Union soldiers, attaching to each a note: "Sewn by an eight-year-old girl." When they visited the daughter of the American consul, the girls took pleasure in waving American flags whenever they passed anyone English, whom they called "Redcoats."

In fact, even some of the Americans were shunned as Confederate sympathizers. Louise wrote: "There are but few loyal Americans of the right sort here, but I am thankful that all of Russell & Company are strong, & when we had a dinner the other night, the gentlemen insisted on having 'John Brown' sung."

After a year in China, Catherine and Warren would have liked to send some of the children back home; the elder ones needed more advanced study, and, more seriously, Phil was in poor health. But not wanting to risk putting their children on a ship that might be captured by the Rebels, at first the family felt they must wait out the war.

However, as the Confederacy weakened, the Delanos decided to let four children go home—Annie, Warren, Sara (now ten), and Phil. In 1864 William Howell Forbes, a business associate of their father's and Dora's fiancé, accompanied them on the voyage. Annie, the eldest of the children and always the organizer, put up her hair in an effort to mark her new maturity. "The most capable of all," Sara remembered of Annie, and "a tower of strength to everyone." They left Hong Kong on a ship that took them to the Isthmus of Suez; since the canal would not open for five years, they proceeded by train to Cairo, where they saw the Pyramids and rode camels before leaving for Alexandria. They traveled on to Marseilles via steamer, and to Paris on another train. A few weeks in London, and then they went back across the ocean on a Cunard ship.

Uncle Ned and Aunt Sarah greeted them in the United States and took over their care. Algonac was still rented—now to A. A. Low, whose eponymous company owned the ship *Surprise* and who was the father of Seth Low (later president of Columbia University and mayor of New York City)—so they went to their grandparents' in Fairhaven. Sara, who always had a healthy appetite, remembered the fantastic meals she enjoyed at her grandfather's house: "And then those breakfasts—never have I had such delightful food—we had the most wonderful biscuits, fish, eggs. I remember my grandfather always had a huge pat of butter before him and would put a big pat on my plate. He was slightly deaf and I would shout at him, 'Grandpa, not so much butter, please.'

"We used to be weighed when we got there to see how much we would gain. And we always gained pounds."

In Fairhaven they heard the jubilant news of General Robert E. Lee's surrender. "Last Tuesday evening we all went out for a walk to see the houses lighted up and the fireworks in honor of our recent victories. I am so very happy! All the bells of the town are ringing and they are firing the cannon near the house," Sara wrote.

Sara was with her maternal grandparents, Judge and Mrs. Lyman, in Northampton when they learned of the president's assassination. Roland Redmond, who later married Sara's niece and namesake, said, "She told me that they had just started their lessons, the judge having left already for his court, when they heard the judge's step coming back into the house, and they couldn't imagine what had happened." Judge Lyman "came into the hall and shouted up the stairs, 'Mrs. Lyman!' and when his wife appeared, he said, 'Mrs. Lyman, the president is shot!'" The entire family went into deep mourning; Sara wore a black ribbon for months. The loss was as if a close relative had died, made more poignant by Mrs. Lyman's childhood memories of the nation's grief at the death of George Washington.

In China the pro-Union Americans celebrated Lee's surrender a few months late. They planned an evening trip on a Russell and Company steamer on July 4, 1865, not having yet received word of the assassination of Abraham Lincoln in April. The night was perfect—the moon was nearly full, and by anchoring six miles offshore, the passengers felt that they were no longer in China. Louise wrote: "It was so enlivening to feel we were under the American flag, & out of an English colony. Midnight found us just returning into the harbor sending up showers of rockets which made some of the inhabitants wish they were Americans for sure."

By 1866, within seven years of setting out to recoup his fortune, Warren retired from Russell and Company a wealthy man. The illness of Warren Sr. accelerated his return home with Catherine and the remainder of the

Delanos. They joined the rest of the family at Fairhaven, until the elder man's death at age eighty-seven later that year. Warren Sr. left the family house in trust to his eldest son and namesake.

In the late summer all the family went to the Paris Universal Exhibition, living in a luxurious apartment on the Bois de Boulogne. Sara glimpsed the entourages of the king of Prussia, Count Bismarck, Empress Carlotta of Mexico, and the French empress Eugénie with the prince imperial, who passed her balcony on their way to the exhibition displays. Sara was impressed but not overawed: she waved enthusiastically as the royal parties promenaded past, a memory she would always keep.

Sara attended school in Paris, and enjoyed rolling her hoop along the bois on her way home each afternoon. The Delanos were actually thinking of remaining in Europe permanently. Warren was disgusted by how certain New Yorkers—those not of his lineage—were being influenced by new money from Industrial Age profits. He called these new millionaires "pretentious" and "boasting." By settling in Europe, he could keep his family secluded from these parvenus. He even wrote that he might "sink for the time being our name of Delano and write ourselves 'de la Noye.'" Realizing that this "might be considered equally snobbish," he eventually dropped the idea.

The next year in Paris, Dora married William Howell Forbes, having followed her father's orders to wait until Forbes had earned his competence. Thirteen-year-old Sara wore a silver dress trimmed in blue to the wedding. Soon after their marriage, the newlyweds left for the Russell office in Macao and lived in Rose Hill, which Warren Delano still owned.

On the heels of the wedding, Sara became seriously ill with rheumatic fever. This was the only severe illness of her childhood, and her parents were sufficiently worried to take her to Germany for the cure. After Sara recovered, she and Annie and Warren Jr. began school in Dresden in order to become fluent in German as well as French. The youngsters took advantage of the winter weather to perfect their ice-skating.

Louise's health was worsening, so the Delanos returned to Algonac in 1869 with her and the younger children. Sara's brother Franklin remembered the snow on the ground and great drifts on the lawn, which they happily fell into, wearing their heavy wool coats. "We thought it was grand," he said.

Annie and Warren missed the experience: they were left to study in Hannover. Sara was nearby in Celle, where she lived with the burgomaster's family while attending a school for young ladies. Uncle Ned and Aunt Sarah, both still unmarried, went to Germany as the children's guardians.

When the Delano trio were released for vacation, their uncle and aunt would take them on holidays—one time to an island in the North Sea; another, to the Harz Mountains. In Switzerland, Sara bought herself a silver thimble in an elegant case, and a tiny violet glass pitcher from Bohemia—starting a lifelong love of collecting fine things.

4

The Contented Spinster

Sara returned to Algonac in 1870 on the last steamship to leave a German port before the outbreak of the Franco-Prussian War. She had been away from Algonac for seven years and had been in Germany when Louise died at twenty-four. Louise's health had seemed stable, and Sara said, "We thought [her illness] cured until it began again." Louise had become her "mother's constant companion," and Catherine felt the loss deeply, commenting quietly, "I've had many troubles in my life, but none of them were the ones I expected. It is always the unexpected that happens."

Yet the family took consolation in the calm way Louise approached her end, softly singing hymns as she sank further from her family. When Sara finally reached home, the Delanos gave her Louise's watch and, drawing on their religious beliefs, helped her recognize that her loss was Louise's "great gain and joy." Now there were eight Delano children.

Sara had ended her formal schooling by age sixteen. She was fluent in French and German and continued cultivating the arts by studying singing and drawing. She was taught the latter by the Hudson River artist Frederick Church, who lived on the east bank of the river in his house, Olana. Sometimes he would use Algonac's own paintings—the portraits of Delano family members, of Sara's grandfather Judge Lyman, and of Houqua—to teach technique.

Sara savored the quiet life at Algonac as much as the thrills of Paris. In the summer she could choose among archery, croquet, riding saddle horses, boating, and picnics. In the winter there were sledding and frequent sleigh rides across the frozen Hudson to visit Uncle Franklin and Aunt Laura at Steen Valetje. The family was busy yet peaceful, lively yet serene. As much as the younger members were physically active, they appreciated more scholarly pursuits and continued their mother's custom of reading aloud.

The family attended the Unitarian Church of Our Father in Newburgh, of which Warren was a major financial supporter. The Delanos and their servants took up three entire rows. Unfortunately, Warren's health was beginning to fail. He went blind in his left eye, which caused him to fall into an elevator shaft and shatter his hip. After a lengthy and painful up-and-down recovery, he walked with a cane. On his sixty-eighth birthday he declared himself "age 50 above the shoulders; age 88 below."

On days other than the Sabbath, there were house parties up and down the river, often with theatricals and charades. Sara would remember a particularly lavish one at the Manhattan house of *the* Mrs. Astor (Caroline, Mrs. William Backhouse), the dowager empress of the Four Hundred, the who's who list that had been established with the assistance of Ward McAllister (who today might be called her publicist). It seemed as if all New York society knew one another. Although Warren allowed his daughters to be a part of the gay groups of young people, Algonac hosted no balls or dances for its daughters. Such activities were far too flashy for Warren to countenance.

As the elder girls were slowly introduced to society—and as Sara advanced to being called "Miss Sara Delano"—the younger ones continued their studies, first at home and then at academies. The boys went to college, except for Phil, who remained ill with frequent seizures ("brain fever") and had to study at home with a tutor. Phil was very tall, over six feet, with fine eyes. Sara said, "He adored me and we always played together."

Phil was clever and had a wonderful memory, being able to read a poem once and recite it afterward. He wrote in his copybook: "I shall never be a President but it seems to me there must be one in the family." The Delanos were convinced of the family's natural superiority and of their ability—or duty—to rule others. Others noted the Delano convictions; as one friend described them: "Ever restless, ever imbued with the itch to make the world over *their* way."

The surviving sisters (Dora, Annie, Sara, Kassie, and Laura) were referred to as the "five beautiful Delano girls." Sara had dark brown eyes, Dora's were blue like her father's, and Annie's and Kassie's were hazel. Laura was the youngest and possibly the most beautiful of the sisters, with a sweet face and silken hair. Annie was a little plump, while Sara and Kassie had sturdy builds. Dora was the sister with the slimmest build, having always been "delicate," according to Sara.

All the Delano sisters were tall. "I think we can afford to stop growing now," Louise once wrote. "Most of the gentlemen of the house are short, and we are as tall as some, and taller than the rest." Sara, the middle sister, was notably aristocratic, with a slender build yet a height of five feet, ten inches—nearly a foot taller than most other women of the era. She had dark eyes, auburn hair, classic features, a wonderful carriage, and a slightly prominent chin that she held high. Even as a young woman, Sara was striking. She read all six volumes of Sir Walter Raleigh's *History of the World*, resting her head on her hands to shut out the noise of her younger brothers and sisters. They teased her and once took a fancy floral box, filled it with old vegetables, wrapped a ribbon around it, and presented it to her, saying that it had just arrived from a young man. When Sara tore off the ribbon and recognized the hoax, she swept regally from the room without a word.

Although sister Dora was already married (after having become engaged at age sixteen), Sara showed no sign of needing a husband to complete her life. She had a number of inconsequential beaux, including several from West Point. One of her gentleman callers took unusual pride in his forebears and was dubbed "the Pilgrim Father" by the no-nonsense family. Fortunately, Sara took her father's advice when the redheaded architect Stanford White—later shot by Harry Thaw in a scandal involving Thaw's wife—came calling. One time, White sent a large bouquet of flowers and Warren remarked, "I suppose that these are from the red-haired trial. Remember that I don't care for that at all." Sara promptly pushed White away. She was both content and happy within the family circle at Algonac, and besides, she would frequently say, "there was no one like my father."

For his part, Warren celebrated his place in the world by having his portrait painted by J. Alden Weir. Sara said that when her father "was in the house, he was usually writing or reading." Weir portrayed Warren just that way: a quill pen in his right hand and his left holding his place in perhaps a journal, with a pair of spectacles resting nearby. He has on a black bow tie and a silk vest with a gold watch chain. His muttonchop whiskers and mustache, now gray, make up for the loss of hair on his head. This portrait was lent back to the artist to be shown in the first exhibit in the Metropolitan Museum's new building in Central Park and won an honorable mention at the Paris Salon.

Of course, the family—having seen most of the world—celebrated what was best about their own country. They traveled to Philadelphia in 1876 for the centennial celebrations, and later took a trip to Niagara Falls. Sara was now allowed to visit her Manhattan girlfriends on Fifth or Madison Avenue off the Twenties or Thirties. Sometimes they would take a carriage up to Central Park to ice-skate at its rink, which was strictly divided into male and female halves. Her best friend was Anna (Bamie) Eleanor Roosevelt, whose young brothers were Theodore and Elliott, of the Oyster Bay family. Bamie had been disabled when her nurse dropped her as a baby, and the twisted spine that resulted caused her constant pain. But Bamie appeared carefree and friendly, and with her, Sara might attend the symphony or a ball in one of her three evening dresses, identical except in color. Now that ladies' powder rooms were being installed in stores and restaurants, women could—for the first time—shop and lunch for as long as they liked.

In 1876 Sara's elder brother Warren III married Jennie Walters of the prosperous Baltimore family renowned for its private collection of French art. Jennie herself was an unusual woman, having attended classes through private arrangement at Harvard College, where Warren was a student. (The Harvard Annex for women was not founded until 1879, and Radcliffe College not until 1894.) Jennie's father fought against the marriage; as a widower, he did not want to give up his daughter's companionship. The wedding finally took place, but few friends were invited and the Delano family itself did not receive an invitation until the last minute. It was a dismal ceremony with no reception afterward.

Having been alienated from Jennie's father, Warren III and Jennie wanted to stay close to Algonac. They were inadvertently successful when childless Uncle Franklin Delano died in 1875 and left his estate, Steen Valetje, to Warren III. When Jennie's father died, she learned she had been disinherited. Fortunately, Jennie's brother, Harry, shared his portion of their father's estate with her. (The art treasures had been bequeathed to the eponymous Walters Gallery of Art in Baltimore.)

A year after Warren's marriage, in 1877, Sara's elder sister Annie, now twenty-seven, left the family to marry—if ever a Delano could be said to leave the family upon marriage. She, like Dora, wed a Russell agent, this one a distant cousin named Frederic Delano Hitch. Annie and Hitch took a short honeymoon, after which they, too, moved to China, where Hitch was a partner.

Sara went to Europe for eight months and also traveled to Hong Kong to visit Dora and Annie. Dora chaperoned her carefully and said of one suitor, "I do not think he is the right person for you, dear." Sara wrote him a note ending their friendship.

Despite Sara's far-flung travels, her schooling abroad, and her frequent trips to Manhattan, she preferred the country to city life. She faithfully kept a diary in which she recorded her many friendships, most of them with kin. In 1880 her friend Bamie asked Sara to visit her in Manhattan. Bamie might have wanted Sara there as a buffer: one of the family's dinner guests was fifty-six-year-old James Roosevelt, a distant cousin whom Bamie was discouraging as a suitor.

Sara was twenty-six and showed no interest in marriage—this at a time when the average age of a bride was twenty-two. However, she had her namesake Aunt Sarah and her beloved cousin Nannie as positive role models. In addition, Sara was content being part of the Algonac family circle and had already been helping her mother manage the large household. She commented years later, "I've noticed families who care more for others, but as I look back we always cared most for each other."

In fact, shortly before Bamie's dinner, Sara had written in her diary that she was a contented spinster. Inevitably, after embracing eternal maidenhood, she fell in love that night in Oyster Bay with Bamie's rejected suitor, James Roosevelt.

5

On the East Bank of the
Hudson River Lived the Roosevelts

The shiny ribbon of the Hudson River laced two families together: the Delanos on the west side and the Roosevelts on the east. The Delanos were Hudson River newcomers, having lived in Massachusetts until Warren moved his family to Algonac in 1852. The Roosevelts, on the other hand, had lived in New York since 1649 and on the Hudson since 1818.

The Roosevelts were true New Yorkers: an original Knickerbocker family whose first-generation members had lived in New-Amsterdam when the one-legged Peter Stuyvesant governed it. The Roosevelt story in America begins with an ancestor bearing a name salted with consonants. He was Claes (for Nicholas) Van Rosenvelt, and both Roosevelt U.S. presidents—President Franklin from the Hudson River clan and President Theodore of the Oyster Bay family—were his direct descendants.

In 1649, the year that Claes and his Dutch wife, Jannetje Samuel-Thomas, most likely arrived from Holland, New-Amsterdam was a bustling town. Just forty years earlier, the English explorer Henry Hudson had been hired by the Dutch East India Company to find a northern sea route to the East. Hudson's ship, *Half Moon*, navigated the Hudson River instead. The company was disappointed at not finding India, but fur traders saw the financial potential of the wildlife living on the shores of what Hudson termed "as fine a river as can be found."

Unlike the Pilgrims and Huguenots who founded Plymouth Colony seeking religious freedom, the Dutch who came to New-Amsterdam did so to worship the almighty guilder. Fur trading was a great source of income, and the Dutch depicted their values clearly by placing a beaver in the center of New-Amsterdam's shield.

When the Dutch arrived at the tip of Manhattan, they encountered the Manates Indian tribe, who sold the island for trinkets and departed north to what is now the Bronx. The Manates left to the Dutch their trails and paths, which account for the irregular pattern of Lower Manhattan's streets today. The Dutch built the first permanent colonial settlement in Manhattan near the bottom tip of the island for easy access to both the Hudson and the East Rivers. However, New-Amsterdam's environment was what might be expected of a colony founded primarily for financial gain rather than a higher purpose; the town was commercial and tumultuous.

In 1647, about two years before the Van Rosenvelts disembarked, Holland sent Peter Stuyvesant as director-general to bring discipline to what had become a mismanaged and demoralized community. Dutch leaders felt that Stuyvesant, a former soldier, would use his command to shape up the colony. Instead, he alienated the colonists by his autocratic decisions: he imprisoned critics, limited alcohol consumption, imposed a curfew, tried to expel Jews from the colony, and tortured Quakers. When he wasn't managing the colony into the ground or defending it against hostile English soldiers and native Indian tribes, he focused on building trade routes. However, fraud and incompetence tainted even his commercial successes.

This rough congeries of about eight hundred people greeted Claes and Jannetje, who had with them barely more than a family Bible as their defense. They suffered through an unusually cold first winter, so cold that "ink froze in the pen." Still, the couple had journeyed to the most cosmopolitan port in America, one where a visitor could hear eighteen languages spoken. Within fifteen years of the Rosenvelts' arrival, the city's population nearly doubled, to about fifteen hundred people.

Claes, despite his grand-sounding surname that means "field of roses," was "very common," a phrase used by both Franklin and Teddy Roosevelt. In fact, Franklin Delano Roosevelt pointed to the fact that no one knew Claes's occupation before arriving in New-Amsterdam, and this prompted him to dryly speculate that "our ancestor must have been a horse thief, or some other kind of a thief and, therefore, a fugitive from justice."

That Claes's ancestry could not be traced back to Holland and that many people thought Rosenvelt "sounded Jewish" gave rise to later rumors that the Roosevelt family was Jewish. However, Claes and Jannetje baptized their children in the Dutch Reformed faith and were themselves later admitted to the New-York church. Centuries later Franklin used the whispers about his ancestors to comment to the *Detroit Jewish Chronicle*: "In the dim distant past they may have been Jews or Catholics or Protestants—what I am more interested in is whether they were good citizens and believers in God; I hope they were both."

Whatever religion or occupation Claes held in the old country, in 1649 he purchased a farm north of land owned by Peter Stuyvesant. It appears that he merely hoped to establish a better life for himself and his family in New-Amsterdam, intentions identical to those of tens of millions of immigrants who followed.

The colony that greeted Claes and Jannetje was unregulated compared with Plymouth Colony to the north. In fact, in 1664, when Charles II of England took it upon himself to deed New-Amsterdam to his brother the Duke of York, the Dutch colonists were too dispirited even to raise a musket in their own defense. The city became, of course, New-York. (It would not lose its hyphen until the 1800s.) The Van Rosenvelt family showed the keen political sense for which it would be known by anglicizing the family surname to the simpler Roosevelt.

By now, the couple had four daughters and one living son, Nicholas, born in 1658. Nicholas would become the great-great-great-great-grandfather of both Franklin and Theodore Roosevelt. As an adult, Nicholas moved up the west bank of the Hudson River to Kingston, where he became a prosperous fur trader, wearing moccasins and a leather jacket as he worked along the Hudson's banks.

In 1682 he married Heyltje Jans Kunst, the daughter of a house carpenter; the couple moved back to New-York in 1690. Nicholas had prospered from trading with Indians and now could live in town and work as a more genteel cloth merchant. He involved himself in local politics and was elected alderman, becoming the first Roosevelt to hold office in America. He always took the side of the colonies against England.

Nicholas had eight living children, including the sons Jacobus (James) and Johannes (John). Here the family splits: Jacobus, born in 1692, was the son whose descendants include James (the man who would be Sara's husband) and Franklin Delano Roosevelt. Johannes (John), born in 1689, was the son whose descendants include both Theodore and Eleanor Roosevelt. Somewhere along the two lines, the Franklin family pronounced their name "Rose-velt," and the Teddy family "Roos-velt." The two presidents were the same number of generations removed from Nicholas, but Theodore's father was twenty-seven years old when Teddy was born on October 27, 1858. Franklin's father was fifty-four when Franklin was born on January 30, 1882, which accounts for Teddy's twenty-three-year head start on Franklin.

In 1713 Franklin's forebear Jacobus Roosevelt married Catharina Hardenbroek, who was of German lineage. Jacobus was a significant landowner and was granted the area of Beekman's Swamp, which became the area of the city's tannery district and is now its Leather District. His task was to drain the swamp and lay out roads. Jacobus and Catharina had eleven children; their son Isaac, born in 1726, grew to be a distinguished man in the community. (The great-granddaughter of Jacobus and Catharina became known as Mother Elizabeth Seton, founder of the Sisters of Charity and the first American-born Roman Catholic saint.)

Isaac established the city's first sugar refinery. He attached his business to his Lower Manhattan residence. His four-story building, plus loft, was taller than anything except the area's church steeples. Isaac advertised "doubling, middling, and single refined loaf sugars, clarified, muscovado, and other molasses, etc." He also sold rum. That he was more prosperous than other sugar merchants may have indicated that he took the laws of Parliament—specifically, the British Molasses Act of 1733 and the Sugar Act of 1764—somewhat lightly. His frustration at English interference in his business probably stirred his desire for colonial independence. In addition, Isaac's rivals in the West Indies sugar and rum trade were British. "And that," said his great-great-grandson Franklin speaking more than 150 years later of his paternal ancestors, "is what made them revolutionists rather than Tories."

Whether it was Isaac's business interests or the politics of his grandfather Nicholas, Franklin was correct in characterizing him as an American patriot. Before the War of Independence, Isaac helped found the first chamber of commerce and the first public hospital in New York. His fellow citizens elected him to the New York Provincial Congress in 1775. After war broke out and General George Washington evacuated the city in late 1776, Isaac fled General Howe's British troops, who had seized Manhattan. He registered as a member of the Dutchess County militia and became a member of the General Committee of One Hundred, which controlled the provincial government. (While living in Dutchess County, Isaac was out on business when British soldiers burglarized his house of most of its silver. Luckily, they missed one silver tankard and the coffee and tea set that would later come into his descendant Franklin's possession.) Isaac also helped organize three thousand men as revolutionary soldiers and was one of a four-person council of war that advised troop commanders.

A month after the surrender at Yorktown, the British removed their troops from New-York on November 25, 1783. (The city was to honor Evacuation Day as a holiday for decades.) Isaac Roosevelt was there to welcome a triumphant General George Washington. On that great night, Isaac was a guest at the Fraunces Tavern celebration for General Washington. (The next month Washington chose the tavern to make his farewell address to his troops.)

Isaac's civic duties continued after independence: he represented New-York and assisted in drafting the state constitution in 1777. He was a member of the New York Constitutional Convention that met in Poughkeepsie (just a few miles from Hyde Park, where Franklin would be born). Here he cast an important "yea" vote on adopting the U.S. Constitution, in New-York's close count of thirty votes for, twenty-seven against. He served in the state legislature for six terms and was a member of the governor's council.

After the Revolution, America urgently needed its own bank. The nation's first bank, the Bank of North America, was formed in Philadelphia and was followed by such state-charter banks as the Bank of New York, which Isaac helped establish in 1784.

Alexander Hamilton wrote the constitution for the New York bank and negotiated a loan to the newly formed federal government, which helped stabilize its credit and economic independence. Hamilton then served as the first president of the bank. Isaac Roosevelt was put in charge of regulating new paper money and followed Hamilton as the bank's second president. In fact, the first corporate stock traded on the New York Stock Exchange eight years later was that of the Bank of New York.

Isaac's role at the bank was significant: New-York not only was the nation's capital at that time but was also becoming the new nation's greatest commercial power. Isaac's friends and associates included John Jay, Robert Livingston, Phillip Schuyler, Nicholas Low, and John Alsop. Through his patriotic endeavors, Isaac rubbed elbows with colonial aristocracy and became the first Roosevelt to be considered a gentleman. He, in turn, was described as "proud and aristocratical." This was at a time when, as a contemporary of Isaac's wrote, "the president and directors of a bank . . . were the only nobility we had. Men could not stand straight in their presence, and woe to them who bowed not down."

Isaac's bank presidency reflected his association with Alexander Hamilton, the young twenty-nine-year-old New Yorker who served as the country's first secretary of the Treasury in 1798. Hamilton was the leader of the Federalist party, which represented "wealth and talent," as opposed to the later Jeffersonian party of the people, a fact that gave Isaac's descendant Franklin some discomfort 150 years later. Yet Franklin would use Isaac to suit his needs. When, during the 1936 presidential campaign, Franklin was charged with disregarding the Constitution, he rejoined: "My great-great-grandfather was a member of that [constitutional] convention. And so you will see that not only in my own person but also by inheritance I know something not only about the Constitution of the United States but also about the Bill of Rights."

Isaac's accomplishments earned him the honorific Isaac the Patriot. He engaged Gilbert Stuart, who then was unknown in America, having just arrived in New York City from his training in England. In 1793 or 1794, Isaac paid Stuart about $50 for his portrait. Stuart also landed a commission to paint Chief Justice John Jay, in town to escape the yellow fever epidemic in Philadelphia, then the nation's capital. With the success of Jay's portrait, Stuart gained entrée to President George Washington and portrayed him in 124 slightly varied portraits. His single depiction of Isaac was similar to other portraits of other well-off men of the day—Hamilton was an exception to his cohorts, being an absolute dandy in comparison—with a frilled white shirt and rounded collar peeking out from a dark jacket. In Stuart's portrait, Isaac's hair is fringed on top but is longer on the side, covering his ears and then drawn back. His chin is prominent. His eyebrows are raised slightly, giving the image of a man curious and intelligent, holding a sheaf of documents in his hands, with an inkwell at his left.

Isaac had married Cornelia Hoffman of Red Hook in 1752, and they had ten children. After the storm of the War of Independence calmed and the task of setting up a new federal government became less urgent, Isaac returned to his sugar refinery in partnership with his son James. He retired from the bank in 1791 and occupied himself with a charitable interest instead, serving as president of the Society of the New York Hospital until his death in 1794 at age sixty-eight.

Isaac and Cornelia's son James had been born in 1760. There is a family tale that George Washington once lifted up young James onto his horse, but the story is only apocryphal. In any case, James grew up and graduated from Princeton College in 1780. He was a merchant, a member of the state assembly, and an alderman. Eventually he inherited his father's sugar refinery and, like his father, became an officer of the Bank of New York. Although Isaac remained in the city except for the brief period when he had to escape the British, James was not happy in Lower Manhattan: he wanted to breed cattle. He bought 150 acres in Harlem, on what is now 110th Street to 125th Street, from Fifth Avenue to the East River. From his house two blocks from Washington Square, he escaped to his farm on weekends.

Lower Manhattan was growing unrecognizable to James; its Dutch roots showed only in the architecture of older buildings, and its narrow streets swelled with taverns and theaters. Washington Irving would later write his sister: "New York, as you knew it, was a mere corner of the present huge city, and that corner is all changed, pulled to pieces, burnt down and rebuilt. It is really now one of the most rucketing cities in the world." James did not want a ruckus: he wanted tranquillity.

James felt the city's northward expansion nipping at his heels. He sold his rocky land—120 city blocks of it—for $25,000 to John Jacob Astor, the wealthy fur trader who was buying up as much acreage in Manhattan as he could. Lacking Astorian vision, James left Manhattan entirely in 1818 and moved seventy miles north to Dutchess County on the Hudson River. James used his windfall to build a grand house north of Poughkeepsie on the east bank of the Hudson River, where his mother's family lived. He named his square roomy house Mount Hope and became a full-time gentleman farmer. His portrait by Henry Inman shows the first Roosevelt to wear spectacles; the glasses draw attention from his long, sharp nose, thin lips, and prominent chin.

In 1790 James and his wife, Maria Eliza Walton, the daughter of an admiral, named their first son Isaac II, after James's father Isaac the Patriot. Although by now the Roosevelts were prosperous merchants, James rose in status when he married Eliza: her great-grandfather had been one of the richest merchants of his time, and her grandmother was descended from a family of Dutch patroons. James and Eliza eventually had seven more children. (After the death of Eliza, James remarried two more times.)

James and Eliza's eldest child, Isaac, graduated from Princeton in 1808. He finished medical school at Columbia University, but it turned out that Isaac the Patriot's namesake was not interested in surgery, for he could not stand the sight of blood or to be in the presence of anyone who was in pain. Such a disposition did not bode well for a man in his specialty. By 1820 he had given up any professional ambition and retired to his father's Mount Hope. There he puttered. He was a withdrawn and solitary man whose only interest outside the estate and its farmlands lay with his Dutch Reformed Church in nearby Poughkeepsie.

Surprising everyone, Dr. Isaac married at age thirty-seven, in 1827. His bride was the wealthy Mary Rebecca Aspinwall, whose family owned entire fleets of ships. However, because Mary's aunt had married Isaac's widowed father, Dr. Isaac was now married to the niece of his stepmother. When their son James Jr.—who would be Sara's husband and Franklin's father—was born in 1828, the baby was his namesake's grandson as well as his grandnephew by marriage. Familial intermarriage was more common than not in what was still an underpopulated nation with restricted social circles, and the practice helped develop strong feelings of kinship. Within the comfort of family, ancestors were revered. Beginning with Isaac the Patriot, the

Roosevelt generations were Isaac, James, Isaac, and James. (It took Sara Delano Roosevelt to break the familial pattern by naming her son Franklin after her rich Delano uncle.)

Now that Dr. Isaac had a wife and baby, he set out to establish his own home away from Mount Hope. Not too far, of course: the family moved across the road and less than a mile north of Mount Hope. They called their gabled estate Rosedale and placed it close to the Hudson, overlooking a placid section of the river. It was attractive but did not have the beautiful sweep of land of Algonac, the home that Warren Delano was to establish twenty years later across the river.

Rosedale was sumptuously decorated, but there was nothing as interesting in its decor as Algonac's Chinese touches. Nor was the household as bustling as Algonac's: young James would be the couple's only child until he was twelve. Home life was also quiet because Dr. Isaac had no professional or political interests that would bring strangers into the house; instead, he devoted himself to the farmland surrounding Rosedale and avoided his neighbors.

6

"A Gentleman of the Old School"

James spent his early childhood in seclusion, but when he was nine, he made friends at the Poughkeepsie Collegiate School, a new institution started as a day school for the sons of Hudson River gentlemen. By all accounts, James was happy and did well. Three years later, now boarding at the school, James was astonished to learn he would have a sibling, a baby brother named John Aspinwall Roosevelt. The baby was quickly dubbed Johnny, a name that stuck within the family. However, there was something about James's maturity that deterred people from calling him Jimmy, Jamie, or even Jim. He was always James.

By the time Johnny was two, James had left New York to prepare for college with a tutor in Massachusetts. He was sixteen years old when he entered the University of New York (now New York University), which was chosen for its proximity to the city residence of his Roosevelt grandparents on Bleecker Street. His Aspinwall grandparents were nearby, too, just a few blocks away, although one Aspinwall uncle objected to James's attending an urban college, fearing that "he will become a Dandy and will walk Broadway with his cane."

James started well at college, joining a collegiate debating society and winning its gold medal. However, by June he had been admonished by the math department and skipped several of his final exams. The next year he transferred to Union College in Schenectady. Its president was the philosophy department chairman and a well-known public speaker on moral values. In fact, under his stern leadership, Union College had gained a reputation for taking in boys who had earlier transgressed. There must have been many disruptive boys from good families, for James was enrolled with a Schuyler and a Schermerhorn. They dressed for class in white shirts with tall collars, frock coats, and top hats.

Imagine the shame that Dr. and Mrs. Isaac felt when the esteemed college president informed them of their son's membership in a forbidden secret society. (This was Delta Phi, which was then an upstart social club but is now honored as the country's oldest fraternity.) Not only was his affiliation shocking, but his fraternity held its meetings in a local tavern. James's actions were appalling, especially after frequent lectures from the school president on the dangers of alcohol, including a cautionary tale about a boy so drunk that he spontaneously combusted!

James's parents pulled him out of school for several months, although the college president thought this punishment too severe and wrote, adjuring them to change their minds. Finally he was released from parental house arrest and went back to school, bearing warnings from his father against reading fiction. James eventually earned an A.B. from Union in 1847.

This was the same year that his grandfather James, who had been the first Roosevelt to establish himself on the Hudson and live the life of a gentleman farmer, died. One obituary read: "Having acquired a small fortune, he retired from commercial life many years ago to spend the remnant of his days in the luxury of sharing it with a large circle of friends, and the richer luxury of doing good in the cause of his Redeemer."

Another account characterized James as "a gentleman of the old school." In fact, beginning with the elder James, three generations of Roosevelt men—James, Isaac, and James—would be characterized in their obituaries as "a gentleman of the old school." Apparently, Franklin, in the next generation, broke the pattern.

In retrospect, the most important action of the elder James was his move to the Hudson Valley, for its way of life shaped every member of the Roosevelt family for four generations. The younger James was too callow to appreciate his Hudson roots, however; he was itching to see the world. After much thought and consideration by his parents, young James was sent on a tour of Europe to help him mature. His father lectured him: "We know not what a day might bring forth. 'Be ye also ready' is the warning voice."

Despite his father's ominous warning, James enjoyed the eighteen-month grand tour that took him to the Holy Land, England, France, and

Italy. It was now 1848, and James took up the cause of the Italian leader Garibaldi and his unification of Italy. James and his pals joined Garibaldi's forces, but after a month of training, their enthusiasm dimmed. Although the Roosevelts would later boast of James's championing a free Italy, he was merely a summer soldier.

After his tour ended, James enrolled in Harvard Law School, graduating on his twenty-third birthday with an LL.B., the degree his grandfather had earned two generations earlier. (Law school was then a two-year project.) James entered the law firm of Benjamin Silliman, who was his uncle as well as a Hudson River neighbor. There, James worked on various corporate matters and, through his close association with Silliman, was named to the board of directors of the Consolidated Coal Company, the firm's client.

Unlike his refined and delicate father, James, with his blue-gray eyes, became a man-about-town and was an athletic figure among the sports-loving Hudson River families. Two years after leaving Harvard, he was elected an honorary member of its Porcellian Club. He was a guest in the best circles and frequently visited the home of *the* Mrs. Astor.

In 1853, at twenty-five, James married plump and pretty Rebecca Brien Howland of *Mayflower* descent and shipping venture fortune. In fact, the couple were cousins: the uncle who feared that James's attendance at New York University would make him a dandy was Rebecca's father. James's grandmother was also a descendant of John Howland, the man who fell off the *Mayflower* and hung from a topsail until rescued by a sailor. After a Niagara Falls honeymoon, James brought Rebecca to Mount Hope, which he had inherited. (Rosedale would go to his younger brother, Johnny.) James left the Dutch Reformed Church of the Roosevelts and joined Rebecca's Episcopal religion.

Soon the young couple was off to Europe. When they returned, Rebecca was expecting a baby. In 1854 their first and only child was born. His name was James Roosevelt Roosevelt: his father disliked the appendage Junior and used the boy's surname as his middle name. The child's nickname was Rosy.

Life was good for James, Rebecca, and Rosy. James loved his old house and closely superintended its land and animals. He was devoted to area affairs and socialized with his neighbors, including Warren Delano across the river at Algonac. He spent weekends riding and hunting in the Dutchess County Hunt. He bred fast horses—his trotter Gloster was the first horse to go a mile in 2:17—and drove a four-in-hand.

Caroline Astor's friend Ward McAllister called the town of Hyde Park "English life to perfection." James took pleasure in the role of country squire and carried it out with a vengeance; he affected muttonchop whiskers, pearl gray leather gloves, and riding crop. His costume made one Roosevelt relative cast a critical eye: "He tried to pattern himself on Lord Landsdown, sideburns and all, but he succeeded only in mimicking Lord Landsdown's coachman."

However, his love for Rosy was real. Both parents took a deep interest in raising Rosy themselves rather than shunting him to the care of servants. James, in particular, was an outgoing and cheerful father, unlike his own father, Dr. Isaac. James would often spend full days with Rosy, teaching him everything about outdoor life and passing down a love of horses. Father and son would fish, skeet shoot, and hunt together. Every aspect of Rosy's life was important. Rebecca took her cue from James and equally dedicated herself to their son. In fact, Rosy slept in his parents' bedroom until he was about ten years old.

Soon James realized that the law was a bore and sought to make a living—or perhaps a fortune—in business. He concentrated on the new forms of transportation that were changing the landscape and commerce of the country. He looked forward and recognized that money was no longer to be made from clipper ships or Eastern exports. Rather than searching outside the nation for his fortune, he concentrated on the transportation infrastructure that would be needed to support a country growing exponentially from its vast tidal waves of immigrants. Some of his investments paid off; some did not. Fortunately, James held interests in railroad companies that offset his losses in canals and steamboats. His railroad investments alone brought him $300,000, as railroads put in motion economic expansion and fabricated sparkling wealth. Coal, which ushered in the Industrial Age in a smoky fog, remained his commodity—in fact, the original purpose of his Delaware and Hudson Canal Company was to carry coal from Pennsylvania to the Hudson River. Another man who had money in this company was Warren Delano.

In the years leading up to the Civil War, James was a Whig, the party of his father and grandfather, as well as of his uncle and former employer, Benjamin Silliman. However, by 1856 the party had failed to take a firm position against slavery, so James changed his allegiance to the Republican party of Abraham Lincoln. However, his pro-Union stance did not mean that he would fight. Perhaps his month's training for Garibaldi had taught him the tedium of war. In any case, as was common among the well-off, James hired someone to soldier in his place for three hundred dollars, in a time when the average man's annual income was only five hundred dollars. (On the other hand, his fourth cousin Theodore Roosevelt Sr.—who also would be father to a president—was ashamed of having avoided fighting and compensated through service work for Union soldiers.)

Halfway through the war, Dr. Isaac died and James, as eldest son, received the lion's share of his fortune. In 1866, the year after the Civil War ended, a fire destroyed Mount Hope. Servants saved a few items, including the Gilbert Stuart portrait of Isaac the Patriot and Isaac's complete George II silver service (the one that the British soldiers missed when they ransacked Isaac's Dutchess County house). Two Duncan Phyfe chairs and five dining-room chairs engraved with the Roosevelt crest of three intertwined roses and feathered plumes were pulled from the fire, as were two rosewood beds and a rosewood bureau.

Rather than rebuild, James decided to relocate, since New York State had already bought the land south of Mount Hope and designated it for an institution for the insane. He sold Mount Hope to the "Lunatic Asylum" and looked for another property to buy. One nearby house belonged to John Jacob Astor, which James turned down as being too pricey at $50,000.

Instead, James and Rebecca moved to an estate on a hundred wooded, rolling acres, whose colonial ownership dated to 1699. The place was eighty miles north of New York City, near Rosedale.

Another attraction of the house was that its prior owner—Josiah Wheeler, who had used it as a summer residence—had built a stable and track, perfect for James's horses. The estate, including its 110 acres, cost $40,000, 20 percent less than the Astor place. Before moving in, James realized that the estate had no gateposts and for sentimental reasons he removed from Mount Hope the brownstone gateposts unscathed by the house fire and placed them at the front of his new driveway, a symbol of continuity.

7

Hyde Park

James decided to call the estate Springwood, but the couple soon realized they did not like designating their home by any name and instead referred to their residence as Hyde Park, after the town in which it was located. The custom of referring to the estate as Hyde Park, rather than Springwood, lasted until the 1940s, when it was turned over to the government for the FDR library. Ellie Roosevelt Seagraves, Franklin and Eleanor's eldest grandchild, said, "We always said we were going to Hyde Park and *not* that we were going to Springwood. It was the U.S. Park Service and the Park Service alone that put on that old name. None of us in the family *ever* used the term 'Springwood.'" Indeed, Eleanor Roosevelt wrote a history of the estate for the National Park Service in 1949 and never once called it Springwood. So the Roosevelt house was called Hyde Park. Having watched Mount Hope's value diminish when the state bought the adjoining property, James added land to the original boundaries; within a few years the estate totaled six hundred acres.

A visitor coming to Hyde Park would pass the brownstone gateposts before the clapboard house would come into view. Its central bloc had been a farmhouse built in the Federal style about 1800. Its previous owner had remodeled it in 1826 to make it larger—fifteen rooms—and now it mimicked the Italianate style of architecture fashionable at the time. Comfortable piazzas ran the length of the front and back, and a three-story tower rose on the south end of the house. From the back, between the pillars with thick vines growing up them, the Roosevelts could see past a small apple orchard to the Hudson below. From the front they would view a gently curved driveway leading out to Albany Post Road. To the house's north side, slopes of hemlock trees edged flower, fruit, and vegetable gardens. The outbuildings included a laundry, a greenhouse, an icehouse that was also used to store coal and vegetables, and, of course, a stable.

Almost nothing survived the fire at Mount Hope, so the couple furnished the house from scratch. However, in went Isaac the Patriot's silver set, a silver tankard, the three rosewood pieces, and two of the crested dining-room chairs (the remaining three went to Johnny at Rosedale). James and Rebecca replaced their old furnishings with items similar to those at Mount Hope, so the house was comfortable, not new or ostentatious. The couple also had a home at 15 Washington Square for James's business trips in town and visits to his clubs—Metropolitan, Union, Century, and University. As often as he could, James brought Rosy with him to his business meetings. Rebecca would join them in the city if she wanted to shop or visit friends. A great event was the annual ball put on by the Patriarchs, organized by Mrs. Astor's friend McAllister specifically as a social club that excluded new wealth. Although James was not asked to be a founding patriarch, he was asked to join within a few years when membership expanded from twenty-five to fifty men, and he served as a host at several balls.

Although the Roosevelt family's wealth was modest compared with that of the Astors, the Vanderbilts, or even their Oyster Bay cousins, James led a comfortable life as a member of the Hudson River gentry. He and Rebecca traveled to Paris and London and were guests in the great English country houses. As a refined American and first-rate sportsman, James was welcome anywhere in society.

However, wherever the couple went, no matter how exotic the capital, they found New York friends nearby. On Sundays they sought out church services in English in whatever city they visited and, rather than stay at a hotel packed with foreigners, would pick one for its appeal to Americans. In Paris, for example, they were guests at Hôtel de l'Oncle Tom. To keep Hyde Park with them, the couple hung drawings of their dogs on hotel walls. James had the *Times* mailed to him so that he could check the value of his stocks. They bumped into everyone they knew; the only problem was sailing on a Cunard ship with, as Rebecca put it, "the greatest number of Jews."

Rosy, of course, went with them to Europe and was tutored wherever they went. With such high expectations for their only child, the couple had a difficult time finding an adequate tutor or governess for him. Still, Rosy must have been learning: according to his attentive father, he talked in his sleep in French, German, and English. Occasionally Rosy enrolled in a local school, but he was not encouraged by his parents to play with schoolmates. Instead, James and Rebecca were delighted that the threesome were inseparable. However, they eventually recognized that their son was lonely and sent for Rebecca's younger brother, only a year older than Rosy, so that he could have a friend.

At home in Hyde Park, James paid close attention to the farm. He built stables for his trotting horses and bred a herd of Alderney cattle that he crossed with Jerseys and Guernseys. In business, his main interest was the reorganization of southern railroads. By now, the Delaware and Hudson's canal route had been abandoned and James was overseeing its conversion to accommodate trains. As president of the Southern Railway Security Company, he wanted to establish routes between the commercial East Coast cities and the principal cities of the South. After the Civil War ended—the Roosevelts were far less caught up in its emotions than the Delanos across the river—James reacted against radical abolitionists and reconstructionists by joining the Democratic party. James had an economic interest in supporting the Democrats: the Republicans' levying taxes on southerners to support Reconstruction harmed the profitability of his railroad lines. Although several other society families were Democrats, James had very few Hudson River friends who were similarly aligned. His cousins the Oyster Bay Roosevelts had been firmly anti-slavery and remained staunchly Republican.

James was content to live within his income, but that did not stop him from investing in several properties that he hoped would make him truly wealthy. He gambled with a small stake and never won big. After the panic of 1873, when the New York Stock Exchange shut down for ten days, his proposed southern railroad network failed and he was allowed to resign from the board. Two years later he suffered another defeat when shareholders of his coal company voted him and his fellow directors out of office. His scheme to build a canal across Nicaragua also failed. Still, James kept his other interests secure and was always financially stable. He was too cautious to bet his starched shirt, but he would have been quietly overjoyed to strike it rich.

James had seen no point in becoming a Union soldier, but he felt strongly the obligations of local elected service. A few years earlier, in 1871, he had run as a Democrat for supervisor of the village of Hyde Park and was elected. He also sat on the Dutchess County board. He took his duties seriously, cutting per diems and payments for supervisors and investigating conditions at the county jail. James was concerned about local education and was instrumental in building a state-of-the-art redbrick schoolhouse for children from grades one to ten. His interest was more than administrative: he took to stopping by classrooms at random and listening to student recitations. Rosy often accompanied him. In 1873 James became a board member of the same state lunatic asylum that sat near his former home. He made spontaneous visits to the asylum, too, and would note his inspections: "Ward 8 overcrowded, twenty-eight in this ward intended for fifteen." He did not take half measures with his obligations.

In fact, his activities convinced the New York Democratic party that James should run for state office. The idea held appeal for him. Rebecca knew her husband was intrigued by the invitation, writing in her diary: "James went to a political meeting. I was dreadfully afraid he would be nominated . . . but he got home safely."

Politics and business were thrown aside when Rebecca developed a heart condition. When she worsened and could not climb stairs, servants carried her. Then James installed an elevator in the Washington Square home for her comfort—an extravagant and rare luxury for the 1870s. In the summer of 1876, James thought the fresh air of a yachting expedition up the Long Island Sound would ease Rebecca's breathing. Instead, she suffered a heart attack on the boat. James brought her back to the house at Washington Square, where she died at age forty-five. Rebecca was buried in the graveyard at St. James Episcopal Church in Hyde Park.

James was forty-eight and he missed Rebecca in particular and having a wife in general. After a suitable mourning period, he began to socialize. On November 19, 1878, James was thrown into the maelstrom of New York society when his twenty-three-year-old son Rosy married Helen Schermerhorn Astor, the daughter of Caroline Astor. Rosy's bride was John Jacob Astor's great-granddaughter. (Sara Delano was by now twenty-four years old and must have read of the Astor-Roosevelt engagement and learned details of the wedding from friends who were invited.)

The Astor-Roosevelt wedding was the most exciting of the season, ranking a front-page *New York Times* story centered directly under the masthead. A NOTABLE SOCIAL EVENT was the capped heading. Rosy was described thus: "He is a gentleman of culture and of leisure, endowed with an ample fortune and with an honored name." All that was needed to say of his bride was "Miss Astor is the eldest daughter of Mr. William Astor."

Hyperbole permeated the story. The bride's mother "wore a rich black velvet, with ample train, and trimmings of lace 200 years old. Her diamonds were superb and abundant." The bride wore a white satin gown designed by Worth, and her Worth trousseau was "one of the most artistic and elegant that it ever fell to the lot of the bride to possess." The ceremony was held at

Manhattan's Grace Church with so many guests that some needed to stand in the aisles.

The English-style reception at the Astor home "has never been surpassed," gushed the *Times*. The families invited fifteen hundred guests, and the arriving carriages blocked Fifth Avenue for four blocks. The newlyweds' gifts included a silver centerpiece, an eleven-piece silver tea service, a diamond tiara, a diamond crescent, pearl earrings, a pearl necklace, and a diamond pendant "of great value." The *Times* further commented of the gifts that "most of them were exceedingly rich, and all were valuable."

Even the capacious Astor house could not adequately display the presents to the crush of guests, but they were "admired by all who could reach them." With the five hundred carriages causing a jam outside the Astor doorway, "the confusion was complete. In the unavoidable struggle at the door, the canopy was carried away and the ruins were gathered up in haste to make way for the [departing] crowd."

Rosy's bride brought him a trust fund of $400,000. The couple moved into a mansion on Fifth Avenue that had been owned by the bride's father, William Backhouse Astor.

James now focused on his friendship with relatives old and new. He began to see his Oyster Bay cousins more often, and soon he formed an attachment to the much younger Anna "Bamie" Roosevelt, who did not return his feelings. In May 1880—the year when the Industrial Age segued into the Gilded Age—fifty-two-year-old James was invited to a small dinner party given at 6 West Fifty-seventh Street, the home of Bamie's mother, Mrs. Theodore Roosevelt Sr. Also at the party was Sara Delano, now twenty-six, the daughter of his old friend Warren. Apparently Sara's presence distracted James from his previous interest in Bamie. His hostess couldn't help but notice James's attention to Sara. "He talked to her the whole time," Mrs. Roosevelt said. "He never took his eyes off her."

8

"A Democrat Can Be a Gentleman"

What attracted Sara to a man her father's age? Perhaps the very fact that James was so much like Warren: James made her feel secure and appreciated, he laughed heartily at her witticisms, and she, in turn, was attracted to the flourish with which he smoked his cheroot. James was courtly, he respected her opinions, and—most important—he was as wedded to the Hudson River way of life as she was. James was comfortable and familiar company; in fact, James and Sara were sixth cousins through Ezekiel Cheever, who was the first headmaster of Boston Latin School and was the well-known teacher of Cotton Mather. And if James was descended from an old Knickerbocker family, certainly Sara—who qualified for membership in the Mayflower Society, the Society of Colonial Wars, the Daughters of the American Revolution, the Huguenot Society, and the Americans of Royal Descent—was his match in lineage. Sara had thought her father was infallible; now she transferred this adoration to James.

Warren and Catherine were initially surprised at James's courtship of their daughter: after all, he had an adult son born the same year as Sara. However, he was a good friend whom Warren respected deeply. In fact, Warren declared, "James Roosevelt is the first person who has made me realize that a Democrat can be a gentleman."

The relationship moved quickly. James embarked on the twenty-mile trip to Algonac, crossing the Hudson on the Beacon-Newburgh ferry. Then Sara's sister Dora, with her husband, Will Forbes, returned the courtesy by staying for five days at Hyde Park. Soon after, James and Sara together paid a call on Rebecca's father, Gardiner Howland. The couple were minding their p's and q's.

In this measured courtship dance, James invited Sara and her female relatives to be his houseguests. One day James asked Sara to arrange the flowers for lunch. His intentions were as clear as if he had proposed on bended knee. Not long after this signal event, one month after their first meeting, James asked Warren for Sara's hand.

The wedding was subdued, since Warren's cousin and Sara's tutor Nannie Church had died the year before and the family had recently lost Aunt Sarah Delano to cancer. A contemporary newspaper account wryly noted that "what had been originally intended to be the most fashionable event of the season in this locality had to be changed at the last moment into a family gathering. The families of Mr. Delano and Mr. Roosevelt, however, are very large."

Algonac was decorated with wildflowers by Sara's sister Kassie and Warren III's wife, Jennie. The gardeners arranged more formal floral decorations and set pots of ferns, tropical palms, and other popular Victorian foliage around the rooms. A few days before the wedding, Warren hired a carpenter and painter for touch-ups, and Algonac's housekeeper, Harriet Wood, went to Hyde Park to arrange Sara's trousseau in the black walnut wardrobe of the southeast bedroom.

October 7, 1880, was the date of the wedding at Algonac. The 1:00 P.M. train that was to take the guests from Manhattan to the ferry was half an hour late, but the carriages sent to pick them up at the opposite landing waited. The fall foliage was colorful and the day was pleasantly cool, following an especially hot summer. As the guests were at last driven through the winding woodland scene to Algonac, locals waved and cheered.

The carriages pulled up to a trellised portico decorated with trailing ivy and evergreens. A more exotic sight—several tiger-skin rugs strewn across the polished floor—greeted the guests in the main vestibule. The twin walnut balustrades of the main staircase were swagged with flowers. To the right, in Algonac's double library with the cardinal red satin curtains, Sara's parents, along with her unmarried sisters, Kassie and Laura, greeted the 125 guests. The room's fireplaces were filled with Sèvres vases holding greenery.

To the left of the vestibule was the west drawing room, where the ceremony was held. It resembled a conservatory, jammed with plants and flowers, its back walls strung with trailing ivy. In the wall niches, orchids in full bloom gracefully drooped from their majolica vases. At both ends of the room, Boston rosebuds cascaded from their containers. The fireplaces were accented on either side with maidenhair ferns.

The wedding started half an hour late because of the tardy trains. The couple stood in the drawing room under a floral canopy as the minister from All Souls, the Delanos' Unitarian church in Manhattan, began the marriage ceremony. Two blue satin pillows were placed on the floor in front of the bride and groom, and when the Reverend Dr. Henry Whitney Bellows pronounced the blessing, the couple knelt before him.

Sara wore a gown of pure white brocade with heirloom lace and a tulle veil. The neckline of her bodice was high to accent her long, stately neck, and it showed off her gift from James, a five-strand pearl necklace. Sara was slim, tall, and majestic. Because the wedding was simple, there were no maids of honor; instead, Sara's sisters and female relatives stood with her as informal attendants, holding bouquets of rosebuds.

Among the guests were James's son, Rosy, and his wife, Helen Astor Roosevelt. The *Poughkeepsie Daily Eagle* noted the presence of James's mother, "Mrs. Dr. Isaac Roosevelt"; his aunt, his younger brother, Johnny, with wife and daughters; his cousins; and, of course, Bamie Roosevelt. A number of Delanos were present, including Uncle Frederick and Aunt Laura Delano. (Laura Astor Delano was both Sara's aunt and the aunt of Rosy's wife.) Sara's eldest sister, Dora Forbes, came in from Shanghai, although sister Annie Hitch had to stay in Hong Kong. The *Daily Eagle* wrote that the wedding was witnessed "by a small number of the best representatives of New York society."

After the ceremony, the guests walked to the back lawn for the catered "breakfast" reception. In the house, they could view the wedding gifts, which included "many rare and valuable heirlooms and art treasures." At 4:20 in the afternoon, the bride and groom departed, riding in a Delano family victoria drawn by the matched horses Meg and Pet and driven by "Papa's coachman French," as Sara wrote in her diary. Sara wore an outfit of gray and black, in deference to the recent family deaths.

Midway between the two estates, the coachman stopped and greeted Hutchins, the Roosevelt coachman. Hutchins was waiting with a tea cart, a small coach with a high seat in the rear. Hutchins held the reins until the Roosevelts took their seats, then jumped into the rumble. James handled the reins himself with his new bride beside him. "James drove me up to Hyde Park, crossing the river in the ferry at Poughkeepsie," wrote Sara in her diary. From there, they drove up Albany Post Road, past the property that had been Mount Hope, past Johnny's house, Rosedale, and home to Hyde

Park. "A perfect October day, bright sunshine and brilliant foliage," Sara concluded.

Sara had been transferred smoothly from Algonac to Hyde Park: from the hands of her father, Warren, to the hands of her husband, James.

9

⁂

"Sallie and Mr. Roosevelt"

Sara embraced her new home that fall of 1880. She knew that in marrying a widower, she would be leaving Algonac for a house that had belonged to another woman, James's first wife. Rebecca was the woman who had selected the design and furnishings of Hyde Park—down to the bed in the blue bedroom where Sara would sleep on her wedding night. Nonetheless, Sara embraced her new home without hesitation or complaint. She knew instinctively that the happiness James had enjoyed with Rebecca would not impair their relationship, unless she herself made an issue of it. This she did not do.

Nor did reminders of Rebecca throughout the cozy house, heavily decorated in the Victorian manner, bother her in the least. An insecure woman might have wanted to replace Rebecca's pictures and china with her own, but Sara admired every item. She thought the decor perfect, including the delicately wrought soft white Dresden china chandelier and mantel set bought by Rebecca in Germany and the silver service with its pumpkin motif that Rebecca had chosen in New York. Also in the house were pieces selected by a younger James, such as the three small spindly chairs that he had shipped home from Ravenna, Italy, during his grand tour. There would be no bridal hesitation step to Sara's pace as she walked into the vestibule at

Hyde Park. She was Mrs. James Roosevelt, mistress of the Roosevelt estate on the Hudson.

As the newlyweds approached Hyde Park, Elspeth (Elespie) McEachern, the Scottish housekeeper originally hired by Rebecca, had alerted the staff and they—Elespie, Lizzie the maid, Allan the butler, Sebastian Bowman the gardener, and a temporary cook—lined up to greet James and Sara. The couple planned to spend a short time at Hyde Park before a long European honeymoon; for them, there was no place more pleasant than their own house. As Sara settled into her new role, it must have seemed that married life at Hyde Park was very much like her maiden life at Algonac. The only difference was that now when Sara glimpsed the river, she watched the sun set rather than rise.

The newlyweds' first days set the pattern for years to come. Awakening with James in the master bedroom, Sara would enjoy an early cup of tea in bed (marriage would not alter her tea drinking, a Delano habit). Only then would she rise and select an outfit from her trousseau. She would not be wearing colors other than gray or black for another six months, for she observed without question the strict rules of mourning. After dressing, she would go downstairs for breakfast with James. Then, leaving James and entering her "snuggery," a favorite cozy sitting room on the ground floor, Sara would consult with the housekeeper about the day's meals and such pertinent topics as what guests might be visiting. She would note any recipe she might want the cook to follow in her household book, a notebook that every bride established in the days before printed cookbooks and other home-organization guides became popular. Boston Cooking-School Cookbook (Fannie Farmer's Cookbook), for example, would not be published for another sixteen years. Sara might suggest a lunch of soup, fish, chicken, and rice pudding, and for dinner, soup, fish, roast beef, and Yorkshire pudding or turkey with squash and mince pie, as well as dessert. Sara would ladle the soup from the tureen, and James would carve the turkey. After she planned the household's day to her satisfaction, she might cut autumn flowers from the gardens and place arrangements throughout the house.

Then Sara would join James outdoors, and they would walk the property closest to the house, checking in at the greenhouse and the stables. She might admire the day's stencil pictures drawn by a groomsman in colored sand that lay on the cement floor in front of each carriage, which would be destroyed when the carriage drove over it, swept away, and then redrawn after the carriage returned. Once they completed their rounds, Sara would change into an English riding habit, including a derby held by a strip of elastic. The couple's mid-morning ride would take them around the farm and into the woods. Their horses would have been brushed to a glow, their hooves varnished, and their ankles wrapped in white puttees. The forest they would ride through had never been timbered off—James forbade cutting any but a diseased tree—and its magnificent trees looked much the same as they had hundreds of years earlier when Henry Hudson had sailed past. As they rode, Sara and James would view the brilliant scarlet and golden foliage and enjoy an occasional glimpse of the sun reflecting off the Hudson below them.

Arriving back home, they would change for lunch. After their meal, they would again ride or, if Sara had changed into her *trotteur* (a walking costume of gray or black serge) perhaps walk on the sloping path down to the boathouse. James would take the oars of his light double rowboat—he also owned a single wherry for his sole pleasure—and row for a short distance on the river, talking with Sara as they went. He would stop occasionally to catch his breath, allowing the boat to drift gently in the current while Sara let her hand trail in the water. Her still hand would make a circular pattern that would seem to travel in an ever-expanding hypnotic circle. In these magic moments, the couple would not speak and would listen only to the sound of birds in the trees onshore, or of geese overhead on their route south.

"We spent a happy month at Hyde Park," Sara wrote in her journal, having symbolically started a new diary that month headed "Marriage of JR and SD." Friends of James who owned nearby estates came by for afternoon tea or stopped over before dinner for something stronger. Sara's parents paid, as Catherine wrote, "our *first* visit to Sallie and Mr. Roosevelt in her new home." One by one, invitations to the couple began to arrive, so many that on many mornings Sara told the housekeeper at their daily meeting to inform "Cook" not to bother with dinner that night. Their first evening out as a couple was at the home of the Livingstons, a family whose ties with the Roosevelt family went all the way back to Isaac the Patriot, who had watched Chancellor Robert Livingston administer the presidential oath of office to George Washington at Federal Hall on Wall Street.

Old New York did not intimidate Sara, with her Huguenot and English ancestry; nor was she shy about her position as the young wife of an older, well-established husband whose family had been New Yorkers for more than two hundred years. She herself belonged to the Hudson River gentry. Manners were the keystone to this society and were a greater indicator of class than money. (In fact, the newly rich were so in need of guidance in how to behave that the first etiquette books were published in this period.) When James's friends met this self-confident woman with the regal bearing, they accepted her immediately. Young she was, but she was undeniably as much a part of their world as any dowager.

Nor did new money threaten the couple. Sara was well rooted in the sound values learned at Algonac—as well as being the daughter of a rich man—and James was prosperous. Sara and James lived in comfort but eschewed ostentation. James and Sara could live life as they wished, and their breeding was unquestioned by the social leaders of booming industrial America. Although they were a part of the New York society that Edith Wharton fictionalized so tellingly in her novels, their preference for "simple" country life kept them a step removed from Wharton's fictional gatherings. (In fact, Sara first met Wharton when Sara was fifteen and Wharton eight. At that time, Wharton was still Edith "Pussy" Jones and lived three blocks from her childhood friends Bamie, Teddy, and Elliott Roosevelt.)

The values of the Victorian era had a strong influence on well-off Hudson River dwellers. Their families were large and patriarchal, although women were revered. Family, religious observation, and Protestant values imbued their lives. Politics also played a role, as Americans linked democratic representative government with the highest form of rule. Still, railroads and the national railroad network were a symbol of progress, one in which James played a role.

James and Sara also eschewed some bluenosed attitudes. James had a smattering of Jewish friends. One of the best known was August Belmont, who represented the Rothschilds' interest in the United States and had a cottage in Newport called By-the-Sea. (Belmont was the man on whom Wharton based her fictional character Julius Beaufort.) Sara remembered her husband saying a number of times that although "he did not have a drop of Jewish blood as far as he knew . . . if he were a Jew, he would be very proud of it."

In early November Sara and James left on their honeymoon, taking with them a copious number of trunks and luggage, lettered and numbered "S.R. No. 1," "S.R. No. 2," and so on. They traveled to fashionable places, sailing to London, where they spent ten days before leaving for France and Italy. They spent a week visiting Sara's sister Dora and brother-in-law Will Forbes at their villa in Genoa. Together, the four toured palaces. Then Sara and James left the Forbeses, were off to Venice, and spent Christmas in Bologna. Throughout Europe, Sara and James visited friends and acquaintances and took their exercise by walking through historic neighborhoods. In Rome, Dora and Will Forbes joined them again for a three-week visit. Sara sent frequent letters to her parents at Algonac, written in the standard nineteenth-century frugal crosshatch style: rows across overwritten by perpendicular rows with the paper turned sideways.

Soon after Rome, the couple left for Spain, where Sara fell ill with a bad cold. "James too devoted to me," she wrote. He nursed her back to health and, as a surprise, brought the landlord's pretty daughter to Sara's bed to model a lovely Spanish lace mantilla he had bought for her. As soon as Sara was up, James came down with the same cold. "I felt so anxious about him that our whole visit [to Spain] was a nightmare." Once both were well, Sara attended her first bullfight. She was appalled, writing that bullfighting is "a cruel savage amusement, not a sport."

Grateful to return to France, the couple went to Biarritz, "where we spent a month to recuperate from our Spanish illnesses. James drove me daily in a picturesque phaeton with a man behind." Wherever they stopped, Sara looked for special Christmas ornaments for the couple's tree. On to Bordeaux, where James ordered wine for Hyde Park. The Forbses joined them again in Paris, and the Delanos from Algonac, including Mama and Papa, and Sara's unmarried sisters, Kassie and Laura, who had missed their married sister dreadfully. Brother Frederick had to remain behind at the Adams Academy in Massachusetts, preparing for his college entrance exams; Annie was in China; and Phil was too delicate to travel. James arranged for Sara to have use of a brougham to drive her family around the city "and we were *most* luxurious." Unless the Roosevelts had made separate engagements with friends, they dined with the Delanos twice a day, and took adjoining boxes at the theater. Sara occasionally wore her wedding dress at formal occasions, for it was the custom for brides to appear in their bridal gowns for a year or two after marriage. By spring Sara's mourning period was over, and her colorful clothing after months of gray and black cheered her when she bade good-bye to her family.

The Roosevelts left together for Holland, where they ordered a grandfather clock for the hallway and a Dutch sideboard for the dining room. They spent two months in Germany. Quick visits to Switzerland, Italy, and Paris engaged them before they returned to England, this time visiting the countryside, where James rowed Sara on the Thames toward Henley. At Norwich, James ordered some wonderful Thorn carriages to be sent to Hyde Park. In his eagerness to please his bride—and perhaps demonstrate that he was a man of means—he commissioned a landau, a dogcart, and a victoria from England's best carriage purveyor. These, in addition to a carriage he had bought years earlier that was made for Napoleon III, made the Roosevelt vehicles a smart collection.

In Scotland in August, Sara wrote: "I nearly fainted at morning service, giving James a little fright, but the feeling passed over." She was five months pregnant, having conceived in Paris the previous April. It was time to go home. "James was untiring and thoughtful in everything, [he] wrote to Elespie and others at home about preparing all for our return."

At the end of the month, Sara received a cable telling her that Uncle

Ned, her bachelor uncle who had lived at Algonac, had died suddenly while yachting at Bar Harbor. Sara could no longer fit into last fall's mourning clothes, so she had to purchase a more capacious black dress. She was not used to ready-made clothing and, in addition, was slightly self-conscious about her changed figure. "James helped me get a black dress and did *every-thing*," she wrote gratefully.

With a baby well on the way, the Roosevelts' ten-month honeymoon was over. They sailed back to New York and were met at the harbor by "dear Papa," Will, and Annie's husband, Hitch. They went straightaway to Hyde Park "and found the house in beautiful order" with the help waiting to greet them. Within two weeks, Sara had hired a new cook, Christine, and James an excellent coachman—"English and well-trained"—with the perfect name of Buckle. (As was the custom, staff outside the house were called by their last names, whereas the female staff within the house were generally called by their first names.) Sara and James took tea that day with James's mother, Rebecca, at Rosedale.

Laura Delano came from Algonac for a five-day stay, and the two women took turns having James row them in his double rowboat. The neighbors revisited the couple, this time to hear all about their European trip and to admire Sara's new parlor grand piano, given to her by James on their first anniversary. Sara immersed herself in James's life and was completely comfortable embracing his friends and family. Of her stepson and his wife who lived in Red House on their property, a quarter of a mile to the north, she wrote: "Of course, we see Rosy and Helen every day." Because of Helen's great Astor wealth, Rosy made leisure his vocation; he was content to drive a four-in-hand excellently and, in recognition of his skill, was granted the great honor of being president of the Coaching Club. Rosy and Helen could also retreat to their land in the Adirondacks, where they "camped out" with the assistance of their chef, valet, butler, and maids.

By now, Sara was six months pregnant and Helen was due to give birth to her second child at the end of the month. (Rosy and Helen had a young son named James Roosevelt Roosevelt Jr., nicknamed Taddy; their second child would be a daughter named Helen after her mother.) Despite this era's prudishness, neither the Delano nor Roosevelt families hid pregnancy. It was a part of life, to be accepted and encouraged in the same manner as good food and exercise. Sara refused to let pregnancy limit her activities, except for riding horseback.

However, she rarely acknowledged the condition in her detailed diary. Sara wrote the words in her household book that she would not inscribe in English: *"Pour compter il faut 40 semaines or 280 jours commencement plusieurs jours après l'indisposition . . ."* (In order to count, it [estimated date of birth] requires forty weeks or 280 days commencing several days after the indisposition [last menstrual period].) Sara also copied a suggested "List for layette" that included such items for baby as "12 white petticoats" and "12 aprons to hold rubber cloth" (bibs), as well as "3 flannel aprons for nurse."

When James needed to go to the city—which he visited as seldom as possible—Sara took the carriage with him to the train station to see him off and back again to meet his return. Once, when she overstayed one of her frequent visits to Algonac and missed greeting her husband at the station, he was so alarmed that he made the twenty-mile journey to her parents' home to find her.

Now that she was pregnant, Sara took Elespie with her when she called on friends. They returned the visits: Kassie often surprised her at Hyde Park, or Bamie Roosevelt from Oyster Bay might send a note saying that she would be visiting. Sara might see James's mother, who, owing to her seventy-one years as well as her many years of living with her reclusive husband, came calling infrequently. Her house, Rosedale, was less than two miles south from Sara on Albany Post Road. (Once called King's Highway, Albany Post Road went north to Fort Orange in Albany and had its origins in a former Indian trail.) When Sara visited her mother-in-law at Rosedale with James, they often rowed down the river and walked up its bank to the house. All in all, her gentle mother-in-law exerted far less influence on Sara than she had on James's first wife; it was almost as if Sara did not have one in the traditional sense.

On December 12, 1881, Sara received a shocking telegram from her father: her twenty-four-year-old brother, Phil, was dead. After years of "brain seizures" that had made him an invalid, he had suffered one last massive stroke. The Delano family, having lost four children from infancy to adulthood, now had seven remaining. Sara took Phil's death stoically. Christmas was celebrated modestly at Hyde Park that year, marked by a wastebasket from Helen and Rosy, a little wall cabinet from James's brother, John, and a brass fender for the fireplace from James's mother. They were also delighted to learn that James would inherit the Gilbert Stuart portrait of Isaac the Patriot. In keeping with the tradition of great families, even in tragedy, Sara noted, "We gave turkeys to our people on the place." In the afternoon they were off to Algonac for a more somber celebration.

Sara refused to be confined to the house in her last month of pregnancy, although medical textbooks of the decade warned that even women who were merely menstruating should remain in bed. The Delanos raised all their children with fresh air and exercise, and when it snowed heavily in January, Sara actually went sleighing on the same day that a trained nurse arrived to help her through childbirth. "I have not seen much of her," Sara wrote in an understatement, "as I am well and go out a great deal."

Jennie and Warren III were usually in Manhattan during the winter and would leave "Baby Warren," their four-year-old son, at Algonac. Kassie liked to bring him across the river to Hyde Park to visit the expectant Sara. James, too, kept busy as he awaited his child, overseeing the crew who harvested ice from the Hudson to store in Hyde Park's icehouse for the warm months. (The Hudson River was not navigable during the winter but was a major commercial source for ice, supplying local river families, residents of New York City, and people as far south as South America.) The house at Hyde Park was unusual in having a large ice pantry near the butler's pantry.

Sara wrote a short entry in her diary on January 29, 1882, and James picked up the narrative the next evening: "Sunday night at half past eleven Sallie's troubles began, was up and down all night." Finally, she was convinced to stay in bed in the soothing blue of the master bedroom. At seven A.M. James sent for the doctor, who arrived mid-morning through the cold and snow. James telegraphed Sara's mother at Algonac with the news of the labor. Catherine wired back that she would arrive in early evening, and James drove through the dark to the station in a Canada sleigh, more useful in deeper snow, to pick her up.

He again made an entry in Sara's diary: "On return, found Sallie was having a very severe time. At eight p.m. Dr. Parker put her completely under the influence of chloroform. At quarter to nine my Sallie had a splendid large boy, but was unconscious when he was born. Baby weighs ten pounds without clothes." It was January 30, 1882.

Catherine was still at Hyde Park, helping Sara with the baby, when she received a telegram from Kassie that four-year-old Warren was very ill with diphtheria and scarlet fever. She left Sara to return to Algonac. A few days later Dora and Will Forbes telegraphed Hyde Park that there was not the slightest hope for the child's recovery. The next day Forbes wired from Algonac: "Baby Warren died this morning."

Sara was ordered to stay in bed while James attended the funeral. The boy was buried at Algonac under the trees and was later reburied at Riverside Cemetery in Fairhaven. The child who had been healthy and rambunctious just weeks earlier was now gone. Waiting back at home, holding her own baby boy at her breast, Sara must have been determined to protect him as best she could from the common fate of childhood disease and subsequent death.

A month after childbirth, Sara was allowed to go downstairs for meals. The couple was in a dilemma about naming the baby. Twenty-eight years earlier, James had named his first son after himself and nicknamed him Rosy. Sara had always wanted to call her son Warren, after her father. Despite their young nephew's death, the couple still set their hopes on giving their baby the same first name. Sara penned in her diary: "We wrote to ask Warren [Sara's brother] if he would object to our naming baby Warren Delano Roosevelt, and he writes that he could not bear it and Jennie also does not wish it."

James and Sara thought about the names the new baby might be given. Sara was in favor of naming her son after Uncle Franklin: her only fear, as she discussed it with James, was the Astor fortune. Would Uncle Franklin think he was being flattered because of his money? The couple concluded that since, in fact, they had no mercenary motive, none would be imputed to them. Still, they were frustrated at not being able to name the baby Warren. Sara wrote: "We are disappointed and so is Papa, but of course there is nothing to say, so we shall name him for Uncle Frank." There was no question about his middle name being Delano, and so Franklin Delano Roosevelt he was.

10

"We Three"

Sara's lifelong devotion to family now extended without reservation to her baby. Even after her confinement to bed ended, "Baby" stayed by her side, nursing or sleeping in his bassinet within arm's reach. They engaged an English nurse who specialized in newborns. She slept in the north room, which was being converted into a nursery. Unlike Rosy, who had spent his first ten years in his parents' bedroom, Franklin was less than two months old when his crib was moved into the nursery. Sara joked about his new location. "In consequence of change," she wrote, "no one slept."

In March, Franklin was christened at the chapel in Hyde Park's St. James Episcopal Church, which had been established in 1811 by Dr. John Bard (the founder in 1860 of St. Stephen's College, which in 1934 was renamed Bard College). Just as Sara changed her politics after marrying James, she also changed her religion, switching from Unitarian to Episcopalian—as Sara was pleased that James was an Episcopalian; that religion was more to her liking than what she jokingly called "Dutch deformed." Both Elliott Roosevelt—Teddy's younger brother—and Will Forbes were Franklin's godfathers, although "dear Will," Sara wrote, was laid low by an attack of gout and was not able to appear.

Soon it was time for the short-term nurse to be replaced by a regular nurse for the baby. The couple paid the English nurse $120 for her six-week stay, rather than the $108 she charged. (The physician later sent a bill for the grand sum of $82 for the delivery and eight home visits, although James insisted on paying him $100.) Dora Forbes, who lived in Manhattan, was charged with the task of finding a suitable nurse for young Franklin. At the end of March, Sara, James, and Franklin paid a month's visit to Dora and Will Forbes's house on Fifth Avenue, bringing Buckle, their driver. James rented a stable near Fifth so the couple might have their horses, brougham, and tea cart at their convenience, for New Yorkers had already started complaining about the cost of hiring city carriages. The Victorian era was waning, and life was becoming faster-paced: instead of spending many hours dining at someone's home, eating in restaurants was becoming socially acceptable. This meant that a couple could dine out—James and Sara often ate oysters and drank champagne at Delmonico's, the top restaurant of the day—and then attend the theater or even the opera afterward rather than spend an entire evening at a private dinner.

When Sara and James returned to Hyde Park, it was with a new nurse named Ellen, whom Franklin would nickname Mamie, a name close to "Mama"—pronounced in the French style—which is what he would call Sara. (James was to be called Popsy, or more formally, Papa.) In April, Kassie married Charles A. Robbins and moved to Brooklyn. Now only Laura and Fred, the youngest of the seven remaining Delano children, were single. Sara spent her time playing with baby Franklin and showing him off to visitors. Mittie Roosevelt (Mrs. Theodore Sr.) went to Hyde Park for a week, which was a great honor to Sara, as Mrs. Roosevelt rarely agreed to be a houseguest. "I love having her," Sara noted. "We have read together, admired baby, driven with James, tea'd with [both] mothers." Before long, Mittie's daughter Bamie came for a visit, and after that, Bamie's brother Elliott. In the summer, young Franklin made his first visit to the Delano family home in Fairhaven.

Although life for such families as the Roosevelts and Delanos seemed completely calm on the surface, there were undercurrents of change: the end of the nineteenth century was actually a turbulent era of vast new wealth and social competition. Well-established families would use visits and ceremonial calls to reinforce their own sense of social order, and they placed great emphasis on these bonds. One way they showed their status was in the gifts they brought. For example, Uncle Franklin returned from abroad with a silver gilt cup, saucer, and spoon from Russia for the baby, while Aunt Laura presented Sara with a gold necklace from Egypt.

Franklin's care was as up-to-date as the best science of the day allowed. He was vaccinated against the croup eight times. If these practices seem excessive today, they were in part a reaction to four-year-old Warren's death. At least the frequent vaccinations caused no harm, for he was a remarkably healthy child, in part because of Sara's nursing him for a full year. Once a specialist asked her at a dinner party what she fed her baby, and her unabashed response was "nature's own food." She wrote in her diary: "Baby very well and laughing all the time." His first photograph was taken, unfortunately, just weeks before two darling little teeth emerged. At ten months Franklin was beginning to articulate "Papa" and "Mama."

Snow lay deep as Franklin's first birthday approached. The family spent much of each day outside, enjoying the accumulation: "Good sleighing," noted Sara; her philosophy was that "all weather is good weather." Even guests were expected to spend part of the day outdoors, no matter what the weather. James might supply his horses for a morning carriage ride in the countryside, exhausting the horse so that after lunch the visitors' coachmen would arrive with fresh horses to transport them back to Hyde Park.

Sara had grown up in the very part of the nation that fostered the Hudson River School artists, whose paintings sparked an American appreciation for the country's natural environment just when industrialization threatened it. With the idyllic landscapes of Hyde Park tugging at James, his ambition was to be a good citizen as an elected town official and to remain an active Democrat regionally. Sara, like Rebecca before her, supported his desire to stay out of politics at any level above the local, for she was concerned about James's age and health. "James went to Hudson to a Democratic convention to *prevent* their nominating him [for Congress]," Sara wrote. Their quiet country life suited them.

Still, any fashionable couple needed a city house, and they rented one a few blocks from the Manhattan house Rosy and his wife owned. James took the furnished house for four months—January through April 1883— for two thousand dollars. Sara noted the price in her diary, showing no awareness of the disparity between, for example, the nurse for her baby earning eighty dollars a month and their paying a monthly rent of five hundred dollars. Sara had no reason to question the given order of her world. She looked forward to returning to her country life of outdoor activities, visits from her relatively simple circle of friends and relatives, and her role as James's wife and Franklin's mother. She characterized her existence as "life as it was meant to be."

In Manhattan in early 1883, Sara and James saw Laura frequently, for as a young unmarried woman, Laura was interested in attending dances and parties, using James as her chaperone. He escorted both Sara and Laura to the annual Patriarchs' Ball, the most important dance in the city for the decades 1870 to 1890. New York, lacking a well-defined aristocracy as could be identified in London, needed organizations that reflected wealth that was rooted: a place where a young woman could be sure to meet men who were from families that were both solid and old.

Sara's only cares were minor ones, and both she and James centered on the natural events of Franklin's childhood. "Baby has kept well tho' not as fat and rosy as he might be," wrote Sara. "He had a bad fall on a tin toy and cut his little nose. I was out and James got a great fright as it bled terribly. The doctor says it will leave no mark." There were more happy milestones: Franklin's first step came at sixteen months and, according to his mother, "he is quite proud of his new accomplishment." Happily, Warren and Jennie at Algonac had a new baby, Lyman, who helped them conquer their lingering sorrow over the death of little Warren. (Jennie later gave birth to a baby girl, whom she and Warren named Sara.) In July, Kassie and Charles's daughter, Muriel, was born at Fairhaven.

Sara, however, would not be having any more children. Her doctor advised her against another pregnancy immediately after Franklin's difficult birth. It would be thirty years before Margaret Sanger introduced the term *birth control*, and certainly contraceptive devices were not yet accepted for married couples. Abstinence would have been the only recourse for Sara and James. Most gentlemen in their late fifties in that era would have lived with this decision. James may not have felt any loss about having no more children: after all, he himself was twelve when his only brother was born, then had a first marriage that produced only one son. (Could the reason for the sole child have been Rebecca's weak heart? Or was it because Rosy had shared his parents' bedroom for his first ten years?) James was familiar with a one-child family. As for Sara, a woman of her era might not have missed the intimacy of marital relations. On the other hand, she had grown up in a loving, large family (eleven births, but five deaths to date), and her natural reaction was to protect and cherish her only child.

On July 12, 1883, Sara made her first visit to the Canadian island of Campobello, on the Bay of Fundy off the Maine coast. The island had been a fashionable summer spot for New Yorkers and Bostonians for several years. The popularity of landscape paintings had helped spur an interest in nature, and with that movement came an urge to tour North America as well as Europe. The family stayed in one of the three luxury hotels of the island. "We are charmed with the fine cool air and pretty scenery," she said. The air was bracing, salt-tinged and pine- and spruce-scented. Franklin's well-being and the need to be outdoors was on their minds: "We have bought a perambulator for Baby so Ellen [Mamie] can keep him out much of the time." Sara formed a group of women to practice French and German and took advantage of Campobello's climate by spending each day "walking, rowing and sailing. James loves this out-of-doors." By September it was decided. Sara and James bought four acres from the privately owned Campobello Company and made plans to build a cottage "to be ready for us in case we wish to come next summer."

Life continued at a comfortable pace. December's snow brought Franklin's first sleigh rides with Sara in the Fort land cutter, as well as his being left behind at Hyde Park while his parents traveled into Manhattan for Elliott Roosevelt's marriage to Anna Hall. In early January, James took Franklin out for his first coast down Hyde Park's sloping ground toward the river. A team of horses would be waiting at the bottom of the hill to pull them back up. Inside the house, Franklin spotted Sara's jacket in his nursery and kissed it, exclaiming to his nanny, "Mama, Mama!" Sara recounted the event in her diary, writing with pride, "Not yet two years old!"

At the beginning of 1884, they were back in Manhattan, showing nineteen-year-old Laura off at dinners and parties. Everyone hoped that she would find a man worthy of her. James's mother was off for the season to Narragansett, the Rhode Island town across the bay from more fashionable Newport. Sara and James were to leave themselves for Europe in a few days, but first Sara visited the extended family at Algonac in July to welcome Annie and Fred Hitch, back from China. (Dora Delano Forbes would remain in Hong Kong, and then in Shanghai, until the turn of the century.) Laura received the guests standing beside her mother in the doorway of Algonac, wearing a white muslin dress with a deep pink sash that matched the excited flush on her cheeks.

On Sunday morning, as everyone was dressing for church, Laura was alone in her bedroom when hair-curling irons that she was warming in an alcohol lamp overheated. The lamp exploded, the noise resounding throughout the house like a gunshot. Laura was doused with burning alcohol that spread instantly over her skin and thin negligee. Her clothes and skin flamed. Laura screamed and, panicked, began to run. As the air spread the fire, her cries became louder. Everybody dashed from their rooms to see her—ablaze—running downstairs to the front door. Sara followed behind her with a small rug to snuff the flames but couldn't catch up. Laura threw open the front door and ran down and off the veranda steps. Just as she reached the grass, Fred Hitch tackled her with a blanket and they rolled on the ground until Hitch was able to extinguish the fire.

Hitch carried Laura, grievously burned, upstairs. The family awaited the doctor. Although they were not hopeful, Laura was conscious and strong in spirit, and she bravely told her family that she was young—not yet twenty—and would heal. The *Fairhaven Star* wrote that even in her "terrible agony . . . she told them [her family] to look up after her room, that it was on fire." Words were not enough to save her: she fell into a coma and died before the next day's dawn. Although Catherine and Warren already had lost five of their eleven children, the unexpected and horrible fiery death of a sixth child—their youngest—jolted them. As for Franklin, he was not quite two and a half. Thankfully, he had only heard Laura shrieking and had not actually seen his young aunt on fire. However, he saw the weeping and sadness that followed. Sara's brother Frederick, now the only unmarried child, hastily arrived at Algonac from Pennsylvania and wrote: "My homecoming was a terrible experience, never to be forgotten."

Franklin and Laura Delano were devastated by the death of their niece and namesake. In early 1885 they purchased property on East 111th Street for a hospital they named the Laura Franklin Free Hospital for Children. They purposely chose this unfashionable neighborhood so that the hospital would best serve the children of destitute families in a time when the poor had to carry a sick child in their arms to the closest charity hospital. The Delano family decided that the facility should follow the same precepts by which the Delanos themselves lived: good food, exercise as possible, fresh air, and a minimal reliance on medicines. The small hospital's start-up cost of $125,000 was paid entirely by Franklin and Laura, who chose not to ask for or accept contributions for further financial support. Besides their bearing its entire support, they eliminated Laura's surname from the hospital's name as they wanted it to be known for its good works and not for the generosity of the Delanos. The hospital was later subsumed into others and is now part of the Terence Cardinal Cooke Health Care Center. The original late-1880s bas-relief commissioned in memory of Laura currently is in the children's ward. (Another New York facility, Roosevelt Hospital—now called St. Luke's–Roosevelt Hospital Center—had been established earlier by a charitable Oyster Bay relative who had benefited from treatments for polio, James Henry Roosevelt.)

The shocked family traveled to Fairhaven with Laura's body for the funeral. Sara said that she would always remember "the angel child"—she could never say the word *Laura* again—as she had been the night before her death, standing in Algonac's doorway in her frothy white dress. Sara and James followed their plans and left for London—once more, in mourning— with Franklin and the nurse and housekeeper. Perhaps having been reminded of life's brevity, James sat for a portrait in London, posing with a walking stick and fine leather gloves. Then the family visited the spas at Tunbridge Wells in Kent (now Royal Tunbridge Wells). When it was time to leave, James insisted that Franklin stay in the country with Mamie and Elespie for the next month while the parents traveled. Sara finally concurred, writing that "it would do [James] good; he had such a sharp attack of congestion of the liver from the shock of our dear little sister Laura's death."

The couple returned to the English countryside for the winter but were anxious to hear that Sara's father was still at Fairhaven, seriously ill. "He never can be quite the same as before Laura's death," Sara said. The Hitches canceled their plans to return to China and lived, instead, with Annie's parents at Algonac. The Roosevelts stayed in England and shopped for furniture for their new "cottage" in Campobello.

Eventually they returned to Hyde Park. Warren Delano had been moved to Algonac, where the couple made many trips to visit him because he was still "far from strong." Then they were off again to their large, rambling house in Campobello for the summer, where James bought a half interest in a sailboat with a neighbor, and were back at Hyde Park in the fall. It fell to Sara, of course, to organize the households for these constant travels and to make sure the possessions at Hyde Park were safe while they were gone— by, for example, bringing their silver and the five hundred dollars in gold that James usually insisted on having at home in case of emergency to the bank for safekeeping, despite their having installed a burglar alarm.

Sara was not only indefatigable and resourceful, she was unflappable. On the journey from England, a storm arose and their ship had dropped into a trough between high waves. Sara recorded in her diary that as the room turned dark she laconically remarked to James, "We seem to be going down." James responded in kind, "It does look like it." They could hear water rushing above them and then saw it flooding in under their stateroom door. Sara wrapped Franklin up in her mink coat and said to her husband, "Poor little boy, if he must go down, he is going down warm."

11

The Oyster Bay Clan

Sara's friendship with Bamie Roosevelt deepened when she married James: after all, the Hudson River and the Oyster Bay Roosevelts were cousins. Bamie; her younger brothers, Teddy and Elliott; and her sister, Corinne, were actually fifth cousins of little Franklin because they were the same number of generations removed from their forebear Claes Martenszen Van Rosenvelt. Although James Roosevelt and his father, Isaac, were prosperous, the other branch of the Roosevelt family had become vastly richer over the past few decades. Bamie's father, Theodore Sr., was a contemporary of James and a powerful figure for reform in New York City. His interest in improving the lives of New York's lowest classes earned him the nickname "Greatheart": he was an early Roosevelt humanitarian. Theodore Sr. was also one of the first Roosevelt Republicans, strongly supporting Abraham Lincoln despite having married Mittie (Martha) Bullock, who came from a Georgia slave-owning family. This Roosevelt family, as was the custom, lived in a house adjacent to that of another family member, in this case, Theodore Sr.'s brother Robert.

Mittie and Theodore's first child, Anna, nicknamed Bamie, was born in 1855. Theodore Jr. followed in 1858, Elliott in 1860, and Corinne in 1861. After the Civil War ended, the family traveled to Europe, and Bamie enrolled in a school called Les Ruches, run by Mlle. Marie Souvestre, a humanist and social activist. Throughout her youth, Bamie acted as mediator between her competitive brothers. Elliott was everyone's favorite, but Teddy overtook him and managed his asthma at the same time by sheer force of will. Teddy was at Harvard, eminently pleased over his election to the Porcellian Club, when he received the news that his father was failing. Theodore Sr. died in 1878 at the age of forty-six from intestinal cancer.

In 1880, the month after Sara married James, Teddy married Alice Lee. Despite the conflicts the brothers had as boys, Elliott served as Teddy's best man. Coincidentally, Elliott was a fellow passenger on the *Germanic* with the James Roosevelts as they set off on their honeymoon trip. The threesome spent time together in London, and Elliott wrote his family: "While I am in London their rooms are to be home." The couple demonstrated their affection for twenty-two-year-old Elliott by asking him to be Franklin's godfather in 1882, the only member of his family to be so honored.

The next year Elliott married Anna Hall, age nineteen, who also descended from various Knickerbocker families. In an era when all ladies were thought lovely, Anna was one of the most beautiful of all. Elliott adored his wife, writing, "When my worship for women began, I cannot tell." The family held great hope for this marriage despite Elliott's flighty ways and his tendency to drink. Although she was young, Anna was wise enough to be worried about both Elliott's drinking and the way he venerated her. Anna's own father had been a wild drunk who had reformed and now preached sobriety—to deaf ears, as both her brothers were alcoholics. She knew enough to see the warning signs, but she married Elliott nevertheless.

Within a year the family knew that the marriage was a disaster. Anna was not strong enough to fight a dissolute husband. She wanted a man who would lead and guide her—much as James was doing for Sara—and without that lodestar, she strayed to the temptations of the frivolous Gilded Age that was rousting Victorian mores. The couple had a yearly income of fifteen thousand dollars that was derived from inheritance, not by Elliott's earnings, and a house given them by Elliott's mother. Anna flitted between Manhattan, Long Island, Newport, and Bar Harbor. Initially, both Teddy and Bamie judged Elliott's wife harshly and placed the blame for their brother's weaknesses on her narrow shoulders: they were certainly not the first in-laws to blame a wife for her husband's faults.

Elliott's real interest lay in the activities of his country house in Hempstead, Long Island. He loved his horses; hunting and polo were his sports. His drinking increased when his beloved mother, Mittie, died unexpectedly in 1884 at forty-eight. Twelve hours later, in the same house, Teddy's wife,

Alice, died after giving birth to young Alice Roosevelt. Elliott's wife was pregnant and in the house when both women died. Anna was naturally frightened, and Elliott exacerbated her fears by crying, "There is a curse on this house!"

He was wrong. His daughter, Anna Eleanor Roosevelt, called Eleanor, was born safely about seven months later, on October 11, 1884. (Franklin was by now nearly three years old.) Elliott was overjoyed; his worship of women naturally extended to his daughter. The baby was surely innocent and pure, and she loved him uncritically—as no one else did. Anna was simply glad it was over. She was distracted from taking care of her baby by her need to be her husband's caretaker: "Please remember your promise not to touch any champagne tonight," she wrote him.

When Eleanor was two, the couple went to Europe for a new try at their marriage. The trip turned out not as they had anticipated: a steamer rammed their ship, pushing its steel plating inward toward the passengers. One child was beheaded; another had his leg torn off. Scores of adults were maimed and killed. Amidst the bedlam, Elliott put his wife and several other women on a lifeboat and then jumped in so that young Eleanor could be lowered into his arms. She was screaming hysterically and held tight to the hands of the seaman who was trying to drop her into her father's arms. The crewman extricated her fingers, one by one, before Elliott could pull her to safety. Eleanor's first memory was of mayhem and fright. Next, in her young mind, came abandonment, for when the couple reached England, they thought it best to leave Eleanor with her great-aunt.

Finally, the couple returned with their daughter to New York. One bright spot was a trip Elliott took with little Eleanor to Hyde Park, where her elder cousin Franklin carried her piggyback around his tower playroom. Elliott's sports were more dangerous. While riding in a charity circus, he fell off his horse and found solace for the pain of an incorrectly diagnosed broken ankle in drugs. Soon comfort became habit. Still, Eleanor was his special delight even after the birth in 1889 of his first son, named Elliott Jr. and known as Ellie. Recovering from childbirth, Anna pleaded with her husband: "I shall never feel you are really your dear old self until you can give up all medicine and wine of every kind. I believe the latter has led to your great difficulty in giving up morphine and laudanum."

Anna escaped her unhappy marriage by immersing herself in the carefree social life of the age, joining her many friends who were happily seeking pleasure over duty. Eleanor grew up aware of tension in the household (compare this disharmony with the serenity that surrounded Franklin at Hyde Park) and made the unsurprising decision to favor her father, who adored her, over her mother, who often ignored her.

In addition, Eleanor thought her mother was "one of the most beautiful women I have ever seen" and felt inferior by comparison. Even her aunt Edith (Uncle Teddy's second wife) coolly commented to Bamie about Eleanor's overbite: "Her mouth and teeth seem to have no future." Yet she added that "the ugly duckling may turn out to be a swan." The family did nothing about Eleanor's awkward bite; at the time, upper-class New York felt that orthodontia was only for showgirls. Eleanor would also never forget that her mother occasionally called her "Granny" because of her serious demeanor. Although Anna did not seem to intend to wound her child, the harm was done.

Yet Eleanor unconditionally loved her father, despite his greater flaws. If her mother was thoughtlessly unkind, Elliott was shockingly mercurial with the daughter who adored him. When Eleanor was five and too frightened to ride her donkey down a steep slope, Elliott dismissed her, saying, "I never knew you were a coward." He rode off and left her alone to navigate the fearsome hill. He also terrified Eleanor with his dangerous carriage driving: he would be drunk at the reins while their carriage was jolting right and left, shaking as if it would break into pieces.

His self-centeredness was not limited to the Long Island countryside. In town, he left her outside his club holding three terriers while he spent the day drinking. "Finally," Eleanor's eldest grandson, Curtis Roosevelt, related, "the doorman said, 'Young lady, who are you waiting for?'

"And she said, 'I'm waiting for my father, Mr. Roosevelt.'

"And he raised his eyebrow, probably, and said, 'Well, young lady, I think we'd best get you a taxi and send you home, because your father left quite a while ago.'

"What he didn't say is that Elliott Roosevelt had been put in a taxi, dead drunk, some time before."

Eleanor's mother tried to make the best of a bad marriage, even after she learned that Elliott had a mistress. In 1889 Anna bore a third child, Hall. She tried to spend more time with her children, setting aside the morning, when she led them in prayer, and the early evening, when she discussed their activities while they enjoyed sweet biscuits. Anna referred to the end of the day as the "mother's hour" and took great pleasure in the children's company. She was only superficially aware that her daughter was sad, nor would anyone else of that time have been able to link what may have been Elliott's depression to the blue moods of his eldest child.

Eleanor must have sensed her mother's stress when Anna learned that a family servant was pregnant and was accusing Elliott of being the father. Teddy, now head of the city's Public Service Commission, investigated and, over Elliott's denials, determined that the servant was telling the truth. (The baby was a boy, named Elliott Roosevelt Mann.) There was no double standard in this upright family: Teddy was scandalized and wrote Bamie that Anna should sever relations with her husband. He told Bamie that for Anna it would be "criminal—I am choosing my words with scientific exactness—to continue living with Elliott. Do everything to persuade her to come home at once, unless Elliott will put himself in an asylum for a term of years." Despite the family's place in society and Teddy's own political ambition, in 1891 he wrote again to Bamie: "You can tell [Elliott] that Anna has a perfect right to a divorce."

The marriage was effectively over, although Anna refused to give up on her husband, hoping that he would be "cured." Anna never said a word against Elliott to any of the children, but the couple spent increasingly long periods apart. When Teddy learned that Elliott had squandered $200,000 of his trust on drugs and fast living, he was desperate to save some of Elliott's fortune for his three children. Teddy went to court to have him declared insane. "Won!" triumphed Teddy, the surrogate father. The *New York Herald* headlined this story; Anna tried to ignore it and spent more time with the three children. Eleanor was a consolation to her now, rubbing her forehead when the migraines would start and sleeping in her bedroom.

In 1892 Anna needed surgery and went into the hospital, where she contracted diphtheria and died on December 7 at age twenty-nine. Elliott was off on a bender and the family could not locate him for days. Eleanor, young as she was at eight, had already insulated her heart against loss and disappointment. She said she was numb, later writing: "Death meant nothing to me, and one fact wiped out everything else—my father was back and I would see him very soon."

The only people Eleanor truly loved now were her little brothers and—despite his negligence—her father. When Elliott was brought back for his wife's funeral, he went to see Eleanor and oddly spoke to her of the home she was to make for him, as if she were his wife rather than an eight-year-old girl. He confused her badly: as she later wrote, "I did not understand whether my brothers were to be our children. . . ."

Because Elliott was unfit to raise Eleanor, Ellie, and Hall, they were packed off to their maternal grandmother, Mary Hall. Then, in 1893, a few months after Eleanor lost her mother, her brother Ellie, age four, died of scarlet fever. The children had been living with their grandmother and their three aunts and two uncles in what was now a three-generation household. Frankly, the Halls were a peculiar group—the aunts were histrionic, the uncles complete drunks, and the grandmother had to support the lot on a miserly dower budget, as her husband had died without leaving a will—and the children lacked the joy one might expect from an extended family.

They spent their winters in a fashionably located yet dreary brownstone on Thirty-seventh Street. In the summer, they traveled to Grandma Hall's dark mansarded house in Tivoli on the east side of the Hudson north of Hyde Park. Eleanor actually felt a stronger bond to the Hudson River families than to the rest of the Oyster Bay Roosevelts because of her summer home. The Hall estate was named Oak Terrace but was called Tivoli by the Halls, just as Springwood was really called Hyde Park by Franklin's parents and everyone else.

If Eleanor's aunts were strange, her uncles were a frightening reminder of her father—they drank out of control. One would shoot out the windows of Tivoli using Eleanor as his target, she later told her granddaughter Nina Roosevelt Gibson. Eleanor would have to run parallel to the driveway, dodging from tree to tree to avoid buckshot in her legs. As Eleanor began to develop, her grandmother insisted she wear childlike clothes into adolescence. Not only did Eleanor think that her dresses were inappropriate, but she felt that her short skirts emphasized her gawkiness and that her long hair tied up with bows drew attention to her overbite.

An unbiased view of Eleanor's childhood is hard to gain, since she herself extensively covered her early years in her autobiography and frequently referred to her unhappy youth in her columns, articles, and speeches. One relative who could never understand why Eleanor's self-image was so low was her first cousin Alice (Uncle Teddy's daughter), who was only half a year older. Alice usually had a tongue that could take paint off a barn wall, but in this case she was sympathetic:

> Many aspects of Eleanor's childhood were indeed very unhappy, but she had a tendency to make out that she was unattractive and rejected as a child, which just wasn't true. She claimed that nobody liked her. Well, *we* all liked her. She made a big thing about having long legs and having to wear short dresses. Well, as far as I was concerned, I envied her long legs and didn't notice her short skirts, if indeed they were short.
>
> She was always making herself out to be an ugly duckling but she was really rather attractive. Tall, rather coltish-looking, with masses of pale, gold hair rippling to below her waist, and really lovely blue eyes. It's true that her chin went in a bit, which wouldn't have been so noticeable if only her hateful grandmother had fixed her teeth. I think that Eleanor today would have been considered a beauty, not in the classical sense but as an attractive, rather unusual person in her own right.

Unfortunately, Eleanor could not see herself as Alice did, and she continued to live for her father's visits. "For many years," she wrote, "[Elliott] embodied all the qualities I looked for in a man." The reality of her father—sentimental about his only daughter yet erratic and moody—could never be as good as the girlish fantasies that he encouraged, telling his daughter that they would travel to Europe together. Eleanor remained mired in her somewhat maudlin emotions, centered on "a dream life, which a less lonely child might never have needed, but which meant many happy hours to me." Her daydreams superseded her own intelligence and common sense; her childhood was setting a dysfunctional pattern for her unrealistic perceptions of others.

Whatever grounding Eleanor enjoyed was shaken by Elliott's inevitable death from alcoholism in 1894. Eleanor's mother had died when she was eight, her brother when she was nine, and now, when she was ten, her beloved father. She also lost her relationship with her father's family when Elliott died. Although Grandmother Hall encouraged the children to see their Roosevelt relatives—and Uncle Teddy himself favored Eleanor (sometimes to Alice's dismay)—Teddy's second wife, Edith, who had despised Elliott and felt proprietary regarding Teddy, kept Eleanor and Hall's visits to one a year.

Although Grandmother Hall would have let Eleanor visit Oyster Bay, she was unsympathetic to many of Eleanor's other preferences. Having been too indulgent with her own children, she tried the opposite tack with her granddaughter. Eleanor said, "I learned in time that when I very much wanted to do things I was more than apt to be told 'no.' So I learned self-discipline as a kind of defense. I learned to protect myself from disappointment by not asking for what I wanted." Instead, she felt happy with only two members of the household: the butler, Victor Overhalse, and his wife, who was the laundress. They were the only ones who smiled when they saw Eleanor.

After Elliott's death, Eleanor's fantasy life ran rampant. She read George du Maurier's novel *Peter Ibbetson* and identified totally with his fictional orphan boy. The book's hero, Peter, lives in a world of fantasy, with his loved ones conjured up into his "private oasis." As an adolescent, Eleanor was so lost and lonely that her only refuge was to invoke her beloved dead father into her daily world. She wrote: "I carried on a day-by-day story [of my father], which was the realest thing in my life. How many afternoons I skated away from my governess on Fifth Avenue, so that I could tell my story to myself without the jar of outside interruptions." Her flights of escapist fancy quickly became a habit, one that would keep her distanced from the world around her.

12

"A Beautiful Frame"

s Eleanor was drifting off into her fantasy world, Franklin, nearly three years older than she, was growing strong and confident. He had graduated from toddling after his mother as she managed the house's affairs to running after his father as he checked the stables and set tasks for the outdoor workers. James was an affectionate husband and a dutiful and loving father. Despite being in his sixties, he was still a sportsman. He raised Franklin exactly as he had raised Rosy, spending full days outdoors with the boy. Although Sara was ahead of other women of her day in her love of outdoor pursuits, James was the parent who taught Franklin to row, sail, sleigh, shoot—all in the acreage surrounding his house. "Up to the age of seven," Franklin said later, "Hyde Park was the center of the world."

In 1886 his parents left four-year-old Franklin in the care of his nurse and two aunts at Algonac while they traveled with Bamie Roosevelt to Mexico, considered too "unhealthy" for a child, for three months. This was Sara's first lengthy trip away from her son, but she sensed that he would continue to thrive while she was out of the country. Before Sara and James left for Mexico, James's mother, who insisted on having the latest household innovations, had a telephone put in at her home and at Hyde Park, over James's fusty objections. She told her son that he did not have to answer it, if he objected so strongly. The Delanos at Algonac also installed a telephone to facilitate communication among the many family members.

To get to Mexico, Sara, James, and Bamie traveled on James's railway car: "the most ideal way," said Bamie. The *Monon* had two small bedrooms and a sitting room, and the Roosevelts hired a permanent Negro cook/porter, William Yapp, who worked for them for years. Upon meeting his parents on their return from Mexico, little Franklin wrapped his arms around Sara's neck and held on tightly as they drove home.

One year, when Franklin was only five, they took up residence in Washington, D.C., as a reward for Rosy's and James's support of Grover Cleveland's campaign for president. (As Teddy was becoming well known nationally, the president had to explain to people that these Roosevelts were Democrats.) James was proud to introduce his wife and young son to President Cleveland. The president shook the boy's hand solemnly and said to him, "My little man, I am making a strange wish for you. It is that you may never be president of the United States."

James was busy designing a new coach house for Hyde Park, complete with a windmill bearing the year and the initials J.R. Neither he nor Franklin was ever bored visiting its tack room, stalls, and hayloft, although the stablemen's second-story living quarters were off-limits to Franklin. The boy's responsibility was a small Welsh pony named Debbie. Once, when Franklin took her without permission to follow a hunt and arrived at its end with an exhausted pony, his father publicly admonished him for tiring his mount. Franklin also kept his new bicycle in the stable, riding it in the company of young neighbor Mary Newbold.

Despite the prevailing image of Franklin as a lonely child, he actually had a good number of boyhood friends besides being part of a large extended family, which meant visiting back and forth among numerous childhood cousins. Rosy and Helen now had two children of their own living in Red House on the Hyde Park property, and at Rosedale, a mile downriver, Franklin had two cousins. (In 1886, when his grandmother Roosevelt died at age seventy-seven, she had left Rosedale to James's younger brother, John, and his family.)

The Rogers family, a mile north, had four boys and two girls; in fact, there was only a six-month difference between Franklin and his best friend, Edmund. In the fall before Franklin turned six, he began two hours of daily classes with the Rogerses at their estate, Crumwold, and had at his disposal its tennis court, golf course, and pond. It was said that Mrs. Rogers enjoyed an income of $1,000 a day and that her house cost $300,000. The stables alone set them back $46,000.

"Rain or shine he would trot at a clip down the winding paths to study

with the Rogers boys, our nearest neighbors and his inseparable companions," Sara wrote. She arranged a course for the boys in manual training so
they could learn woodcraft and other practical skills. The families were so
near that the Dutchess County Hunt started on the Rogerses' property, ran
over James's land, and continued on John's acres.

By current standards, it may look as if Franklin had little schooling, but
his life was typical of children of the upper class. In fact, neither rich nor
poor children attended local public schools. The wealthy were often educated at home until about age twelve, when they went off to boarding
school. The poor or working-class child was put out on the farm or in the
factory and had neither schooling nor childhood. The most telling difference between Franklin's youth and others of his set was that he was an only
child. Sara noted that "he enjoyed a kind of kinship with older people that
children of large families almost never experience—so one might say, does
the law of compensation go about its work of equalization."

Franklin was actually more fortunate than other rich children of his era
by having parents who were usually present in the house. The typical rich
child of that era rarely saw his parents or understood how they spent their
time. Franklin was part of his mother's and father's day; in fact, he was the
central star of the family constellation. Whatever disadvantages his childhood may have brought, Franklin was content. "In thinking back to my earliest days, I am impressed by the peacefulness and regularity of things both
in respect to places and people," he said.

In the evenings before Franklin's bedtime, Sara would spin tales of her
childhood voyage to China and of his seafaring Delano forebears. She
would sing him the chantey that she heard from the sailors of the *Surprise*
as they were preparing to pull into Java Head, *"Down the river hauled a Yankee
clipper and it's blow, my bully boys, blow!"* Which of his friends had a mother
like his? The boy would listen, transfixed. He was devoted to her, and she
focused her energy on him.

There was little that Sara feared. When Franklin became ill with his various throat ailments, she naturally grew nervous; in an age before antibi-
otics, what mother would not? Still, she kept her anxiety from the boy,
taking her mother's philosophy as her own: "I've had many troubles in my
life, but none of them were the ones I expected. It is always the unexpected
that happens."

Franklin learned to take illness and even death in stride, it happened so
often and so unexpectedly. When his friend Archie Rogers, Edmund's
brother, died of a childhood illness, Franklin was taught to keep going and
not dwell on his loss. As for Sara, she did not worry about the future. The
one incident she reacted to with fear was James's first heart attack, when

Franklin was only seven. Despite Franklin's young age, he instinctively understood that his behavior should never upset his father. Rather than being brought closer to Sara by this decision, he learned to keep problems to himself—not even mentioning them to his mother—as Sara shifted her focus from her son to her husband.

Encouraged by Sara, Franklin spent whole days in the woods by himself. "I believe that even a little child needs time for thought—time to sort out all his impressions and absorb them," said Sara. Off for a free afternoon, Franklin and Edmund Rogers built a raft to navigate the Hudson—no doubt inspired by *Huckleberry Finn*, which Sara had read to Franklin. The Mississippi River raft was made by a better craftsman than the Hudson River raft, which sank a few feet from shore. Less ambitiously, Franklin also fashioned acorn shells into little sailing ships, complete with tiny masts, which he watched sail on the brook that ran through woods filled with ferns and jack-in-the-pulpits. Each summer, he would watch for a blue heron that liked to visit the marsh below the house, close to the river.

Ellie Roosevelt Seagraves said that "James taught Franklin about wildlife, about knowing trees, about the responsibility of being a landowner, caring for the environment. James taught him caution and respect for living creatures. His father had everything to do with instilling that value in Franklin."

When he was eleven, Franklin asked James for a gun and began to collect birds native to Dutchess County. "Had I had my way," said Sara, "he should never have gotten off to such an early start." Once, when Franklin forgot to engage the safety and accidentally fired into the ground—nearly shooting his mother, who was walking with him—James took his gun away for a full year.

His father also forbade him to come home with more than one male and one female of a species: collecting birds was a fine hobby, but shooting to kill merely for sport was wrong. James also taught him never to shoot a nesting bird. In all, Franklin collected three hundred Dutchess County birds, which the family displayed in the big mahogany cabinet in the library. Franklin kept a detailed record of his specimens in his bird diary. The boy must have liked to imagine that his collection was much like the bird grouping displayed in the recently opened American Museum of Natural History in Manhattan—which it was.

Or he would take out his red setter, Marksman, a gift from Uncle Warren, and run behind as Marksman ran badgers to ground. He climbed trees and, with Edmund, built crow's nests in the branches high aboveground, perhaps pretending as he looked over the Hudson that he, like his mother at his age, was sailing a ship to a distant place. On azure summer days he would naughtily break in to the icehouse to cool off, sniffing the woody aroma that rose from the sawdust layered in between the ice blocks.

Winter meant sledding, sleighing, skating, ice hockey, and ice yachting. Uncle John, James's younger brother, led the American Challenge Pennant for Ice-Yacht Racing, and Franklin and his cousins loved to ride down the river on the *Icicle*, John's wooden sailboat skeleton on steel blades, known to seamen as a gaff rig. These boats could go up to six times the speed of winter wind, more than a hundred miles per hour. At this speed, they could rise up and, if the rear runner left the ice, the boat could spin and propel its driver across the ice. When the ice sailors got too cold, they brought their boats to shore, where bonfires awaited to warm them.

Franklin's hobbies were influenced by his parents' interests. Besides his birds and his boat models, he began a stamp collection founded on Sara's Chinese stamps and enhanced by postage on Uncle Frank's missives from around the world. He might bring his albums to Red House, for Rosy had given his daughter, Helen, his own voluminous collection, and the children would trade stamps. At home, Sara often read to Franklin as he worked, attributing the tone of his upbringing to her husband. "If any outside agency could be said to have been responsible for this quality it was his father, who believed in keeping Franklin's mind on nice things, on a high level; yet he did it in such a way that Franklin never realized that he was following any bent but his own," she said. She was disappointed, though, at Franklin's lack of interest in piano lessons and drawing.

The Roosevelts' lives reflected a popular phrase of the time, "the joy of life," coined by the contemporary playwright Henrik Ibsen. They moved as one unit from Hyde Park to Manhattan to Europe, where Franklin traveled every year from ages seven to fifteen. (Sara was a full-figured statuesque beauty, set off by her lovely clothes ordered from Worth in Paris.) July and August were always spent at Campobello, where Franklin was free to explore a coastline more rugged than the Hudson shore. The family was always content to return to Hyde Park, with Sara noting "how much nicer it is here than in New York."

Franklin led a magical life without having to resort to the fantasizing that Eleanor was doing. As his aunt Dora Forbes noted, "He was brought up in a beautiful frame."

13

⚜

Groton School

Along with Sara's duties organizing the household at Hyde Park, she had two other permanent residences—in Manhattan and at Campobello—to oversee, as well as supervising the household in various European locations. Always, at least two staff—Mamie, Franklin's nurse for nine years, and Elespie, Sara's housekeeper—traveled with the family. The staff remaining at Hyde Park sent baskets to Campobello "twice a week . . . with delicious grapes and fresh vegetables." Sara also piloted Franklin's education, hiring governesses as well as tutors of French and German, with whom she conversed until assured of their competence. Back home at Hyde Park, the Roosevelts might sail their forty-five-foot schooner with an auxiliary naphtha motor, the *Half Moon* (named after Henry Hudson's ship that brought the first Europeans up the river), or they might travel on tracks owned by one of James's railroad interests, riding in luxury in their private railway car.

James was appointed an alternate commissioner of the Chicago World's Fair and traveled there a number of times. Once, the entire Delano family went with him, even though Catherine was recovering from scarlet fever and Warren was relegated to a wheelchair. Franklin was allowed to bring his friend Edmund Rogers. In Chicago, Sara bumped into an old friend who had divorced and then remarried for love. Sara wanted to renew their friendship, but "James feels so strongly on the subject that I give up seeing [my friend] again. It's not easy to make up my mind!" she wrote in her diary. In a tale Edith Wharton might have written, she dropped her friend, as James wished.

When Franklin was a teenager, James gave him a twenty-one-foot boat of his own. He explored the river and the acres of woods on both shores. When he happened upon a Roosevelt worker or even a neighbor's worker— for 175 of Hyde Park's 900 residents worked on the Hudson River estates— the man would tip his cap as he said hello to Master Franklin. He listened to tales from Bowman, the gardener, who had found British cannonballs on the property, from warships sailing up the Hudson to join General Burgoyne's army coming down from Canada. No wonder the boy loved history.

The Roosevelts had signed Franklin up at birth for Groton and were delighted that he would be influenced by the school's mission to instill the spirit of Anglophilia in their sons: British character, strong minds and muscle, combined with true-blue Christian precepts. Groton was as close as an American school could come to the English school Cheltenham. In fact, the students were even required to use British spellings, writing *colour* rather than *color*. Groton's Episcopal headmaster was the Reverend Endicott Peabody, who was called the Rector. (One of his later students, Louis Auchincloss, would novelize his experiences at Groton in *The Rector of Justin.*)

Franklin wanted to succeed, even developing the personal traits that the Rector encouraged in his students. For example, he admonished them to be pleasant, no matter what, which reinforced Franklin's tendency to wear a mask of superficial cordiality and may have decreased his ability to engage emotionally with others. The Rector also admired public service. For a man who stood for tradition, he was also a righteous reformer and exhorted his boys to make a difference in the world for those who could not do for themselves. Because Franklin had started to follow news of his cousin Teddy's public service career, Franklin was thrilled that the Rector's teachings dovetailed with the actions of Teddy, who was now the police commissioner of New York City. Groton's atmosphere was nevertheless elite; the motto the Rector chose for his school was *Cui servire est regnare*, "To serve is to rule."

Still, the three Roosevelts were so closely bound that when it was time for Franklin to enter Groton School, his parents felt he should stay home a few years longer. As he saw his friends go off, he was too curious not to want to explore the world outside Hyde Park on his own, but he was bound by his father's illness to stay home. At a young age, Franklin learned to keep his own counsel and master both the trait of evasiveness and the charm that would allow him to remain independent of the persuasions around him.

~

Finally, in 1896, at age fourteen, Franklin entered Groton, thirty-five miles north of Boston, taking his place in the third form along with twenty-one other boys. It was James—not Sara, as commonly believed—who made the decision to delay Franklin's formal education. James had started boarding school at fourteen and had made the same decision for Rosy. Sara frankly noted of her son, "His road, I realized, would be none too easy to travel, for nearly all the boys in the form he entered had already been at school for two years. During that time it was only natural that they should have chosen their friends, found their special interests, and might easily regard a new boy as a good deal of an interloper."

She was right. Soon after Franklin arrived, the boys hazed the short stranger in their midst—for he was only five feet three inches when he entered Groton—by making him dance on a wooden floor while they slid by, hacking at his ankles with their hockey sticks. Franklin turned a poker face and took the punishment good-naturedly; finally the boys became bored and left him alone.

After the Roosevelts and Mrs. Rogers had settled the boys at Groton—Edmund, Franklin's close childhood friend, was entering the second form, a year below him, and Rosy's son, Taddy (James Roosevelt Roosevelt Jr.), Franklin's half nephew, was a class ahead of him—the couple continued on to Germany, where they hoped their annual Bad Nauheim spa visit would improve James's heart. Although Sara wrote that "James and I both feel this parting very much," she also wanted to take advantage of Franklin's absence to devote herself to James's care. "I could hardly bear to leave Franklin at Groton," she wrote, "and *nothing* but James's health would induce me to cross the ocean without Franklin!"

While taking the waters, the couple received a telegram from Groton telling them that Franklin had scarlet fever. Sara wrote in her diary: "I am so anxious for James to take his cure that I encourage him to stay and not go home." Nevertheless, when they received a telegram that "Franklin's developed inflamed kidneys," they made plans to leave Germany on the first ship back. Upon their apprehensive arrival at Groton, the Rector told them that Franklin was quarantined and that neither of them could see him without being confined themselves. Sara was torn, writing in her diary: "I have to choose between going in to him and staying in and deserting James or merely seeing F. thro' the window and being with James. As the infirmary is full and F's room has 2 other boys and 2 nurses in it, I decide not to go in."

Later she wrote that "in spite of my husband's anxiety, he was tremendously amused, as were the others there, by the way I circumvented the 'no visiting' rule. Several times each day I would climb a tall, rickety ladder, and, by seating myself on the top, manage to see into the room and talk with our small, convalescing scapegrace. He loved to see me appear over the window ledge, and, at first sight of me his pale, little face would break into a happy, albeit pathetic smile." She also brought toys and games for all the boys in the infirmary. This was the only time that Sara visited Groton without being invited. Although Franklin was often sick, his mother said that she put the impulse to coddle "promptly behind me. We stayed away from the school" for his own good. In fact, only when Sara's stepgrandson, Taddy, was quarantined at Groton while Rosy was in London (Taddy's mother, Helen, had died there four years earlier, in 1892) did she again pull up a ladder to visit a lonely boy.

Franklin adjusted to school life during his first year at Groton, although it was a difficult period for the Roosevelts. Besides Franklin's frightening illness and James's ongoing heart disease, Sara's beloved mother, Catherine, died, as did Dora's husband, Will Forbes, who had been one of Franklin's godfathers. Sara again dressed in black and arranged the long black veil that fell below her shoulders. With the death of his grandmother Delano and Uncle Will on his mind—as well as his father's own ill health—Franklin did not want to worry his parents with minor complaints. He wrote them optimistic letters from school: "I am getting along finely both physically and mentally."

Sara's outlook on her son's Groton years was cheerful. "Almost overnight he became sociable and gregarious," she wrote, although Franklin later said, "I always felt hopelessly out of things." Maybe he was referring to being the only Democrat among 124 Republicans. Alternatively, perhaps he was thinking of his lack of athletic ability, which even Sara acknowledged when she said he had "a hearty interest" in sports but "did not play any of them conspicuously well."

Although Franklin was not a brilliant athlete or student, his grades improved as he applied himself. Rector Peabody had written in Franklin's first report home: "He strikes me as an intelligent and faithful scholar, and a good boy." Scholarship was not the only topic on his mind. In 1898, shortly before his fifteenth birthday, he lost his grandfather Warren Delano. "Franklin loved and admired his grandfather. We are thankful he is old enough to remember him always," Sara said. Sara's father was buried in the family tomb at Fairhaven's Riverside Cemetery. (The year before, the Delano servant Harriet Wood, who had laid out Sara's trousseau at Hyde Park, had died and was buried in the family cemetery. Her grave lies outside the Delano circle, facing the family across the gravel road in a sort of upstairs-downstairs relationship for eternity.) Warren's will provided that Algonac remain the property of his children, just as the home in Fairhaven had been. Franklin's aunt Annie and uncle Fred Hitch lived in it year-round. All the siblings would visit in the summer, just as they had the Homestead. Still, a chapter had closed on Algonac, as Sara said: "All so changed by the absence of *both* parents."

There was a subtle difference in the James Roosevelt family, too. Sara was now a rich woman, far wealthier than her husband, who had years earlier been left $300,000 by his own father. Warren had left Sara and her four surviving siblings the staggering sum of $1,338,000 *each*. Sara's inheritance came in a year when an average family's annual income was about $650. Despite this new wealth, nothing changed, for Sara hoped to leave the money intact for Franklin and his future children. The only addition to Hyde Park that year was a new icehouse to replace the fifty-year-old one.

In fact, the Roosevelts were busy monitoring the incredible estate being built just a few miles north of them on the Hudson River. Both old and new money sprouted along Albany Post Road. In 1899 Frederick William Vanderbilt and his wife—they had no children—moved into their new Beaux Arts mansion (now known as the Vanderbilt Mansion). Everyone up and down the river was curious about this monument to unbridled luxury. The house was designed by the top-drawer architectural firm of McKim, Mead & White (White was, of course, the "red-haired trial" who had courted Sara) and sat on 635 acres. The residence had fifty-four rooms, with sixty-two servants year-round. It was decorated in the eighteenth-century French style by Ogden Codman, who had just published the country's first guide to decorating with his coauthor, Edith Wharton. Codman's decor called for, among other luxuries, seven hundred square feet of seventeenth-century tapestries. Yet the Vanderbilts used their palatial mansion for only two months in the spring and two in the fall. For the other eight months, the couple split their time between their estates in Manhattan, Newport, Bar Harbor, and Palm Beach and their "camp" in the Adirondacks.

Even with Sara's cash infusion, the Roosevelts' bank account could not come close to matching the Vanderbilt fortune. Still, couples such as James and Sara represented the quiet Hudson River society to which the Vanderbilts aspired, even though the gilded family had been accepted sixteen years earlier by Rosy's mother-in-law, Caroline Astor. In 1883 she had loftily announced: "We have no right to exclude those whom the growth of this great country has brought forward, provided they are not vulgar in speech and appearance. The time has come for the Vanderbilts."

Perhaps, but time flowed more slowly upriver. Inevitably, the Roosevelts received an invitation to dine at the mansion that epitomized the vulgar Gilded Age. Sara was naturally eager to see the estate. James warned her, "If we accept, we must return the invitation." The couple sent their regrets.

14

Allenswood School

In the same year that eighteen-year-old Franklin was finishing preparatory work at Groton, with an eye toward Harvard (only two boys in the class went to Yale), his fifth cousin once removed Eleanor was sent to England to enroll in Allenswood School. It would be Eleanor's first and only experience with formal education. She was fifteen, a year older than Franklin was when he left home. As it turned out, Eleanor would be as strongly influenced by her headmistress, Mlle. Souvestre, as Franklin was by Rector Peabody. Aside from her father, Souvestre with her "liberal mind and strong personality," as Eleanor later described her, was the most significant influence on her intellect and emotions. Bamie, Eleanor's aunt and Sara's close friend, was influential in having Eleanor sent to Allenswood because she herself had studied with Souvestre outside Paris decades earlier. Now it was Eleanor's turn to awaken intellectually as her aunt had done.

Souvestre immediately recognized Eleanor's sharp intelligence and her potential to be the teacher's protégée. Souvestre welcomed a chance to mold the impressionable young woman. When Eleanor learned that Souvestre also had a father whom she adored and had lost him when she was young, Eleanor identified completely with the woman. Eleanor blossomed under her guidance and was asked to call Souvestre by her nickname, Sou.

Allenswood's atmosphere was more bohemian than Groton's. Whereas Franklin was discouraged from developing close relationships with his classmates, at Allenswood "young girls had crushes and you left [gifts] in the room of the girl you were idolizing," remembered Eleanor's cousin Corinne (named after her mother), also a student. "Eleanor's room every Saturday would be full of flowers because she was so admired."

Sou wanted the girls' thoughts to remain independent, and Eleanor was developing a worldview that was radically different from most people's in New York society. While Franklin had never known anything other than Anglo-American sentiments, Eleanor was learning to inquire: she watched Sou's fury, for example, when her English students celebrated the defeat of the Boers.

Yet even Franklin remonstrated with his parents on this subject: "I cannot help feeling convicted that the Boers have the side of right and that for the past ten years they have been *forced* into this war." James and Sara disagreed with him, and Sara wrote: "Still, I like you to form your own opinions and to look into things more deeply than your Mummy does." Yet both Franklin and Eleanor were exhorted to do good. It was at Groton that Franklin met the muckraker Jacob Riis, author of *How the Other Half Lives*, and it was through Groton that he worked at the Boys Club of Boston and at a missionary summer camp for underprivileged boys.

Moreover, Franklin was very impressed when cousin Teddy came to give a talk at Groton, telling the students: "If a man has courage, goodness, and brains, no limit can be placed to the greatness of the work he may accomplish. He is the man needed today in politics." Franklin made as strong an impression on his cousin as Teddy did on the young man. Teddy, who was now governor of New York, told Sara in his straight style, "I'm so fond of that boy, I'd be shot for him."

Franklin was developing his own strengths and was growing independent of his parents. He became especially interested in the goings-on at Oyster Bay. When Sara turned down an invitation from Bamie on his behalf, Franklin wrote her an unusually sharp note: "I am so sorry you have refused Cousin Bamie's invitation and I wish you had let me make my own plans as you said. As it is, I have accepted the Theodores' invitation and I hope you will not refuse that too."

In 1900, Franklin's last year at Groton, he was among the top students in the class—although Sara noted that he "was far from being a prodigy"—winning the Latin prize and breaking the school's record for the best high kick. He had gained nearly a full foot during his Groton years and was now six feet one inch. The papers had been full of Teddy's exploits during the Battle of San Juan Heights in 1898—in fact, Franklin and a classmate planned to run away and join the war, until an embarrassing case of the measles struck. (More embarrassing, in retrospect, was the pince-nez Franklin affected to imitate his cousin.) Influenced by Teddy's propaganda and his own love of the sea, Franklin told his father that he preferred enrollment in the Naval Academy over Harvard. James, again, told him that he should go to Harvard University and then Harvard Law School for a sound background in managing his estate, as both he and Rosy had done. (This may have been the first time that Franklin learned the extent of his mother's wealth, for Sara's sister Kassie had written that she did not want her own son "to know anything about it until he is a good bit older" so that the money would not "make him an idler.")

Franklin never defied his father, so he entered Harvard at age eighteen to matriculate with the class of 1904: "We all three went to N.Y. and our dear Franklin left us for *college*, a great step," Sara wrote. At that time, Harvard sponsored a two-tier dormitory system: there were attractive dorms for those who could afford them and older dorms where the majority of the undergraduates lived. Franklin lived in a Gold Coast dorm that looked like an English manor, with leaded windows and oak wainscoting. Franklin set up housekeeping with a Groton buddy, Lathrop Brown. Franklin had gone furniture shopping with his parents, and he and Brown worked on covering every inch of wallpaper with photos and drawings of Groton life. Rather than eat in the common dining halls, they joined the Groton Club.

As Franklin looked toward the future, James knew that his own life was coming to a close, entreating Sara, "Only tell Franklin to be good, to be a good man." James had gradually dropped his sporting activities—Sara wrote that "my dear James is not very well and gives up much of his sailing, which he misses"—and by now was left with only his intellectual and civic interests. He continued to chair school board meetings and pass the collection plate at St. James. Once, though, he spoke sharply to Sara when she suggested that he let the coachman take the reins: "I am not dead yet."

Yet he would become suddenly stricken, and his doctors seemed of no help. Sara wrote: "Dr. Russell says he just escaped pneumonia. I know it was a heart attack." She centered her activities entirely on her husband, renting a house in Aiken, South Carolina, so he might have a more moderate climate for the winter. But then she realized that he was too ill to travel there. Finally, Sara hired a nurse and moved James to Manhattan so he could receive a more sophisticated level of care. At Thanksgiving she told both

Franklin and Rosy that she thought their father's time was near. "James is happy to have his two sons. James very delicate and tired looking in a velvet coat, but it was sweet just to be together."

Franklin went back to college but was called to New York only ten days later. On December 7, 1900, James died in his sleep at seventy-two. (This would again be a terrible date for Franklin forty-one years later.)

"All is over," wrote Sara. "As I write these words I wonder how I lived when he left me." Sara had been married twenty years. She was forty-six; Franklin, not quite eighteen.

15

Mother and Guardian

T he men who worked the farm at Hyde Park carried James's coffin and placed it in a receiving vault in the cemetery behind St. James Episcopal Church. Burial would have to await the spring thaw. Then the men would bury James to the left of Rebecca, his first wife.

Sara wrote in her diary: "I returned to this house without him. I am grateful to have had Franklin here these first dreadful days." Despite many visitors—including sisters Dora, Annie, and Kassie, and brothers Fred and Warren—Sara was left in a lonely house. "I see him every minute—I hear his voice at every turn," she wrote.

As Sara shook off the paralyzing grip of grief, she slowly took on the role of father as well as mother to Franklin. Her new duties had been specifically delineated by James, whose last will, written only six months before his death, made it clear that he left his wife head of the Roosevelt household. Although Franklin was nearly twenty-one, both his Victorian parents considered him still in need of guidance. Indeed, Franklin had never openly rebelled against their control and regarded their influence over his actions as natural. James further increased Franklin's dependence on his mother by leaving him only the income from a trust and not any money independently.

Sara, as has been noted, was an enormously wealthy woman in her own right. She had never commingled her fortune with James's smaller one but kept it in her own name and held on to it for Franklin's future. James, for his part, divided his liquid assets so that the three most important people in his life would receive equal shares of about $100,000 each: Rosy and Franklin in trust, Sara in cash. Rosy's and Franklin's trusts paid them about $5,500 annually in dividends.

Of course, James left the house at Hyde Park and its china and silver to Sara, who also took charge of four hundred acres of land, including the farm, subject to James's wish that at her death the Hyde Park property go to Franklin. She had the furnishings and farm equipment for her lifetime; she was to leave them proportionately to Rosy and Franklin. James left Rosy the two hundred acres of land on which Red House sat—again, with the requirement that the land eventually pass to Franklin rather than to Rosy's own children, perhaps because they were heirs to their mother's Astor fortune.

The most telling part of James's will read: "I do hereby appoint my wife sole guardian of my son Franklin D. Roosevelt, and I wish him to be under the influence of his mother." Others have interpreted James's intention only in light of the control that Sara was to have over Franklin. Yet in 1900 it was necessary for a man to appoint his wife as his children's guardian because married women in New York and most other states did not have an automatic right to guardianship of their own offspring. (However, when a child's mother died, the father automatically became sole guardian.) A male who was a stranger to the family could have been appointed by the court to direct Franklin's affairs if James had not included a provision naming Sara guardian. To exacerbate this unfairness, a guardian could actually bill a widow's estate for his unwanted supervision. For example, when young Marion Dickerman, who became Eleanor's close friend, lost her father, his law partner became the Dickerman children's guardian and not their mother.

The issue of guardianship for children of widows had been visited several times by the New York State Assembly. In 1848, fifty-two years earlier, New York had passed the Married Woman's Property Act, which among other provisions allowed a mother to have guardianship over her own children. It was the first law of its kind in the United States. In 1862 the legislature repealed several sections of this law, including the part that gave mothers equal guardianship. Then, four years later, the assembly reasserted in a revised and more encompassingly discriminatory act that women were not considered equal to men under the law. And so in 1900 court officers were still designating guardians for minor children.

James's will sent a multitude of messages. To the court, he said that Sara was to be the legal guardian of Franklin. To Sara, he said that she should be Franklin's anchor on James's behalf. To Franklin, he communicated that his mother should steer his course, reinforcing this message by giving his son only a trust income.

Franklin's first act was not that of a dependent child but rather of a protective and responsible young man. He wrote his dean at Harvard to request an extended leave of absence. "As my mother is all alone and as the end of the term is so near, I feel sure that you will not mind my staying at home with her." Mother and son spent a joyless Christmas together at Hyde Park, and Franklin returned to college on January 3, 1901. A few weeks later they marked Franklin's nineteenth birthday with a restrained celebration; Sara gave him a red bound volume of Shakespeare's works.

Although Franklin's social life was curtailed by his six-month period of mourning, he competed for a space on the school's newspaper, the *Crimson*, and was accepted the second time he ran, in the spring. He planned to clip a year off his four-year term in order to graduate early, which was not unusual for someone out of a rigorous preparatory school—30 percent of his Harvard class finished in three years. Franklin's scholarship was merely decent, and his athletic skills were slight: although he was tall, he was still very slim and had not yet attained the weight and strength that would characterize him in his late twenties and thirties. He did not make the varsity football team; instead, he ushered at the games and helped lead cheers. Some students found Franklin a tad arrogant and thought his old-fashioned English mannerisms (copied from James) silly. They giggled that F.D. stood for "feather duster"; perhaps his lightweight status as a scholar and athlete made his superior attitude rankle.

Franklin was definitely taken down a peg when he was not elected to Porcellian, the most exclusive of Harvard's "final" clubs, founded in 1791 and named for its founders' appetite for roast pig. Rosy was a member, Teddy was a member, and both James and Rector Peabody had been honorary members. Franklin felt the blow and would tell intimates that it was "the greatest disappointment in my life," despite his eventual fellowship in the inner-circle club Fly (Alpha Delta Phi).

As for Sara, she sought no shelter behind her stepson or her brothers. Although she had shown a typical Victorian female dependency by never crossing either her father's or her husband's wishes, by now she had gained the strength and direction she needed to stand tall. She was an oak and not a weeping willow; she would manage her estate—and her son—just as James had expected her to.

Initially, Sara went about her duties from a sense of obligation and as a way to fill her time, noting that "the days drag on. We have to bear them." Soon she realized that she enjoyed her new responsibilities. She became Hyde Park's manager and filled her time with these tasks: grief could not interfere with spring planting, business affairs had to be resolved, and Hyde Park's employees looked to their mistress for guidance and support. To show her mastery, Sara symbolically mounted James's horse Bobby and rode through her fields on the east side of Albany Post Road, checking on the men and the crops. She modestly wrote in her diary: "I am all right and have my duties clearly defined although I fear I do not do them all very well."

Rosy helped plan James's memorial stained-glass window for St. James Episcopal Church. He also helped Sara understand the cash flow of the estate and its working farm, becoming frustrated when he saw that it was difficult for her to keep within a budget. To make up the difference, she began to spend out of her seemingly endless Delano inheritance, which she had intended to keep entirely for Franklin.

Sara rented an apartment in Boston on Commonwealth Avenue. To remain at Hyde Park by herself during the long winter immediately after her husband's death "just then was unthinkable." Her temporary stay in Boston was not unusual: many well-off parents took quarters near a preparatory-school- or college-age child. Thirteen years earlier the widowed mother of Nicholas Longworth—who would be Alice Roosevelt's husband—had taken a place in Cambridge to be near her son. When Sara rented her Boston dwelling, for example, a young cadet named Douglas MacArthur was in his second year at West Point. His mother, whose husband was a brigadier general dispatched to the Philippines, lived for four years in the nearby Thayer Hotel, from whose rooms she watched for her son's burning lamp in his academy quarters. Unlike Mrs. MacArthur, Sara was in Boston for only two months during 1901 and only three months the next winter.

Sara's intention in moving to Boston for several months during the first two winters of Franklin's undergraduate years was to be "near enough to the university to be on hand should he want me and far enough removed not to interfere with his college life." She was also careful to cross the Charles River only when asked: "I never believed that mothers should be much in evidence at college and I visited Franklin only on those occasions that I was invited for some specific function."

Sara did not want to dominate Franklin. She had never respected weak men. She adored her father, who had steered the Delano family with a firm hand, and she had followed her husband's guidance in all matters. Sara was not submissive—she expressed her own opinions and lived according to her values—but she gave no quarter to meek and docile men. Sara's wish for Franklin—and she told him this repeatedly—was that his character be as close as possible to that of his father and grandfather.

Sara made her own friends in Boston and marveled at the Titians, Rembrandts, and Vermeers in the private art collection of Mrs. Jack (Isabella) Gardner, whose Venetian-style palace on the Fenway later became the Isabella Stewart Gardner Museum. Her pictures were much more pleasing than those of such emerging Ash Can artists as George Bellows and John Sloan. Sara also visited Julia Ward Howe; "a dear old thing," Sara wrote, "gentle and cordial."

That summer of 1901 neither mother nor son had the heart to return to Campobello. Sara chartered a trip through the Norwegian fjords, Germany, Switzerland, and Italy. Franklin's chum and cousin Theodore Robinson went with them. In Europe they read that an anarchist had shot President McKinley in Buffalo on September 6. They were returning home when they received the startling news via a megaphone from a Nantucket lightship that the president had died of his wounds. Cousin Teddy was now president of the United States.

Both Sara and Franklin admired Teddy. Franklin analyzed his presidency with an eye to political tactics, while Sara viewed Teddy's first critical situation through an ethical prism, without letting her financial interests sway her position. One of Teddy's first crises as president was the anthracite coal strike of 1902, which became one of the most important events in labor history. Mine workers struck—150,000 of them—for shorter nine-hour workdays, union recognition, and higher wages. Five months of violence ensued until Teddy intervened, calling for a commission to adjudicate a settlement. Five hundred witnesses described shocking conditions that included child labor, "company towns," and unsafe working conditions.

Sara and Franklin disagreed on Teddy's intervention. Franklin criticized the president for overreaching the powers of the executive office to end the strike—an ironic position in view of his later policies. Sara responded, "One cannot help loving and admiring him the more for it when one realizes that he tried to right the wrong, even though it may injure his own prospects." Sara's view was certainly contrary to the typical sentiments of the widow of a mine owner.

Having a cousin in the White House definitely buoyed Franklin's confidence at Harvard, although his classmates saw no indication of Franklin's brilliant future. A strong base was set, the rest of the figure had yet to be molded. For better or worse, Franklin's dual setbacks—the loss of his father and his failure to make Porcellian—gave him the opportunity to exercise his nearly bottomless optimism and bear his trials with his characteristic reserve. Fortunately, a sea change washed over him when he fell in love with his cousin Eleanor Roosevelt. This was one emotion he would let sweep him away.

16

Sparks and Smolders

When Sara and Franklin were on the train from New York City to Hyde Park in the summer of 1902, Franklin left his mother to exercise his long legs by walking the cars. Striding through the coaches, he spotted Eleanor quietly reading as she whiled away the journey to her grandmother's house in Tivoli. The two young people had not seen each other since they danced together at a Christmas party four years earlier when Franklin was sixteen and Eleanor, thirteen. Then, Franklin had noticed Eleanor sitting off to the side with a sad face and had gone out of his way to rescue her. After the party Franklin wrote his parents of Eleanor's "very good mind," but nothing more came of the friendship.

Now, as the train continued its journey, the couple began chatting and an hour flew by before Franklin remembered that he had left his mother alone in the parlor car. He suggested to Eleanor that she go with him to say hello to the woman she called Aunt Sallie. Eleanor was particularly fond of Sara because she had asked Eleanor's father to be Franklin's godfather, and Eleanor was grateful to any relative who remembered her father tenderly.

Eleanor had not seen Aunt Sallie since Uncle James's death, and when she approached Sara in the parlor car she was filled with awe at Sara's dramatic beauty. Sara, eighteen months after her husband's death, was still in full mourning, wearing a deep black gown and a long veil. Although Sara had put on some weight since her youth, her firm, proud profile was striking and she presented an imposing figure to the impressionable Eleanor. The two women affectionately held hands as they chatted.

The chance meeting of Eleanor and Franklin sparked feelings between the couple that flamed in the fall and winter. Two years had gone by since the death of Franklin's father. Although James's passing had not come out of the blue, the loss was a great blow to a son who for many years had enjoyed an intimate, twenty-four-hour-a-day relationship with his father. Franklin felt the lack of someone to confide in. Stoically, he would not burden his grieving mother with any of his personal doubts. No wonder he was susceptible to falling in love.

That winter was Eleanor's debutante season, and Franklin continued to run across her at parties and family gatherings. Despite her gowns from Paris designers, Eleanor dreaded her debut. She felt that she was still spending long evenings sitting on the sidelines as her girlfriends danced with eligible young men; the only men who asked her to dance did so out of pity, she claimed.

Her memory was colored by her own self-doubt and insecurities. A member of her circle contradicted her: "I hasten to tell you that you are far too modest about your appeal to the gilded youth of 1902," he said. "I remember well that when we asked you to dance it was because we wanted to, contrary to your story." His assertion was not mere gallantry: a dowager of the era described Eleanor as "most attractive" and "very much sought after." In fact, when Eleanor debuted at the Assembly Ball, curtsying before Mrs. John Jacob Astor with her four Roosevelt cousins, including Alice, the newspaper columnists dubbed them the "Magic Five." (Although Eleanor and Alice would not be friends later in life, they were very close during the period surrounding their debut.)

On January 30, 1903, Rosy gave Franklin his twenty-first birthday party and invited Eleanor. Hyde Park was rich with young people at the holidays and during the summer: besides Franklin's friends visiting from Harvard, Edmund Rogers brought fellows home from Yale. Eleanor began going to Hyde Park regularly that summer and fall as Franklin entered his third year at Harvard. Sara never gave Eleanor's visits a second thought; there were many young people around for weekends and holidays, and this particular girl tended to remain in the background of the noise and gaiety.

As for Eleanor, she certainly needed a break on weekends. Since her mother's death ten years earlier, she had been a perpetual guest in other people's houses. Most recently she had stayed with Aunt Pussie in the Hall brownstone on Thirty-seventh Street that was filled with Pussie's vivacious friends but had become nightmarish for Eleanor. When her drunken uncles came to stay, the nineteen-year-old had to install triple locks on the inside of her bedroom door.

On a visit to Aunt Corinne, as Corinne wrote in a letter to her daughter (also named Corinne), "Eleanor came to see me. [Her] path is not roses. She burst into tears and said, 'Auntie, I have no real home,' in such a pathetic way that my heart simply ached for her." Another cousin, Susie Parish, ended up sheltering Eleanor in her specially built double house, whose address was 6–8 East Sixty-seventh Street. One part was occupied by Eleanor's widowed great-aunt Elizabeth Livingston Ludlow and the other by Mrs. Ludlow's married daughter, Susie Parish; her husband, Henry; and their children. Dual dwellings, with double doors that opened in the common wall, reflected the importance of kinship in New York society. Fifth Avenue was lined with them, including the twin mansions of William H. Vanderbilt and his adult daughters. New York's hierarchical groupings made kinship paramount: nothing could demonstrate family ties more clearly than these two-generation dual houses.

Eleanor lived with her cousin's family, dedicated to Mlle. Souvestre's continual admonition "Where is the duty?" Between 1890 and 1915, 15 million immigrants from Ireland, Italy, and Eastern Europe streamed into Lower Manhattan, and women, not men, were initiating the settlement movement to assist the immigrants' adjustment. Eleanor found *her* duty in teaching at the Rivington Street Settlement House on the Lower East Side, nervously taking the trolley to a marginal part of town to teach dance and exercise to young children. These boys and girls attended class after a twelve-hour workday at the factory or after doing piecework in their tenement dwellings, touching Eleanor with their joy in childish activities. Eleanor worked under the auspices of the newly formed Junior League, and she also had joined the National Consumers League to investigate the working conditions of girls and women. (Franklin could boast that Sara had been an early and regular contributor to Greenwich House, another settlement for Lower East Side immigrants.)

Despite Eleanor's social work and her great pride in Uncle Teddy's presidency, she was apolitical. Without the right to vote, most women did not follow political issues. Nor did many link civics and social issues: certainly government did not perceive the poor or disenfranchised as its responsibility. The community relied on individual philanthropy and churches to alleviate social problems, and the upper class generally took on a certain amount of personal responsibility for those less fortunate.

The only female family member who was involved even tangentially in politics was Sara's old friend Bamie, who was also Eleanor's aunt. (Nicknames ran riot in the Delano and Roosevelt families, perhaps because members of different generations had the same given names. Eleanor would also address Bamie as Auntie Bye.) Bamie lived in Washington with her husband, Will Cowles, a navy admiral, and continued to be Teddy's greatest confidante. The president would stop at Bamie's N Street house to talk over political affairs so frequently that it was called "the little White House"; in fact, Teddy held his first cabinet meeting in Bamie's dining room. Eleanor loved the intellectual stimulation of visits there: "The dinners, luncheons and teas were interesting, and people of importance, with charm and wit and *savoir faire,* filled my days with unusual and exciting experiences." Despite Eleanor's frequent trips to Washington, she did not yet see a nexus between the crushing working conditions of women and children and the responsibility of government.

As Eleanor fell in love with Franklin, she was eager to show him the things that were important to her. And his reaction, as Nina Roosevelt Gibson said, was that "Franklin Roosevelt apparently was fascinated by the fact that this was a woman who thought about things that he had never seen in his own backyard. This was a woman who thought about things, who had opinions, who had developed an intellect, was well read, and wasn't afraid to talk about her opinions and her feelings. And this was quite uncommon for many of the young women that FDR had known."

When Franklin was in the city, he would pick up Eleanor at the settlement house when her day ended. Franklin had done his share of charity work at Groton and Harvard, but he saw poor and working-class boys only in institutional surroundings when he met them at outdoor camp or the Boys Club. He never had a firsthand glimpse of what poverty actually meant until Eleanor needed him to take a sick child home. Franklin carried the little girl up three flights of stairs to her tenement quarters. The conditions he saw shocked him: filthy, unlit stairwells; a pervasive stench coming from the building's communal toilet; and seven people sleeping in three dark rooms that had no natural light or fresh air. Eleanor remembered that he was "absolutely shaken." He confided, "My God, I didn't know people lived like that."

Although it may have been a pivotal moment for him, he did not wallow in others' miseries and was capable of enjoying life. In April 1903 he left for a spring trip with his college friends rather than spend his holiday week with his mother. Sara wrote to reassure him: "Of course dearest Franklin I shall miss you but I am not silly and I have no intention of 'tying you to my apron strings.'" She again instructed him: "I want you to be self-reliant."

Sara went aboard Franklin's ship to see him off, as was the custom. Much has been made of Sara's bursting into tears when the ship's whistle blew, signaling guests to go ashore. Yet her quick tears were hardly unlike other mothers' emotions when they say good-bye to a college-age child leaving for a first trip alone to Europe. In fact, Franklin's own feelings threw him off-kilter. He wrote his mother a short note as soon as his ship set sail and gave it to the ship's pilot to mail when the man disembarked in Long Island.

With Franklin's growing independence, Sara had more free time on her hands, especially after she routinized her farm supervision. She intensified the charity work that she had started as a married woman: she sewed dresses for dolls given to sick children at the Laura Franklin Hospital, and at Christmas she and her Delano siblings decorated the hospital's tree. Sara also organized her friends into sewing parties, each one producing dozens of sheets, pillowcases, and pajamas for other hospitals. For years Sara had taught a sewing class "on the new system of sewing" at Hyde Park's public school. She had bought needed materials and, for twelve years, actually paid the salary of a second sewing teacher. She wrote Franklin at Harvard: "Yesterday was my last sewing class of the season and I gave ten prizes, little leather bags, really very nice and the children were delighted." She organized a cooking class for the girls at St. James's rectory, too.

Sara also took food to the sick, sent flowers from her garden to the local hospital, and became a trustee of the Gallaudet Home of Dutchess County for the deaf and mute. She even took on the role of an unofficial caseworker at the state hospital for the insane, following up with newly released inmates to teach them how to live independently. Her philanthropy was immediate and hands-on; she did not dismiss the poor by writing a check, as did so many others in her set. She felt she was fulfilling James's work by doing good within her own community.

Although Sara confined her activities—but not her financial bounty—to Dutchess County, she was quite familiar with tenement work. Her sister Annie Hitch, who lived in the family house Algonac, was an early and influential social-reform advocate who was recognized regionally and nationally.

That summer, distracted by her many activities, Sara had no reason to notice that Franklin was anything other than a carefree college man. Franklin skillfully hid his emotions from her. She had no idea—none—that her son and Eleanor were falling in love. Eleanor, on the other hand, was distracted and moody, signing her letters to Franklin "Little Nell," her father's nickname for her. She also called Franklin "boy, darling": this was a relative's pet name for her father. Eleanor was transferring her uncritical love of her father, whom she had always perceived as her rescuer, onto this young man.

As autumn progressed, Sara was still unaware of Franklin and Eleanor's relationship. In early November, Eleanor invited Sara to lunch at Sherry's. "Is that not nice of Eleanor?" Sara wrote Franklin. Sara was a great fan of the social reformer Jacob Riis, and it would have been natural for the women to discuss the lecture Sara had attended a few weeks earlier when Riis talked about "good government."

Sara and Eleanor did speak about Sara's invitation to become a founding member of the Colony Club, the first club of its kind for women. They agreed that the concept of a woman's social club was silly, and Sara declined.

17

"For Life, for Death!"

Franklin was busy in his fourth year, taking graduate courses while going full tilt as editor in chief of the *Crimson*, which gave him a taste of being a public figure—albeit on a small, yet influential, campus. As Thanksgiving approached, he invited Eleanor to see him cheer at the Harvard-Yale game. After Harvard's defeat, the couple (and Eleanor's maid) traveled thirty miles to Groton to visit Eleanor's little brother, Hall. They managed to find a few minutes to themselves, and Franklin took the opportunity to propose.

"It seemed an entirely natural thing and I never even thought that we were both rather young and inexperienced," Eleanor said later. However, she did not accept immediately. She returned to Tivoli to discuss her situation with Grandmother Hall, who simply told her that the answer should reflect whether she loved Franklin. Eleanor wrote Franklin, telling him that her answer would be yes if he could answer in the affirmative to the words she remembered from Elizabeth Barrett Browning:

> *Unless you can swear "For life, for death!"*
> *Oh, fear to call it loving!*

Franklin pledged his love—and the couple agreed that Franklin would tell his mother at Thanksgiving, when he joined the Delanos at Fairhaven. On that day, the extended family attended morning services at Mercy Unitarian Church, admiring the new building with its stained-glass window commemorating the Delano family. They also followed family tradition by bringing flowers to the Delano crypt at Riverside Cemetery, staying for prayers.

In the afternoon Franklin took his mother aside and told her that he had proposed to Eleanor. Sara was shaken by the news. Then Franklin informed her that it was a fait accompli: Eleanor had already accepted. They were to marry. And they wanted to marry as soon as possible.

Franklin was naive to assume that his mother would be joyful at his tidings. Sara would scarcely have thought Franklin old enough to marry, at twenty-one. It would be understandable if she had resented his deciding without ever giving her the slightest hint of his intentions; however, this is only supposition.

We do know that rather than focusing on her own feelings, Sara zeroed in on practical points. Franklin was still a college student and if this engagement was announced, propriety would demand that he and Eleanor marry within six months. It was ludicrous to think that a young college man would marry, especially in a day when a bride inevitably returned pregnant from an extended honeymoon.

After all, Eleanor had just turned nineteen in October and Franklin was twenty-one. Sara reminded her son that her beloved father had been thirty-three at his first marriage: "A man who had made a name and a place for himself, who had something to offer a woman." Franklin had yet to finish Harvard, much less graduate from its law school, where he was bound. Coming from an era when men were expected to earn their "competency" before marriage, Sara was dismayed at Franklin's lighthearted approach to the responsibilities of a married man. Moreover, Sara suspected that Franklin's trust income, although generous, would not be enough to support the couple and their children as they expected to live. Eleanor's income from her trust would help, but she had no estate of her own, either.

Rarely did Franklin's wishes meet with Sara's opposition. Now he was unnerved by her reaction. Sara extracted a promise from him to keep the engagement private for a year. This had not been his intention, but it seemed a small compromise, especially as he realized that Sara would need to support him and his family at least until after he passed the bar and established a career. He realized that his mother's approval of their plans was critical.

~

Undoubtedly, Sara must have pointed out that few of Franklin's friends were engaged, much less married. His proposal to Eleanor in 1903 was definitely not the norm for his social group. Rector Peabody kept files on each of his graduates: in Franklin's class of 1900, both the average and the median year of first marriage was 1912. Franklin wanted to marry in 1904 and was persuaded by his mother to wait until 1905, when he coincidentally would be only the third of twenty-one classmates to marry. By 1912, when half of his classmates still were single, Franklin's wife would already have given birth to four children. Sara had a point: Franklin seemed to be rushing into a lifelong decision.

Sara may also have noticed the great difference in the couple's personalities and may have correctly sensed that this would be a union fraught with difficulties. (Years later the couple's firstborn, Anna, commented, "You couldn't find two such different people as Mother and Father.") However, Sara could never be faulted for being an ambitious woman. She had no keen desire for Franklin's marriage to be as brilliant as Rosy's wedding to an Astor, which had rated a front-page story in *The New York Times*. Certainly, Sara did not object to the marriage of two fifth cousins once removed. When Franklin was at Groton, he had written his mother asking her to suggest a few girls to invite to a dance. Sara suggested four names: two of the girls were cousins, one was Franklin's childhood friend, and the last was Rosy's daughter, Franklin's niece.

The two returned tight-lipped to the Thanksgiving festivities. Sara must have found it painful to banter with her brothers and sisters as she struggled to keep Franklin's secret. And she must have keenly missed James's strong shoulders and his influence over Franklin. That night Sara wrote starkly in her diary: "Franklin gave me quite a startling announcement."

Franklin and Eleanor's eldest grandson, Curtis Roosevelt, disputes any theory that his great-grandmother did not want her son to marry Eleanor. "Sara saw it as a good match and a logical one. Eleanor was someone from the other side of the family. There was no upward or downward mobility on either side of the family.

"Sara was not against the marriage, just against it happening too early," Curtis continued. "Franklin would barely have finished his undergraduate work. Her objection was youth. It was inappropriate for them to marry so young. She just wanted them to delay it until it was a bit more sensible."

Sara's nephew-by-marriage Roland Redmond later said that she was very much for the marriage. "I think that old Mrs. Roosevelt was intent on having her son marry somebody that was going to be of good family, good background, et cetera, and Eleanor was everything in that line."

He also said that "Sara Roosevelt may well have thought that Franklin and Eleanor could have waited until he was established in business but the Delanos were well off in those days and there was no compelling reason for avoiding an early marriage."

Eleanor herself provided some perspective many years later when she wrote: "My mother-in-law had sense enough to realize that both of us were very young and very undeveloped, and in spite of the fact that she thought I had been well brought up, she decided to try to make her son think this matter over—which at the time, of course, I resented." Just as Sara's shock at the engagement is understandable, so is young Eleanor's grudge at Sara's reaction, especially considering the depth of Eleanor's nineteen-year-old adolescent need for love and approval.

The next week Sara received a letter from her son. He wrote:

Dearest Mama—I know what pain I must have caused you and you know I wouldn't do it if I really could have helped it—*mais tu sais, me voilà*. That's all that could be said—I know my mind, have known it for a long time, and know that I could never think otherwise: Result: I am the happiest man just now in the world; likewise the luckiest—And for you, dear Mummy, you know that nothing can ever change what we have always been & always will be to each other—only now you have two children to love & to love you— and Eleanor as you know will always be a daughter to you in every true way.

Franklin's happiness was Sara's first concern, so she did her best to smooth the relationship with Eleanor. In early December she wrote Franklin from Manhattan that she and Eleanor went "to the shops for nearly two hours and had a nice talk." Eleanor was eager and optimistic: if she remained resentful of Sara, she did not show it.

After this short visit, Eleanor wrote: "Dearest Cousin Sallie, I must write you and thank you for being so good to me yesterday. I know just how you feel & how hard it must be, but I do so want you to learn to love me a little. You must know that I will always try to do what you wish for I have grown to love you very dearly during the past summer." Eleanor signed it, "Always devotedly."

Just two days after seeing Eleanor, Sara wrote Franklin sensibly: "I know that in the future I shall be glad and I shall love Eleanor and adopt her fully when the right time comes. Only have patience, dear Franklin, don't let this new happiness make you lose interest in work or home."

Eleanor visited Hyde Park soon after Christmas, when Franklin was back at college. Sara wrote him that she "had a long chat with the dear child."

Years later, after Franklin became president, Sara good-naturedly recounted her surprise at Franklin's engagement. "Franklin, unknown to any of us, had become engaged, to his distant cousin, Anna Eleanor Roosevelt, a delightful child of nineteen, whom I had known and loved since babyhood. Even Lathrop [Brown], who had roomed with Franklin, shared in our surprise and had known nothing of the impending romance until he had a letter from Franklin telling him the wonderful news."

Franklin, instead of withdrawing, was openly elated at the secret engagement. He behaved as if the three were bound together in some type of clandestine conspiracy. He wrote to his mother about seeing Eleanor secretly in Manhattan and of his various plans to avoid relatives, saying dramatically that Rosy "would be sure to smell a rat" if he saw the couple together and that "*not a soul* need know I have been there at all." His juvenile tone makes it clear why Sara worried that he was too immature to marry.

In January 1904 Sara started to spend more time in the city than she had since her husband's death, partly to facilitate Franklin's seeing Eleanor. Sara was discarding the outward symbols of mourning, and she even took in a play, the first she had seen in three years "since my great sorrow." In the theater district, she could see the "fire signs" (outdoor electric advertisements) that had lit the theaters since 1891, giving rise to its name the Great White Way. She also dined with a friend, a European prince, who introduced her to a new dish: "Prince T. [Pierre Troubetzky, a painter] made a 'risotto.'"

Sara raised the topic of renting a house in Boston for the winter, as she had done briefly for Franklin's first two winters at Harvard. He demurred, perhaps feeling that his mother would feel deprived of his company because he planned to travel frequently to New York to see Eleanor on the weekends. Instead, he suggested a cruise to the West Indies for Sara, himself, and Lathrop Brown.

Of course, this would mean missing six weeks of graduate work. (Franklin had stepped down from leading the *Crimson* at the end of the first semester.) Actually, he had nothing to lose by skipping a great many classes. Franklin had failed to earn a B average during the first semester of his fourth year and would not receive, in any case, the A.M. degree that would have been his had he maintained a higher average. Neither he nor Sara seemed concerned in the least about this missed opportunity; the phrase "gentleman's C" was coined for men such as Franklin.

In February, Franklin sailed with Sara and his housemate Lathrop. Although this cruise has famously been tagged as the device Sara hoped would permanently tear Franklin from Eleanor, evidence shows otherwise. Decades later Sara criticized a biography of Franklin. She corrected the book's text to Franklin: "*1st fib* (to use a mild term) That your Mother whisked you off to the West Indies to prevent your leaving Harvard to be married! Going to the W.I. was your idea, rather than for me to take a house in Boston."

She continued: "2nd fib. That 'I tried to defer your marriage'—the most I ever said was that you were both very young—18 and 21." (Eleanor actually had just turned nineteen when Sara learned of Franklin's proposal.)

In fact, Sara gave Franklin and Eleanor a chance to be together before the West Indies trip by inviting Eleanor up to Hyde Park for a quick day visit. She also arranged for them to meet at Bamie's house for the day when the ship docked in Washington on its way back to New York.

Eleanor was doing her own plotting regarding the couple's relationship with Sara, advising Franklin on how to handle his mother. After Sara and Franklin returned from their cruise, Eleanor wrote him: "Don't let her feel that the last trip with you is over. We three must take them together in the future, that is all, and though I know three will never be the same to her, still someday I hope that she will really love me and I would be very glad if I thought she was even the least bit reconciled to me now. I will try to see her whenever she comes in town."

Eleanor was true to her word, seeing Sara as often as she could. The two women spent many afternoons together riding in the park, visiting, and lunching. Sara was delighted. In return, she invited Eleanor to Hyde Park, writing that it was "always a pleasure to have the nieces and added joy to have Eleanor now."

Still, Sara thought that Franklin could benefit from holding a paid position between college and law school. In the 1890s Rosy had served as secretary to the American ambassador to the Court of St. James's in London after he had donated ten thousand dollars to the successful campaign of Grover Cleveland. Now Sara approached the current ambassador, an old friend, and asked him about a job for her son. The ambassador declined, saying that Franklin was far too inexperienced.

Law school looked inevitable. Franklin told Sara that he wanted to attend law school at Columbia University rather than Harvard so that he could be geographically closer to Eleanor. Rather than pushing for her son to follow his father at Cambridge—and to keep away from Eleanor in Manhattan—Sara told him: "I want you to think seriously of coming to the Columbia law school which now stands very high." After all, Teddy had attended Columbia's law school two decades earlier, although politics pulled him from completing his degree. Sara and Franklin agreed that Columbia would be Franklin's best choice. It would provide him with a solid background for whatever future work he chose, it would place him in the same city as Eleanor, and Sara could rent a house for Franklin that would provide her a residence when she came to town. All three were satisfied with the situation.

However, plans for the next year were not enough to combat Sara's loneliness following Franklin's return to school. She wrote him with a rare heavyhearted feeling: "I am feeling pretty blue. You are gone. The journey is over & I feel as if the time were not likely to come again when I shall take a trip with my dear boy."

Sara urged patience to Franklin as well as to herself: "You *know* that I try not to think of myself. I know that in the future I shall be glad & shall love Eleanor & adopt her *fully* when the right time comes." She continued this theme in another letter: "I must try to be unselfish & of course dear child I *do* rejoice in your happiness & shall not put any stones or straws even in the way of it."

18

"Keeping the Name in the Family"

ara was a Victorian—she could no more have altered her breeding than she could the color of her eyes—and she held a magnetic sway over her son, typical for a mother and son of their time and class. Sara asked Franklin to attend a wedding of one of the Russell sons on her behalf—she was eager for him to remain a Delano and to respect the family's history, intricately tied as it was to the former Russell shipping firm. Franklin, however, was bored by the thought of an event at which he would know so few people. Sara added as a sweetener, "I am going to have Eleanor here next week, so you will find her, and I think you will be willing to do what I ask."

Sara knew her power, and Franklin and Eleanor—both the children of Victorians—became part of a triangular drama. They complied with Sara rather than confront her, but thought they could play around her. Eleanor, in particular, took over the role of subtle manipulation, often telling Franklin the best way to handle his mother. "We will have to learn to accept the little things, and not show our annoyance," she wrote him. "I know it is harder for you."

Sara was sincerely fond of Eleanor, whom she described as "as sweet as ever" when she wrote Franklin about the women's now frequent encounters.

Sara had been lonely since her husband's death, and Franklin was bringing someone into the family who was not only part of the Roosevelt clan but whom she had known since birth. Although she wished the couple would proceed more slowly with their engagement, there is no evidence that anything else about the marriage except their youth disturbed her.

Eleanor's family approved of Franklin, partly because they held Sara in high regard. Sara called on Susie Parish, Eleanor's de facto guardian, who told Eleanor how "sweet" Sara was to her. Eleanor excitedly wrote Franklin of the meeting, adding, "I don't think, Honey, your Mother could be anything else. Everyone has to fall in love with her."

Sara was slowly introducing Eleanor to the Delano relatives. An astonished and delighted Eleanor wrote Franklin that Sara's sister had asked Eleanor to call her Aunt Kassie and that Sara's brother, rather than calling Eleanor "Miss Roosevelt," had addressed her by her first name. In that formal era this was surely a tangible sign of acceptance.

Next, Sara planned a gathering of all the Delanos at Fairhaven to meet Eleanor. Despite having been warmly accepted by those Delanos she had already met, a deeply insecure Eleanor dreaded the reunion. Eleanor misjudged: the Delanos were just what Eleanor had hoped for in a family. Here, finally, was the embracing group that she had longed for all her life. She later wrote: "They were all very kind and warm in their welcome that I quickly began to feel that I was part of their clan."

Besides their love and affection, Eleanor was entranced with another Delano characteristic. She couldn't help noticing their wealth—that they had it, that they enjoyed it, and that it gave them freedom from care. Eleanor, an orphan living on a fixed income from a limited trust, always knew that she would need to watch her budget. Her years growing up under the supervision of a grandmother who had been left too little money to meet her needs, and watching her erratic aunts and uncles constantly plagued by debt, had made her realistic about her own finances. Like Sara, who had needed financial advice from her stepson when she was widowed, Eleanor, when she moved in with the Parishes, had to be taught by her cousin's husband, Henry, how to manage her income. Money was always a worry for her.

Eleanor later wrote of Sara's family that she was struck by "a sense of security that I had never known." She continued: "The Delanos were the first people I met who were able to do what they wanted to do without wondering where to obtain the money." She explained with a hint of irony that the Delanos "were a clan, and if misfortune befell one of them, the others rallied at once. My Hall family would have rallied, too, but they had so much less to rally with."

On June 24, 1904, Franklin, who had been elected permanent chairman of the class of 1904, graduated from Harvard. Sara and Eleanor and the many family members who came to show the family flag were immeasurably proud of his position onstage as a class officer. Eleanor also interpreted Franklin's stride to accept his diploma as one more step toward the altar.

Sara and Franklin returned home to Hyde Park. His mother ceremoniously recorded the college graduate's vital statistics, writing in her journal: "F. weighed today, 161½ lbs. In silk pajamas and barefooted. Measured 6 Ft. 1 in." Physically, Franklin was coming into his own. He had always been handsome, but now with his adult weight he was a beautifully built man, athletic with long muscles. Both he and Eleanor were proud of his good looks; Sara particularly reveled in his strong resemblance to his Delano side.

In July, Eleanor was visiting relatives in Maine when Franklin, who sailed in to see Eleanor's group, deceived his mother by telegraphing that he was fogged in and could not return to Campobello for a few days. Before leaving Maine, Franklin induced Eleanor to visit the "beloved island," as Sara and James had called it. "Campo" was nearly as dear to him as Hyde Park, and he was eager to show his idyllic summer home to his future bride. There was a complication in Eleanor's travel plans, however; the shortest route between Maine and Campo might have necessitated an overnight stay if the trains failed to connect. Eleanor reminded him that even with her maid accompanying her, the couple could not be together for that period. "That is one of the drawbacks, dear, to not announcing our engagement, and though we did not think of it at the time, it is one of the things we gave up until January 1st."

Finally arriving for her August visit, Eleanor quickly adopted Campo as her beloved island, too. The couple spent many leisurely hours walking and talking about their future. The summer passed quickly; Franklin entered Columbia Law School in autumn 1904, and took up a comfortable residence in a house belonging to William Waldorf Astor that Sara had rented for him at 200 Madison Avenue. Sara brought Elespie and a few other servants from the Hyde Park house and hired a few new city servants for Franklin's comfort.

Sara was competently managing three households (and one farm): in Manhattan, at Campobello, and in Hyde Park. Besides overseeing the move into the Madison Avenue house, she hired tinsmiths to mend Hyde Park's roof and directed men to test its plumbing with peppermint. (The peppermint oil would travel through the pipes, and the odor would pinpoint the fissure.) Fortunately, Sara wrote that she "found only one or two slight leaks."

As soon as Franklin began classes, Eleanor dashed off a lighthearted note inquiring about his first day "and whether you found any old acquaintances or had only Jew Gentlemen to work with!" Franklin did not rise to Eleanor's jibe in his response, nor did he point out the dissonance between her phrase and her work for desperately poor immigrants, many of whom were Jewish. He had been raised by parents who may have had class prejudices but whose bias did not extend to different races, ethnicities, or religions. When Sara, for example, agreed that Franklin should change law schools, she never pointed out that a goodly percentage of his Columbia class might be Jewish. (In fact, Jewish students made up nearly 30 percent of the 1907 Columbia law class, compared with about 6 percent of Harvard's 1907 class.)

Franklin seemed more fascinated by the details of his upcoming engagement than by the law. In October he went to Tiffany & Co. to select Eleanor's engagement ring, which he presented to her on October 11, her twentieth birthday. She was ecstatic but showed it to no one. "I love it so," Eleanor wrote with thanks, "yet I know I shall find it hard to keep from wearing it!"

Sara sent Eleanor a note on her birthday: "I pray that my precious Franklin may make you very happy and thank him for giving me such a loving daughter. I thank *you* also darling for being what you are to me already. This is straight from my heart."

The secret engagement was weighing heavily on the couple. Eleanor found it difficult not to giggle when her aunt and cousin noticed Franklin's attentions and warned her against leading the young man on. (Apparently, Eleanor could disguise her joy at being in Franklin's presence—although rarely her dark moods—while Franklin, conversely, could control any unpleasant emotions but not his happiness.)

Franklin did poorly in his first semester and seemed to draw no connection between his bad grades and the amount of time he was spending with Eleanor. Franklin knew instinctively that a comfortable life lay ahead merely by virtue of his birth. In his circle, many men—including his half brother, Rosy—never engaged in much of anything that required actual work.

At Thanksgiving, Franklin had dearly wanted to travel with Sara to Fairhaven to announce his engagement to the Delanos, but he was ill and had to settle for writing them the exciting news. They, in turn, immediately telegraphed their congratulations. On December 1, a week after Thanksgiving, Sara wrote in her diary: "Franklin and Eleanor announce their engagement." Two days later the news was included well inside *The New York Times*, in the column "What Is Doing in Society," and was placed as a relatively insignificant item, seventh down.

Now it was time for the Oyster Bay Roosevelts to weigh in with their thoughts on the union. In Washington, Sara's old friend Bamie was all for the marriage. Surely if Sara had indicated any reluctance about the engagement, her oldest friend would not have been supportive. In fact, Bamie paid Franklin the highest compliment by telling Eleanor that his "character is like his Father's whom Uncle Will & I always feel was the most absolutely honorable upright gentleman (the last in its highest sense) that we ever knew."

Also from the capital city, its most prominent resident wrote the future groom from the White House: "I am as fond of Eleanor as if she were my daughter; and I like you, and trust you, and believe in you." Alice wrote: "Oh, dearest Eleanor—it is simply too nice to be true." Only one Oyster Bay aunt asked rhetorically about Eleanor, "What does she see in him? I don't understand."

A few critics of the tight-knit group mocked the Roosevelt-Roosevelt engagement: "They never fell in love except with cousins because they never met anyone outside their own families."

As for Eleanor and Franklin, their engagement briefly took a backseat to their thrill at Teddy's winning the presidency on his own, two years after assuming office following McKinley's assassination. On March 4 Sara, Franklin, and Eleanor traveled on a Roosevelt relative's private train car to Washington for the exciting occasion of the inauguration and to hear Teddy exhort, "All I ask is a square deal for every man." Franklin as yet had given no serious thought to a political career, and his fiancée commented on what she thought was a once-in-a-lifetime experience: "I never expect to see another inauguration in the family!"

The three stayed with Bamie, who was the best-known Roosevelt outside Teddy and his already infamous daughter Alice. Franklin enjoyed being teased about a possible political future growing from his double connection (blood and marriage) to the Oyster Bay Roosevelts. As Franklin and Eleanor danced at the evening's ball, the thought of their wedding—just thirteen days away—surely added to their happiness.

As March 17 approached, the papers paid little attention to Franklin but more to Eleanor, for she was the president's niece, who had debuted with her news-making cousin Alice. Eleanor—the self-styled wallflower—was actually the first of the "Magic Five" to be married, which made Alice envious. Eleanor remembered that "it was all very exciting, and the wedding plans were complicated by the fact that Uncle Ted, at that time president of the United States, was coming to New York to give me away, and our date had to fit in with his plans."

Actually, Teddy had wanted Franklin and Eleanor to marry in the White House, which would have been far more convenient for him than traveling to New York. Alice—pleased though she may have been by whom Eleanor was marrying—raised a ruckus. She proclaimed that she would be the only White House bride during her father's presidency. As Bamie often remarked on Alice's tantrums, "Alice came in with her amber-colored hair and shed an amber-colored tear."

Alice's father had himself earlier admitted, "I can either run the country or I can run Alice, but I can't do both." Alice won: there would be no White House wedding for Eleanor. The president traveled to Manhattan to give his niece away.

Teddy selected a wedding date of St. Patrick's Day so that he could head Manhattan's grand parade and then zip over to East Seventy-sixth Street to give away the bride. Coincidentally, that was the birthday of Eleanor's mother, who would have been forty-two years old.

The morning of the wedding, Teddy paid a visit to Sara's Madison Avenue house to pay his respects to her and to josh with the groom. (The night before, Sara had written in her journal: "This is Franklin's last night at home as a boy.") Teddy proceeded to the parade after visiting Sara and Franklin, and the *Poughkeepsie Daily Eagle* commented that "he seemed to greatly enjoy the typical Irish welcome." At two-thirty Sara and Franklin set out for the Parish-Ludlum home on East Seventy-sixth Street, between Fifth and Madison Avenues, where Eleanor was nervously dressing for the upcoming ceremony.

The Parish family had offered to host Eleanor's wedding, and their dual residence was perfect for the ceremony and reception, as the doors of the drawing rooms on the first floor could be thrown open to provide a more spacious setting. Palms and pink roses punctuated the decor that day, with long rose stems in tall vases lining the fireplace.

Eleanor was soon dressed in her stiff satin dress covered with rosepoint Brussels lace, the same lace her mother and grandmother had worn at their weddings, so valuable that it was stored in a bank vault. She also pinned her lace veil, which belonged to Susie Parish, to her hair with her mother's diamond crescent and wrapped her neck in Sara's generous wedding gift of a high-necked pearl dog collar with diamond bars in a style made popular by England's Queen Alexandra. (The cost of the Tiffany & Co. gift was four thousand dollars.) Eleanor looked fashionable yet painfully stiff and uncomfortable in such elaborate apparel. Holding her huge bouquet of lilies of the valley, she said she felt "decked out beyond description."

Relatives and a few close friends, about a hundred in all, were invited to the ceremony, and twice that number received invitations to the reception. Some of the wedding guests were irate at arriving late, delayed by tight security. The guests included members of the families Vanderbilt, Riggs, Burden, Sloane, Winthrop, Belmont, Mortimer, Van Rensselaer, and Chanler. The seventy-five police officers anticipated the arrival of the president—and, perhaps more important, the city's former police commissioner. The Delano clan was there in full force, having traveled from Europe and China to show the flag. Sara, according to *The New York Times*, "was in white silk, covered with black lace" that had been her mother's.

Eleanor was attended by six bridesmaids in cream taffeta. Alice, her maid of honor, privately ridiculed the young ladies' pretentious headdresses: three small white ostrich feathers tipped with silver, adopted from the knight's panache on the Roosevelt family's putative crest, clipped onto foamy tulle veils. Franklin, on the other hand, took the family escutcheon quite seriously. He gave his ushers three-feathered gold pins, and his bride a watch pin adorned with three diamond-encrusted feathers.

Tumultuous cries greeted the 3:30 P.M. arrival of good-humored and top-hatted Teddy Roosevelt. The police and Secret Service officers wedged him in through the double front doors; panting, he took the steps two at a time and greeted the waiting crowd with delight. The popular and colorful president was outshining the bride at her own wedding.

With Eleanor on Teddy's arm, they proceeded through the open double doors to meet Franklin. Candlelight set off the rich yellow brocade walls. The groom had asked Rosy to serve as best man, but he was ill and Lathrop Brown substituted. Susie Parish had to throw the drawing-room windows open because of the unseasonably warm weather. Guests strained to hear the pianist play "Oh Promise Me" as the lively brass of the Ancient Order of Hibernians blasted out "The Wearing o' the Green," oom-pahing from nearby Fifth Avenue. Reverend Endicott Peabody officiated at an Episcopal ritual in front of the altar set up in Mrs. Ludlum's drawing room. He would marry nearly all his students, but this would be the only service that was punctuated by street cries of "We want Teddy!"

When Rector Peabody ended the solemn ceremony, Teddy broke in. "Well, Franklin, there's nothing like keeping the name in the family."

The president kissed the bride and immediately strode toward the refreshments in the next room. The bride and groom tried to form a receiving line, but their guests were more interested in talking to the president. Family and friends alike homed in on Teddy where he was holding forth in the library. Within minutes, Eleanor and Franklin were standing alone.

There was nothing they could do but follow their guests into the library and gather around the infinitely fascinating Teddy, who was already entertaining the crowd. Promptly at five P.M. Teddy left the reception to attend the dinner of the Friendly Sons of St. Patrick. When he departed from what he called his "scuttling visit to New York," so did the rest of the friends and relatives. The wedding was over. There was a reason why Alice said that her father wanted to be the bride at every wedding.

Sara stayed in Manhattan while the newlyweds journeyed to Hyde Park for their first night together. Sara wrote a note to the newly married couple and addressed them as "Precious Franklin and Eleanor." She said it was "a delight to write you together & to think of you happy at dear Hyde Park."

19

Roosevelt and Roosevelt

For a young man striking out on his own, it's notable that Franklin chose to replicate exactly his parents' honeymoon a quarter of a century earlier. The newlyweds did not spend their wedding night in a plush hotel suite or in the brownstone on Madison Avenue, instead taking the train north to honeymoon at Hyde Park, "just where," Sara wrote them, "my own great happiness began." Then, precisely as his parents had done, Franklin delayed the extended honeymoon to the beginning of the summer, when he and Eleanor planned to leave on a lengthy European trip.

First came their week together at Hyde Park, where Franklin hoped to imbue in Eleanor his own sentiment for the place. To Franklin, Hyde Park was home; he would always remain deeply attached to its house, its land, and the river. On their last leg of the journey from Manhattan on the evening of March 17, after disembarking the train, Franklin and Eleanor sat close together on the leather-cushioned carriage seat, a blanket spread over their laps to protect them from the cold, clear night. As the newlyweds turned into Hyde Park's long driveway, they glimpsed welcoming candles that Elespie had lit in every window facing the road. The housekeeper, feeling sentimental about having welcomed Sara as a bride so long before, greeted Franklin warmly at the door. Elespie's presence, however, increased

Eleanor's discomfort at being "Mrs." rather than "Miss" Roosevelt. As Eleanor remembered the moment, "she looked me over critically and appraisingly, wondering if I could come up to her expectations as the wife of 'her boy.'"

After dinner, the couple retired to spend their first night together. Years earlier, when Eleanor and her cousin Alice were girls, Alice teased Eleanor about sex, having gleaned a very small amount of knowledge from both the Bible and her pet rabbits. Alice tried to make Eleanor listen to how "it" was done. Eleanor leapt to hush her, saying Alice was "blasphemous." "I think she probably went to her wedding not knowing anything about the subject at all," Alice remembered. The only thing we need to know about the couple's wedding night is Eleanor's later comment to her daughter that sex "was an ordeal to be borne." (Sara's view was not much more positive. She told a relative, "We were Victorians. I knew my obligations as a wife and did my duty.")

What Eleanor herself described was her own personal terror "on the dreadful day after I was married." As she put it, "Franklin had given me one of his precious first editions to look at" and she accidentally tore a page. "I held it in my hands, while cold shivers went up and down my spine." Sick with anxiety and convinced that her beloved husband would denounce her clumsiness, she screwed up her courage and confessed. Franklin immediately consoled her: "If you had not done it, I probably would." Waves of relief swept over Eleanor, and she realized how they differed in self-confidence. "He had always been so secure in every way and then he discovered that I was perfectly insecure."

Their happiness as a couple made all differences seem minor. They received a lovely note from Sara, who wrote: "My precious Franklin and Eleanor, it is a delight to write to you together & to think of you happy at dear Hyde Park. You have a real spring day and I can just see the sun and feel how you two are resting and reveling in your quiet time together."

Sara also complimented Eleanor on the wedding ceremony and reception. "Everyone says it was the most perfect wedding so simple and yet so elegant and so refined. Eleanor dear you were a perfect bride and I was very proud of both my dear children." It was a kind note for Sara to write, for in truth Eleanor's family had used a miserly hand in throwing the wedding, serving poor food and stingy refreshments. In fact, Sara may have been cushioning Eleanor from a snide write-up that had just appeared in New York's *Town Topics*. Among its sniping criticisms was that Mrs. Vanderbilt stayed at the reception for a mere ten minutes and that there was "only a fleeting glimpse of a bottle of champagne!" It also noted that the bridegroom was "surprisingly handsome" for a Roosevelt, no doubt pleasing the Delanos, whom Franklin so clearly resembled.

The remainder of the week at Hyde Park went by quickly, and on Sunday, Franklin returned to the city for classes. Sara had rented a brownstone for Franklin's first semester that she had used occasionally as her own pied-à-terre. Although it was large enough for both her and the young couple, Sara knew that her presence would detract from the newlyweds' privacy. Instead, she encouraged Franklin to take a suite at the nearby Hotel Webster and paid all costs for the couple's accommodations, including those of Eleanor's brother, Hall, when he visited from Groton. The arrangement was perfect for Eleanor because the hotel supplied its own staff and she could avoid the terrifying—to her—tasks of supervising household help. "I knew less than nothing about ordering meals," Eleanor said.

Sara visited the suite before the couple's arrival to arrange bunches of flowers from Hyde Park's greenhouse. Then she left so Eleanor and Franklin could arrive to solitude. She went on to her French lecture and then reappeared at the hotel: "Returned to find my children and brought them home to lunch with me."

Despite Eleanor's awkwardness with domestic details, she had learned to manage money from her cousin's husband Henry Parish. Now she and Franklin painstakingly set up a household budget. Their annual income from paternal trusts was about $12,000 ($240,000 today), with Eleanor contributing about $7,000 and Franklin $5,000. They decided that Eleanor would pay household expenses and the cost of their children's clothing with her own money. Franklin would pay for the children's schooling and the family's doctor bills. They each would pay for their own clothes; they split the cost of gifts, unless they were "very personal"; and they each gave to favorite charities. Eleanor asked Sara to review the new budget: Sara told her to set aside money for large unexpected expenses.

No matter how generous an annual livelihood of $240,000 might seem, the income was not quite enough to keep this couple in the manner to which they—Franklin, especially—were accustomed. As exemplified by their suite at Hotel Webster, Eleanor and Franklin gratefully relied on Sara's gifts and became financially dependent on her without questioning the appropriateness of their actions or the implications of her largesse. Their planned budget, therefore, did not translate into reality; but still Eleanor felt secure having a system, and it gave her a feeling of partnership with Franklin.

In the spring warmer weather beckoned Sara to Hyde Park, and she offered her Manhattan house to her grateful son and daughter-in-law.

Eleanor was pleased to move from the hotel into a house that was already fully staffed "so I still did not have to display the depths of my ignorance as a housewife." "I was beginning to become an entirely dependent woman," she later admitted. She was beginning her married life in a protected cocoon financed by Sara, and at the time, she was deeply grateful for her safe shelter that she "slipped into with the greatest of ease."

With Franklin married, Sara set to work busying herself with the same Hyde Park tasks that had occupied her after James's death. Her friend and biographer Rita Kleeman later pointed out: "Some of Mrs. Roosevelt's friends expressed surprise that she did not have them [Franklin and Eleanor] come to live with her. The latent and surprisingly discovered independence of a few years before had developed into an integral part of her nature." Sara enjoyed her freedom.

Now that Sara was unencumbered, she began taking breakfast in bed, as there was no point in going down to an empty table. When she finished, her cook would go upstairs to discuss the day's meals. Menu planning was especially important because of frequent visits by friends and relatives, especially the peripatetic Delanos. Warren, who had inherited Steen Valejte from Uncle Frederick, visited frequently, as did Annie, who lived at Algonac. Others traveled farther to see their sister: Fred from Chicago, and Dora and Kassie from Europe and China.

Left on her own, Sara ran a tight ship: she ordered a new well dug and purchased a younger bull for the farm. Her cook of several generations retired, so Sara needed to interview and try out potential cooks as well as find a new butler who would meet her exacting standards. She also needed to work out household communication problems stemming from Elespie's encroaching deafness. Sara was truly chief executive of her household. She supervised Elespie, as well as the butler and second man (who did such odds and ends as stock the fireplace with wood, light lamps, wash windows, and sweep the porch). She also oversaw the work of the cook, kitchen maid, parlor maid, chambermaid, laundress (who hand washed Sara's silk lingerie), and, of course, personal maid. Each one of her eight household employees received a notebook of instructions and list of duties that let him or her know madam's expectations, and a wage book in which they recorded their monthly cash wages.

Sara organized a system that supplied her three residences with her favorite bouquets of roses and carnations or freesia that were grown in her Hyde Park garden and greenhouse. Although the estate was without electricity, the fruit, vegetables, and milk produced on the farm—and sent to Manhattan and Campobello for Sara's pleasure—were delicious despite the paucity of labor-saving devices. Sara's best china, silver, and damask also traveled to the city for dinner parties. A fine table was a symbol of her skills: at Hyde Park, Sara even began shopping for the household's groceries herself in Poughkeepsie or went into town personally to make sure her butcher gave her the finest cuts.

Before overnight guests arrived, Sara would ensure that their beds were freshly made with ironed percale sheets and perfectly smooth cases on the square pillows. (Sara, Eleanor, and Franklin slept on monogrammed linen sheets.) Both immediate family and guests dried their hands on towels bearing the initials SDR in a modern angular design and stepped out of the bath into fluffy white towels embroidered with a large red R. Her guests understood that she would leave them on their own for a short time when she went to the high school to teach her sewing class. Before dinner Sara would write out the menu in French in her slanting handwriting.

In May, after the weather became reliably pleasant, Eleanor and Franklin went to the country two Sundays in a row. "Annie gave them eggs and asparagus," wrote Sara, pleased at the availability of spring treats. The couple returned for two days in June, excited about their approaching honeymoon in Europe.

20

❧

"Dearest Mama"

On June 5 Sara wrote in her journal: "Franklin got all their luggage put on board the *Oceanic* & lots of friends came to say goodbye. We had Rosy, Helen & Teddy [Robinson, Helen's husband, who was also Eleanor's first cousin] to dine." Helen and Teddy had just returned from their own extravagant worldwide honeymoon, financed in part by Helen's Astor inheritance from her mother. Because Helen lacked a mother to help her with her wedding arrangements, Sara stepped in to fill the void, just as she had for Helen's brother, Taddy, when she visited him at Groton's infirmary atop her ladder when his father was in London.

Sara added a poignant sentiment to her journal: "My dear F. & E." The next morning Sara went back to the *Oceanic* to watch them set sail at 8:30 A.M.

Eleanor feared that seasickness would spoil her voyage, but to her amazement, she was never ill. The couple strolled on deck, read, and socialized with their fellow first-class passengers, charming them with their youth and good looks. Eleanor did look into life in steerage and was dismayed at the contrast to her own staterooms. One night Franklin nearly sleepwalked out of their cabin. Eleanor was frightened, but she handled the situation coolly, gently leading him back to bed.

Franklin and Eleanor took turns corresponding with Sara, each sending her a daily letter. Eleanor wrote: "You must forgive me dear if my letters are long and dull for I can't write like Franklin and I'm really quite ashamed to send you such stupid epistles after his amusing ones." Of course, she was overly modest: Sara enjoyed her letters immensely, and both Eleanor and Franklin told her of their activities, of their plans and hopes, and of their happiness together. Eleanor addressed her notes to "Dearest Mama." In an early letter from the ship, she wrote: "Thank you so much dear for everything you did for us. You are always just the sweetest, dearest Mama to your children and I shall look forward to our next long evening together, when I shall want to be kissed all the time!" She signed, "Ever and ever so much love my dearest Mummy from your devoted Eleanor."

Upon disembarking in England, the couple checked into Brown's Hotel, only to find that the staff had associated their name with the president's and therefore had placed them in the royal suite. Eleanor was embarrassed by the misunderstanding and the suite's extravagance, but Franklin reveled in both the Roosevelt connection and what he perceived as their good luck at staying in the most expensive suite, despite the additional cost.

The couple spent the next three months visiting major European countries, going to some of the same sites that Franklin's parents had visited. They walked goodly distances, dined in sidewalk cafés, and admired the artwork inside museums and the scenery outside. They spent an enormous amount of time at a pastime that they both enjoyed: shopping. Using Sara's gift money, they spent prodigious sums on Franklin's first editions and artwork, including a Rembrandt engraving. Eleanor was fitted for dresses, Franklin for suits, and together they selected furniture and linens. In Italy, Franklin ordered custom-made Murano stemware etched with the Roosevelt crest. In Venice, riding in a gondola, Eleanor admired the brass horses atop the gondola's poles and fancied the horses for andirons. She bought them from the gondolier on the spot.

They were not shy about letting Sara know of their purchases, although Franklin typically teased her by making their expenditures sound much more lavish than they already were. In Paris, where they were entertained beautifully by Sara's sister, Eleanor wrote: "Aunt Dora has been an angel and trotted from shop to shop with us every day. This A.M we went out and Franklin got me such lovely furs." A few weeks later Franklin sent a quick note: "Also I got an old library—about 3,000 books—and had them shipped to London."

Franklin and Eleanor's honeymoon passed nearly without unpleasant incident. Only once did Eleanor's Griselda mood emerge: Franklin left her to take a four-hour hike with an attractive—and more athletic—woman. "I never said a word [but] I was jealous beyond description," she wrote. She admitted to "feeling like a martyr and acting like one."

In July the couple began planning for Franklin's second year of law school. They enlisted Sara's assistance to rent a house for them, beginning in the fall. After some back-and-forth, Franklin telegraphed his mother on July 22 from St. Moritz: WILL TAKE DRAPER HOUSE IF IN ORDER. Sara got them "a bargain" on the house, using a negotiating skill that Eleanor admired.

Two days later Sara wrote in her journal: "Went to town to see 125 E. 36th St., belongs to Mrs. Draper, small, but it is to be put in good order." Franklin wrote that he and Eleanor were *"delighted."* He asked on Eleanor's behalf if Sara would purchase servants' sheets and towels for the house. Eleanor wrote her three days later: "Poor Mama, I am afraid we've given you lots of work about the house, but I shall be so glad if we get it and it is quite near you."

On August 1 Eleanor again was apologetic because a letter from Sara that contained a large check for the couple was delayed in transit and Eleanor had not yet written a thank-you note. "How I would like to kiss you and tell you instead of writing my thanks." She added details about additional clothing she planned to buy with Sara's check, joking, "Are you horrified at my extravagance?" Then she gave her mother-in-law more tasks regarding the house—plumbing work and painting needed to be done, and a telephone and safe installed. Eleanor admitted that "altogether we feel very jubilant over it and I am looking forward so much to getting it in order with you to help us. I am afraid my unaided efforts would not be very successful!" Altogether, Eleanor wrote Sara five letters during her honeymoon in which she thanked Sara for finding them a house.

Eleanor was not rejoicing when she wrote Sara in mid-August. Franklin had just wired his mother to have some law books sent to Europe, but he had not explained why he needed them. He left it to Eleanor to break the news: "Poor Franklin is sad at having failed in two exams, particularly as he got good marks (B) in all the others and if possible he wants to take them again this autumn, as otherwise it will mean very hard work all winter." She moves from "poor Franklin" to social topics, then signs her letter, "Best love, dearest Mama, I do so want to kiss you and in a little over a month I will be able to."

Sara was less sympathetic to Franklin's plight. She shipped his law texts to the couple's European address, admonishing Franklin to study on the voyage back: "You can do a good deal even crossing an ocean, if you set apart two or three hours a day for work."

With her son and daughter-in-law away for the summer, Sara kept herself active. Besides seeing to the couple's city rental, Sara returned to Hyde Park to have a new stable floor laid with asphalt bricks, and a new interior added to the old cow stable. She supervised the farm's threshing, proudly noting in her journal a harvest of 235 bushels of rye, 582 bushels of oats, and 7 bushels of wheat. She also took time to visit Bamie at her country house in Farmington and the Delanos at Fairhaven, then returned to her house in Campobello. In mid-July, in Hyde Park, Sara broke the social barrier James had wished to install between the Roosevelts and their neighbors immediately to the north: "This evening I dined on the *Warrior* with the Vanderbilts. *Very* hot."

In the city, Sara visited nearby friends, including the Pells and the Newbolds, and dutifully attended her committee meetings at the Laura Franklin Hospital. She rented a small electric brougham and hired a driver—who perched outside the conveyance like a coachman—to take her around the city. She enrolled in history and French classes and attended lectures and fund-raisers.

Sara had always been sympathetic to the cause of Negro education, reflecting her own father's sentiments. In late August she attended a meeting featuring Booker T. Washington, who was by then recognized as the county's foremost Negro educator. (He was on a speaking tour to advocate egalitarian education for the races and an end to lynching.)

She reintroduced herself to him, reminding him that in the early 1880s he had called on her father. The men, in their white linen, had sat together on Algonac's veranda, drinking lemonade and talking about how Warren could assist Washington in making his dream of schooling for Negro students a reality. The initial introduction of Washington to Warren probably had been made through mutual acquaintances in the Unitarian Church, which gave news of Tuskegee Institute in its newsletters. Warren made a substantial contribution to Washington's vocational college and lent his name in support.

In fact, the year before Sara saw Washington again, he had written Sara's nephew Allerton Delano Hitch, saying, "I am very glad to receive your kind letter of January 25th and to be reminded that we met at the home of your grandfather some years ago. I remember Mr. Delano very well and my visit to his home."

No doubt, Sara proudly told Washington that her son had married the niece of the president, since Teddy had invited Washington to dine at the White House in 1901. The event made Teddy the first president to host an African-American at an Executive Mansion dinner, an event etched in history by lithographers, who drew Teddy and Washington around a table whose cloth was embroidered EQUALITY.

Eleanor and Franklin were in Scotland as their honeymoon approached its end in early September. Eleanor encountered a rough spot when her hostess asked her to explain the relationship between state and federal government. Eleanor—the niece of a man who had been New York's governor and was now U.S. president—could not explain the different levels of American government. She deferred to Franklin and pledged to learn something about her country's governance on her return home. Sara seemed to understand Eleanor's insecurities better than Franklin and wrote to reassure her: "*Everyone* says lovely things about my Eleanor. Those who had not seen her say they have heard she was charming and so I am quite puffed up with pride."

Also during their Scottish estate visit, Franklin subjected Eleanor to a frightening nightmare in which he shrieked and screamed. She quieted him so that he did not wake the household. She could not cure the hives that had plagued him throughout their honeymoon, however.

From the Scottish estate, Eleanor wrote Sara to tell of a couple who came to lunch, a Mr. and Mrs. Webb, who wrote "books on sociology." Apparently Eleanor had not learned of the Webbs from her days at Allenswood, even though they were England's leading social reformers and had founded the London School of Economics ten years earlier. When Eleanor and Franklin met the couple, Beatrice was just beginning her work as a member of a royal commission that ultimately led to radical revisions of the Poor Law. Unfortunately, Eleanor could not anticipate how much she would have in common with the British woman who strove to help the poor through national programs. Eleanor wrote Sara—with some sense of irony—that "Franklin discussed the methods of learning at Harvard with the husband while I discussed the servant problem with the wife!"

Eleanor also wrote her mother-in-law: "Franklin and I have been discussing the electric light question. Of course we would rather have it than gas and you are a dear, sweet Mama, to want to put it in for us." Franklin eventually decided that it would not be rational to pay for such an installation on a rental property. However, his decision was not based on thrift or concern for his mother's expenses. As Eleanor expressed it, "If you really want to give us something we would rather have something we can keep, such as furniture."

Both Eleanor and Franklin were busy sending Sara last-minute messages before they left for New York. "We will have such long arrears of kisses and cuddly times to make up when we get home," Eleanor said. "I shall want to be kissed all the time!" Eleanor's son Elliott later criticized his mother's letters to his grandmother as "almost fawning," not recognizing Eleanor's ceaseless craving for Sara's approval and love during these early years.

In any case, Franklin took a more practical tone than his wife, asking Sara, "By the way, before I forget it, will you bring down to the dock when you come to meet us a small sum of gold? I ordered a most wonderful [silver-mounted] tandem harness and we must pay on that as well as on the linen."

Sara was on the dock at ten A.M. to see Franklin and Eleanor disembark from the *Kronprinz Wilhelm*. It had been three months since they had sailed. Sara wrote: "They are well and we are all so happy. I brought Eleanor up, and Franklin [who was left to manage the luggage] came uptown by 3. We all stayed in town." The Draper house was not ready, so the couple moved into Sara's Madison Avenue house for a short time. Sara left for Hyde Park the day after the couple arrived in order to give them privacy and to allow Franklin some quiet time to study for retaking his exams before second-year classes began on Monday. The couple joined her in Hyde Park for the weekend. Sara noted that "Eleanor [is] very tired so she keeps quiet."

The couple returned to the city without Sara and continued to live in her Manhattan house. Sara supplied them with her caretaker, a cook, a waitress, and a housemaid. She enjoyed hearing of their activities: "They loved to have people around them and entertained as much as they could without interfering with Franklin's studies, which was not a great deal." The guests they hosted were from their set; their home circle had not yet expanded outside old New York. However, Franklin did tackle his exams a second time and passed them.

In mid-October the rental house on Thirty-sixth Street was finally ready. The couple purchased some furniture of their own with Sara's money, and the rest of the household goods—from chandeliers to pots and pans—Sara supplied from her own houses. Franklin joked that their narrow house was his "fourteen foot mansion." They were now members of the brownstone society.

Eleanor was grateful that Sara took on the task of hiring servants for the rental—three staff for two Roosevelts—as she knew she was still an incompetent housekeeper. Curtis Roosevelt would later sum it up: "Sara was self-confident. Eleanor was not." Franklin unwittingly reinforced Eleanor's poor self-image by sentimentally calling her Babs, his diminutive for "baby." He used the word affectionately, yet—characteristic of his humor—the term had a bite.

Eleanor would later write: "For the first year of my married life, I was completely taken care of. My mother-in-law did everything for me." At the time, her own letters showed a deep gratitude at Sara's taking over the simple chores that frightened her so inordinately. There was absolutely no indication that Eleanor resented her mother-in-law's help; indeed, she saw it for what it was intended to be—an expression of love. As for Sara, she was delighted in her daughter-in-law.

Eleanor was disappointed that she had been sick on the sea voyage back from Europe. Now on terra firma, she was still nauseated and unusually fatigued. A trip to the doctor confirmed that Eleanor was in her first trimester, having become pregnant on her honeymoon trip. Although the physician pronounced Eleanor healthy, Sara noted with concern that she looked "white and tired."

Eleanor's pregnancy brought out her latent moodiness. She listlessly remained in bed when Franklin left for classes. Her fantasizing had not ended: like the hero of her favorite childhood novel, *Peter Ibbetson*, Eleanor lay in bed pretending to be flying above Franklin, watching him as he went about his day. She seemed eager to see no one but her mother-in-law and rarely socialized with other young women. Eleanor did take cooking classes, but she learned only elaborate menus suitable for formal occasions and could not translate them into everyday meals.

At Thanksgiving the entire Delano family gathered at Fairhaven. In the weeks before Christmas, they indulged themselves in Manhattan by going to the theater. They saw *Sapho*, which Sara termed "a bad play, well acted by Sara [*sic*] Bernhardt." They much preferred *Peter Pan*, with a charming Maude Adams in the title role.

On Christmas Eve the couple went up to Hyde Park to join Sara. She gave them a grand gift, presenting them with a sketch of a house with five full stories. Under her drawing, she wrote: "A Christmas present to Franklin & Eleanor from Mama. Number & Street not yet quite decided—19 or 20 feet wide—"

Eleanor had the impression that this would be a single-family house because of Sara's description of its width, which was a third wider than their current cramped rental. As Sara and Franklin's plans segued toward the two families living in a thirty-five-feet-wide double house, any misgivings that Eleanor might have had were suppressed—perhaps even within herself. Eleanor's granddaughter Nina Roosevelt Gibson later said, "The dynamics between Sara and her own son were that Sara's decision on where they should live was fine by him. Franklin never seemed to object, and my grandmother, feeling that it was her role to just go along with it, went along with it." As far as anyone could tell, Eleanor was delighted with Sara's generosity.

On Christmas Day, Franklin, who avoided church whenever he could, skated on the frozen river. Sara went to services at Trinity Church, and Eleanor took Sara's suggestion about exercise and made the cold walk up from the estate to meet Sara as she returned home. The threesome went to see the Rogerses' tree, and Rosy came for Christmas dinner. After the holiday, Sara returned to the city by herself, leaving Franklin and Eleanor to stay at Hyde Park until after the New Year.

In Manhattan, Sara worked out a routine for Eleanor that seemed healthier than having Eleanor lie in bed, imagining Franklin's day. At ten A.M. Sara expected Eleanor at her door for their morning walk together. Then the women would have lunch, and afterward they would take Sara's victoria through Central Park. Several days a week they took a literature class, and afterward Sara nearly always had a meeting to attend while Eleanor went home to rest. Sara took another step in distancing herself from the traditional seclusion of widowhood by giving a large reception at the end of January that both Franklin and Eleanor attended: Sara's first in the six years since James's death. However, she had no thought of remarrying: "No, it would have been a sacrilege," said Eleanor's friend Marion Dickerman years later. "I don't think that ever entered her head."

In mid-February, a mere eleven months after Eleanor's marriage to Franklin, Sara and Franklin traveled to the nation's capital for Alice Roosevelt's wedding to Nicholas Longworth. Alice later explained Eleanor's absence: "She couldn't go because that was indecent. A pregnant woman at a wedding, going around *showing* herself! That just wouldn't do." Eleanor remained in Manhattan as her cousin Susie Parish's guest.

Sara and Franklin stayed at Bamie's house, and Bamie took Sara to the White House to see Alice's many gifts. Franklin and Sara attended the White House wedding together. The next day Bamie gave a luncheon at which Sara was delighted to be seated next to Justice Holmes, whose physician father treated Sara for whooping cough when she was a child.

After returning to New York, the three Roosevelts continued their daily routine. As her pregnancy drew to an end, Eleanor's terrible fear of childbirth panicked her, but she could not bring herself to disclose this to Franklin or Sara, which made her feel doubly a coward. Sara had no idea. "She is wonderful," she wrote of her daughter-in-law, "always bright and well."

Eleanor kept her terror to herself as she assumed her worries "would have shocked my husband and my mother-in-law." Sara had told her about Chinese women who expressed no pain, "but this was not as encouraging as perhaps it should have been," Eleanor later noted. Instead, Eleanor grimly confided her own blue funk about the approaching birth: "The child would come when it would come, as inevitably as death itself."

Eleanor found that her foreboding, at it usually was, was worse than the experience itself. In early May, Sara noted in her journal that "Eleanor had some discomfort" while they were playing cards. Sara went home and immediately laid out a change of clothing on her bedroom chair so she would be ready at a moment's notice. On May 3 "Miss Spring [the nurse] called me at 9. I went over, Dr. Ely soon came. At 1.15 a beautiful little girl was born, 10 lbs. and 1 oz."

The next night she noted: "Dear Eleanor had a good night. All goes well. Franklin dined with me." The following week Sara moved up to Hyde Park. Except for occasional weekend visits, Franklin and Eleanor stayed in the city with their first child.

Eleanor would name her daughter Anna Eleanor Roosevelt, after her mother and herself, and she and Franklin would call the child Anna.

21

"Modern Ideas"

Now with a child of his own, Franklin was determined that Anna—and any siblings she might have later—enjoy the kind of halcyon childhood that had been the bedrock of his development. However, Franklin had little income available for a country place of his own and, in fact, no desire to leave the warm shelter of Hyde Park. Something else weighed in favor of using Sara's house as their own home: Eleanor had no parents, so the usual pull between different sets of in-laws was absent. As for Franklin and Eleanor's country house, it would be Hyde Park or nothing.

Therefore, the couple usually traveled with baby Anna to Hyde Park two weekends a month and for longer visits at holidays. Franklin was maintaining his parents' Victorian custom of keeping relatives as one's closest friends, which also reflected the convention of Eleanor's own Oyster Bay family. That family thought Eleanor had made a good marriage—a handsome cousin with a close and loving mother-in-law who had a Delano fortune that gave Eleanor every luxury, including a beautiful estate she could call home.

As for Sara, her attitude was straightforward: she focused on her son, his family, and their happiness. As long as Franklin was content, Sara was satisfied. Initially, Eleanor showed no sign of resenting Sara's central role in the couple's life; indeed, if her letters are sincere, Eleanor craved Sara's love and attention. Eleanor had few friends her own age, and those she relied on—for example, her cousin Susie—were as traditional as her mother-in-law. Kinship was more important than age in choosing confidants. Everyone thought it right and proper for the young Roosevelt family to make Hyde Park their country residence.

Years later Anna pointed out that "[Father] grew up with all this—this was his home, and this was his mother who'd always, always looked after him very, very personally, and Mother had never had a home, really, that she liked." Franklin was an only child and had always been somewhat self-centered. He did not recognize his wife's growing impatience, never seeing—or perhaps not fully caring—that Eleanor failed to embrace Hyde Park as the wonderland he pictured.

A few years earlier, on their honeymoon visiting the estate Osberton-in-Worksop in England's Sherwood Forest, Franklin had picked up some grand ideas on farming and cattle raising. He had written his mother that he planned "not only a new house, but new farm, cattle, trees, etc." Of course, he could not buy his own place to put his ideas into practice. In fact, he felt he did not even have enough money to live separately from his mother in his own house as Rosy had done, financing Red House with his wife's fortune. Instead, Franklin tried to persuade Sara to implement *his* plans on *her* land. This she would not do, but she did agree that he might purchase some parcels of her property at a small price so that he could experiment with forestry, eventually planting 300,000 trees.

This compromise worked for both of them, although Franklin would have preferred to take over Sara's role as farm manager, oversee their tenant farmers, and modernize Hyde Park's operations: perhaps even, as he would joke, try to turn a profit. "But Mrs. Roosevelt," said biographer Rita Kleeman, "wished to run it as her husband had, as a gentleman's place."

In truth, the estate Franklin and Eleanor called home belonged to Franklin's mother. Within its house, Sara sat at the head of the table, nearest the kitchen. Franklin took the host's position across from his mother, who has been criticized for not ceding her hostess position to Eleanor. Why should Sara have done so? It was Sara's house, not the home of the young couple.

They were guests. The many biographers who find fault with Sara most likely did not visit their own in-laws and declare that *their* position should be at the head of the table and that their mothers-in-law should sit elsewhere.

Then there was the issue of Sara and Franklin having favorite chairs in the wood-paneled library. They sat in front of the fireplace, below the Gilbert Stuart portrait of Isaac the Patriot, Franklin on the left and Sara on the right, while Eleanor sat on the floor between them. Eleanor's inferior position during these tricornered conversations was her own choice: she simply elected not to pull up another chair. Again, Sara has been criticized for not relinquishing her favorite chair. Who of her faultfinders would ask their own mothers-in-law to vacate their chairs, and who among them would not find their own places to sit? Of course, Franklin might have helped Eleanor find her niche in the daily life at Hyde Park by courteously fetching his wife a chair. Nevertheless, he did not, and Eleanor remained at their feet—perhaps her subtle indication of feeling an outsider.

Many years later Anna would say, "If Mother had then put her foot down and said, 'I want a house of my own out here at Hyde Park for the children and us,' then Granny would have been left in the old house herself, but Mother would have had her house. There was plenty of room, God knows, as far as land goes. But at that time she wasn't [assertive]."

Anna's eldest son, Curtis Roosevelt, who has strong memories of Sara, does not feel that Eleanor and others have been fair in blaming Sara for her daughter-in-law's blues. He said, "To go back in time to that period, a mother-in-law welcomed a daughter-in-law to the house. [The daughter-in-law would be expected] to be respectful but also to make her place" in a way that was neither aggressive nor passive. This is certainly how Sara handled her own potentially awkward position as James's second wife with a mother-in-law who was seventy-one years old. Self-confident Sara had relied on her own sound instincts and "disciplined herself," as Eleanor later wrote, in living the life of the wife of an older man. Curtis believes that Sara may have been "dismayed that her daughter-in-law lacked confidence."

On the other hand, he thinks that Eleanor was looking for a mother-in-law who would view her as material to shape, as Mlle. Souvestre had done. He said, "Sara did not expect she was acquiring a student. It was not in Sara's style to make an issue [of Eleanor's dependence on her]; it *was* in her style to make decisions." Which, given Eleanor's withdrawal—and Franklin's passivity—Sara did.

Anna's birth brought out another contrast between Eleanor and Sara, this one in their mothering skills. Sara had nursed baby Franklin and made him and James the focus of her life while keeping busy with estate duties, volunteer work, and the obligations of entertaining a large family circle. Now that Sara had her first grandchild, she took great delight in caring for Anna in the only ways a baby understands—feeding, bathing, and holding.

Sadly, Eleanor would never be at ease with young children. Although Eleanor often criticized her late mother for being aloof, she did not compensate with demonstrations of love toward her own offspring. She had difficulty breast-feeding and assumed that a hired nurse would be a better caregiver than she would be—the feeling of many upper-class women of that time. Eleanor entreated Sara to interview and select a nurse for Anna, even though, according to Curtis, she should have said, "'Mama, I will interview the nurses.' But that takes a certain amount of confidence."

In contrast to her daughter-in-law, Sara was assured, experienced, and practical. She realized that it was necessary to hire a good nurse, and allowed an insecure Eleanor to lean on her so that baby Anna would receive the care she needed. Sara must have sensed that Eleanor did not feel up to the task, and pragmatic Sara's first instinct was to ensure her granddaughter's health and happiness. Soon Sara hired Blanche Spring to help with the newborn baby, becoming Eleanor and Franklin's fourth household staff member. Eleanor acknowledged that even Miss Spring became frustrated with her inexperience and lack of interest in her firstborn. "I never had any interest in dolls or in little children, and I knew absolutely nothing about handling or feeding a baby," Eleanor remembered. Apparently, the birth of her first child did little to change her point of view.

Yet there were good reasons besides even Eleanor's own difficult upbringing for her relative coolness toward Anna and the later children. At the beginning of the 1900s, childhood experts were, for the first time, making mothers feel anxious about raising children. Psychologists and pediatricians stressed "scientific methods" and "warned against kissing and cuddling children," according to the writer Ann Hulbert. Wealthy mothers relied on such tomes as Dr. L. Emmet Holt's *Care and Feeding of Infants*, for the author became pediatrician to John D. Rockefeller's children. Even Uncle Teddy had entered the child-care arena by heading the 1908 advisory committee of the National Congress of Mothers. He referred to mothers as "soldiers" and did not sentimentalize their role.

While Sara's loving and somewhat confining child-rearing practices represented her Victorian era, Eleanor's generation was taught by such experts as Dr. Holt, John Harvey Kellogg (memorialized in the novel and movie *The Road to Wellville*), and Dr. G. Stanley Hall, author of *Youth: Its Education, Regiment, and Hygiene*. Although progressive educator John Dewey kept calling for more insight into children and less fact-gathering, men such as Hall—who warned against playing with infants or toddlers (then called "runabouts") and who believed that children should be kept to a bland diet and toilet trained by three months—must have captured Eleanor's attention, as they did other middle- and upper-class women.

Eleanor also felt intimidated by her own baby's doctor, noting that "while he was kind to them [mothers], he still felt a great contempt for the ignorance and foolhardiness of any young woman who would have a baby without knowing even the rudiments of how to care for it." Curtis Roosevelt mocked Eleanor's excusing her lack of ability. "Eleanor would complain, 'I had no experience. I didn't know how to do it.'

"Come on, now," Curtis scoffed, believing that Eleanor "was making excuses" for herself. "Granny [Sara] would have picked this up, shaken her head, and said, 'My God.' Things like that came to her so easily."

In fact, in 1933 Sara published a book titled *My Boy Franklin*, in which she describes her relationship with her own baby: "I used to love to bathe and dress him, although I took the responsibility of lifting and turning him rather seriously. I suppose all young mothers are a little fearful in the beginning of dropping their babies, and in that respect I was no different from the rest. Still I felt as I do now, that every mother ought to learn to care for her own baby, whether she can afford to delegate the task or not."

Yet Eleanor's generation was being told just the opposite. A 1908 article in the *Atlantic Monthly* was ominously titled "Why Mothers Fail." It advised: "If a mother would strive to put less heart into it all, and more mind!"

Sara may well have thought Eleanor's fears and lack of interest in her newborn odd, but Sara's loyalty was strong and she never criticized her daughter-in-law. Instead, Sara compensated for Eleanor's shortcomings with a grandmother's love. Sara's journals show that Franklin and Eleanor often left baby Anna with her in the city or in Hyde Park for days on end. She reveled in her first grandchild and felt complimented that Eleanor entrusted her with Anna, cheerfully writing: "Baby is lovely. Eleanor [is] so bright and well."

Eleanor could not cope with Anna as gracefully. One evening Eleanor decided to give a dinner party on the nurse's day off. Before the guests arrived, she dutifully gave Anna a bottle and put her down. The baby continued to fuss. Eleanor panicked and called the baby's doctor. He told her that Anna had gas: Eleanor should lay her stomach-down and rub her back. The doctor's recommendations relieved Anna's discomfort, but Eleanor remained agitated and left her guests every few minutes to run upstairs to check on the sleeping baby. By the end of the evening, Eleanor was exhausted. Rather than learning from this experience and becoming less fearful, Eleanor's reaction was: "I registered a vow that never again would I have a dinner on the nurse's day out."

Yet in later years Eleanor wrote: "If I had it all to do over again, I know now that what we should have done was to have no servants those first few years." Her often-repeated notion about ridding the family of servants certainly seems in conflict with her many admissions of being unable to run a household or raise her children without help. Once, when she found herself with dinner guests expected but without a cook to prepare the meal, she dashed from agency to agency to hire someone in time to make dinner for the small party. She was apparently convinced of her own inadequacy.

And despite Eleanor's earlier budgeting plan that designated Franklin responsible for their children's medical bills, Sara paid all of Eleanor and Franklin's doctor bills. She even picked up the cost of having the couple's babies delivered and, later, the bills of the children's pediatricians and specialists. Years later James Roosevelt wrote that his "mother did not question it when [Franklin] sent insurance and medical bills to his mother." Nor did anyone criticize Franklin for not upholding his share of the family's medical bills as he had pledged to do.

In the first years of their marriage, Franklin and Eleanor employed a butler, housemaid, cook, and nurse. Within a decade, their personal staff would expand to nine. Certainly, even if Franklin had gone along with her idea to live without help, the couple would have been viewed as wildly eccentric by their own family and friends. As a matter of fact, Eleanor and Franklin could not have led their lives without servants to smooth their way. As Sara noted in her journal on June 20, 1906, when the nurse departed and another nurse arrived in her stead: "Miss Spring left. Poor little Eleanor is upset by it tho' she is brave."

One fact Eleanor knew about babies came directly from her tenement work: children need fresh air. Eleanor's mothering sensibilities, though, were slightly off-kilter. Rather than taking Anna out in her perambulator for a stroll, Eleanor had a wire box attached high above the ground on a side of the house that received no sunlight. Into this jerry-built contraption went baby Anna, much as one might place a pot of geraniums, or perhaps a plant that did best in the shade. Eleanor decreed that the baby be left hanging outside for a certain length of time every day. Anna screamed from the cold and neglect, and finally a neighbor threatened to call the New York Society for the Prevention of Cruelty to Children. Only then did Eleanor cease the daily airing. Yet baby expert Dr. Holt opined to mothers of Eleanor's generation that crying was an "exercise" for babies "necessary for health." No wonder Eleanor was confused. Sara, who had taken little Franklin for long walks and pony rides, never criticized her daughter-in-law, even in this extreme. She merely noted in her journal the "interesting modern ideas" of young mothers.

22

"The Chicks"

In July 1906 Anna was christened in a Roosevelt gown with cascades of roses on it. The ceremony was held at St. James Episcopal Church, with a luncheon for thirty-four people following, hosted by Sara at Hyde Park. Right after, the Roosevelts were off to spend the summer at Campobello, where Franklin golfed, Eleanor walked, and Sara sailed. The young family were Sara's guests at her cottage and on her sailboat, the *Half Moon* (this was the family's second boat of that name). Sara would give her captain his orders, allowing Franklin to take charge when he was hosting his own guests. Eleanor's brother, Hall, was also Sara's guest at the summer island; friends noticed that Eleanor seemed to take greater pleasure in her adolescent brother than she did in her baby daughter. (In fact, when the couple would visit Hall at Groton, they left Anna at Hyde Park.)

Sara stayed at her Canadian island house only a month, leaving it in Eleanor's care in August when she visited Fairhaven and then when she returned to Hyde Park in September. That same month, Franklin began his first job, using family connections to snag a one-year, unpaid clerkship position with the Wall Street firm Carter, Ledyard and Milburn, which represented the Astor estate, of which Rosy and his family were beneficiaries. Soon he began to specialize in admiralty law. Franklin had passed the bar earlier in May and decided to go straight to work in the autumn rather than return for a third year at Columbia to finish his law degree, despite the dean's dire warning that he was ruining his future. He had ambitions—although not for the law—but he was careful to keep them from his wife and mother. That Franklin would not be paid his first year was not a problem with the couple's trusts of about twelve thousand dollars and Sara's largesse; after all, the average man's wages were about seven hundred dollars a year.

Sara, too, went back to work, picking up her heavy responsibility for "aftercare" duties, monitoring women who had recently been released from the local psychiatric asylum. Before the end of September, Eleanor, Franklin, and the baby went up to Hyde Park for an extended visit. Franklin commuted between the country and his new job in the city; Eleanor and Anna remained with Sara. The couple eventually returned to the city after a ten-day visit, taking with them their five trunks but leaving Anna behind. It was left to Sara to take the baby for her well visit to the local doctor, writing: "On our return, I held Baby from 6:00–7:00 and she was so lovely."

October again found Sara taking care of the six-month-old. Franklin and Eleanor went up for a day's visit to see Sara and their baby. Sara wrote: "After a lovely day, darling Baby was very ill. *I was thankful her parents were here* [emphasis added]. We got Dr. Tuthill at 11." The family was again together at Thanksgiving; at Christmas, Sara hosted everyone, including Hall, for the two-week break: "Such a nice boy," Sara wrote.

The family spent New Year's Eve with the Rogerses. Following afternoon festivities of sledding and ice-skating, the two families were joined by fifty guests for dinner and dancing. Eleanor "does not seem at all well," Sara wrote; subsequently, the women went home early. Franklin, however, stayed at the dance all night, returning before dawn. Sara did not take kindly to Franklin's partying. Eleanor's cousin Corinne, also a guest at Hyde Park, wrote of Franklin that morning: "He was pale as a sheet and furious. His mother had upbraided him for staying out so late, especially with his wife unwell, and had forced him to come down for breakfast at 8 A.M." Sara saw to it that Eleanor had her breakfast in bed.

Sara's Christmas gift of 1905, the promise of a newly built house for the family, was becoming a reality. In mid-January 1907 Sara drove the couple up to see 47–49 East Sixty-fifth Street. It was to be Eleanor's last ride for a month; less than a week later, "my dear Eleanor was operated for hemorrhoids by Dr. Ely. Pretty serious and she was very weak." Sara wrote later: "After two very suffering days, Eleanor is a little better and I spent the afternoon with her very quietly. Baby Anna is well and very fascinating." Eleanor remained in bed for three weeks, with Sara visiting her every day. On January 30, Franklin's twenty-fifth birthday, Sara sent over a cake with candles, which the three ate in Eleanor's bedroom. On February 6 she wrote: "Took Eleanor for her first drive since her operation. It could not do her any good, so snowy and bumpy."

On February 25, with Eleanor nearly healed, both women lunched with "Miss Wald at the Nurses' settlement." Lillian Wald had been born to a wealthy New York family but, like a significant minority of women of her class, opted for a life of public service. Wald chose to enter the nursing profession. By 1907 she was already an early leader for public health nursing and a pioneer for social reform, including being a strong voice against child labor. Both Sara and Eleanor quizzed her about her work and agreed that she was inspirational.

When Hall's classes at Groton School ended in June, Franklin and Eleanor brought him back to town and cared for him following surgery to remove his tonsils and adenoids. Sara kept Anna with her at Hyde Park so that Eleanor could take care of Hall. Eleanor was also pregnant again, but that did not keep the young family from leaving for Campobello in July.

Instead of making her annual trip to the Canadian island, Sara sailed to Europe. In England she went foxhunting in Sherwood Forest: "22 hounds— a wonderful picture with a handsome huntsman in red coat, the hounds all so happy and keen under the trees and obeying the huntsman." She received a boastful little letter from Eleanor about her care of Anna: "I am to take charge of her and put her to bed tonight as nurse is going to Eastport." She also received a note from Franklin, listing the boots ("1 Pair black lace boots like the last; 1 Pair black riding boots, a little bigger on the instep and ½ inch more at the top") he wanted from Peal and the suits, riding trousers, and single-breasted evening waistcoats he needed from Tautz.

In Paris in August, Sara's beloved Dora became her companion. Sara's visit was marred, though, when Dora informed her that Franklin had bought some merchandise two years earlier on his honeymoon and had never paid for it. The shopkeepers were complaining to Dora about her nephew's bad debt. Sara was mortified and wrote her son: "I am not accustomed to this way of doing business." He responded that "I simply haven't had the money till now."

The women were together through September, when Sara left for home. On the ship *Baltic* on her fifty-third birthday, Sara received a telegram from Eleanor and Franklin: HAPPY BIRTHDAY, ALGONAC. Sara added in her journal: "This last means 'all well.'"

On her return, Franklin met his mother's ship at the dock. Sara, on her first day back in the city, wrote: "Dear little Anna knew me after 5 minutes and said, 'Gaga.'" Sara returned to Hyde Park to check on the construction of a three-section greenhouse for roses, carnations, and ferns, but by the end of October she was again attentive to Anna's care. "I spent yesterday in town, busy about plans for the new houses. Baby Anna is so bright and so very good. She no longer cries at night as I told Nurse Watson she *must* get up and turn her over and soothe her."

Eleanor, entering her last trimester, wrote Sara at Hyde Park: "It is a very active infant or infants (!), and I have never felt so well but it will stick out in front and I have great difficulty keeping my clothes from rising up to my chin! Miss Spring says if it is twins she will run away!"

After Thanksgiving, Sara went back into town, where Eleanor was to remain until giving birth. Sara said admiringly of the nine-months-pregnant Eleanor, "She and Franklin and Hall dined with me last evening and walked home at 10:30." At eleven-thirty Eleanor's labor began; Franklin sent teenage Hall back to Sara's house to wait it out. "Franklin called me by telephone at 2:45," Sara wrote. "I flew over and found Franklin to greet me with 'A son, all right, Mummy.'"

The baby had arrived at 3:15 A.M. on December 23, 1907. "A fine baby boy," wrote Sara. "10 pounds, 5½ oz. And very fat and handsome. Dear Eleanor got through quickly and has a comfortable day." The next day Sara wrote of her first grandson: "I hope he will be *James*."

The couple agreed, and Eleanor expressed her joy at giving birth to her first son: "My heart sang when James was safely in the world."

After her confinement ended, Eleanor joined Sara in shopping for their new houses, looking, for example, for "wall papers." Eleanor was becoming house proud and, with Sara on Palm Sunday, took Franklin's uncle Warren to see the building of "our new houses," as Eleanor called them. Anna was thriving and was toddling so actively that Eleanor often put her in her "cage" (playpen). However, infant James seemed sickly, and in the summer of 1908, Campobello was passed over in favor of Sea Bright, New Jersey, because twenty-five-year-old Franklin was required to work over the summer—for the first time. From Seabright, he could commute into Manhattan.

"We spent a great many hours on the beach in the sun, and the children throve," wrote Eleanor. However, she was unhappy. "I played no games, I could not swim, I was feeling miserable [although she did not know it, she was at the beginning of her third pregnancy], all day long I spent with the children or walking up and down that boardwalk." Franklin bought "a little Ford car" for commuting, which Eleanor promptly drove into a gatepost and was so dismayed that she did not take the wheel again for a decade.

When Eleanor wrote Sara a complaining note about the badly furnished house they had rented, Sara replied pragmatically: "I think the cottage on the ocean sounds perfect, as the *air* is what you go for, and really if it is healthy the furniture makes absolutely no difference." However, Sara must have intuited that Eleanor was at the end of her rope, for she left the "delicious breeze" on Hyde Park's veranda to go help Eleanor with the children, making several short visits over the summer.

In fact, Eleanor wrote about Sara's influence on Anna in a note from Seabright to Franklin, who had left on a hunting trip—shades of Uncle Teddy. Eleanor amused him with an anecdote about little Anna's refusal to give up a favorite chair. When the girl realized that her mother had diverted her from her preferred seat, she shrieked and cried. Eleanor wrote:

> When she ceased to weep, I said "Oh! Anna where did you get all your determination from?"
> She looked up at her mother and said, "Gaga!"
> Of course I almost expired for it did hit the nail so beautifully on the head.

Sara had her own chores to attend to and returned to Hyde Park to oversee the installation of electricity on the estate. She spent the morning riding and the afternoon overseeing the work of her farmhands. On Labor Day she wrote of their labors: "Garden rests." (Because the Roosevelts usually spent summers and early fall away from Hyde Park, its outside gardens were designed to bloom in the spring.) On September 18, 1908, she underlined in her journal: *"Electric light is turned on."*

A week later baby James was christened at St. James Episcopal Church in Hyde Park. As was the custom in great houses, Sara wrote that she "gave presents on the place and in house in honor of the name."

Eleanor had become pregnant for the third time even before James's christening. Anna was only two years old. James was a sickly infant, and although he outgrew his illnesses, he gave his family a scare with his colds and frequent bouts of influenza in a time when the virus could be fatal. Baby James's doctor also diagnosed a heart murmur and a "nervous affliction." Franklin was told to carry him up and down stairs, even after he was a toddler, and Eleanor and Sara were enlisted to read to him while he lay flat and still on the floor to "relax his muscles."

Eleanor, with no natural affinity for children, felt trapped. She quietly expressed a desire to return to the tenements to work; what she could not do for her own children she might do for others. She had tried to satisfy her active mind with reading, foreign language lessons, and charity board work—to no avail. She wanted to go back to social work. Franklin, Sara, and cousin Susie thought her wish bizarre and frankly told her so, and Anna's pediatrician also said no. Her duty lay with her toddler and sick infant, they said, especially given the real possibility of bringing home a disease from the slums in a world that was absent any miracle drugs. If Sara was disheartened by a daughter-in-law who wanted to escape her children, she never expressed it. Instead, she made sure that she was Eleanor's—and her grandchildren's—fail-safe.

For example, Franklin would call Sara when James became ill, and she would arrive in the city forthwith to pick up Anna and take her back to Hyde Park. Once when Eleanor and the children were visiting Hyde Park, both children caught colds at the same time: Sara took care of them so that Eleanor could return to the city and enjoy some time to herself. Even with servants and Sara to help out, Eleanor felt cornered.

Also grating on Eleanor's nerves were the cramped quarters at East Thirty-sixth Street. James would cry all night long, and his wails would start his sister screaming, too. Eleanor and Franklin felt squeezed and, desperate to separate the children, turned their second living room into James's own bedroom. The couple eagerly looked forward to moving into their new home, the house Sara had promised them at Christmas three years earlier.

By the end of 1908, the families settled at 47–49 East Sixty-fifth Street, with the servants having moved in three days before the Roosevelts. There was so much showing off to be done that the family spent Christmas in their new location rather than going up to Hyde Park.

Yet decades later Eleanor wrote: "This winter of 1908 I still think of as one of the times in my life which I would rather not live over again." She referred to James's precarious health and to her unexpected reaction to living in a double house side by side with Sara. The houses were designed in the Georgian style by Charles A. Platt, the architect for the Smithsonian's Freer Gallery of Art in the nation's capital. The thirty-five-foot-wide building was buff brick on the street facade, with a limestone ground floor and limestone window cornices, and a second floor with iron balconies. It was five stories high and had a partial sixth floor. There was a utility basement belowground, with a full cellar under the basement.

Guests would enter a dual vestibule that served both families. Once inside, to enter Sara's house you would knock on the door to the left at 47 East Sixty-fifth Street. If you were Eleanor's guest, you would turn to the door on the right, 49 East Sixty-fifth. The houses were not only adjacent but also interconnected, just like the Parish-Ludlow houses where Eleanor had lived during her engagement. Besides the common front entrance, the house connected by sliding panels in the dining rooms and the drawing rooms, which could then be expanded into more capacious entertainment areas. Another connecting door was on the fourth floor: this is where the

Roosevelt children and nannies lived on one side, Sara's servants on the other. Floor three, where the adults had their bedrooms, was not joined.

Platt added a distinguishing feature to the dual house. At its core, where dual walls were typically the darkest, he added a large rectangular light well from the roof down to the second floor, bringing natural light into the house. Each side of the mirror-image house contained fifteen rooms and four baths. A generous stairway extended from the first floors to the fourth, and a narrower flight of stairs served all eight levels. There was a small courtyard at the rear of the house.

Despite Eleanor's initial excitement, once inside the house she felt trapped. She had spent part of her childhood and her adolescence as a guest in other people's houses, and now she was only one wall and a connecting door from Sara. Friends found the double houses charming and cozy, but Eleanor felt claustrophobic. Soon after moving in, Eleanor timed her tears for Franklin's arrival from work, weeping at her dressing table to show him her deep unhappiness.

Franklin was dumbfounded. Eleanor later wrote: "When my bewildered young husband asked me what on earth was the matter with me, I said I did not like to live in a house which was not in any way mine, one that I had done nothing about and which did not represent the way I wanted to live." Franklin asked why she had not spoken up earlier, when Sara sketched out her proposal. She had not whispered a word of discontent and spoke only of her eagerness to leave their cramped rental quarters. He asked why, when Sara and he had tried to draw her into consultation about the building, she had demurred and now claimed that the house was not what she wanted.

In truth, Eleanor had avoided many of the house talks, perhaps believing it her duty to let her husband take the lead. Contrary to her saying years later that she had "left everything" about the house to Sara and Franklin, in 1907 she actually had written Sara that "Franklin and I have been working over the plans for lighting, bells and telephones, which [Platt] sent us two days ago. All the arrangements seem very good except in one or two bedrooms where I think he has made a mistake as one would want lights over dressing tables."

Now Eleanor honestly could not express any sensible answers to Franklin's questions—her sobbing emotions were stronger than her reason. He could not deal with his distraught wife, who noted, "It became part of his nature not to talk to anyone of interior things." Franklin walked out after rebuking her in gentle tones that she was "quite mad."

Despite Eleanor's breakdown that evening, she continued her regular activities with Sara. They took embroidery lessons together through the winter and, with Franklin, went to the theater about once a week. Although

Eleanor confided her newly expressed feelings about Sara's presence to a few contemporaries and to Sara's sister-in-law Jennie Walters Delano, she could never bring herself to speak honestly either to her husband or to Sara. Those to whom Eleanor had revealed her unhappiness were uncomfortable because she had pledged them to secrecy, and there was nothing they could do to solve her problems. They did offer Eleanor sympathy, which was all she seemed to want.

Sara was either oblivious to or confused by Eleanor's hidden emotions— all interpretations other than Eleanor's (which were made only after Franklin's death) are conjectural: Sara never referred to these issues in her comprehensive journal or in her many letters. Although she may not have understood her daughter-in-law—nor did Franklin—she continually offered love, helped with the children, and gave constant support to the family, including large chunks of her personal fortune.

Sara also juggled her considerable volunteer work while keeping the happiness of Franklin's family and the care of his children her priority. She was on the boards of the Henry Street Settlement Visiting Nurse Service and of the Babies' Ward of the New York Postgraduate Hospital, and a member of various Red Cross committees. She supported the Junior League, helping entice wealthy women into social causes, and was one of two hundred members of the tony Thursday Evening Club, which brought cultural events to its attendees. Sara had joined the Colony Club after it moved uptown, and enjoyed taking her friends there for lunch. Her wide-ranging curiosity included exploring other religions. In February she hosted the annual Plant, Flower and Fruit Guild that, despite its name, sponsored public affairs talks. "Rabbi [Stephen] Wise [the Reform Jewish activist who was a crusader for social justice] spoke very well. Father McCloskey not so well."

The next month saw Sara touching both the past and the future. After a long illness, her husband's younger brother, John, died at age sixty-eight. Sara herself was now fifty-three years old and was about to become a grandmother for the third time. On March 18 she wrote: "Eleanor had her beautiful hair washed, etc. and nails done. At 2:00, she went to drive with me. We got home at 4:00. At 5:30 Dr. Ely came. At 8:10 her second son was born. The baby is really lovely and very big, 11 lbs." The baby was named after his father—Franklin Delano Roosevelt Jr. "Eleanor continues to do perfectly," Sara said the next month.

In May, unusually early, the families traveled to Campobello to look at a possible summer house for the growing family. Sara's beloved neighbor Mrs. Hartman Kuhn of Boston, who lived to the south of Sara's island house, had been a great admirer of Eleanor's. Before her death that year, she had made an offer in her will for Sara to buy her furnished two-and-a-half-story

Dutch colonial shingled house on the Friars Bay waterfront for an inexpensive five thousand dollars. Her sole condition was that Sara turn over the thirty-four-room house and five acres to Eleanor and Franklin. Consequently, in late spring the three spent a long afternoon, said Sara, "going over Mrs. Kuhn's house, which I have bought for Franklin and Eleanor."

Now that Franklin and Eleanor had their own gift house on Campobello (with taxes paid over the decades by Sara), there was little doubt that they would continue to spend their summers on the island. The 1897 house was lovely, with acres of shorefront.

Later in the season Sara traveled to the island resort with her summer staff and the toddlers, Anna and James. Franklin and Eleanor followed with baby Franklin Jr. and their staff—which included Miss Spring for the baby, and an English nurse and German girl for the two elder children, as well as their usual retinue. Despite the occasional foggy weather, Eleanor enjoyed every minute, decorating the first house she regarded as her own and reading by the fire in inclement weather to her "chicks," as she began calling the children.

Eleanor saw how much Franklin had taken to the newly popular sport of golf, and sweetly took secret lessons so that she might join him on the links. After practicing for weeks, she invited her husband for a game. She was nervous and kept tearing at the green. After watching her play for a few holes, Franklin unkindly informed his insecure wife that she should give up golf. "My old sensitiveness about my inability to play games made me give it up then and there!" she wrote.

Years later Anna commented that "Mother's written about how she used to try to do things that Father wanted her to do, like riding horseback, playing golf, learning to drive a car. At all of these things, she was a flat failure. But I think she just gave up too quickly." Surely she did, but given her husband's brusque dismissal of her attempts, no one can blame her for being easily discouraged.

Franklin and Eleanor were now free to invite however many guests they wished to stay with them at Campobello, although Sara was perplexed by Eleanor's friendship with the baby nurse, whom Eleanor asked to visit in the late summer when she was no longer in their employ. Miss Spring was probably Eleanor's first friend outside her social set. Again, Eleanor could not be forthright with her mother-in-law about this outside-the-circle friendship. She wrote Franklin, who was back in the city: "I broke it to Mama [that] Miss Spring was coming up and put it all on you."

Despite this unusual friendship with a member of her household staff, Eleanor could be traditional when it came to paying help. She wrote Franklin to oversee the summer cleaning of the Sixty-fifth Street house:

"Ask Harriet to do the library & tell her to take all the books out, wipe them & put them back. She ought to do it in three days & as she can't work steadily, I would tell her that we will only pay her $1 a day. The other cleaners get $1.50."

At Hyde Park in the fall, it was time to christen Franklin Jr. at St. James Church. "A sweet sight, but my heart sank a little because Baby looks so delicate and exquisite," Sara said. Eleanor and Franklin left for town, having established their three children and nurses at Hyde Park with Sara. On weekends the couple returned to visit their three children.

By October the baby and the toddlers had caught influenza, but the vulnerable baby was Sara's first concern. A week later she wrote in her journal: "Find Baby Franklin not very well tho' he takes his food." The next day, "Baby does not eat well today. Dr. Gribbon finds a 'murmur' in his heart. It might come from being anemic. I feel anxious."

On October 23 Eleanor and Franklin went to Hyde Park to see Dr. Gribbon and returned to the city, leaving the sick infant with Sara. Several days later Sara wrote: "Baby lamb gained 1½ oz. in two days but continues the rapid breathing, and now it is quicker." The next day, "Baby cried often in the morning, but was sleeping sweetly in his perambulator at 12:30," when Sara left for a luncheon.

She continued: "At 2:00 Annie the housemaid telephoned me to come as Baby was ill. I *flew* home. Dr. Gribbon was here, holding precious Baby. He just got here in time as the little heart had almost stopped. Dr. G. got to the house in 20 minutes. I telephoned Eleanor. She and Franklin came at 8.30. Dr. Gribbon stayed till 11:00."

The next day Eleanor and Franklin, with Dr. Gribbon, took the declining baby back to Manhattan for further medical consultations. They hoped that the specialists would disagree with Dr. Gribbon's diagnosis of endocarditis, an infection of the inner lining of the heart.

With the baby out of Sara's care—although she still had the elder two children—she hid her worries and wrote "Dearest Eleanor" as reassuring a letter as she could:

The children have gone to the farm with both nurses and as they left they were laughing and playing. I have been reading up "endocarditis" in Flint's book. He says the outlook is hopeful, of course sometimes it *leaves* delicacies or produces bad after effects, but no doubt with a baby the after effects are more likely to be outgrown—I keep seeing that lovely little *patient* expression! And I realize what it all means to *you* dear. It certainly seems incomprehensible but I feel it must proceed from some *natural* cause—Love to my dear Franklin. Devotedly, Mama.

A few days later Franklin and Eleanor had a difficult telephone call to make to Hyde Park. They told Sara that the Manhattan specialists had agreed with the country doctor: it *was* endocarditis. After the conversation, Sara went to her snuggery to write the couple another worried yet reassuring letter:

> I am still *aching* over your telephone message, to think that our fears are true. I am thankful he is in your own town house & can be quiet, *absolutely* so, and it is well for the other babes to be here. I feel it is a question of time and nursing but he must and will get well.
>
> I also had to tell Aunt Annie [Hitch], as she had no idea of the darling being ill, she is very very sorry & full of sympathy for your anxiety.

She continued to tell them how she took Anna and James to feed the chickens at the farm "and they ran about & played & had a lovely time."

On October 31 Sara felt she must leave the elder children at Hyde Park and return to town to be with the couple and the baby, even though Franklin had instructed her to remain in the country. When Sara arrived at the house, Eleanor cried out, "Oh, I am so glad you came." Sara wrote of her sick grandson that she "could hear every cry all night from my room where I lay, useless."

Sara wrote of the next morning, November 2, 1909: "Franklin telephoned to my room, 'Better come, Mama, Baby is sinking.' I went in. The little angel ceased breathing at 7:25. Franklin and Eleanor are most wonderful, but poor Eleanor's mother's heart is well nigh broken. She so hoped, and cannot believe her baby is gone from here. He was 7 months and 9 days old, a beautiful flower he always seemed."

Now that Sara could no longer do anything for the baby, she turned her energies to Eleanor and Franklin. She made sure that they could be alone with their grief, yet she felt she could not leave the infant alone, so she sat watch by her grandson's still body for an excruciating twenty-four hours after his death, departing only when it was time to take his tiny coffin to the train.

At Hyde Park the night before his funeral, with Eleanor and Franklin still secluded, Sara wrote: "Again last night I sat five hours beside the little angel and wondered why he had to go."

The next morning Franklin, Eleanor, and Sara took the infant's coffin back to Hyde Park and buried the "little lamb" at the churchyard at St. James. Rosy was there; he and Sara's driver had dug the tiny grave. Sara's sister-in-law Jennie, with daughter Laura, had made a bed of flowers to lay down after the burial. Hall, who was now a student at Harvard, had arrived from Cambridge. Sara wrote that Eleanor was "brave and lovely" during the service. Of her youngest grandson, she said, "It is hard to give him up and my heart aches for Eleanor."

After the funeral, Franklin and Eleanor returned to town, leaving Anna and James with Sara. Two weeks later they returned to pick up their two remaining children and take them back to the city.

23

"A Really Fine and Dignified Position"

Eleanor was despondent in late 1909. She had viewed motherhood as a duty rather than a joy and now blamed herself for her baby's death: perhaps if she had been more maternal—done something different— Franklin Jr. would have survived. "I felt . . . in some way I must be to blame. I even felt that I had not cared enough about him." Ellie Roosevelt Seagraves said, "She thought there must have been something she could have done. She could have contacted this doctor or that doctor." Eleanor was terribly hard on herself, given that in this era one out of every five children died before reaching a fifth birthday. Although Eleanor saw no "alienist" to diagnose her terrible sadness and hopelessness—in 1910, psychiatry was scorned by social New York—it would not take a medical specialist to determine that she was severely depressed.

Sara, who surely had seen more than her share of childhood death, believed that people worked through their grief by getting on with life. Of course, her inborn disposition was durable and optimistic; it must have been difficult for her to watch Eleanor's great misery and be unable to alleviate it. Sara did what she could: she encouraged Eleanor to take vigorous walks, go to concerts, visit relatives, and attend afternoon classes and meetings. Sara gave up many of her own activities to be with Eleanor. She also took

responsibility for Anna and James so that Eleanor would have fewer obligations. Perhaps, too, Sara was afraid of how Eleanor's melancholy would
affect her grandchildren.

Franklin shrank from thinking about the tragedy. Eleanor later described
his own quiet grief at his son's loss: "It was like closing a door." He did not
understand his wife's unceasing mourning and did his best to avoid her.
Whatever sympathy he might have shown was diminished by her acting the
silent martyr when he came home late from, say, the Knickerbocker Club. At
work, Franklin was just as uninvolved—one of the firm's principal partners
mentioned to a shamed Sara his disappointment at Franklin's inattention.

However, to his fellow law clerks Franklin sketched a glowing future:
first, he would be elected to the New York legislature. Then he would be
appointed assistant secretary of the navy. Afterward, New York would elect
him governor. He would cap his career—as had three previous New York
governors Van Buren, Cleveland, and Uncle Teddy—by becoming president of the United States!

At home, Franklin bridged the gap between him and his wife in the marital bed. About a month after their baby's death, Eleanor became pregnant.
She later told Anna that she entered marriage "totally ignorant of any
method of contraception whatsoever." By 1909 a number of prominent society women supported birth control, so Eleanor would have had some
inkling of how to avoid pregnancy. In fact, the nation's birth rate had
already dropped to 3.5 children per family from double that number in
1800. However, there was little in Eleanor's character that would have
allowed her to suggest abstinence or any form of contraception to her husband. Duty was Eleanor's leitmotif, although a pregnancy at this time was
probably the worst thing for her emotional well-being.

The family was heavyhearted as Christmas approached. Sara wrote sympa-
thetically of Eleanor's insistence on having the family over on December 23
to see her tree, "so lovely of her when she misses baby so." The next day
everyone went up to Hyde Park for Christmas. Eleanor and Franklin
returned to the city a few days later, leaving their children with Sara.

Still, Franklin and his family were spending more time with Sara at
Hyde Park. To his mother's delight, Franklin took on many of the same
local responsibilities that his father had shouldered. He became a warden
of St. James Episcopal Church (even though he still found the actual service
tedious) and was a more enthusiastic member of the Rescue Hook and
Ladder Company of Hyde Park and of the Dutchess County Society. Sara
joined her family in outdoor sports; at fifty-six, she still relished sailing and

riding horseback in the warm months, coasting and skating during the winter.

In February sister Dora arrived from France for minor surgery, and Sara and Eleanor spent most of their time with her. (Sara went solo, though, to the house of the Ralph Sangers, where she sat next to Columbia University's esteemed president, Nicholas Murray Butler.) In mid-February, Eleanor lost Sara's able assistance when news came that sister Kassie had become ill while visiting Bombay. As soon as Kassie could travel, she left India for medical treatment in France. Sara and Dora sailed immediately from New York to be with Kassie during her recuperation in Paris. Sara did not return until April 28, when she wrote: "My little Anna and James have not forgotten me."

Poughkeepsie is where Franklin was "kidnapped," as he liked to put it, into politics by local Democratic leaders. (Note the aristocratic denial of ambition in his wording.) For years, an apocryphal story has circulated that Franklin reacted to their invitation to run for the New York State senate by responding, "I'd like to talk to my mother about it first."

There's no proof of that story, nor should credence be given to the common claim that Sara dismissed politics as "dirty." In fact, the senior leader of the Dutchess County Democratic party was Sara's longtime friend and neighbor Thomas Jefferson Newbold, termed "the aristocrat in politics" by Eleanor. Newbold's son Archie was one of Franklin's oldest and best chums.

The men had great hopes in electing Franklin to the Twenty-sixth District senate seat, last won by a Democrat—the elder Newbold himself—before Franklin's birth. Surely Sara would have regarded Newbold's choosing Franklin as a compliment. Although she might not have wanted a public life for her son, she could never have thought that politics was not a place for a gentleman, not after cousin Teddy's accomplishments. Wasn't Isaac Roosevelt a member of the state's very first senate? Moreover, relative Robert B. Roosevelt had battled New York's Boss Tweed. Her friend Lewis Stuyvesant Chanler (not just a Stuyvesant but also a great-great-grandson of John Jacob Astor and brother of the painter Robert Chanler) had served as lieutenant governor of New York in 1906 and as a state assemblyman representing Dutchess County since 1909. Young Corinne's husband, Joe Alsop, was active in Republican politics in Connecticut, and Teddy Robinson, Eleanor's first cousin and Rosy's son-in-law, was considering a run for the New York State Assembly.

No matter what Sara's private concerns, as her friend Kleeman wrote: "All her life she had been accustomed to accepting the decisions of the men of the family whom she loved and respected." She may also have realized that Dutchess County politics would keep her son closer to Hyde Park.

In early July, Sara, Eleanor, and the children left for Campobello. Eleanor was both pregnant and dressed in mourning for her last baby. Franklin had to spend part of his summer in Hyde Park, shoring up support for his nomination. On September 1 Eleanor left Campobello with her maid to await the baby's birth in Manhattan, leaving her two children with Sara. Mid-month, Sara accompanied her grandchildren on the long trip back to Manhattan. Sara, Anna, and James visited Eleanor and Franklin in Manhattan and then left for Algonac on September 17.

Sara was with the grandchildren at Hyde Park on September 23, 1910, when, as Sara wrote, Eleanor gave birth in Manhattan to "a fine boy, 11 lbs. 14 oz. Born this morning at 6:45. I went to town on the 9:38." She visited Eleanor and her newest grandson, Elliott—named after Eleanor's beloved father—and returned to Hyde Park the next day to continue watching over the elder children. Anna and James did not return to Eleanor until October 5, having been away from their parents, except for a few short visits, for six weeks.

The day after Elliott's birth, Sara wrote triumphantly in her journal: "Franklin recd. *nomination* for State Senate. Franklin will be here now a great deal." As soon as he had secured the nomination, Sara made a generous campaign contribution—a gesture that local politicos probably would have already assumed was coming. Franklin raised $2,500, with some two-thirds (more than $1,700) coming from Sara.

A week after Elliott's birth, Franklin began his campaign. He took on his quest with real vitality, a vigor that he had lacked for the law. He became the first Dutchess County politician to campaign in a motorcar—a rented red Maxwell roadster, without a windshield or a roof, nicknamed the Red Peril and equipped with an eighteen-pound repair kit from Hammacher Schlemmer.

Franklin's district was large: it comprised three counties (Putnam, Dutchess, and Columbia) and ran one hundred miles up the Hudson and to the borders of Connecticut and Massachusetts. In fact, Franklin's driver became so disoriented on the area's meandering roads that once Franklin gave an enthusiastic speech to great applause—in Connecticut.

He would begin his speeches either simply and sincerely—"My friends"—or with a quip—"I'm not Teddy." The jest adroitly distanced Franklin from the Republican party yet reminded the listener of the familial relationship. In areas close to home, he would mention his father, "You have

known how close he was to the life of this town," and said that his own campaign was "to follow in his footsteps," remarks certain to have made Sara
proud.

He worked harder than he ever had in his life and focused his campaign
on local and state issues, particularly "bossism" in Albany. Franklin was at his
best during a campaign—the process of politics engaged his mind. He
began a lifelong habit that must have pleased Sara to the core: at the end of
the campaign, the final speech would always be made from her home at
Hyde Park.

Although Democrats were a distinct minority in the district, Franklin
won the election by a slight margin. He was just shy of his twenty-ninth
birthday. Sara later reminisced, "I shall never forget it. I was one of the few
sympathizers Franklin had among his own people. Many of our friends said
it was a shame for so fine a young man to associate himself with 'dirty' politicians. But by this time I knew Franklin's ideas and ideals in going into politics. I knew not only that I would always be proud of him, but I predicted
the time when their ideas, too, would change and when the younger members of other old families would enter politics and take their places in the
government. I was happy indeed when he won."

Sara must have taken pride, too, in knowing that she had helped jump-
start his campaign with her contribution. Eleanor, though, was less
involved; her health kept her confined in Manhattan until October 29.
Eleanor focused on little Elliott and did not fret at being left behind, writing
later: "It never occurred to me that I had any part to play." She made one
campaign trip with Sara and Franklin's uncle Warren in early November to
Tivoli, home of her Hall family. Of her future, she admitted, "I felt I must
acquiesce in whatever he might decide and be willing to go to Albany."

Eleanor organized their move into a sunny rented house, fully furnished—
"very large," said Sara, "a fine house. Can be made comfortable." Eleanor
and Franklin took their good fortune as routine. Most legislators rented a
single room in a boardinghouse and left their families in the home district.
The Roosevelts, however, rented this house for $1,500—the same amount
as Franklin's state salary. Sara again paid for their rental, more than happy to
pick up such costs necessary to further Franklin's burgeoning political
career.

Sara also sent upriver vast amounts of fresh food from Hyde Park's farm:
vegetables, fruits, eggs, and milk. She has been criticized over the years for
her "extravagance" by sending her family homegrown products. People have
forgotten that, at that time, commercially sold cow's milk "was recognized

as the source of a large number of different infections, including typhoid fever, bovine tuberculosis, diphtheria, and severe streptococcal infections," according to a recent scientific paper. In fact, the chief cause of infant mortality was diarrhea from impure milk and "community standards governing sanitation and safe milk were either very lax or non-existent." Sara was merely protecting her grandchildren in the best way she could.

Eleanor also brought with her to the state capital three servants for the household and three for the children. Eleanor said, "I was so nervous about this new baby we took a wet nurse to be sure of having him properly fed." She also took an English governess and a German nanny. There were five in the family and six in help. The couple rented 49 East Sixty-fifth to the Stanley Mortimers, Eleanor's aunt and uncle.

The first thing Eleanor had to tackle the day following Franklin's swearing-in was a lunch—albeit with the help of a professional caterer—on January 2, 1911, for 250 people from his district. Eleanor asked Sara to come to Albany with the family to help with the household and her first official party. Sara claimed not to have been needed: "Eleanor managed splendidly." As soon as everyone had left and the debris was cleared, Eleanor and Sara rearranged the furniture to Eleanor's taste. Sara left for Hyde Park soon after, writing: "When I said goodnight after hymns to the children, Anna and James both said, 'I *wish* you were not going away, *do* come back soon,' and were very sweet and loving. I hate to leave my grandbabies."

She also wrote Eleanor and Franklin when she arrived back home on the evening of January 5: "It seems like a very strange dream to be here & to think of you dear things all settled in that big Albany house and my boy sitting in the state Senate, a really fine and dignified position, if only lived up to as it should be and I know it *will* be by my dear one."

Sara continued: "Every man who has the highest conception of his country's good & of the great trust reposing in its government must & will help others to the same high standard of honesty & truth & the welfare of the people."

As for Eleanor, in Sara's absence she realized that "for the first time, I was going to live on my own; neither my mother-in-law nor Mrs. Parish was going to be within call." (Elliott would later comment that it was Susie Parish who dominated Eleanor.) Eleanor found that she enjoyed her new freedom, although she felt unsettled when strangers recognized her as a political wife. She continued to write Sara daily about her new activities, and the couple went down to Hyde Park when Sara hosted New York's Governor Dix and his wife.

Occasionally Eleanor watched the goings-on in the capitol gallery, attending from a sense of obligation to Franklin. She would return home in late afternoon to read and play with the children, staying with them until their bedtime, just as her own mother had done during the "children's hour." She coddled baby Elliott—the first child she would treat this way—out of a lingering grief over Franklin Jr. Only once did Eleanor and Franklin have lunch with Anna, their eldest and only daughter. Eleanor later reported that Anna had spent "a solid hour over the meal" and was banished back to the nursery. The experiment did not work, so Eleanor and Franklin returned to the custom of wealthy couples dining without their children. Although the elder children lived with their English nanny above the library in the back of the house, Eleanor placed Elliott and his German nanny in the bedroom next to his parents'.

In the evenings Franklin began bringing home his fellow officials and Democratic henchmen. As Eleanor wrote, she was beginning "to learn to get on with people of varying backgrounds." Unfortunately, the visitors' cigars in the library polluted the elder children's bedroom, as rising fumes percolated through the ceiling. Eleanor was forced to move the children and their nurse to a higher level of the house that she had not planned on opening. Little James still had to be carried upstairs, so this accommodation was a backbreaking sacrifice.

At the end of the session, Eleanor gave up this house and arranged to rent another for the next fall session. Then life continued as normal: late spring at Hyde Park and summer at Campobello at the island house that, as Eleanor said, "became a great source of joy to me."

Much to Eleanor's twenty-year-old brother's dismay, she began to meddle in his love life. She was delighted that Hall was friendly with a young woman she liked, so she told the girl's family that Hall was serious about the romance—which he was not. Hall wrote to his sister: "I am now under obligation to the family all bound in such a manner as I had always carefully avoided. I prefer to do my own choosing and to carry out all such diplomatic relations without expert assistance." Eventually he was bound to tell the young lady that his feelings were merely those of a friend. When she reported the news to her family, Hall wrote Eleanor that he had "incurred the hatred of the whole tribe." Sara is often portrayed as a meddler, but she would never have interfered in Franklin's affairs this blatantly.

In the fall, when it was time to return to Albany, the Roosevelts found kin waiting: Teddy Robinson had won his election to the State Assembly and arrived with his wife, Helen. They took a house not far from the Roosevelts, which comforted Eleanor, as she was more at ease with relatives than with anyone else. However, she was briefly reminded of her grief over Franklin Jr.'s death when the Robinsons' baby died of whooping cough.

Franklin now became entangled in one of the couple's first open disagreements with Sara from which he would not cut his way loose. The Mortimers had moved out of East Sixty-fifth Street and the house lay vacant. Franklin and Eleanor, without a new tenant, wanted to economize by closing up the house for the winter and making other arrangements for their servants. Sara thought this a shortsighted economy; perhaps she had hoped that they might come to Manhattan more often if their house were open. From Hyde Park in September, Franklin wrote to Eleanor in Albany: "She began about the New York house. I told her we had made all arrangements to have all the servants board out. She was quite upset and although I said it didn't matter I think she has written you to have the servants stay! I don't know quite what to say about it; it would certainly be nice to have them there in November and December, but on the other hand we have practically decided not to. Do just as you think best dearest and you know I'll back you up!"

Franklin was backpedaling from an agreement he had made with Eleanor and was now merely offering to support her rather than simply standing firm against Sara's objections. Eleanor held her ground and the house lay vacant, but she was angry with her mother-in-law for pressuring them to go back on their decision. Rather than being vexed by her husband's lack of backbone in the matter, Eleanor focused her resentment on Sara.

The women did agree on one thing: they were shocked when Franklin came out for national women's suffrage. Neither Eleanor nor Sara initially saw any purpose in women having the vote, even though a significant number of their wealthy acquaintances—Mrs. Alva Belmont, for example—were suffrage leaders. Of course, it would have been nearly impossible for Franklin to oppose women's right to vote, with Vassar College and its many professorial suffragists in his district. Eleanor came to support suffrage in time—ironically, out of duty to her husband. "I realized that if my husband were a suffragist, I must be, too." Eleanor was feeling her way in Albany and was in no sense yet a political partner to Franklin.

Sara had purchased a car and had her driver, Plog (pronounced "plow"), take her up to Albany for short visits. Anything important to Franklin was interesting to her, so politics now came within her domain. Sara was particularly proud of her son's fight against Tammany corruption, which even upstate voters were noticing. In fact, *The New York Times* wrote that Franklin had the face and body of a matinee star, which pleased his mother greatly, although she must have thought the description silly. More tangibly, she—like Eleanor—disliked the cigar smoke of his colleagues and during her visits spent much of the time outside with the children: "Took dear little Jamesie for a walk while Anna coasted."

March 1911 was a difficult month for the family. It was the second anniversary of Franklin Jr.'s death. Sara wrote: "Eleanor met me at Pough-keepsie and went to Hyde Park" to visit the baby's grave at St. James Epis-copal Church. Three days later Sara's brother-in-law Fred Hitch, Annie's husband, died at Algonac. Sara, Eleanor, Franklin, and a contingent of rela-tives attended services in Fairhaven. On the last day of the month, Franklin's uncle Frederick Delano lost his twelve-year-old daughter, Matilda, to tuber-culosis of the spine.

A month later, a cataclysm at sea caused Sara to write Franklin, who was off on vacation while Eleanor and the children were with her at Hyde Park. "I have not been able to get my thoughts away from the awful disaster, it seems too terrible to be true. The confidence in the 'unsinkableness' of the great ship, the shortage of lifeboats, of long distance glasses, no search lights, all these faults are doubtless common to all the great liners. Rosy is much upset over poor Jack Astor's death [Rosy's brother-in-law John Jacob Astor IV]. Mr. Millet, Mr. Widener, Major Archie Butt and Mary, others were well known but oh! the tragedies in the steerage as well."

Sara also wept over the heroic deaths of the Isidor Strauses. Although she did not know them, she thought the couple courageous and loving to give their lifeboat seats to others and die together on the *Titanic* rather than be separated after four decades of marriage.

In May, Sara was back taking care of the grandchildren at Hyde Park, and she hosted Elliott's christening party on the thirtieth. In June, Franklin was sick with "sinus and tonsillitis, some fever all the time." Eleanor went ahead to Campobello, leaving her husband with his mother. On July 5 Sara took him to the doctor's office, where he "had cocaine and was miserable all day."

As the fall session approached, Franklin realized he "needed an automo-bile," Sara noted on October 5, "so we got a little 'Hudson.'" It was actually an early birthday present, but she wanted him to have the gift right away, as he had to have a car to reach his constituents. The next week the family cel-ebrated Eleanor's birthday in Hyde Park.

In late 1911 Franklin made a long motor trip to Trenton, New Jersey, to get better acquainted with Governor Woodrow Wilson, who would run for president the following year. The otherwise insignificant state senator was welcomed because both his late father and half brother Rosy were ardent party supporters. The governor reacted favorably to his first impression of Franklin. His staff, thinking of Teddy, wondered whether the cousin was a Republican. Wilson responded, "No, this one comes from the Democratic branch of the family, and he is the handsomest young giant I have ever seen." Eleanor, still a political neophyte, was disappointed that Franklin seemed to be tending toward standing behind Wilson rather than Teddy and his third-party Progressive (Bull Moose) party. The Oyster Bay clan took Franklin's disloyalty hard, and fissures began to open between the once-close Roosevelt families.

Eleanor retreated to Campobello in the summer of 1912 after a few days at the Democratic National Convention in Baltimore. Franklin stayed and wrote her devotedly. It was his first national convention: hot, smoky, noisy, and dirty. He loved every moment.

After the convention, Franklin joined Eleanor at Campobello but soon left for New York to begin his campaign to retain his seat. The couple, who had sent the children on to Hyde Park, arrived ill in Manhattan. Franklin took to his bed, and Eleanor, despite her own fever, nursed him. Sara came to the rescue, putting Eleanor comfortably to bed and calling the doctor. The diagnosis was typhoid. With the grandchildren at Hyde Park, Sara made the long round trip by train every day to keep an eye on both houses.

The campaign looked doomed, especially as Franklin faced not just the Republican opposition but also a candidate from Teddy's Bull Moose party. Enter an unlikely-looking knight to the rescue: the short, skinny, pock-marked, and ill-kempt Louis McHenry Howe. The brilliant strategist had recognized Franklin's potential and had written him only weeks before as "Beloved and Revered Future President."

These were certainly the words that Franklin wanted to hear. Now, sick in bed, he needed Howe and telegraphed him to come manage his campaign. As a result of Howe's cleverness and hard work, Franklin won his second term in the state senate. (His fellow Democrat Woodrow Wilson, by the way, also won the presidency.)

Eleanor and Sara both took an instant dislike to Howe and thought him a chain-smoking, ill-bred "nuisance," to use Eleanor's word. Howe was bright and realized he would need to win over his candidate's wife before his candidate could win over the voters. Eleanor said, "I was as determined that I would not like him as he was that I should. He kept coming to my desk and talking to me, day after day, until I became interested in spite of myself, and eventually I realized how much he had to offer." In January

1913 Eleanor and Franklin were back to Albany, but in March they traveled to Washington for the presidential inauguration.

Earlier, Franklin had let Wilson know that he would like a political appointment. Several positions were floated by him. The morning of Wilson's inauguration, Franklin walked into the lobby of the capital city's Willard Hotel, where a previous president, Ulysses S. Grant, had coined the term *lobbyist* to describe the men waiting in its lobby for a chance to solicit his support for their causes. There Franklin bumped into the man who was to become Wilson's secretary of the navy. "How would you like to come to Washington as assistant secretary of the navy?" he was asked.

Franklin said, "I'd like it bully well."

After two years in Albany, he and Eleanor would be leaving for Washington, D.C.

24

"Launched in Your Work"

In March 1913 Eleanor received indirect word of her husband's confirmation as assistant secretary of the navy and wrote Franklin a subtle rebuke. "A telegram came to you from Mr. Daniels [the secretary of the navy], so we know you are confirmed and finally launched in your work." Then she added: "Many happy returns of today, dear. I ordered your 17th of March present as we couldn't do anything else together!" Franklin immediately sent her an apologetic note, excusing himself both for not telling her of his confirmation and also for forgetting their eighth anniversary in his excitement over the political appointment.

He next wrote his mother a happier letter: "I am baptized, confirmed, sworn in, vaccinated—and somewhat at sea!" Sara was thrilled, and as a reflection of his new importance, she admonished him to "try not to write your signature too small as it gets a cramped look and is not distinct!"

At thirty-one, Franklin was delighted with his prestigious job and pleased to learn that he was to use the same desk that Teddy himself had as assistant secretary. With this tangible symbol of his success, and with Louis Howe as his assistant, Franklin foresaw smooth sailing ahead. Sara was proud and touched by the honor her son brought to the family. Eleanor felt inadequate in her new role but was determined to do her best. She traveled to Farmington to speak with Bamie Roosevelt Cowles, the Roosevelt family's most experienced and politically attuned Washington hostess. Bamie gave Eleanor sound advice on both Washington and navy protocol—but most important, she generously offered the couple her comfortable house at 1733 N Street NW, on a tree-lined street and with a backyard rock garden and rose arbor. The rental would include the house's caretaker couple. Eleanor also would have her own four servants and two nurses to look after the family of five. However, Eleanor would take her own staff with her when she and the children left Washington on their many holidays. Bamie's couple suited Franklin perfectly, as he would have them to keep everything shipshape.

The house would not be available until the fall, so Eleanor and the children rotated among Sixty-fifth Street, Hyde Park, and Campobello while Franklin lived in a Washington hotel for the spring and summer. He joined the Metropolitan Club and, of course, the Army and Navy Club. He left the nation's capital to spend weekends at Hyde Park with his family and to enjoy a short summer vacation at Campobello. In the autumn Eleanor and the children joined him. Eleanor wrote: "When we moved to Washington my mother-in-law, as usual, helped us to get settled."

After the move was completed, Sara returned home. She left for Europe in late fall when she received word of Kassie's husband's sudden death. From abroad, she wrote Eleanor and Franklin a pleasant note in December about her visit with a friend who had remarried a Jewish man. "He is a very nice man, does not look Jewish at all, and of course is very clever and not only financially." She mentioned having just received a telegram from Franklin that said simply ALGONAC, so she knew all was well. Sara told them they should not meet her at the dock in New York because she knew they were too busy in Washington.

At Christmas the family joined Sara at Hyde Park for their Victorian celebration. Hall did not join them—he had married and was celebrating Christmas with his wife. The traditions remained the same, though: on Christmas Eve everyone, including the adults, hung stockings on the fireplace mantel in Eleanor and Franklin's bedroom. The tree downstairs had already been decorated with Sara's and Eleanor's collections of ornaments from around the world and lit with wax candles. A crèche with ceramic figures sat under the tall pine.

"We always had a party the afternoon of Christmas Eve for all the families who lived on the place," Eleanor said. "The presents were piled under the tree, and after everyone had been greeted, my husband would choose the children old enough to distribute gifts and send them around to the guests." Sara would give out her envelopes with money, and Eleanor would repeat the gesture. This was the first Christmas since the passage of the Six-teenth Amendment, but the new federal income tax that would be so far-reaching in its impact had no effect on Sara's or Eleanor's generosity. "The cornucopias filled with old-fashioned sugar candies and the peppermint canes hanging on the tree were distributed, too, and then our guests would leave us and enjoy their ice cream, cake, and coffee or milk" in the kitchen.

After the "guests" had departed, the family enjoyed tea while Franklin read *A Christmas Carol*, selecting parts suitable for the younger children to hear. He squeaked his voice soprano when Tiny Tim spoke; when it was Scrooge's turn, his voice turned harsh and gruff. When Franklin tired, they dressed for their Christmas feast and he finished the reading afterward. Eleanor attended midnight service "so the religious aspects and significance of the Christmas celebration were never out of my mind."

In the morning the younger children were bundled into their parents' bed to open their stockings while Eleanor tried to get everyone to drink a glass of orange juice. Breakfast came late, and following it, Eleanor and Sara would take whichever children were willing to attend services. "My hus-band resented having to go to church on Christmas Day and sometimes flatly refused," his wife said.

After returning home, the children opened their outdoor gifts—"I remember the excitement as each child grew old enough to have his own sled"—and ran outdoors to coast on the hill behind the stable. Franklin, though, was the only one allowed to pilot the bobsled. When they reached the bottom, thrilled and excited, Franklin would chase the children up the hill to begin again. In late afternoon the remainder of the gifts were opened, including Eleanor's homemade sachets of dry pine needles from Campo-bello and her embroidery—"perfectly useless handwork," she would later disparagingly call her thoughtful attempts. Franklin loved her generosity and would savor her special gifts, often opening only one each day between Christmas and New Year's.

After the 1914 New Year, the family returned to Washington, leaving Sara in New York. Franklin had decided that Eleanor should have a chauffeur drive her to her prescribed afternoon social calls. Eleanor ordered calling cards and practiced repeating, "I am Mrs. Franklin D. Roosevelt. My hus-band has just come on as assistant secretary of the navy." Only then did she set off on her calls.

The protocol was stifling: Monday, she paid visits to the wives of the Supreme Court justices; Tuesday, the wives of congressional members; Wednesday, at home to receive calls; Thursday, the wives of senators; and

Friday, the wives of diplomats. Then on Monday morning it began all over again. Her schedule was tedious but also challenging; it made Eleanor meet new people and learn to put others at ease. She was becoming more self-reliant and later admitted that she could never have taken on such duties three years earlier in Albany. She also began to take official trips with Franklin on navy ships, noting that "my mother-in-law always had an eye to the children when we were away, so there was really no cause for anxiety."

On top of a grueling daytime schedule, a lovely Eleanor accompanied Franklin to a formal dinner nearly every evening. She was tall, with soft sun-streaked brown hair, and slim—despite meals that included cream of oyster soup, filet of beef, fresh asparagus, peas and mushrooms, and ice cream with strawberries. Sometimes Eleanor found her dinner companions unpalatable. In 1913 she wrote Sara: "I've got to go to the Harris party which I'd rather be hung than be seen at. Mostly Jews."

Two days later she was sneering again. "I went to a Jew party . . . for the Baruchs on Sunday night. It was appalling. I never wish to hear money, jewels and sables mentioned again!" Later, when Franklin invited Felix Frankfurter (whom he would appoint to the U.S. Supreme Court) to lunch, Eleanor's response to Sara was that he was "an interesting little man, but very jew." Whereas Sara's comments on Jewish acquaintances reflected the inbred attitude of the times tempered by her innate generosity, Eleanor's anti-Semitism seems surprisingly mean-spirited.

She was often displeased by the behavior of those outside her group. Eleanor wrote a candid letter to Sara about the president's daughter: "Miss Eleanor Wilson, who is nice, but dear me, breeding is somewhat lacking in this political flower of the land."

Eleanor's words reflect her own insecurities. Her orphaned childhood made her uncertain of herself; unlike Sara, Curtis Roosevelt has pointed out, Eleanor had no deep roots. Sara could accept others without being judgmental because "she knew who and what she was," said Nina Roosevelt Gibson. "Sara had no insecurities, unlike Eleanor."

Eleanor and Franklin at least enjoyed their own smart social set, people who were from recognized families. Lathrop Brown, for example, was now a congressman from a Manhattan district. The young couple also dined at 1718 H Street, the home of a group of young bachelors who called themselves "the Family." Among them were Andrew J. Peters, the future mayor of Boston, and David Bruce, who would marry the daughter of Andrew Mellon and be the first American diplomat to win the "triple crown," becoming ambassador to France, Germany, and Great Britain. On one relaxed visit to the Family, Eleanor facetiously signed the guest book, "Eleanor Roosevelt and husband."

On other occasions, Franklin and Eleanor visited frail Henry Adams, the grandson of John Quincy Adams and the author of *The Education of Henry Adams,* an influential book that explained his theory of history. Adams had just turned seventy-five and still entertained in his house on Lafayette Park across from the White House. (The house is now part of the Hay-Adams Hotel.) He would call on the Roosevelts on N Street but remain in his horse-drawn victoria while they and the children would come out to greet him.

Every few weeks the couple would have their younger friends in for a casual buffet supper. Foreseeing what might be sensitive conversation about the approaching war in Europe, Eleanor told her servants not to enter the dining room unless called. She would ring her mother's sterling silver bell, which depicted Old Mother Hubbard with her dog tucked under her arm. Cousin Alice caustically summarized their suppers: "very indifferent wine and a good deal of knitting."

Once again, Eleanor and Alice lived in the same city, although now Alice was the wife of a defeated congressman and had no official rank, unlike Eleanor. The two women, formerly closest friends, realized that they had little in common. The newspapers insisted on linking them, however. The twenty-six-year age difference between Eleanor's husband and Alice's father led most writers to report that Franklin was Teddy's nephew, rather than his fifth cousin. (Since Eleanor was Teddy's niece, this inaccuracy left the impression that Eleanor and Franklin were first cousins.) Sara would clip any news article mentioning Franklin, and if there was a reference to his being Teddy's "nephew," she carefully crossed the offending word out and firmly inked "cousin" above it.

Sara was also surprised that Rosy, who had been a widower for about two decades, was planning to marry his longtime companion, a lower-middle-class Englishwoman. Sara was taken aback by news of his proposal to Betty Riley and tried to lure Eleanor to voice an opinion for or against the marriage. Sara was, according to Eleanor, "enraged" when Eleanor would not rise to the bait. As soon as Sara met Betty, she accepted her and wrote: "She is very nice and of course absolutely unselfish & devoted to him & he seems devoted to her." In the end, Sara relented and invited the couple to hold their wedding ceremony and reception at Hyde Park. The newlyweds lived in Red House and became frequent visitors to Sara's home.

Eleanor was becoming independent in her own home, too. She did not become pregnant with her next child until after Elliott had turned three in September 1913. One assumes that the couple planned this three-year abstinence so that Eleanor could take a break from constant childbearing.

Elliott later said that his mother's "shyness and stubborn pride would keep her from seeking advice from a doctor or woman friend" about birth control. Abstinence had been her solution. Now it was time for Eleanor to resume her marital duties, and by late fall her pregnancy and the crush of duties necessitated her hiring a part-time social secretary.

Twenty-nine-year-old Eleanor selected as her secretary a lovely woman six years younger. Lucy Page Mercer descended from both the Carroll family of Maryland and Lord Baltimore, the founder of the Maryland colony. A Mercer was a member of the Second Continental Congress, as was Charles Carroll, who also signed the Declaration of Independence. In fact, Maryland's state anthem contains the line "Remember Carroll's sacred trust." Unfortunately, Miss Mercer's grandfather squandered away the family fortune, and her father, like Eleanor's, was a drunk, so Miss Mercer had to work for a living. However, she had been carefully raised and had been educated in an Austrian convent. Despite her reduced position, she kept her dignity as well as her infectious sense of joy. She was slim and tall, like Eleanor, but had the advantage of a soothing voice.

Miss Mercer was at least the social equivalent of the Roosevelts and could successfully substitute for Eleanor at any official luncheon. At the N Street house, the two women worked together on the living-room floor, spreading out and sorting Eleanor's invitations and correspondence. The children found her a welcome respite from their own frosty governesses. Sara, too, thought Lucy was lovely: "She is so sweet and attractive and adores you, Eleanor."

Eleanor was pleased to have an extra pair of hands, especially now that she was expecting in August 1914. Franklin was the only family member who totally enjoyed being in Washington. No longer a man who practiced law in a leisurely way, Franklin exuded vitality, especially on those few days when he was acting secretary of the navy. He explained his feelings of addictive pleasure to Eleanor: "It is a little like a drug habit." Eleanor, of course, was against intoxication of any kind. Even her pleasant N Street house was not really home to her, with its walls covered with photos of Bamie's family and her nautical prints, which pleased Franklin—as did the house's link to Teddy. Nor was Eleanor, who allegedly was held back from tenement work after her first pregnancy, interested in improving her community. In 1914 Eleanor was pregnant with her fifth child and perhaps because of that strain she did nothing to support Mrs. Wilson's tireless attempts to improve living conditions in Washington's black neighborhoods. Instead, Eleanor and the children looked forward to summer, when they could leave muggy Washington for fresh Campobello, where Eleanor planned to give birth.

Eleanor remained blissfully detached from the European war that had broken out in July and from Franklin's burgeoning campaign to garner the Democratic primary nomination for U.S. senator from New York. He was on a break from his campaign, visiting his family at Campobello, when Eleanor went into labor late at night. Their well-laid plan to send for the Manhattan doctor who had previously attended Eleanor's births fell apart when the contractions came early.

Franklin ran down to the bay, shouting to the groundskeeper to ready *Half Moon* so that he could set sail to pick up a Maine physician. (There were no telephones on the island.) Sara heard the commotion from her house and went running down, with her robe flapping over her nightgown. Hearing what was happening, she dashed next door to await the baby with Eleanor and Miss Spring. No one needed to rush: the labor was long and Eleanor's son was not born until the following day, on August 17, 1914. It was the couple's fifth child in nine years and he was given the same name as the baby who had died: Franklin Delano Roosevelt Jr. He was their only child able to have dual citizenship with Canada. The Roosevelts were surprised and relieved at the country doctor's competence, and he, in turn, privately exclaimed to Miss Spring about Eleanor, "She is just like one of us!" The children—Anna, James, and Elliott—had eagerly anticipated this new baby after their nearly four-year wait. After the birth, Franklin returned to Washington while his family went to Hyde Park with Sara.

Franklin campaigned through the fall. Two years after Teddy had been defeated in the presidential election as the Progressive candidate, he was back in the fray, this time stumping for the party's congressional aspirants in, among other places, Dutchess County. Sara had written asking him to stay overnight at Hyde Park and apparently his son, Ted Jr., had accepted for him. Franklin wrote Uncle Teddy from Hyde Park on September 23: "I am perfectly delighted to hear from Helen that you and William Davenport will spend the night of October 5 here. *Nothing* could give me greater pleasure and I am counting on seeing you."

When Teddy learned of these plans, he worriedly wrote Sara:

I am more than pleased at your letter. It was the first notice I had that we were supposed to stay with you. Now, Sarah [sic], I am very doubtful, from Franklin's standpoint, whether it is wise that we do so and I have communicated with [Ted Jr.] to this effect. I shall be in the middle of a tour in which I am attacking the Administration and I think it might well be an error, from Franklin's standpoint, if we stayed with you. If it were only not during the campaign there is literally no place where I would rather go. And, of course, if the matter has been made public, it may be fine to go anyhow.

I hope you understand, dear Sally [*sic*], that it is the exact truth to say that I am only thinking of Franklin's interest.

The news had not yet spread, so Sara scuttled Teddy's visit. Sara wrote Franklin of her decision and added: "Of course it is very kind of him, but why he should go on a tour deliberately to attack the Administration, is what I cannot see the wisdom of. I think no one gains by pulling others down. It is not a noble or high-minded viewpoint." (Despite Teddy's tact in not visiting Franklin, the younger man still lost the primary nomination for the Senate seat and continued as assistant secretary, an appointment that he prudently had never resigned.)

Two weeks later Eleanor rejoined her elder children and Sara at Hyde Park. Sara now had Eleanor to watch over, as well as the chicks. She wrote Franklin of Eleanor's renewed attempts to nurse her newest baby: "All going well, but I think in consequence of Eleanor's having had two hard days, and being up rather late, Baby is a little fussy and hungry. I am sure all will be as well as ever tomorrow, and Eleanor is very cheerful this afternoon and will get to bed early."

In November the family anticipated Franklin Jr.'s christening at St. James Episcopal Church. Franklin telegraphed his mother a few days before: PLEASE TELEPHONE THE FORBES MORGANS, ASTORS AND DERHAMS TO COME TO CHRISTENING AND LUNCH."

25

"The Traditions Some of Us
Love Best"

With an additional grandchild and Franklin's family as constant houseguests, along with Franklin's political visitors and his growing collection of *things*—books, stamps, coins, and prints—Sara agreed that it was time to enlarge her Hyde Park house. She realized its necessity, but she also felt trepidation that her home would no longer be a tangible link to the husband who had brought her to it.

Franklin would boast, "The main house was remodeled by my mother and myself in 1915." The actual architect was Francis L. V. Hoppin, related to the family by marriage. Sara wrote: "Franklin constructed, in a most ingenious little model, the whole 'new' house as we visioned it in our long family talks by the open fire." The long family talks did not include Eleanor, who again showed little interest in the planning.

The construction was well under way by June, with Sara overseeing every detail. "I keep busy and have Plog, Goertz and the carpenter busy," she wrote Franklin. "I have decided to have Brown do the water supply and not connect the pond, he will leave things so it can be done later if necessary. Brown puts the pump near the spring. I hope it will prove a perfect arrangement." Brown cleverly erected a protective pyramidal roof over the pump and also built an enclosed stand-alone porch that Sara's grandchildren would call "Granny's bughouse" or, in a takeoff on her snuggery, "Granny's buggery."

The remodeling doubled the friendly Victorian home in size and turned it into an impressive mansion. Franklin and Sara had the house's clapboards pulled off and replaced with gray stucco. They added a third floor to accommodate more bedrooms for children and guests. Seven baths in all were added, a great improvement over the house's former single bath for the entire family of three adults and four children, and the single bath for servants. On the second floor, Sara kept her southeast second-floor master bedroom where Franklin was born.

They also added a south wing to the house. On its second level, a hall running east-west contained the rooms of Franklin and Eleanor and two new baths. The west room was Eleanor and Franklin's master bedroom, the east room was their shared sitting room, and the room in between served as Eleanor's dressing room, with a vanity and desk. Franklin also had a small dressing room off the master bedroom. French doors led to an outside deck.

Within a few years—no one knows when—both Sara and Eleanor moved into different bedrooms. These newer arrangements are what is shown to visitors, who can see that Eleanor chose to move out of the master bedroom and into her cramped dressing room. Sara moved into the couple's east sitting room.

Sara said, "We flung out a wing at each end, took off old-fashioned porches which darkened the ground floor rooms, and made a graceful, round portico and central entrance." They also added a trunklift behind the front stairs to transport luggage to and from the second-floor bedrooms.

Both wings were fieldstone. On the north end was a ground-floor schoolroom and, above, servants' quarters. For the front hall, Franklin had a glass-front display case made to order for twenty-seven of his stuffed birds, which still stands in position. The south wing boasted a huge ground-floor library and extra bedrooms on the second floor. The library was the most carefully designed room. Sara wrote Franklin: "Personally I think you want plenty of room for books, books, books!" He planned specially built display cases and bookshelves—some with tiny shelves for smaller volumes—to exhibit his collection. Each end of the library boasted a marble fireplace; above each fireplace Franklin had the Roosevelt coat of arms carved. Conversation groupings in front of each fireplace and in the middle of the room left visitors inevitably facing one crest or the other.

The house contained a larger snuggery for Sara. She furnished it with her favorite red chairs and, despite its generous size, wanted it as crowded as ever with pictures, vases, and china figurines. She ran her household from its desk and, if close friends visited, invited them in for tea.

~

While the construction was going on in the spring and summer, the family retreated to Campobello. Sara's greatest concern was the European war. In August 1915 she wrote Franklin, who had just left Campobello and was on his way back to Washington: "This war is the greatest calamity of our age or of any ages, and it seems too dreadful to be true." Although sister Dora was in Fairhaven, and sister-in-law Jennie and her daughters were assumed to be in Switzerland, Sara worried about their safety. Ten days later Sara, always mindful of Franklin's extra expenses in Washington, sent another letter: "Please cash enclosed cheque to restore the necessities of life!"

Franklin stayed in Washington, but when he sent word in July that he was ill, Sara left New York immediately. A few days later Eleanor left the children with their nannies in Campobello and was on the train when she received a telegram from Howe: FRANKLIN DOING WELL, YOUR MOTHER-IN-LAW WITH HIM. The women took Franklin to Hyde Park to recuperate. They all felt that the children should remain at Campobello; there was a polio epidemic on the East Coast.

That summer Eleanor was pregnant with her last baby. Franklin realized that he should not let his growing family rely on Sara's largesse in case something happened to him. He took immediate action to protect his family—but typically, the independent gesture was limited. He wrote his mother: "I enclose an insurance card on my life but your pocket."

By the end of August, Sara was visiting sister Kassie at her house in Tuxedo Park, New York, and was disappointed that Franklin could not visit as planned because of the Wilson campaign. Sara clearly positioned herself in sympathy with Franklin's politics: "It is a pity T.R. cannot keep quiet, he certainly has only stirred up trouble by his speech."

In September 1915 Sara was at Algonac, awaiting a visit from Eleanor. She wrote Franklin: "Your two servants came and are watching for the trunks. I can hardly wait for Eleanor and the children to arrive." At the end of the month, still at Algonac, she sent him shocking news: someone had stuffed wood shavings under the first floor of Hyde Park, which was still being remodeled, and lit the excelsior with a torch. Her night watchman saw the flames and called the local fire department. Little damage was done to the new $50,000 building. Sara wrote to Franklin: "No danger done, but it makes me sad that *anyone* could do such a thing."

Another fire, with more devastating effect, burned Algonac to the ground in early March 1916. Annie Hitch, now widowed, was living there with only the servants as company. The fire began in the attic and got a good head start before anyone noticed it. Finally, a maid began to strike the

Chinese gong outside the house to attract the neighbors' attention. Even then, the nearest town of Newburgh had no fire department. Friends across the Hudson saw the flames and rowed furiously across the dark water to help, chopping into reflected fire as they plied their oars. Brother Frederick wrote: "Thanks to neighbors from far and near, most of the books, furniture, pictures and bric-a-brac on the first and second floors were saved, but, even so, much was lost, and it was a pathetic sight for poor Annie, as she sat on the lawn, wrapped in her fur coat, to watch her beloved home burn down."

It was a great loss to the Delanos that many of the carefully saved family papers were now ashes. Later Sara wept with Kassie at Hyde Park at the family's loss. Warren and Frederick went up immediately and had the house rebuilt while Annie camped out in a cramped rental cottage for another eighteen months.

Eleanor was expecting, but she would no longer be confined. She was eight months pregnant when she hosted 225 people at an official navy function. People were amazed at her ability to take on a number of tasks and accomplish them in a short time. Eleanor stayed in Washington for this birth, and her baby was born at eleven P.M. on March 17, 1916, at the N Street house. His parents named him John Aspinwall, after the younger brother of Franklin's father. (Now Franklin had five living children to Teddy's six.)

The day after the birth, Sara took a maid and traveled to Washington. When she left a week later, she had the elder children with her; they had the whooping cough and Eleanor wanted them away from the baby. After they recuperated under Sara's care at Sixty-fifth Street—she would read to them for hours to keep them from talking and thus set off their coughing— she enrolled Anna in Miss Nightingale's class at Mrs. Bartlett's on Park Avenue for half days. (This class was the precursor to the Nightingale-Bamford School, founded four years later and now located on East Ninety-second Street.) James was privately tutored for ninety minutes each day.

The three younger children remained in Washington with Eleanor. When Franklin was in Manhattan on April 14, he did stop by to see Anna and James. Sara noted in her journal: "Franklin came at 6:30 P.M., stayed 15 minutes." In mid-May, Eleanor, Franklin, and the three youngest children left Washington for Hyde Park. Sara and the elder children did not join them until the end of the month, after Anna and James were released from their lessons. Franklin again returned to Washington, but Eleanor and the children stayed with Sara.

At the end of June, Eleanor and the children returned to Campobello. Sara did not arrive until August 9, in time for Franklin Jr.'s second birthday a week later. She wrote to Franklin, who was starting his campaign for Wilson's reelection: "This awful disease infantile paralysis is spreading. I trust our Island will be 'immune.'" But when she returned to Hyde Park on August 30, she wrote ominous news in her journal about her coachman's three-year-old daughter: "Butler's little Mildred ill." Two days later she noted: "Mildred Butler has Infantile paralysis." The next day: "The case is a very slight one thus far. Quarantine Butler etc." Sara also paid for a private nurse for the child and had the woman stay six weeks until Mildred was doing well.

When Franklin learned that polio, no matter how mild, had struck Hyde Park, he insisted that Sara fumigate all its dwellings before the grandchildren returned. Eleanor and the children did not go back to Hyde Park from Campobello until October, when the virus was less of a danger. With his family in Canada, Franklin had more time to continue campaigning for the president. However, by now Eleanor and her children were the only summer people left on the island. Franklin, who loved taking command of boats and ships, dramatically picked up his family at Campobello in the secretary's official yacht *Dolphin*, sailing down the Atlantic and up the Hudson River to drop them at Hyde Park's dock.

The Democratic party was successful with the Wilson slogan, "He kept us out of war." Teddy's Progressive party was in shambles. Sara, however, paid a courtesy visit on election night to the Progressive party headquarters to reinforce the blood, if not the political, ties between the families. Franklin, of course, retained his political appointment, and now that the situation was again stable, his family returned to Washington. Sara wrote Franklin when she returned to her Sixty-fifth Street house: "I am so happy over the President's splendid majority and that your party is triumphant. Lucky you to get Eleanor back!"

On March 4, 1917, Wilson was again inaugurated. On April 6 Wilson asked a joint session of Congress for a declaration of war against Germany. Eleanor saw it all from her gallery seat. Franklin stayed in Washington while his family traveled to Manhattan to join Sara at East Sixty-fifth Street. He telegraphed Sara the day after the country went to war: OBLIGED TO STAY WASHINGTON. LOVE AND HAPPY EASTER TO YOU ALL.

Sara wanted to help her family and her country at the same time. Over the summer she pledged a large sum for Liberty Bonds for the grandchildren. Franklin wrote: "It is too dear of you to put each of the children into the Liberty Loan Bonds & I am glad too that you have been able to subscribe for $10,000 [$140,000 today]."

In no way were the children allowed to learn of their grandmother's generosity. In fact, Eleanor's enthusiasm for having them learn about the sufferings of others led her, as James later wrote, to "set an empty place at our dinner table as a symbol of food being saved in support of Herbert Hoover's program to feed starving children abroad."

Sara did her part, too, hiring undergraduates from Vassar College to plant vegetables and fruits in her fields to help mitigate the world food shortage. She would let them take home whatever they needed for themselves. She gave the grandchildren each a small plot of land on which they were to grow vegetables and purchased the produce back from them at "outrageous prices," James remembered. She continued to send produce, eggs, and milk—as well as cream "so thick we could eat it with a spoon," James said—to Washington, just as she had to Albany.

In July *The New York Times* sought out the wife of the assistant secretary of the navy for a feature on how her household enacted the administration's new wartime food-saving program. Eleanor responded, "Making the ten servants help me do my saving has not only been possible but highly profitable."

Franklin wrote her, teasing that "I am proud to be the husband of the Originator, Discoverer and Inventor of the New Household Economy for Millionaires!"

Eleanor blamed the reporter, and "yet some of it I did say. I never will be caught again, that's sure, and I'd like to crawl away for shame."

In August sharp-eyed and sharp-tongued Alice Longworth was driving in the country when whom did she see but Franklin and Lucy Mercer, out for a drive. (Lucy had left Eleanor's employ in the spring to enlist in the navy when the war began.) Alice telephoned him when she returned home, purring with malicious pleasure: "I saw you 20 miles out in the country. You didn't see me. Your hands were on the wheel, but your eyes were on the perfectly lovely lady." Alice was so tickled that during the many weeks Eleanor was out of town, she began inviting Franklin and Lucy to her parties. They accepted her invitations. Alice explained that Franklin "deserved a good time. He was married to Eleanor."

Alice had other, more self-serving, motives. She was bored and had acquired a dangerous habit of playing with other people's lives, and she was envious of Eleanor's good, solid reputation and that of her successful husband. She may have been wryly pleased to see Eleanor's husband flirting, as her own husband was a flagrant womanizer. And Alice was determined to see only her brothers as the rightful heirs and successors to Teddy's lost throne: she would do whatever she could to keep Franklin out of it.

Back in Washington in the fall, the family moved to a larger house on R Street, having increased their size by two children and several servants since moving into Bamie's house. The Roosevelts were exceedingly fortunate to find spacious lodgings; one wartime Washingtonian wrote: "Houses

were commandeered and lawsuits to get rid of tenants so that more profitable ones could be put in were an every-day occurrence. People rushed
back to Washington from all corners of the earth to save their homes from
being taken by the Government. You hardly dared leave for a moment, for
while you were away a blue sign might be put up, saying that the house had
been commandeered."

Travel was difficult, too. When the Roosevelts could not get back to
Hyde Park for winter weekends, Franklin took the children coasting on a
hill behind the U.S. Naval Observatory on Massachusetts Avenue.

With the changes brought by the world war as the backdrop, Sara and
Franklin, on Sixty-fifth Street in the fall, had a stormy discussion about their
respective values and outlook on life. What began the tempest, no one
knows firsthand. (Later James said that his mother told him it was over the
disposition of the land at Hyde Park: Sara wanted it kept in the family, and
Franklin would not give her his pledge. This doesn't make sense in light of
Franklin's later insistence on keeping the estate intact and turning it over to
the Department of the Interior in perpetuity.)

Whatever the undercurrent, Sara listened to what Franklin had to say
and she was distressed. Immediately upon her return to Hyde Park on
October 14, 1917, she wrote her son and daughter-in-law:

> I am sorry to feel that Franklin *is* tired and that my views are not his, but per-
> haps dear Franklin you may on second thoughts or *third* thoughts see that I
> am not so far wrong.
>
> The foolish old saying "noblesse oblige" is good and "honneur oblige"
> possibly expresses it better for most of us. One can be democratic as one
> likes, but if we love our own, and if we love our neighbor, we owe a great
> example, and my constant feeling is that through neglect or laziness I am
> not doing my part toward those around me.
>
> After I got home, I sat in the library for nearly an hour reading, and as I
> put down my book and left the delightful room and the two fine portraits, I
> thought: after all, would it not be better just to spend all one has at once in
> this time of suffering and need, and not think of the future; for with the *trend*
> to "shirt sleeves," and the ideas of what men should do in always being all
> things to all men and striving to give up the old fashioned traditions of fam-
> ily life, simple home pleasures and refinements, and the traditions some of us
> love best, of what use it is to keep *up* things, to hold on to dignity and all I
> stood up for this evening.
>
> Do not say that I *misunderstood*, I understand perfectly. . . . Well, I hope
> that while I live I may keep my "old fashioned" theories and that at *least* in
> my own family I may continue to feel that *home* is the best and happiest place

and that my son and daughter and their children will live in peace and keep from the tarnish which seems to affect so many.

Sara's admonitions have been interpreted as an example of her attempt to impose her ideas on Eleanor and Franklin. Rather, Sara, whose Delano family was Republican, understood better than Franklin the prevailing view throughout America—a country that had elected only two Democratic presidents (Cleveland and Wilson) since the Civil War.

By writing Franklin that he "may on second thoughts or *third* thoughts see that I am not so far wrong," Sara was trying to head off her son's headstrong disregard of the sentiments of most Americans. Indeed, Sara's belief in "old fashioned traditions" reflected the beliefs of most voters; her warning to her son was prescient, for the next three presidents (Harding, Coolidge, and Hoover) would be Republican.

26

"A Kaleidoscope of Work"

The Great War was a machine fueled by more than 3 million servicemen. The effort demanded a huge infrastructure of a size and complexity that the nation had never before provided. Every man and woman was needed to make it work. Opportunities abounded outside the house for any woman willing and able to volunteer, and Eleanor responded to this rallying call.

It took Eleanor a while to hit her stride. No wonder: as she later observed, "For ten years, I was always just getting over having a baby or about to have one, and so my occupations were considerably restricted." In the first months of the war, she dabbled. She distributed free wool for volunteers to knit into warm clothing and washcloths (imagine a dank wool washcloth on your face), learned to drive to be more self-sufficient (remember the car accident in Seabright), and hosted naval missions from allied countries (for her, dutiful social events).

In May, Eleanor's search to find her place on the home front was broken by a house full of sick children. Sara took the ill chicks back to Manhattan so that their parents could focus on war work. She wrote them from Sixty-fifth Street: "James still has fits of coughing quite often, Anna hardly at all, but she was ill first and really had far the worst case. Elliott's is not bad, only his being a nervous child he gets easily upset." Sara had her hands full, but her notes purposely included something cheerful about the children's recoveries. In this note, she mentioned their having short fresh-air breaks on the second-floor balconies.

In July, Sara was at Hyde Park, writing that "Albert (in our stable) is drafted. I could easily let him go now, but I fancy he will wait here, and then probably not pass the physical examination. He is strong as a horse but butler says he is 'flatfooted.'" Domestic help everywhere were doffing livery and slipping out of their employers' back doors to don factory aprons or khaki uniforms. One Washington wife wrote: "In the twinkling of an eye, servants became as extinct as the dodo, and not even fossils remained." Everyone was making do with less—and that included fewer servants. Even Sara and Eleanor would be hit by this phenomenon.

Eleanor was spending long hours being helpful where she could, until Franklin and Sara, who feared she was overworking, talked her into taking a break at Campobello. Her intuition, though, told her that there might be other reasons Franklin wanted her out of town. Eleanor wrote him in Washington and intimated this. Franklin rejoined in a letter dated July 16: "I really can't stand that house all alone without you, and you were a goosey girl to think or even pretend to think that I don't want you here *all* the summer, because you know I do! But honestly *you* ought to have six weeks straight at Campo, just as *I* ought to, only you can and I can't."

In late July and August, Franklin was ill with another throat infection and had been taken by his uncle Frederick Delano (a governor of the Federal Reserve Board) to the naval hospital (now called National Naval Medical Center, commonly called Bethesda Naval Hospital). Eleanor left Canada to take care of him in Washington. Sara was still at Hyde Park, torn between leaving to take care of the five children and deferring her trip until she learned that he was better. She wrote her son as he recovered: "I think [you] fortunate to have the most lovely person rush to you as she did and stay."

Once Sara left for Campo, she spent the day with the children outdoors or at their house, and then walked back to hers once they were asleep. Sara hoped Franklin could take a break from work, telling him in mid-August, "Do come there just to get your strength and eliminate poison in the breezes of Passamaquoddy." She told him of a cure for sore throat that she had learned from a friend whose father was a doctor: "Nothing is so good as a gargle as a half cup of water with a small teaspoonful of turpentine in it."

When Sara returned to Hyde Park with Eleanor and the children, she also took on war duties and was an active member of the Hudson River War Relief Committee along with her neighbors Mrs. Frederick Vanderbilt, Mrs. Archibald Rogers, and Mrs. Charles DeRham. She supplied a navy unit of

volunteers with wool and individually inspected each sweater before passing it along. She also became vice chairman of the women's section of the
Navy League in New York and wrote letters asking for donations of goods
for the fighting men. She was horrified to receive a letter from a sailor
telling of inequities in the distribution of free clothing and forwarded the
charges to her son, hoping he would go right to the top regarding the waste
in the free-woolens crisis. "I enclose a letter which ought to be read by the
Sec. of the Navy and the Sec. of War."

Eleanor returned to Washington in late October after having spent several
months with Sara and jumped back into the most rewarding activity since
her days at the Rivington Street Settlement House: she volunteered for the
Red Cross canteen at Union Station. The Red Cross had set up more than
eight hundred canteens across the country at transportation stops where
men in uniform could enjoy short breaks as they traveled east. They could
dash out of trains or buses to purchase candy, cigarettes, stamps, and magazines or, most important, get a free hot meal from one of seventy thousand
women volunteers.

Eleanor and Franklin were working so hard that she wrote: "The winter
of 1917–1918 wore away and remains to me a kaleidoscope of work and
entertaining and home duties, so crowded that sometimes I wondered if I
could live that way another day. Strength came, however, with the thought
of Europe and a little sleep, and you could sleep, and you could always
begin a new day." Through all this, Eleanor had the invaluable Miss Mercer
to assist her with the formal invitations that kept rolling in.

Eleanor was not braced for an unpleasant encounter with Alice at the
Capitol. Eleanor wrote, hinting, to Franklin, who was out of town: "On the
way out I parted with Alice at the door not having allowed her to tell me
any secrets. She inquired if you had told me and I said no and that I did not
believe in knowing things which your husband did not wish you to know so
I think I will be spared any further mysterious secrets!" Alice, again, was trying to force Eleanor into hearing "the facts of life," and Eleanor was again
resisting.

In January, Sara wrote Franklin a thirty-seventh birthday note from
Sixty-fifth Street: "God bless you and keep you well and in the constant useful life you have chosen with strength of mind and character to cope with
the many problems which constantly come up. I am very proud of you and
all my happiness is in you and our dear Eleanor and children."

Franklin took a minute out from his nonstop work to write Sara in March
with apologies for his delayed thank-you note: "I have been trying to write

you for many days about many things, first of all to give you loads of thanks. I have loved my very extra nice shirts and ties and they will make me very comfy and cool this summer. And you have saved my life, or, rather, the various Doctors' lives, by making it possible for me to pay them promptly!"

Eleanor also wrote Sara, acknowledging that without her services she could never have accomplished all that she was doing for Franklin's career and for the country. Eleanor realized "how lucky we are to have you and I wish we could always be together. Very few mothers I know mean as much to their daughters as you do to me." A few weeks later she wrote again: "I wish you were always here. There are so many things I want to talk over and ask you about & letters are not very satisfactory, are they?"

By now, Sara had sold *Half Moon* to the navy. Teddy volunteered his services to Wilson—Sara wrote to her children: "I do wish your Uncle Ted could go to France. I *hope he* will be allowed to go"—but he was denied a war role. His feeling of uselessness began his decline. Hall tried unsuccessfully to enlist—he was already doing vital work for General Electric—and Eleanor was horrified when her grandmother Mary Livingston Ludlow Hall suggested that he pay someone to take his place instead. Mrs. Hall, in turn, was shocked to learn that substitutes were no longer permitted.

Over the summer of 1918, when Franklin was inspecting the U.S. naval forces in Europe—and where he had a chance, in Paris, to see his aunt Dora—Eleanor was able to devote herself entirely to canteen work. Unlike the winter, when, as she said, she "was obliged to be at home, if possible, to see my children before they went to bed," she could use the absence of her children—who were being watched over the summer by Sara at the newly enlarged Hyde Park—to work until well past midnight.

Sara, from Hyde Park, proudly wrote Franklin at sea: "When you get 'over there' the interest and responsibility will redouble and you are well fitted for it. The children are all very well . . . they feel quite important at having been told by you of your plans." Later she was amused to write him that the *New York Herald* "has quite an article, and say you are now on a 'cruise.'" She also reported that "James has been to the Y.M.C.A. pool for 3 lessons, and today I let him go to the pond with butler who put a rope around James, and James got on very well, and butler was very careful of him."

Sara also met her neighbors the Henry Morgenthaus, who had lived in Dutchess County on a dairy and apple farm for five years. Morgenthau, who would eventually serve as Franklin's secretary of the treasury, was an Exeter graduate and had attended Cornell University for two years, studying agriculture. During the war he played a role by sending tractors to France.

Sara told Franklin, "Young Mr. Morgenthau and his wife called this P.M.

and while they were here Mrs. [Vanderbilt] came bringing 5 people and we had a pleasant tea, young Morgenthau was easy and yet modest and so nice and intelligent. The wife is very Jewish but appeared very well."

Sara also paid him compliments on his work and on Eleanor's. Rosy had written to tell her that he had seen an article in the *New York Herald* "about T.R. and the four sons at the front, and saying do not forget the member of the family who is doing a man's job in Washington and not talking about it!"

Sara also told him that "Eleanor is working very hard, I saw Aunt Kassie at Algonac yesterday and she said Eleanor is the 'willing horse' and they call upon her at all hours, all the time."

Canteen work was Eleanor's ultimate choice to help the war effort. She volunteered two or three days a week, arising before most of her servants. She was proud to wear the starched gray poplin uniform that was accented by a white collar and cuffs, which made her feel crisp and efficient. (And it had been tailored for a better fit by her seamstress.) After being served breakfast, she drove to Union Station (with her chauffeur, Huckins, perched next to her on the running board to help navigate), where she presided over a corrugated shed that housed an iron stove with a wood fire burning inside. Hot meals would come off that stovetop from dawn to late night, ready for Eleanor and the other volunteers to begin dishing out to the men waiting in line.

It was sooty, dirty work. By noon Eleanor's uniform was usually stained with food and damp from perspiration from a combination of the hot sun beating on the tin roof, summer humidity, exertion, and the constantly burning fire. However, the drudgery of repetitive work thrilled her: even swabbing the floor late at night gave her pride in running a tight ship. She reveled in immersing herself in gritty, get-your-hands-dirty work, writing: "I loved it. I simply ate it up." None of the men who thanked her recognized her family name or her husband's title. All they knew was that she was a nice lady who gave them a meal, and they appreciated her efforts. Eleanor realized that she was being accepted for her work—for what she *did*—and not for her family history or station in life. Yet she did not seem to make any female friends at the canteen and never knew the wartime camaraderie that so many others felt.

Eleanor felt free: she had served her husband in Albany and in Washington. For the last three and a half years, every afternoon she had introduced herself to other wives so that they would mention Franklin's name to their husbands. During the other hours, she efficiently organized a complicated peripatetic household with ten servants. When her five children (whose ages spanned ten years) were in her house and not with Sara, she assumed their care, carefully working out schedules for their nannies and for Huckins, who drove them to their various schools and lessons. Sara, a woman who had raised only one child in an impeccably run household, complimented Eleanor on her efficiency at working out her children's overlapping schedules.

Although Eleanor previously had not cared to be drawn into any community work in her new city—nor was she taken by Washington, its manners or customs—all of that changed with the Great War. Just as young men were dashing off to war in hopes of great adventure, women, too, were exploring expanded horizons. This new world dovetailed with Eleanor's fresh desire to create a more meaningful life for herself. Just as the United States was rising to fight a ferocious war overseas, Eleanor, too, was waking up.

Her new skills were acknowledged perceptively by Sara, who had written Franklin that "Irene spoke to aunt Kassie of Eleanor with such admiration and affection, she is clever enough to see how different E. is from some of her friends!" Eleanor was now also working at St. Elizabeth's Hospital, filled with shell-shocked men, and she persuaded the Red Cross to set up an occupational-therapy room. She wrote Sara about another task: "I'm going to have charge of the knitting at the Navy Department work rooms. It is going to mean part of every day now except Sundays taken up at one place or another, but that doesn't seem much to do, considering what the soldiers must do." She found duty liberating rather than oppressive. Duty pushed her to transcend her limits and made her a meaningful part of activities that were difficult for her but had to be completed because they were right.

Eleanor heard that Sara's childhood friend Edith Wharton, who was childless and living in France when the European war broke out, was establishing many French relief groups funded by wealthy Americans. The Children of Flanders Rescue Committee was responsible for the lives of one thousand French young people, and the Flotilla Committee was started for "surgical motors [ambulances] for the advanced trenches." However, Eleanor had to settle for the fact that the involvement of her family—that is, the Delano family, with its French ties—would be limited to financial donations and board work for Wharton's numerous war charities.

Eleanor would have loved to do such work in Europe, too. She craved helping; she wanted a taste of the European adventure that appealed to men. When she was asked to go to London in May to set up a Red Cross unit, she wrote Sara: "I really won't go abroad but it is a fearful temptation." Still, she was good at resisting temptation; leaving her family to go to England would be too radical a move, and she turned down the offer with deep regret. She seems to have made the decision on her own; although both Sara and Susie Parish are offhandedly blamed for influencing Eleanor—and although thoughts of what would have been their disapproval may have served as a damper to Eleanor—she knew she could not do it even before telling Sara, as her letter indicated.

Franklin's summer tour of European naval capability came to a dramatic end. Eleanor received a telegram saying that she needed to meet his ship at the dock in New York with an ambulance: tight quarters on the ship led to a horrific outbreak of influenza, and many men had already been buried at sea. Frightened Eleanor and Sara met him as commanded, but to their great relief saw that he was not as badly off as feared. The two women took Franklin to Sara's Sixty-fifth Street house (number 49 was being rented), and the children remained in Hyde Park, away from their contagious father.

When he was well, Eleanor—eager to get the children back to Washington and into school—returned in mid-October, only to have her entire family hit with the influenza that had spread from the western front. Three of her servants were sick, and Eleanor sent for a trained nurse, as Miss Spring was unavailable. The Roosevelts' cook was preparing meals for the family and was asked by Eleanor to make extra dinners that Eleanor dropped off at Red Cross hospital units for other flu victims, particularly the single war workers who had surged to Washington and had no family to care for them. Every day hundreds of health workers entered Washington boardinghouses to see if the rooms housed dead tenants or people in dire need of hospitalization. Thousands died in Washington before the epidemic ended; the dead in the United States totaled 500,000 people.

Finally, peace came and the armistice was signed on November 11, 1918. The world exhaled with a collective sigh; Eleanor wrote that the "the feeling of relief and thankfulness . . . was beyond description."

Yet her own household had just been swept over by a tidal wave. When Franklin was at Sixty-fifth Street, recuperating from the ship's influenza epidemic, Eleanor unpacked his trunks. Inside one, she found a packet of letters tied with string. They were to her husband from Miss Mercer. Now Eleanor thought that she was drowning.

Five Delano sisters in 1883: (standing) Laura, Sara (Roosevelt), Kassie (Collier); (sitting) Annie (Hitch) and Dora (Forbes).

Algonac, Sara's girlhood home on the west bank of the Hudson River, 1880.

Delano Kindred in 1890. Typical Victorian family photo after member's death: Franklin in center, James behind him, and Sara behind him to the right; Laura, "the Angel Child," shown in portrait to right.

Hyde Park, 1890. FDR Library

Hyde Park after remodeling in 1915. FDR Library

Franklin Delano Roosevelt and parents, 1899. FDR LIBRARY

Eleanor Roosevelt and Franklin Delano
Roosevelt as an engaged couple, 1904.
FDR LIBRARY

Sara's 1905 gift to Eleanor and
Franklin, the house at East
Sixty-fifth Street.
FDR LIBRARY

Eleanor and Franklin with James and Anna at Hyde Park, 1908.
FDR LIBRARY

Sara's 1909 gift to Eleanor and Franklin, the house at Campobello.
FDR LIBRARY

Eleanor in 1911 with children James, Elliott, and Anna.
FDR LIBRARY

Three generations in 1919: (seated) Franklin with Franklin Jr.; Eleanor; Sara with John; (standing) Anna, Elliott, and James. FDR Library

Lucy Mercer, circa 1920.
FDR Library

An uneasy trio: Sara, Franklin, and Eleanor in 1920. Corbis

"He-shes"?: Marion Dickerman, Eleanor, Nancy Cook, and Dickerman's sister, Peggy Levenson, during a 1926 trip. FDR Library

Sara's first cover: *Time*, 1933.
TIME INC./TIME LIFE PICTURES/GETTY
IMAGES

Sara's eightieth birthday party with family: (standing, left to right) Franklin Jr., Elliott, James, and John; (middle row) Eleanor, Sara, and FDR; (front) Ruth (Mrs. Elliott), Betsy (Mrs. James) with daughter Sara Delano Roosevelt, Eleanor and Curtis Dall with their mother, Anna Roosevelt Dall. FDR LIBRARY

Queen Elizabeth and King George with Franklin, James, Sara, and Eleanor at Hyde Park's St. James Church, 1939. FDR Library

NEWS-WEEK

JULY 10, 1937

THE PRESIDENT'S MOTHER:
'I AM THE CHILD OF MY SON'
[SEE HEADLINER]

Mirror images: Franklin, fifty-eight, and Sara, eighty-five, in 1940.

Sara with Franklin Jr., Franklin III, and Franklin in 1940. FDR LIBRARY

Last photograph of Sara Delano Roosevelt, heading home from Campobello in 1941 with Eleanor at the wheel. FDR LIBRARY

Sara's death makes headlines.
DES MOINES REGISTER, FRONT-
PAGE SCAN BY FISHY DESIGN

THE WEATHER
****
Partly cloudy, showers.
Day's record, page 12. Radio,
page 9.

The Des Moines Register
THE NEWSPAPER IOWA DEPENDS UPON

PRICE 5 CENTS — DES MOINES, IOWA, MONDAY MORNING, SEPTEMBER 8, 1941.— SIXTEEN PAGES

She Lived to See Her Son Elected to White House Three Times--

SARA ROOSEVELT DIES AT 86
President Postpones Important Radio Address to Thursday

ROOSEVELT AT MOTHER'S SIDE THROUGH NIGHT

Circulatory Collapse Hastened By Age.

HYDE PARK, N. Y. (AP)— Mrs. Sara Delano Roosevelt, 86, who lived to see her only son elected to three terms as president of the United States, died Sunday at the ancestral Roosevelt home overlooking the Hudson river.

Mrs. Sara Delano Roosevelt. "My Son, the President."

Sunrise at Campobello, 1958 Broadway play starring Ralph Bellamy as FDR and Anne
Seymour as Sara. CORBIS

27

Miss Mercer

It seems odd that a married man—much less a political appointee with great ambition—would stow away a sweetheart's love notes rather than immediately jettison them. Eleanor would never have found Franklin's packet of letters from Lucy Mercer in autumn of 1918 if he had not inherited the Delano habit of collecting and saving every scrap of personal paper. Such writings are priceless to historians—and biographers—but this time, the family trait would cost Franklin dearly.

Yet Franklin often acted obliquely: could he subconsciously have wanted Eleanor to learn of his romance? If so, could he have intended to inflict the trauma of her stumbling onto his love letters? She had hinted her suspicions to her beguiling husband several times over the past couple of years, giving him a chance to answer her honestly. He dodged these opportunities and turned her misgivings against her, taking shameless advantage of her low self-esteem: "You were a goosey girl to think or even pretend to think that I don't want you here *all* the summer."

Fifteen years and six children earlier, before their engagement was announced, Eleanor had written Franklin a few lines from Elizabeth Barrett Browning:

> *Unless you can swear "For life, for death!"—*
> *Oh, fear to call it loving!*

Eleanor's percipient fears had come true. Her handsome husband—full of easy banter and light flirtation, equally comfortable with women or men—had betrayed her and then lied about it at her "goosey girl" expense. The premonitions she had during her engagement when she sobbed to her cousin, "I shall never be able to hold him. He is so attractive," had come true.

One of Eleanor's nieces illuminated her aunt's despair: "The way that my Aunt Eleanor felt about Franklin was the way she had felt about her father. It was the fantastic love that she felt would be total. When she discovered that Franklin had an affair, she was so stunned and didn't know where to put this hurt." Trude Lash, the wife of Eleanor's friend and biographer Joseph Lash, said, "I think the greatest hurt was that Franklin had broken his word. It was like her father, who had made promises and not kept them."

Eleanor's absolute, often harsh judgment rendered Franklin's relationship with Lucy proof that he had *never* truly loved her. Of course, she was wrong, but she could not pull herself out of her despondency. She must have thought back to Barrett's poem, ironically titled "A Woman's Shortcomings." The poet lays out the near impossibility that love can last. The poem ends:

> *Unless you can dream that his faith is fast,*
> *Through behoving and unbehoving,*
> *Unless you can die when the dream is past—*
> *Oh, never call it loving!*

When Eleanor read Mercer's letters, her heart went cold. *Never call it loving,* she must have thought. Her romantic love for Franklin died. He was imperfect; she had allowed herself to be vulnerable; she would not let it happen again.

This, of course, is speculation. What we know with certainty is that there were words—angry words on Eleanor's part and placating ones on Franklin's. There was not, according to Ellie Roosevelt Seagraves, as much weeping by Eleanor as other biographers have written to dramatize the crisis. Instead, Eleanor was so deeply hurt, so betrayed, that to cut off her pain, she immediately offered Franklin a divorce. She could keep her sanity only by clutching her dignity.

Eleanor herself alluded to this period a few times and spoke openly about it to her daughter, Anna. Later Anna wrote in an unpublished article that Eleanor would have agreed to set Franklin free. She asked him only that he "take time to think things over carefully before he gave her a definite answer. . . . He voluntarily promised to end any 'romantic relationship' and seemed to realize how much pain he had given her."

However, at the same time, Eleanor knew how to stack the deck against receiving a quick "yes" from Franklin. She sought out Sara to safeguard her and her marriage from Franklin's rash emotions. Sara must have been wounded by her son's moral shortcomings: perhaps she thought back to that Thanksgiving when she told him he was too young to marry. Sara would have been furious at his hurting her beloved, vulnerable daughter-in-law and distraught about her grandchildren growing up in a split house-hold. In this instance, Sara's point of view about Franklin's behavior was identical to Eleanor's: there were no gradations of right and wrong.

Franklin well knew Sara's feelings about even the most innocent of flirta-tions outside marriage. In 1914 Sara wrote Franklin an aggrieved letter about Helen's husband, Teddy Robinson. He enjoyed a friendship with a former girlfriend and joked with Sara that he was going to spend the after-noon with "his best girl."

She described Robinson's quip, saying that it was "all very silly and not a dignified joke for married people and heads of young families. Do you think I am too old fashioned? I think people go too far now with this sort of joke, and also that very deep love does not permit it. This tirade is for you alone dear and to be destroyed." (Note that he did not obey her immediate direc-tion any more than he heeded her larger point.)

Now that her own son was guilty of a more serious flirtation, Sara real-ized that the world of her past had shattered. She saw clearly that her son had done wrong and was nimbly trying to dance his way clear. She must have thought about James and what would have been his disappointment in their son and, perhaps, felt that she herself had failed James as Franklin's guardian. Where Sara differed from Eleanor was that she saw no choice to be made: a divorce was to be avoided at all costs. If Franklin would not respect his marriage vows, Sara would continue to love him but flex her muscle by immediately stopping her immeasurable financial support.

Eleanor's aunt Corinne learned of the crisis and told both her daughter, Corinne, and her niece Alice. "I don't think one can have any idea of how horrendous even the *idea* of divorce was in those days." The younger Corinne Alsop repeated what her mother had said, writing of Sara: "[She] was regal, autocratic and adamant. She refused to give a penny if he got a divorce." Franklin might have been able to leave Eleanor, but he knew he could never leave Sara.

At the same time, Louis Howe—who was slowly becoming Eleanor's friend as well as Franklin's—told the couple that Franklin's chances for the presidency would be scuttled by a divorce. He surely pointed out that even

Franklin's current administration position would be jeopardized as soon as word leaked out. The secretary of the navy was a traditionalist Christian who had fired his own sister's husband when the couple divorced, and then ran him out of town. Howe was serving as an intermediary, "going back and forth and just reasoning, convincing Father he had no political future if he did this," said Elliott later. "Louis did a selling job." Franklin was astute; he knew that in the case of a divorce, brownstone doors would slam in his face up and down the East Coast.

So, in addition to Franklin's real devotion to his wife and children, he perceived the negatives of a divorce. He recognized that he craved politics and would never be happy without trying for the presidency. Less flattering, he also had to acknowledge he could never live without his mother's extensive financial support—even *without* the added costs of a second family—despite his ability to earn a good income augmented by a trust. If it had not been for Sara's pulling the purse strings tight, Franklin might have divorced Eleanor and would never have become president. We are obliged to her: everybody has said she didn't want him in politics, and yet if it hadn't been for her decision here, he would not have been able to remain in politics.

Franklin also felt guilty. He had failed—worse, disappointed—the two most important women in his life. Franklin, too, had a strict Victorian conscience instilled by his parents—remember his elderly father's words to Sara, "Only tell Franklin to be good, to be a good man"—and would have feared stepping this far out of line.

In fact, when he was at Harvard, Franklin reacted pompously to news of his nephew's transgression. Taddy had dropped out of Harvard at twenty-one upon gaining his *annual* Astor income of $100,000. Soon after, Taddy disappeared into the Tenderloin section of Manhattan and resurfaced with a wife, a woman nicknamed "Dutch Sadie" (she was actually Hungarian). Rosy located his son's West Side apartment and broke up the marriage. Someone tipped off a reporter, who used the story to embarrass Teddy Roosevelt, and so the scandal went public.

Young Franklin was appalled and wrote Sara: "I do not wonder that it has upset Papa but although the disgrace to the name has been the worst part of the affair one can never again consider him a true Roosevelt." Although Miss Mercer was from an entirely different world than Dutch Sadie, what Franklin was thinking of putting his family through was just as bad. Perhaps Sara reminded him of his earlier words, "the disgrace to the name."

The situation was resolved. Franklin told Howe first—not Eleanor—and she was once again wounded that he did not see her role as principal. Mercer was told that it was over, and she accepted the decision, having been reluctant as a Catholic to marry a divorced non-Catholic. The three Roosevelts, and Mercer, destroyed all documents that referred to their turmoil. Sara's journals for 1918 and the beginning of 1919 are missing—probably tossed into the fireplace by her own hand, for their subject matter was certainly incendiary.

There was bound to be punishment for Franklin besides his own guilty conscience. Eleanor decided to end their marital relations. Most likely, this is when she moved from their master bedroom into her small dressing room. Her decision hardly bothered her: she disliked sex, had borne six children already, and was still young enough to have the prospect of another decade of unwanted pregnancies. "My mother," said Elliott years later, "had an iron stubbornness of her own and she was bound and determined that she would have nothing to do with my father, even though he was quite abject in seeking to rehabilitate himself in her eyes."

Eleanor's expulsion of her husband came at little cost to herself, except for her continual faultfinding at her own ongoing anger. When she had been an adolescent living with Susie Parish, her cousin warned her about her inability to forgive and suggested that she read 1 Corinthians 13, the famous passage ending "And now abideth faith, hope, charity, these three; but the greatest of these is charity." Eleanor wrote: "Then Susie talked to me a long time on the subject of forgiveness. She says I do not know the higher meaning of the word, because I never forgot."

This may have been the only unworthy trait of Eleanor's that she would give up trying to change. She would later tell people, "I have the memory of an elephant. I can forgive but I can never forget."

"Eleanor could be hard," said Marion Dickerman. "I know she tried to forgive but hers was not a forgiving nature, really." She added that "Eleanor never forgot a hurt, never. There was a forgivingness in Franklin in many instances but I never found it in Eleanor."

Perhaps Eleanor realized that her anger was, to use an old-fashioned term, "unchristian." She felt spiritually shipwrecked by her reaction to Franklin's affair and, for the first time in her life, denied herself Communion.

What constituted the Mercer affair, as it is commonly called? Most people automatically brand Miss Mercer Franklin's "mistress," which certainly puts a modern overlay on a relationship that most likely went not much further than hand-holding and kissing. Part of the couple's attraction to each other was the forbidden nature of their situation. Lucy Mercer was a conservatively reared, convent-educated young lady who was a faithful Catholic.

She lived with her mother during her romance with Franklin—and her parents' former house, only a few doors down from the Roosevelts on N Street, was a constant reminder to her of her parents' own broken relationship. Even when Eleanor was out of town, Mercer and Franklin were not alone in the N Street house: at least two servants—whose loyalty was to their employer, Bamie—were around. Any assignation on N Street (or later, R Street) seems unlikely; a hotel, even more so. Alice, who already had her telescope focused, never reported anything as tawdry as a rented room. And certainly Miss Mercer was not "kept," as the word *mistress* implies.

There was also the issue of pregnancy. Franklin and Eleanor had used no artificial device to prevent pregnancy, only abstinence. Mercer, as an observant Catholic, would not have been comfortable using a birth control device—even if she had been willing to seek one out. And in the end, people who knew her said that Mercer would never have married Franklin—even if he had left Eleanor—because she would not marry a divorced man.

Ellie Roosevelt Seagraves said, "It was a love affair, but I doubt that it was consummated. Lucy Mercer was a very nice person, a Catholic, and it was hard to find contraceptives then. A woman in those days would not just go out and get fitted with a diaphragm—you just didn't do it." Arthur Schlesinger Jr., too, thought that people exaggerated the gossip and that their involvement was only "emotional."

Even Alice later said that she wished it could be put in capital letters that "I DO NOT THINK THAT ANYTHING EVER HAPPENED!"

Of course, Franklin and Eleanor remained together. He was chastened but determined to put things right with his wife, whom he loved. He was ashamed at his behavior and recognized how badly he had hurt her. Even if it was unintentional, he knew the harm he had done. To reassure her of his love, Franklin sought special permission to take Eleanor with him on a navy cruise to visit the peace conference and resolve some navy affairs. In January 1919 they shipped out together. Sara kept the children while they were abroad.

28

❧

"Our Boy"

Eleanor and Franklin embarked on their journey to Europe on January 1, 1919, on the *George Washington*. The evening before, the ship's captain was Sara's guest at the Colony Club, along with Eleanor and Franklin. Eleanor alluded to her fear about her weak stomach: she had not sailed to Europe since her honeymoon fourteen years earlier. As it turned out, the sea voyage did not make her ill—although her shipmate Bernard Baruch was quite seasick—and she went out of her way to seek out all kinds of shipboard activities and to chat with individual seamen. She was assertive and social, not at all shy.

They were aboard ship on January 6 when word came that Teddy had died. Eleanor was not as saddened as she might have been over the loss of the closest thing she had to a father figure. Instead, she wrote: "Another big figure gone from our nation and I fear the last years were for him full of disappointment." Eleanor was part of the growing distance between the two Roosevelt clans, in part because she could neither forget nor forgive Alice's knowledge and encouragement of Franklin's romance. Sara wrote them in reaction to Teddy's death: "I am keeping some pictures and cuttings for you [of the newspaper accounts] and only send the small ones, for I know you both want to read all you can of that splendid Uncle of Eleanor's."

Upon disembarking, the couple were taken aback by France's deep grief over its war losses. So many families had lost men that traditional long mourning veils were forbidden by law for fear that it would be demoralizing to see such a sea of black. Eleanor noted, however, that elderly women were allowed to wear their black veils "to their knees" without interference.

Eleanor and Franklin saw Aunt Dora, who had remained in Paris during the war. The two women paid visits to hospitalized men who had suffered severe face wounds. Their disfigurement deeply disturbed Eleanor, although Aunt Dora took the hideous injuries in stride. "I was lost in admiration," Eleanor said, "because she found something to say to each one." Despite the mournful atmosphere, both Eleanor and Franklin took time to shop, with Eleanor ordering several sumptuous evening gowns from Worth. In England she nearly turned blue from the city's cold weather and heating economies, chiding herself, "Decidedly we are growing effete at home from too much comfort and I always thought myself something of a Spartan!" She was also solicitous of Sara: "I hate being away from you and the children and the next time we must all come together if we come!"

In Manhattan, Sara spent the six weeks the couple was gone busily watching the children and supervising their governesses. On January 12 Anna, James, and their governess left Sara to return to Washington for school. Elliott followed them a few days later, while the two youngest children stayed with Sara at East Sixty-fifth Street. Sara passed the time by being with the children—they sang hymns together on Sunday night—attending some family functions, and continuing her work at the Laura Franklin Hospital. She also ordered Hyde Park's first electric washing machine and mangle. She wrote Eleanor and Franklin frequently to fill them in on details about their children.

Later in January, Sara's niece Kassie (sister Kassie's daughter) was to marry. Sara used the occasion to relay kind words from Kassie's mother-in-law to Eleanor: the woman "spoke with tears in her eye of her happiness" at having such a wonderful daughter-in-law. To which Sara remarked, "Well, Kassie, you are running a close second to my Eleanor as daughter-in-law!" and Kassie said, "Oh, Aunt Sallie, I never could be as good and lovely as Eleanor is. . . ."

Eleanor must have enjoyed hearing of the conversation, for she responded, "I do hope we never have to separate again. As I grow older I miss you and the children more and more. I think instead of becoming more independent I am growing into a really clinging vine!"

At the end of January, Sara told Eleanor and Franklin of how she arranged for her friends to visit their children in Washington to check on them and make sure the household was running on an even keel. (Eleanor either had not thought of having a friend do so, or, more likely, she had no close friends she could ask.) Sara added: "I am glad my dear Eleanor ordered two dresses from Worth for they will be 'stand-bys,' if as good as mine from Worth."

In early February, Sara alluded to the storm of the preceding autumn:

I was talking with Fred Weekes yesterday about Kassie and Sallie [Sara's namesake and niece] and I said I thought my sister Kassie and I were very different, she always thinks anything her daughters do is the right thing. With me my love for my own makes me more critical than I would be of strangers.

He said: "Well, you will never be disappointed in Franklin, he never will do anything you would not like, he is a splendid fellow."

Was that not nice of him? I agreed. Susie says, "Eleanor is an angel," and I agreed with her and said, "An angel with a heart and a mind."

So you both get bouquets, frequently.

Sara was pleased that her son and his wife were both involved in events of global import, and she followed their progress through Europe in the newspapers. "I can't tell you how happy I am that you are both doing all these interesting things and seeing these interesting people and it seems to me public life is so peculiarly what you are fitted for even tho' you are so extremely nice when leading the simple life at Hyde Park! Well, at least I can help my son by not giving him much trouble about the country place, etc."

She continued to keep them abreast of the news at home and of the American reaction to events in Europe. "People are so nasty here about the Peace Conference, and League of Nations, that when anyone is full of admiration of our President and his ideals it is a pleasant surprise." Sara had so thoroughly rid herself of her Republican roots that she declined one invitation, telling Eleanor and Franklin that "I am rather tired" of spending time with critics of Woodrow Wilson.

In mid-February the couple sent ahead a radio message that they were coming home. The president's work was finished; the covenant to the League of Nations was completed. Eleanor and Franklin sailed home with President and Mrs. Wilson, and Franklin took the opportunity to spend time with him.

After landing in Boston, the couple took a train to Washington with the presidential party. Sara had taken the youngest children down to the R Street house so that their parents would see them immediately upon arriving home. She dropped them off and left the house so that the parents could have their reunion alone with the children.

Earlier, Eleanor had written her from London: "I am anxious to hear how you find my household." Sara did not think that the household help had fared well in their mistress's absence and, complying with her daughter-in-law's request, left Eleanor a note, explaining to Franklin: "I hate to leave a worrying letter for Eleanor about servants, but I felt before complimenting them, she ought to talk with her two faithful nurses."

Soon after, Eleanor rid her household of two servants (two had already left). It was Eleanor's decision alone, though, to replace her white butler, housemaid, cook, and kitchen maid with cheaper African-American help. She said nearly two decades later that she hired black help because she did not want to have to travel to New York to hire white servants—as if none were available in Washington. More likely, Eleanor needed to economize because she and Franklin were always behind on their household bills. She was also still insecure with her help and felt that she would receive less back talk from an African-American staff because they were "pleasanter to deal with," as she wrote to others, telling them that her new serenity was due to "a complete darky household."

Others have interpreted Eleanor's hiring African-American servants as an early sign of her liberal leanings, yet in a letter to Sara—who was never known to use a deprecating term about anyone's race or ethnicity—Eleanor wrote: "Well, all my servants are gone and all the darkies are here and heaven knows how it will all turn out!"

Before Eleanor's first large party, she was worried about how "my darkies manage," and to her delight, her staff worked competently. However, she kept a watchful eye on her butler's illness, writing: "With darkies, one is always suspicious even of a death in the family."

With Eleanor's work as an assistant secretary's wife winding down, she had time to question her role in life and her place in her husband's family. Eleanor's exposure to modern ideas made her reflect on the standards by which she was raised and which she herself had represented over the past fifteen years of married life. She began to break away from her past by critiquing Sara and her sisters. She wrote Franklin: "They in all their serene assurance and absolute judgments on people and affairs going on in the world, make me want to squirm and turn bolshevik."

It was bold to criticize Franklin's mother; perhaps Eleanor was taking advantage of her husband's now sympathetic ear and felt comfortable confiding in him. Had Eleanor merely had one woman to call her friend, someone to talk to when her household, children, husband, and mother-in-law seemed too much to bear, her attitude might have been healthier and her actions more effective. Instead, Eleanor would lash out at Sara, criticize her to Franklin—who was careful never to get caught between the two women—and then follow her outbursts with overwrought apologies to both mother-in-law and husband. It must have been difficult for them as well as for Eleanor.

She was terribly worried about the violence in Washington. During the Red Scare, anarchists exploded bombs and socialists called for restructuring the government. And after wholesale harassment by soldiers, Washington's black residents rioted, with whites joining against them in response. The capital was in upheaval. As soon as school let out, Eleanor took the children to Hyde Park but hesitated at making the lengthy trip to Campobello without Franklin. Eleanor wanted him to reassure her that he would be safe working in Washington during the summer. In all honesty, he could not promise her that, and he instead evaded answering her questions, which angered her.

Eleanor expected to stay with Sara for the summer. In early July she realized she wanted an escape and planned a trip to Fairhaven for herself and her three younger children. After she departed, she wrote Franklin that "I feel as though someone had taken a ton of bricks off me and I suppose she feels the same." Although Eleanor was happy to be free of her mother-in-law, she saw nothing the matter with leaving two of her children for Sara to watch.

At the end of the summer, the elder children were at Hyde Park with Sara. When school started at the beginning of October, they switched places with the younger ones—Anna, James, and Elliott went back to Washington while Franklin Jr. and John stayed at Hyde Park with Sara. She treated her grandchildren with as much care as she had her own son, lovingly recording in her journal details of their health, weight, and growth. When they were ill, she kept a record of their temperature fluctuations.

Eleanor was unhappy at what she saw as her mother-in-law's usurpation of her children, just as Sara may have been displeased by Eleanor's lack of steady involvement. Unfortunately for our understanding, Sara did not write about their strife. Only Eleanor put her thoughts down, although she was confiding solely in Franklin: "Mama and I have had a bad time. I should be ashamed of myself but I'm not."

Yet three days later she wrote Sara a note: "I know, mummy dear, I made you feel most unhappy the other day and I am so sorry I lost my temper and said such fool things for of course as you know I love Franklin and the children very dearly and I am deeply devoted to you. I have, however, allowed myself to be annoyed by little things which of course one should never do and I had no right to hurt you as I know I did and am truly sorry, and hope you will forgive me."

There seemed to be no middle ground for Eleanor between arguing with Sara and abjectly pleading for forgiveness. As for Sara, she never put down any record of these crosscurrents either in her many letters or in her journal.

Just as Franklin was trying to be more considerate of Eleanor, she was going out of her way to be more sociable for his sake. Occasionally her efforts backfired, as when Franklin's frivolity at a Chevy Chase Club dance irritated her and she left him and went home by herself. She did not realize that she had no house key. Locked out, she did not awaken her servants; she did not go to a neighbor's house; instead, she sat silently on the porch all night long until Franklin returned at dawn—just as she had patiently waited for her drunken father outside his club. Franklin was embarrassed at seeing her sitting there like "a wilted green bean," Alice said, and thought her martyred behavior somewhat bizarre.

So did all the people in their set, when they heard about the incident. Alice told the story all over town, ending her rendition by intoning, "So noble, so noble."

Eleanor herself realized that something was wrong with her. She was constantly fatigued, saying that she felt like "a dead dog." Sometimes she could not keep her meals down. On many days she spent sad hours at the statue known as *Grief* in Rock Creek Park, constructed in memory of Clover Adams, the wife of Henry Adams who had committed suicide. Eleanor was beginning to see that even when Franklin paid more attention to her, he did not always succeed in making her happier. Yet at the same time, thirty-five-year-old Eleanor finally was recognizing that peace and joy come from within and cannot be supplied by another person.

The realization may have frightened her. She wrote in her diary at the end of 1919: "I do not think I have ever felt so strangely as in the past year, perhaps it is that I have never noticed little things before but all my self-confidence is gone & I am on edge though I never was better physically I am sure."

At the beginning of 1920, Eleanor was still recovering from the loss of her ideal of marital romance. Although some biographers cite this period as the beginning of Eleanor's independent life, most of her activities revolved around Franklin's schedule, a great amount of personal travel—some of it with the children—and visits to Sara. Although her war work had been extraordinary, she put it behind her like a mustered-out soldier. The only work she continued was at St. Elizabeth's Hospital. Eleanor had regressed with the blow to her ego of Franklin's dalliance. She was still rudderless and went to a tea meeting of the International Congress of Working Women in Washington only to translate for some French speakers.

She also had financial worries. Shifting to an all-black staff to economize was not enough. Franklin continued to order custom-made shoes and clothes and to increase his collection of prints, books, stamps, and coins. Even with his 1919 income of nearly $27,000 and his "Principal Account" of $273,000, there was never enough money.

Sara was used to sending Franklin a large check on his birthday. This year he wrote her on February 11 to thank her: "You are not only an angel which I always knew, but the kind which comes at the critical moment in life! For the question was not one of paying Dr. Mitchell. . . . The Dr. can wait, I know he is or must be rich, but of paying the gas man and the butcher lest the infants starve to death and your cheque which is too much of a Birthday present will do that. It is so dear of you." (Ted Morgan, a biographer of FDR, has joked that at Franklin's birthday party, where guests were to come in costume as characters from their favorite books, Franklin should have gone as Dickens's Micawber, "who spent more than he earned.")

At the end of the summer, when Eleanor had separated from Sara for the season, her grandmother Hall had died. Now, in February, Eleanor suffered another break with her past—Aunt Pussie (Mrs. Forbes Morgan) suffocated to death from smoke inhalation along with her two little girls in a house fire. Horrified neighbors watched them through the upstairs window gesturing frantically to be rescued. Then they sank from view. Pussie's husband and son were spared because Forbes was out of town and the boy at boarding school. Eleanor traveled to Manhattan to arrange the ghastly memorial service—battling a snowstorm that blasted through the city—and the funeral at Tivoli, where she had just mourned six months earlier.

Soon after, the couple was at a tea party when they learned that Miss Mercer had married the widowed Winthrop Rutherfurd in a small private ceremony. She had been working as his children's governess. (Winthrop's grandson Lewis Rutherfurd would marry Jacqueline Kennedy Onassis's half sister Janet Auchincloss Jr.) Franklin "started" when he heard news of the marriage, "like a horse in fear of a hornet," a family member wrote. Eleanor reacted only in a note to Sara: "Did you know Lucy Mercer married Mr. Wintie Rutherfurd two days ago?"

In June the Republicans held their national convention in Chicago. One of the potential nominees was General Leonard Wood, who had been a Rough Rider with Teddy. In a political and social landmark, Eleanor's aunt Corinne seconded the nomination of Wood and gave the first address by a woman before a presidential convention.

Despite Aunt Corinne's demonstration of women's new role in politics, Eleanor refused to commit to the suffrage campaign as it neared its successful conclusion. "I was very noncommittal," she said. One of its leaders asked her to throw her weight behind it; she refused and asked Sara to oppose suffrage, too.

Indeed, Eleanor had little interest that summer in accompanying Franklin to San Francisco, where he was a delegate to the Democratic National Convention. She refused to read an influential biography called *Woodrow Wilson: An Interpretation* because its author, Eleanor said, was "such a loathsome little Jew." Franklin kept his hope of winning the vice presidential nomination quiet: in fact, he responded to a reporter's question with "I can't afford the honor. I have five children." Although the quip disarmed the reporter, Franklin knew that if the honor went to him, his mother would continue to fund his family's daily expenses, the couple's personal luxuries, *and* his political ambition.

Franklin left his wife and children at Hyde Park with Sara on June 20. Sara wrote him five days later: "It was nice to get you your telegram last evening and I can imagine that the time at San Francisco will be most interesting and I hope 'elevating' as the old letters would say, but I fancy the last epithet is not very likely in a crowd of every sort of politician." She continued: "Langdon wrote me that if you run for Vice President it will strengthen the ticket very much!"

She also kept him up with the children's riding: "Anna on 'Bobby,' James on 'Truepenny' . . . Eleanor and Elliott and I shall meet them at the pond and see them swim. The little ones are out with bare feet." She added that "Eleanor looks well and lovely. She is very regular about her exercises and I think they have helped her wonderfully and account for her carrying herself much better and adding to her weight."

On July 4 Eleanor and the children left for Campobello. Four days later Sara crossed the river to the newly constructed Algonac to visit Annie and was outside when Annie sent a servant to tell her of an important telephone call. Her neighbor Thomas Newbold was on the telephone: the convention had just selected Franklin for the vice presidency. Eleanor was without a phone at Campobello and Rosy was camping at his palatial digs in the Adirondacks; Sara telegraphed both with the good news that Franklin would run with the presidential nominee, Ohio governor James M. Cox. Sara wrote Franklin immediately—"I received your dear telegram"—and proceeded to send him all the local news. "Now Hyde Park wants you to come this way, stop your train at Hyde Park, be met there by our own village men. . . . They much fear Poughkeepsie getting ahead of them." She continued: "Now if you can possibly do this on your way back, quite aside from my feelings, I think it would be wise. They are all worked up to it now and plan a rousing welcome.

"If and when you are elected, you will belong to the nation, now you are 'our boy' of Hyde Park and Dutchess."

Sara's letter of July 16 shows that she did not hesitate to express her complete pride in Franklin's political success. "I will say nothing of my feelings on Tuesday last and in fact always for you know. I know you and I will never forget . . . I kept wishing for your Father but I believe he knew and was with us—altho' I am not 'going in for spiritism,' just old fashioned religion, that those we love are always helping us."

She signed her letter, "No more only my love and blessing. Today is Papa's birthday. I am going up with some roses. Ever, Mama."

Eleanor, too, wrote a note, but hers was to Sara: "Whatever Franklin achieves must be largely due to you."

29

∞

"Rainy Day"

In August 1920, soon after Franklin received the vice presidential nomination, Sara and Eleanor went from a leisurely summer—Sara at Hyde Park, Eleanor at Campobello—to a cascade of activities. Eleanor raced back from her vacation, taking Anna and James with her, to travel with Franklin to Dayton, Ohio, for the official notification, as it was called, of Governor Cox's presidential nomination. Just after Eleanor began traveling southwest, Sara was dashing northeast to Campobello at her son's request to pick up Elliott and take him back to Hyde Park. The two youngest children, Franklin Jr. and John, remained at the island with their nanny. Sara, who would celebrate her sixty-sixth birthday in a month, must have felt—to use her expression—"like a boiled rabbit."

Sara arrived at Hyde Park with Elliott on Saturday, August 7, in the early evening. Franklin, Eleanor, and the eldest children returned from Franklin's campaign on August 8. On August 9 Sara hosted a grand open house for Franklin's vice presidential notification at Hyde Park, writing afterward in her journal: "About 500 came in house. About 8,000 in all outside." (The final estimate was 5,000 people.) "Franklin's 'Notification' very fine and impressive," she added.

Franklin talked from the portico of the newly designed house, and it was as fine an image for the photographers as he had hoped it would be when he sketched it five years earlier. Dutchess County friends were there to hear him, along with the requisite politicos and even the Tammany Hall crowd. The *New York Post* wrote: "The physical impression leaves nothing to be asked—the figure of an idealized college football player, almost the poster type in public life . . . always with a smile ready to share . . . a strong clear voice . . . [an] intangible, utterly charming and surely vote-winning quality."

Only Eleanor, still a bystander, was immune to Franklin's charm. She said, "I was glad for my husband, but it never occurred to me to be much excited." Eleanor's aloofness was noticed by the sharp eyes of the press, one member of whom reported that she was a woman who "seems particularly to dislike the official limelight, and to resent the pitiless publicity given the private and personal affairs of people who are prominent in official life. Just how she'll ever endure the Vice-president status . . . remains to be seen."

Despite Eleanor's distaste for politics, the event went splendidly. Sara shone: she arranged to have lemonade and cake served to the thousands on the property and ordered enough luncheon for the five hundred inside the house. She gave her son a kiss on the front portico, but the photographers missed the shot and asked her to buss him again. She shook her head: she would express genuine feelings but would not seek publicity. Then, after Franklin's invited guests had left, she found a Poughkeepsie tailor and his wife munching in her dining room. "She greeted them with the same graciousness that she might have bestowed on any of the invited guests," said Rita Kleeman.

Eleanor later wrote: "I sympathized with my mother-in-law when I saw her lawn being trampled by hordes of people." Eleanor's statement is often used out of context to characterize Sara as a woman who disdained the common man, yet Sara actually reveled in the crowds for her son and Eleanor meant only to praise her mother-in-law* Eleanor continued, adding an explanation that is rarely, if ever, quoted: "My admiration for her grew through the years as I realized how many political guests she had to entertain in her house, where for so many years only family and friends had been received. Mrs. Roosevelt was quite remarkable about this plunge into the national political picture and made the necessary adjustments in her life in a remarkable way."

---

*Joseph Lash, for example, in *Eleanor and Franklin*, gives an incorrect citation, claiming that Kleeman's biography, for which she interviewed Sara in the early 1930s, has Sara complaining about her lawn. There is absolutely no such item in Kleeman's book. Other biographers have repeated this inaccuracy. Kleeman's actual statement about the event was "In a very real sense, her home was always her son's home; its doors were always open, its table ready to welcome whomever he wished to receive."

At the same time, Sara never sought recognition for what would be just the beginning of opening her house and grounds to thousands of people. Whatever Franklin asked her to do, she did, and she served him well. In June, for example, she had received a telegram from her son: ARRIVE FRIDAY EVENING WILL WIRE THAT MORNING FROM NEW YORK. EXPECT TO HAVE TWENTY TO LUNCH SATURDAY ONE O'CLOCK AND ABOUT 150 FOR LAWN PARTY AT 4:00.

In July a reporter from the *New York Evening Post* had attempted to interview Sara. She refused, except to say that her son had always been devoted to the town of Hyde Park. She made an impression, however, for he reported that "there is a stark and undeniable atmosphere of noncompromise about this house and its lady."

Sara's stamina was amazing: she never complained about the tiring round trip to Campo to pick up a grandchild only thirty-six hours before her son's enormous campaign kickoff. Sara took such events in stride, doing what she could to support Franklin's political ambitions. Not the least was her adapting to a public life after sixty-five years of assuming that her name would never appear in the newspapers. She had already accepted with dignity the attention his nomination brought her.

Sara was raised in a world, noted biographer Kleeman, where sisters and brothers could find "a complete life together, when other than material things (good manners and social grace) were handed down from generation to generation. . . . Added to this training was an inherent warmth and friendliness which impelled her constantly—and never with condescension—to put people at their ease and make them comfortable and happy."

Sara made an adept transition from old Hudson Valley, where everyone knew one another and their ancestors, to being stopped on the street by total strangers who wanted to shake her hand. Franklin had brought her into a very different life indeed, and she embraced it—or nearly all of it—to further her son's aspirations. Moreover, Sara did it competently and without complaint. She also added two thousand dollars* to her son's election fund, which was the second-largest (behind Franklin's) personal campaign contribution.

Now that Franklin had his moment in the spotlight, Sara assisted Eleanor so she could return to the vacation she sought. Sara accompanied her daughter-in-law and the three elder children back to Campobello—three days after having left there and the day after hosting a crowd of thousands on her lawn. Franklin had already jumped into the campaign—it didn't matter to him that the unpopularity of the Wilson administration doomed the

---

*Some accounts cite three thousand dollars, although her receipt reads two thousand dollars.

ticket. The electorate liked Franklin—he was hard *not* to like—but Cox and the League of Nations were unappealing.

Optimistic as always, Franklin mistook his fans for the nation's voters. He confidently told a Dutchess County Democrat that he would need the man in Washington after the election. "Listen, Frank," was the candid response. "You're not going to Washington."

On the trail many people mistook Franklin for Teddy's son and would shout their compliments: "I voted for your old man!" and "You're just like your father!" These misunderstandings did not please the Oyster Bay family. Ted Jr. made that family's feelings clear, trailing Franklin's campaign stops and announcing, "He is a maverick. He does not have the brand of our family." Eleanor refused to speak to her cousin for many years after his gratuitous disavowal.

Sara had a pithier response when she was asked why the Oyster Bay Roosevelts were antagonistic: "I can't imagine, unless it is because we are better looking than they are." (It must have been the Delano genes.)

Louis Howe slowly coaxed Eleanor into becoming a political wife, persuading her to start talking before crowds. "I was flattered," Eleanor responded, "and before long I found myself discussing a wide range of subjects." Still, it was difficult for her to listen to political speeches all day and then sit alone in a hotel room as Franklin plotted strategy while playing poker with the men. But she was needed—Franklin must have hoped that her presence might win over some of the women's vote. She stayed on the campaign longer than she had originally expected and had to dash off an urgent note to Sara, saying she needed "1 clean nightgown & shirt & 3 chemises & 3 drawers & any black stockings & handkerchief."

Just as the campaign was in full swing, Sara received awful news. On September 9 her journal reflects an uncharacteristic outburst: "My brother Warren was taken from us suddenly—thrown from his wagon at the station—God help us!" Warren Delano III was buried at the family mausoleum in Fairhaven, with his family and the vice presidential nominee in attendance. Of Catherine's eleven children, the only ones left were Sara, her brother Frederick, and her sisters Annie, Dora, and Kassie. Less than a week later, Sara was back in Hyde Park taking care of all five Roosevelt children, whose parents placed them with her through the campaign's end in November.

The American people selected the Harding-Coolidge ticket not by a landslide, as one of Wilson's men quipped, but by an earthquake. The Cox-Roosevelt ticket suffered the worst defeat of any presidential election in a hundred years. The national ticket pulled other Democrats down with them: even Al Smith lost New York's governorship. Voters wanted no more change; they wanted a return to peacetime routine and prosperity. Harding had pledged this, whereas Franklin had criticized those who wished "to restore 'normal' conditions."

It was also a blow to suffragists, who were convinced that the women's vote would lead to pacifism, which, in this election, translated into support for the League of Nations. Nine days after Sara's massive political kickoff for her son in August, the Nineteenth Amendment was ratified, changing the American electorate for all time. The election of 1920 was an incredible experience for both Sara and Eleanor: they cast their first votes, and for Franklin at that. As soon as Sara returned home from voting in town, she opened her house to feed hundreds of supporters, who trekked inside for shelter from the rain.

Franklin characteristically took his defeat with grace. He took only a few days to recover before he began referring to himself as "Franklin D. Roosevelt, Ex-V.P., Canned. (Erroneously reported dead.)" Actually, the doomed campaign had served its purpose: at thirty-eight, he was certainly young enough to have another chance; he had sharpened his campaign skills and was now a national presence. But still, Franklin had taken a political gamble in running for vice president, as *no one* to that date in U.S. history who had lost the vice presidency had ever been able to win election later as president.

Sara took his loss calmly. "Rainy day," she reported aptly. "Harding and Coolidge elected. Quite a landslide for Republicans. Franklin rather relieved not to be elected Vice President."

Two days later, on November 4, she wrote her son: "We all feel very badly over the result of the elections." She also mentioned that the two youngest children, Franklin Jr. and John, who had been with her since August along with their three siblings, were returning to Eleanor at East Sixty-fifth Street. James had just started Groton School. Anna and Elliott would remain with Sara for the entire academic year and continue their tutoring with Vassar undergraduates. Their parents would see them on weekends.

30

"Solidly Important Individual"

Now Franklin needed a job, so he became a $25,000-a-year vice president of one of the nation's largest surety bond firms, Fidelity & Deposit Company of Maryland. (The firm issued bonds guaranteeing that the government or private businesses would fulfill their financial obligations or forfeit the bond.) This was the first job that paid him real money, befitting his status and the beginning boom of the 1920s. Earlier in March, Franklin had formed a law firm with two friends and was a principal partner. With the election over, he began his work at Emmet, Marvin & Roosevelt—although not before going on a hunting trip in Louisiana to recover from the campaign. Despite Eleanor's dutiful attendance on the campaign trail, Franklin went on vacation solo, leaving Eleanor in New York. She enrolled Franklin Jr. in a Manhattan school while John attended an informal class across the street.

When Franklin got back from his boys-only vacation, he spent mornings on Broadway at his Fidelity office and his afternoons on Wall Street at the law firm. Thursday evenings, Eleanor took Franklin Jr. and John to Hyde Park to join Anna and Elliott for three-day weekends. Franklin usually joined them on Fridays.

~

The family had been relieved to see James enter Groton School in September. Sara had written Franklin the previous June: "James's examination marks are so low that poor Eleanor is most troubled and vexed and he does realize it for he is quite cast down and looks badly. . . . Meanwhile I feel rather sad about it." Thankfully, Reverend Peabody admitted James, and when he left for school, Eleanor took him by herself—her husband, the Groton man, was too busy campaigning. Eleanor realized in hindsight that James was too young to go away to school, but she explained in her autobiography that "it was a tradition in the family that boys must go to boarding school when they reached the age of twelve . . . so of course we had to send him." (Her memory was faulty: Franklin had started school at age fourteen.)

James no sooner started Groton than he came down with stomach problems and needed the family's attention. Eleanor stayed at Franklin's side on the campaign trail. Sara decided that James took priority now, and she left the other four children. She traveled to Massachusetts, just as she had done several times in the 1890s when her son and her stepgrandson, Taddy, became ill.

Sara arrived at Groton on September 29 and took James to see a Boston physician. She rented a suite at her father's favorite hotel, the Bellevue, and stayed with James for five days until his doctor released him. Then Sara took the boy to Hyde Park to recuperate for another five days, leaving again with him for Groton on October 9. She stayed in town for several days, until she was sure of his health, before she returned home to the four children waiting for her.

As it happened, James's problems were due to his anxiety and shyness over asking the location of the bathroom. "Hard as it may be to believe," he later wrote, "I did what had to be done in my pants or in the bushes. My soiled pants were stuffed in a box, which I buried. Holding back as long as I could, I started to suffer stomach pains."

"It was my grandmother, not my mother or father, who came for me," he added. Eleanor excused her absence: "It was probably a very good thing for the children to learn that they could not always be my first consideration."

James's crisis at Groton was just one sign of the problems caused by his upbringing, which included cruel nannies and governesses, inattentive parents, and the rigid child-rearing beliefs then in vogue. Eleanor unwittingly replicated with her children aspects of her own childhood, especially the harsh, repressive discipline inflicted by her grandmother Hall that was popular at the turn of the century and fostered by such child development experts as Kellogg and Holt. Franklin, on the other hand, had grown up deeply loved by two parents who focused on his needs, but he, in contrast, was often absent from his own children.

The child-rearing problems began soon after the children were born. Eleanor's early hanging contraption that aired Anna, and then James, out the second story was definitely one of her strangest ideas. Shortly after, when Eleanor noticed them sucking their thumbs, she attached wire guards to their tiny fingers. When Eleanor saw little Anna touching herself in bed, she told her nanny to tie her little wrists to the top bars of her crib each night. Many years later Anna—who never forgot this treatment—asked her mother why. Eleanor answered her "in a tone which precluded any further question. The indication was clearly that I had had a bad habit which had to be cured and about which one didn't talk." Child experts termed masturbation a "vice and sin" when Anna was young; by following their advice, Eleanor must have thought she was doing what was best for her child.

Whereas Eleanor's actions were well intentioned, her children's governesses were mean and abusive. One time Anna's governess caught her in a lie and she "was sent to school with cotton in her cheek," Marion Dickerman related. "The teacher said, 'Why, Anna, take that out,' and she said, 'I can't, I told a lie, I have to keep it in.'" The girl was punished regularly by the same woman, who, James said, would "push Sis to the floor" and kneel "on her chest and cuff her around a bit in order to drive home the importance of conducting one's self as a lady at all times."

James was not immune, either. Eleanor severely lectured him after catching him walking home from kindergarten with a little girl, arm in arm. The next year his governess caught James in a lie. She forced him to put on Anna's dress, wear a sign, I AM A LIAR, and walk up and down his block on East Sixty-fifth Street. A few years later she compelled him to eat an entire pot of hot mustard, which burned his mouth and made him vomit for several days.

Elliott came in for his share, too. When he accidentally knocked John's high chair over—with John in it—the governess locked him in a dark closet for three hours. Franklin rescued him when he returned home and heard the boy screaming; although Franklin was livid with rage (in fact, his fury exacerbated Elliott's fright), he did not discharge the governess. Nor did Franklin's anger stop the woman from locking Franklin Jr. in the closet again. The help was sadistic and realized that they could do nearly anything to these children and get away with it.

Eleanor said of her children's caregivers: "As a rule, they kept the children in pretty good health and I think were really fond of them"—making

James walk his block in a dress with a placard on his back?—"but I had a silly theory that you should trust the people with your children and back up their discipline. As a result, my children were frequently unjustly punished, because I was unprepared to be a practical housekeeper, wife or mother." Eleanor also admitted that the most serious mistake she ever made was "possibly too much belief in discipline when my older children were young . . . although I am not sure."

Eleanor's cousin Corinne characterized Eleanor's mothering as "She did her duty. Nobody in the world did her duty more than Eleanor Roosevelt. But with the children I don't think you can have an understanding of them unless you enjoy them."

Eleanor, who was so sensitive about her own adolescence, minimized her children's fears. They were, in fact, terrorized. Eleanor fired the worst of her governesses only when she found a bottle in the woman's dresser drawer. As James critically noted, "Secret drinking was a much more serious crime than child abuse."

Although her sons were hard on their mother, she did not purposely harm her children. Eleanor was deeply insecure as a mother and later felt so guilty about her children's treatment that she blamed their horrific governesses on Sara, saying that her mother-in-law had hired them. This blame has been repeated many times, although it is inexplicable that Sara would employ cruel women for her grandchildren after she had hired only loving nurses for her son. In fact, none of these abuses happened at Hyde Park.

The first nurse Sara hired was Miss Spring, who became Eleanor's friend. Sara's contemporaneous writings indicate that she interviewed one governess at Eleanor's behest—this woman turned out to be the one the children nicknamed "Old Battle-ax"—but was required to use Eleanor's own standards to select her. In 1915 she wrote Franklin about the woman who would cause terror in her grandchildren's lives: "I engaged an English nurse, just landed, 32 years old, fresh, young, thoroughly trained and highly recommended. . . . It is always a chance but she promises well and accedes to Eleanor's rules."

Although sadistic punishment would eventually color the children's adult lives, they managed to have some fun, too. In Manhattan, Anna and James would sneak up onto Sara's roof and drop water bombs on the pedestrians below. Then they'd streak back to their rooms at 49 East Sixty-fifth, wide-eyed and innocent, claiming that they had been there the whole time. The boys kept reptiles in one of the bathtubs, and Sara would indulgently send down a bucket of "slimy brook vegetation" every Sunday afternoon from Hyde Park for the creatures.

They also remembered good times with their parents, although as James said, "We spent so little time alone with our parents that those times are remembered and treasured as though gifts from gods." When Franklin was with his children, he was a joy: he picnicked, played baseball, and led them in a game called Hare and Hounds. He and Anna bird-watched. There were always the winter sports of skating and sledding. His life centered on the water, and he loved to take the children sailing and taught them to race model boats.

James later wrote: "When he was around, which wasn't nearly often enough for us, he inundated us with fun and activity, and with love too—but in his special way, which was both detached and overpowering. Sometimes we felt we didn't have him at all, but when we did have him, life was as lively and exciting as any kid could want it to be."

The children called Franklin "Pa," except for Anna, who often called him "Father," and Elliott, who used "Pops." Anna was his favorite—she was the first baby he could play with and the two bonded tightly. She adored him and called him her childhood hero. As it turned out, perhaps Anna's relationship with her father gave her a resiliency that the boys lacked.

Eleanor had a favorite, too: Elliott suffered poor health—here was a boy she could do something for and fulfill her sense of duty. She may also have recognized that he, as a middle child, was left out of the sibling cliques or worse—"everyone ganged up on him," James said.

Eleanor usually stayed behind when the kids and their father enjoyed outdoor sports—"I was never really carefree," she admitted—but she would spend quieter times with them. When at home in the evenings—a rare event, given the couple's political socializing—she would read to them in the living room or play the piano. These were enjoyable moments.

However, Eleanor often appeared unloving to her chicks. Anna noted that if she interrupted her grandmother in the snuggery, "she would manage with a pat on the head or shoulder and a remark that she'd talk to me later," whereas her mother "had a far more chilling way of putting me in my place" using a "low but cold voice" to ask her what she wanted. When the boys became adults, they were especially harsh on their parents. Elliott wrote of "the father we loved, the mother we respected." James wrote that "Mother loved all mankind, but she did not know how to let her children love her."

Eleanor's most unmaternal behavior occurred during the Red Scare in 1919 when a bomb exploded at the Washington house of the U.S. attorney general, just across the street from where the Roosevelts lived. Franklin and

Eleanor were parking their car when they heard the explosion. They ran toward their house, with Franklin in the lead. The anarchist had accidentally blown himself up: there were body parts strewn on the street and blood on the steps of the Roosevelts' house. Police and firemen were arriving on a wave of sirens.

Franklin ran upstairs, using his long, athletic legs to take the steps two at a time to see if James, who had a front bedroom, was safe. When Franklin threw open his son's door and saw him staring out the window at the commotion, James later remembered, "he grabbed me in an embrace that almost cracked my ribs." Then Eleanor dashed in: "Whatever are you doing out of bed at this hour, James?" she said to her son, who was standing barefooted with broken glass all around him. "Get yourself straight to bed!"

Luckily, the children had a safe harbor in their grandmother. James said, "For the most part, Father left our rearing to Mother. And she, for the most part, left it to our grandmother." James noted that Sara constantly took care of the children when they were sick, "where we might contaminate our grandmother but not the rest of the family." They also knew that it was Granny to whom they should go to with their problems. James, several years before he left for Groton, told his grandmother that his mother was "up at five this morning to go to the canteen. Do you not think that Mother should not go so early?"

Anna wrote that her grandmother was "the most solidly important individual in this category in my earliest childhood." Her original draft used the phrase "puzzling important individual," indicating, perhaps, the children's confusion at their grandmother's position in their lives. Sara, according to Anna's second husband, John Boettiger, was the "most reliably loving and available parenting figure" to the children.

Nina Roosevelt Gibson, daughter of the youngest Roosevelt son, John, said, "The children had to make quite a few adjustments to the fact that their parents were both very busy and not home on a consistent basis. Again, they had a grandmother who was constantly available to them. Their household ran smoothly so that the children had a sense of stability and they knew in terms of the household what was happening."

Even as the five grew older, there was little change in their relationship with their parents. Although Eleanor went on to give advice in her newspaper column and her other writings, James said, "I cannot imagine going to my parents with a problem. When we had problems, we handled them ourselves or went to our grandmother." Even so, Sara had her limitations: "But you did not discuss *personal* problems with Granny."

Each morning, the children received "perfunctory morning kisses" at the breakfast table from their parents, Anna said. Eleanor admitted that "I do not think that I am a natural-born mother. I think I approached my own motherhood with a keen sense of responsibility but very little sense of the joy which should come through having babies." Franklin would kiss his sons, always, as his father had kissed him. "On the other hand," said Anna, "when I was sent down to say good morning to Granny, as she finished her breakfast in bed, her kiss and hug were indeed warm." The children would also receive a hug and a kiss after evening prayers from Eleanor, unless their nurse had complained about their behavior. Then Eleanor's "disapproval was quite evident, usually expressed by dampening down the warmth of her goodnight hug and kiss," Anna said.

James said of his mother: "She felt a tremendous sense of duty to us. It was part of that duty to read to us and to hear our prayers before we went to bed, but she did not understand or satisfy the need of a child for primary closeness to a parent." Apparently Eleanor never did understand this, for in her writings later in life she explained that the most important part of motherhood was that the "children's lives were planned in a manner which I felt was right for them."

By the end of 1920, the children ranged in age from four to fourteen. They had lived in houses in five locations: Hyde Park, Manhattan, Campobello, Albany, and Washington. Although their horrific nannies traveled with them, at each house they would find different household staff members. "We never had the day-to-day discipline, supervision and attention most children get from their parents. Ours was not an ordinary way of life," James remarked. He told John Gunther, the journalist, that he felt "rootless" as a child. Still, he said, "When I was growing up, Hyde Park seemed more like home to me than the many others I had."

His sister concurred: "Hyde Park was home, and the only place I ever thought was completely home. Hyde Park was very definitely my most favorite place in life," she added. The magic of Hyde Park came only partly from its woods and fields, its trees and river. The warm feeling of Hyde Park came from their grandmother. Sara took care of her grandchildren when they were sick and focused her attention on their needs at all times.

It was true that she said to them, "Your mother only bore you. I am more your mother than your mother is." No one would claim that this was an appropriate thing for her to say. However, even Eleanor admitted that it was true. "As it turned out, Franklin's children were more my mother-in-law's children than they were mine." She blamed Sara for the situation, not her own actions. What else could Eleanor have expected when Sara had to serve as her grandchildren's antidote to their father's ambition and their mother's lack of interest? Anna, too, said that she was brought up "more by my grandmother than by my parents."

At Hyde Park, Sara's butler would tap her Chinese gong—brought from Algonac—once thirty minutes before lunch or dinner. At five minutes before the meal, the butler struck the gong again. Sara brooked no complaints or excuses for tardiness; if the children claimed they didn't have time to finish what they were doing, she would remonstrate, "You had all the time there was." Nor was there a good reason for not washing before meals. "Do I smell horses?" she would ask if the children ran in from riding, and they would excuse themselves to wash their "soiled"—never "dirty"—hands. If they complained about the weather, she'd retort, ""All weather is good weather for something."

There were the usual generational differences. Sara expected her grandchildren to dress for dinner and was disappointed that her only granddaughter was a tomboy. "Anna, darling, why do you wear those ugly blue jeans?" she said. "I can hardly believe you are the same girl who [used to enjoy] looking like a beautiful golden-haired fairy in a pretty little muslin dress with blue ribbons." In this, she was like many others of her generation.

Sara noticed that her grandchildren's governesses were overly harsh, and she knew that Eleanor believed in strong discipline. Although that was not her way, she did not think it her place to question Eleanor openly. Instead, she overcompensated by being too generous with the grandchildren. It was the only way she could make up to them for what they were missing.

The children learned this in no time. "We 'chicks' quickly learned that the best way to circumvent 'Pa and Mummy' when we wanted something they wouldn't give us was to appeal to Granny," said Anna. Therefore, if a child suggested that to have a pony would be lovely, "then suddenly one would appear in the stable in Hyde Park. Moreover, this was never discussed with the parents. It was just provided for by Sara Roosevelt," said her great-granddaughter Nina Roosevelt Gibson.

Worse, sometimes Sara would provide these things even after Eleanor had said no to the children. Certainly Sara was being unfair to Eleanor and inconsistent with the children, but she did think she was using "the law of nature" to give a material item when she saw that something less tangible had been taken away. Nina Roosevelt Gibson said, "I don't believe Sara was trying to drive a wedge between her grandchildren and their parents. I think she felt, as the grandmother, that this was her right to spoil the children and that they weren't really being spoiled. And as long as she could provide these lovely things for her grandchildren, she was going to."

Eleanor and Franklin felt entitled to the many checks Sara wrote them for everyday expenses and luxuries—but when Sara wished to spend for their children, Eleanor and Franklin wanted to limit her gifts. The couple wanted to be able to control their own children and not let them be spoiled—a common intergenerational complaint between parents and grandparents.

Eleanor did slowly learn that children could be deeply wounded by cruelty disguised as discipline. Marion Dickerman noted that "Eleanor had not been happy about some of her experiences with her older children. James and Anna and Elliott, she felt, had been subjected to types of punishment that Eleanor felt quite wrong, but she never had the spiritual or intellectual strength to protest. She made up her mind that young Franklin and John would have quite different experiences." To this end, Eleanor hired a young Scottish governess, Elspeth Connachie, who was nicknamed Connie, and the children's lives—especially Franklin Jr.'s and John's—became more joyous and spontaneous. Regardless of the quality of their help, all five siblings saw their grandmother as the one constant loving person in their lives.

31

" 'I Got Up This Party for You' "

The summer of 1921 was off to a choppy start for Franklin. Vengeful Republicans, in office after the devastating 1920 Democratic defeat, were taking full advantage of their strength in the Senate to lead an investigation of Franklin's role in a scandal over homosexuality in the navy. A Senate committee was examining whether Franklin had known about the crackdown at the Newport naval base in which sailors were being lured into homosexual acts by undercover agents who actually arrested the sailors after having sex with them. *The New York Times* ran a headline: LAY NAVY SCANDAL TO FDR with the subhead "Details Are Unprintable." Luckily for Franklin, the Senate committee dropped the issue when its members realized that the nation was growing weary of the investigation.

Although the hearings had ended, the experience had drained Franklin's energy in a hot and humid Washington summer when the air was cooled only by ineffectual electric fans. He yearned for Campobello; he thirsted for cool sea breezes and dips in the refreshingly chilly bay; and he anticipated seeing Eleanor and the children, who were already there with Mrs. Howe and her son, Hartley. Louis Howe had been detained on business, too, but was expected soon.

Sara had left on July 7 for Paris and London, her first European trip since the war had ended. Her letters to Franklin in Washington and to Eleanor at Campo detailed visiting with Dora, taking in art at the Louvre, and seeing plays whenever possible. Of course, she tantalized her son and daughter-in-law with gifts she had bought: a beautiful English couture dress for Anna and rugs that Eleanor wanted.

On August 5, as soon as he could, Franklin left Washington. Rather than traveling straight to Campo, he visited a group of Boy Scout camps at Bear Mountain on the Hudson Palisades, then sailed to Campo with a friend on the man's yacht. Franklin was worn to the bone from the strain of the past three years: the war, the European trip with Eleanor, the election campaign, and, recently, the navy scandal. Even the hunting trip that followed the campaign had been more strenuous than relaxing. Looking forward to Campobello ahead, Franklin expected an easy sail; instead, maneuvering through the rocks and islands of the Bay of Fundy in fog made for a difficult trip. Franklin, familiar with those waters, unexpectedly had to pilot for many hours. Finally, Franklin and his friend arrived safely and were greeted warmly by Eleanor and the children, as well as Mrs. Howe and her son.

He was delighted finally to enjoy his summer cottage, although his son James later wrote that Franklin arrived still angry at the Senate committee: "When Father was mad, his way of working off steam was through an outpouring of physical vigor—and Campobello was the place where he could do it. Immediately on his arrival, we began having a wild, whooping, romping, running, sailing, picnicking time with him." On August 10 he and Eleanor went out fishing on the yacht's tender. Engrossed in baiting a hook for cod while crossing the deck, Franklin slipped on the varnished plank and fell overboard into the icy Bay of Fundy. Franklin later wrote: "I'd never felt anything so cold as that water! I hardly went under, hardly wet my head, because I still had hold of the tender, but the water was so cold it seemed paralyzing." When he was pulled out, the contrast between the hot sun beating down on deck, the hazy heat rising from the tender's engine, and the frigid water seemed especially sharp to him.

Still dedicated to enjoying his vacation, the next afternoon Franklin dressed in his bathing suit—a cotton one-piece that covered shoulder to thigh—and went for a relaxing sail with his family. From the boat, they spotted a brush fire on a nearby island. After docking, all seven did their part to beat it out with evergreen boughs Franklin cut on the spot, working strenuously for several hours. "Our eyes were bleary with smoke," Franklin remembered, "we were begrimed, smarting with spark-burns, exhausted."

Sooty and sweaty, Franklin and the children left Eleanor to return home while they jogged several miles to a freshwater pond, bathed, and then quickly plunged into the icy bay to enjoy the waves. When they reached the cottage, the children felt chilled and changed into warm clothes. Franklin said he was too tired to dress and sat reading in his wet cotton bathing suit. After an hour or so, he was chilled through and still abnormally fatigued. He decided to skip supper and said he would go right to bed to warm up. Franklin climbed the stairs to his bedroom. It would be the last time that he would make that walk unassisted.

The next morning, August 11, he woke up feeling no better. When he swung out of bed to use the bathroom, he noticed his left leg lagging. "I managed to move about and shave," he recounted. "I tried to persuade myself that the trouble with my leg was muscular, that it would disappear as I used it. But presently it refused to work, and then the other."

Franklin was spiking a fever and experiencing stabbing leg pains. Eleanor called in the local doctor from Maine, the one who had helped her deliver Franklin Jr. This man diagnosed a cold, though it didn't seem like a cold to Eleanor, who decided to watch Franklin at night and slept on his bedroom's cushioned window seat. Howe had arrived, and he began to assist her, taking catnaps when he couldn't go on any longer. "He has been the greatest help," she wrote Rosy on August 14 as she brought her brother-in-law up-to-date on Franklin's health. She told him to conceal the severity of Franklin's illness, however, saying, "I do not want particulars to get into the paper."

Within a few days Franklin could not move his body below the chest. Eleanor and Howe were deeply frightened; Howe looked for a city doctor who might be vacationing in the nearby resorts. In Bar Harbor, Howe found an experienced Philadelphia physician. By now Franklin was "completely paralyzed, even his face," Elliott said later. The esteemed doctor examined Franklin and said he had more than a cold: he had a blood clot or a type of lesion on his spine. Franklin *must* receive massages around the clock. Eleanor and Louis followed the doctor's orders and tried to ignore Franklin's screams as they kneaded his legs.

Franklin was completely helpless, so Eleanor took on the most personal aspects of his care. She sponged him clean, brushed his teeth, shaved him, learned to insert a catheter, and administered enemas. Franklin must have been shattered by the breach of his essential reserve. When Howe relieved Eleanor for the more ordinary nursing tasks, she saw to the children and the household summer staff of five and wrote short notes in response to any urgent correspondence.

Rosy kept up a worried exchange of messages but remained at Red House with Betty, his second wife. The news of Franklin's strange illness, of course, had traveled through the family, and the entire Delano clan, in

Sara's absence, was grouping to help her son. Sara's recently widowed sister-in-law Jennie Walters Delano and her daughter Ellen arrived to assist Eleanor however they could. Sara, of course, was in Europe and still knew nothing. Yet on August 19 Franklin and Eleanor received a letter from Sara, in London with Dora, that must have disquieted them both. Sara wrote: "We went to Peal today, I longed to order shoes for you, but feared I might not get what you want." Then she signed the letter with a message to Eleanor: "I hope you are very well & taking good care of the dearest son on earth."

Eleanor again wrote Rosy four days after her first letter, growing more frightened by the situation. Two weeks had gone by and Franklin showed no improvement; in fact, he was getting worse. Although there had not been a severe polio epidemic that summer, and three of its four known victims were children, Eleanor and Howe still feared it for Franklin; she told Rosy that "the symptoms so far would be much the same." She continued: "On Uncle Fred's urgent advice, which I feel I must follow on Mama's account, I have asked . . . for a consultation to determine if it is I. P. [infantile paralysis] or not. I am sure Mama would feel we must leave no stone unturned to accomplish the best results."

Howe had thought Frederick's recommendations sound, and without even waiting for Rosy's response, he telegraphed Frederick with Eleanor's go-ahead to look for specialists in Boston. Frederick immediately found an expert who read Eleanor's and Howe's letters describing Franklin's symptoms and quickly diagnosed polio. The physician ordered the massages stopped *at once*—the excruciating rubdowns were destructive to muscles affected by polio and had actually caused damage. This doctor, however, was not free to go to Campobello at the time.

Fred found another well-known polio specialist in Newport who went to Campobello and confirmed the diagnosis, although he told Eleanor that it was a mild case. (Anna was hiding in a closet and learned of her father's polio before he himself was told.) Eleanor and Franklin almost felt relieved to know the truth—although his reaction was hard to read as "there was never the slightest emotion that was allowed to show," his wife said. Still, the couple was greatly encouraged by the allegedly mild nature of the case. On August 27 Eleanor pulled her courage together to write Sara a note that Rosy would bring to the pier to be delivered to her as she awaited customs. Eleanor wanted to give Sara a hint of her son's illness, yet not tell her so much that she would be unduly worried during the long trip from New York to Campobello.

Eleanor used her old R Street stationery and jotted down:

Dearest Mama,

Franklin has been quite ill & so can't go down to meet you on Tuesday to his great regret, but Uncle Fred and Aunt Kassie both write they will be there so it will not be a lonely homecoming. We are all so happy to have you home again dear, you don't know what it means to feel you near again.

The children are all very well and I wish you could have seen John's face shine when he heard us say you would be home soon.

Even before anyone had made an accurate diagnosis, fear was not allowed in the house. The adults kept any private misgivings to themselves. Eleanor and Franklin remained cheerful and told the children that he would have a quick recovery. For their part, the chicks initially believed it, and they were allowed to say quick hellos to him. "He grinned at us, and he did his best to call out, or gasp out, some cheery response to our tremulous, just-this-side-of-tears greetings," said Elliott, who was ten. (Anna was fifteen; James, thirteen; Franklin. Jr., six, and John, four.)

Even Howe, an intense man, kept up the almost jovial atmosphere. They continued to keep the news quiet, warning the telegraph clerks not to repeat their messages and even employing one physician who did not know who he was going to examine. However, Franklin later told Elliott that he despaired; he thought God had deserted him.

Eleanor continued her backbreaking work, now focused on getting Franklin into the bathtub for as many hot baths as the water supply of their cottage would allow. Howe helped her until, finally, a trained nurse came up from New York. Only then did he leave the island to quell rumors in New York about Franklin's health and to greet his daughter, sailing home from France. He announced that Franklin was ill but did not disclose the diagnosis. On the morning of August 30, the day before Sara's ship arrived from Europe, Howe took Frederick to breakfast to talk with him candidly about Franklin's illness. They became so friendly that they decided to dine together that night and take in a movie.

Waiting at Campobello, Eleanor received a letter from the Philadelphia doctor who had diagnosed a spinal clot and ordered the devastating massages. He sent a note excusing his misdiagnosis and referred to what was his final bill: "As to the financial side, will you kindly send me at your entire convenience a thousand dollars."*

Frederick and Kassie went down to the Manhattan harbor to meet Sara

---

*Although a bill of six hundred dollars, based on a complaining letter that Eleanor wrote Rosy, is mentioned in biographies, the physician's own correspondence refers to a thousand-dollar fee.

when her ship docked on August 31. Rosy traveled to the pier separately. It was next to impossible for Sara to leave New York that same day, so Eleanor made train reservations for first thing the following morning.

Sara walked into the Campobello cottage with a smile on her face and as relaxed an attitude as she could muster—as she always had done regarding illness, whether it was one of Franklin's many childhood sicknesses or her own husband's ill health. She greeted Eleanor and the children with kisses, taking her time to hug and speak to each one before she went upstairs to see her son.

Franklin greeted her jauntily. Sara responded in kind. She later said, "I realized I had to be courageous for Franklin's sake, and since he was probably pretending to be unworried for mine, the meeting was quite a cheerful one."

She wrote Frederick the day after arriving:

> I got here yesterday at 1:30 and at once . . . came up to a brave smiling and beautiful son, who said, "Well, I'm glad you are back Mummy and I got up this party for you."
>
> He had shaved himself and seems very bright and *keen*. Below his waist he cannot move at all. His legs (that I have always been proud of) have to be moved often as they ache when long in one position. He and Eleanor decided at once to be cheerful and the atmosphere of the house is all happiness so I have fallen in and followed their glorious example.

Dora, at home in Paris, received a letter nearly immediately from Sara. "It was a shock to hear bad news on my arrival on the dock, but I am thankful I didn't hear before I sailed, as I came directly here, and best of all am strong and I could copy the happy, cheerful attitude of Eleanor and even our poor Franklin who lies there unable to move his legs, which are often painful and have to be moved for him, as they have no power."

She added: "He looks well and eats well and is keen and full of interest in everything. Dr. Lovett, the greatest authority we have on infantile paralysis, pronounced it that and says he *will* get well. At best it will be slow. . . . They are lucky in their nurse, but Eleanor does a great deal. This again illustrates my point that the lightning usually strikes when we *least* expect it. And this is such a splendid young life, may God grant him complete recovery."

Sara stayed only two nights, encouraged by Franklin's insistence that she attend a family wedding with Anna and by her own fears that she would be more burden to Eleanor than relief. She stopped at Fairhaven on September 4 and sent Eleanor a letter whose words are casual but whose writing is extremely shaky and barely resembles her usually confident hand. Sara began with a small item of news, and then continued:

> My thoughts are with you and our dear invalid all the time and I ever wake at night with a longing to know how Franklin is and if there is continued gain. It seems so dreadful I can do nothing to help you at this time when I know you are so full of grave anxiety. Your dear [nurse's] presence will I am sure be a help at a time where your responsibility seemed too much. We all have faith in Franklin's good constitution to help him thro' & I know his patience and courage will do everything.

Sara's brother, the only remaining male Delano of his generation, dedicated himself throughout the crisis to Franklin's recovery. "Uncle Fred," Elliott later wrote, "has been mostly forgotten by some historians as a key factor in Father's battle to get well." (In fact, Howe has received credit for finding the capable physicians who diagnosed polio, but Frederick Delano was actually the one who insisted that Franklin have better care and located them for Eleanor. Howe was merely their go-between and was, unfortunately, responsible for locating the Philadelphia doctor whose misdiagnosis damaged Franklin's legs.)

Now Frederick wrote Franklin words imbued with the Delano philosophy of life: "I realize that you are up against a hard problem and hard, cruel, fact, and yet I feel the utmost confidence that you will emerge a better and stronger man." For his part, Franklin continued as if he would be well soon, pledging to lead Vassar College's upcoming fund-raiser and joining an executive committee of New York Democrats.

Eleanor, Howe, Frederick, and Sara realized that Franklin should begin a specialized hospital-care program as soon as possible; what puzzled them was how to get Franklin to New York. Rosy lightheartedly responded, "What a pity he is not still in the Navy, and a destroyer [at] hand to take [him] right through to Hyde Park!"

Howe coupled his strategic planning with Frederick's influence and Sara's money. Frederick was now a railroad director (he had left the Federal Reserve Board) and, with Howe, arranged a special train for Franklin that would take the invalid from Campobello to a Manhattan hospital with a minimum of public exposure. Naturally, Sara paid the complete expense of the private car. Dr. Lovett noted, "This will be the better way, perhaps as she [Sara] can pay the bills."

Howe made elaborate plans for September 13, the day Franklin would escape from Campobello. He schemed to get Franklin from the cottage down to the pier into a boat for the two-mile crossing, up wooden steps to the dock, and over toward the rail lines. That morning Franklin had his favorite fedora placed jauntily on his head. He cradled the family Scottie (not yet Fala) in his arms, opened his teeth for Howe to put in his plastic cigarette holder, which someone lit for him, and was off. Before he was hoisted up, he turned to his children, thrust his chin "out like a bulldozer blade," and managed "a big flashy smile and a wisecrack that was for the benefit of us kids," James recalled.

Crowds had gathered to see Franklin and wish him well at Eastport, Maine—but in the wrong area, thanks to Howe's advance work. Franklin was privately laid on a stretcher and passed through the window of his personal railroad car. Then he was carefully positioned in his seat before reporters came bounding toward him. A duped *New York World* correspondent reported that "Mr. Roosevelt was enjoying his cigarette and said he had a good appetite."

Two days later Howe told the public the truth, and the front-page headline in the *The New York Times* read: F. D. ROOSEVELT ILL OF POLIOMYELITIS. RECOVERING, DOCTOR SAYS.

Sara was at the train station in Manhattan to meet Franklin and Eleanor and help move her son to Presbyterian Hospital, where he would stay for nearly two months.

32

Grit and Grace

At Presbyterian Hospital, Franklin was under the care of Dr. George Draper, an associate of Dr. Robert Lovett and an acquaintance of Franklin's from Harvard. After studying Franklin's reaction to his disease, the physician wrote: "The psychological factor in his management is paramount. He has such courage, such ambition, and yet at the same time such an extraordinarily sensitive emotional mechanism that it will take all the skill which we can muster to lead him successfully to a recognition of what he really faces without crushing him."

Draper realized that until polio struck, Franklin had been on the cusp of success: at thirty-nine, he was nationally recognized and still hoped to occupy the White House. The doctor was concerned because he saw that Franklin was working toward total recovery, which Draper knew was unlikely. Franklin's unrealistic goal meant agonizing hospital therapy. He did not seem to have a moment's peace: when his body was not being manipulated, his mind was engaged in an ever-flowing correspondence to those hundreds of people (possibly thousands; few letters survive) who had sent him good wishes. Franklin's aim was to stay out of sight—yet remain in the public eye.

One message to a well-wisher less than three days after making his painful orchestrated exit from Campobello typified the lighthearted mood he affected: "I have renewed my youth in a rather unpleasant manner by contracting what was fortunately a rather mild case of infantile paralysis."

Franklin's tone disguised his unexpressed fears, which surfaced only at night when he torpidly slept through his own screaming nightmares. What were his dark apparitions? Perhaps he hallucinated that he lay paralyzed on a golf course, tennis court, or skating rink. Maybe he dreamed that he lay with immovable limbs while his children called him to join in Hare and Hounds or to pilot the bobsled. Franklin would continue to scream in his sleep for the rest of his life, but he never shared his dreams with anyone. He kept his fears private and genially pretended that all was well.

Franklin's paralysis altered the lives of everyone around him. After the Cox-Roosevelt ticket was defeated, Louis Howe found a new position with an oil firm. He was about to begin when Franklin fell ill. Howe quietly quit his job and moved his family to Poughkeepsie (Manhattan was unaffordable) to devote himself to Franklin's recovery. Finally, a distracted Eleanor realized that Howe had been away from work for months and asked him how he could take so much time off. Howe replied, "*This* is my job—helping Franklin." Franklin's legs may have started to wither, but Howe would not let their shared dream of the presidency die on the vine.

Eleanor, Howe, and Sara had a common mission, which was to keep Franklin as healthy and as pain-free as possible. Sara tenaciously protected her son's health, but Eleanor and Howe were also looking ahead to his future. It wasn't that Sara was oblivious to his ambitions; rather, she could see that her son would not have much of a future if he did not make his health top priority. Sara felt strongly that Franklin should return to the country, to Hyde Park, where he could rest and recuperate.

Sara admitted that she wanted Franklin to go to the country to get his strength back immediately following his hospital release. "In the meantime I arranged for his return to Hyde Park where I hoped he would devote himself to his restoration to health and to writing perhaps the book he had always longed to get on paper. But Franklin had no intention of conforming to my quiet ideas for his future existence. He was determined to ignore his disability and carry on from where he had left off. Eleanor entered wholeheartedly into this plan."

Eleanor was fearful that Sara's Hudson River estate would hypnotize Franklin into a peaceful Rip Van Winkle reverie, in which time would lazily drift on and on before he awakened. However, Sara's desire for Franklin to recuperate at home did not necessarily mean that she felt Franklin should remain Hyde Park–bound forever. Perhaps Sara did assume that the presidency was now out of the question—*anyone* in 1921 would have thought so, save Eleanor and Howe—but that does not mean Sara wanted to bury her son alive. Instead, her emphasis was on recuperation as a first step. She was not thinking beyond her son's return to wellness. Sara was not from a background where one worried about long-term planning. You lived your life fully and did your duty, but ambition, if you had it, was to be camouflaged. So Franklin's political hopes were secondary to her at this time.

As she later wrote to Franklin, "All I did was say that if the doctors thought best for you to have for some months a quiet life, I would keep Hyde Park open and live there for a time."

There is certainly external evidence that Sara's fear for Franklin was real. His own nurse was concerned over the extent of his outside activities and wrote a report to Dr. Lovett expressing her worries: "If only his wife could be persuaded that he does not need urging on all day and entertaining all evening, I think he would not be too tired and would do better physically." Franklin's physiotherapist also told the doctor, "The nurse seems to think that there is a good deal too much pushing ahead being done by the wife and Mr. H." Franklin's two professional caregivers knew that Dr. Lovett thought that overexercising a leg muscle was "worse than its disuse" and would lead to "permanent loss." Sara's concerns for her son's physical recovery were well founded.

Eleanor, of course, also had Franklin's health as her primary concern. Yet both she and Howe were completely reliant on Franklin for their own future and were determined to have a hand in his plans. Although Eleanor had initially questioned whether Franklin still had a political future, Howe assured her that Franklin would be president. This is what she worked toward. Also, Eleanor had strong likes and dislikes—even if she did not always articulate them—and certainly she did not want to be isolated in her mother-in-law's country house with her entire world composed of an inactive husband and five children. Howe, too, was thinking of his own prospects. He had bet on Franklin as presidential material and had already nudged him to the candidacy of the nation's second-highest office. Howe's ambitions for the future would sink or swim with Franklin's.

Franklin also needed to stay on course with life as he knew it. Together, Eleanor, Franklin, and Howe opted for Franklin to return from the hospital to the house on East Sixty-fifth rather than Hyde Park. Sara was disappointed but continued to make life as easy for her son and his family as she could. Eleanor, for example, had worried about how she and Franklin would pay their children's school tuition. Her husband told her not to fret; they could count on Sara for their financial needs. Once Sara realized that Franklin was not returning to Hyde Park, she refocused on helping him at East Sixty-fifth Street. "She was not trying to control his life," said Nina

Roosevelt Gibson. "She was sincerely concerned about his health; most mothers would be!"

Franklin's release date was October 28, 1921. Because Presbyterian Hospital was only a few blocks from the Roosevelt home, Franklin planned to be pushed in a wheelchair from the hospital to the house. Franklin had only one request—to travel at night, in darkness.

"It was not long," wrote Sara, "before he was once again in close touch with all the things that interested him most." Franklin's conduit was Howe. He was by Franklin's side every day—and night, as he actually had moved into 49 East Sixty-fifth and visited his upriver family only on weekends. Howe kept both Franklin and Eleanor in touch with the political world.

Soon Franklin resumed a small amount of law work every day. When he had started at his law firm, he hired Marguerite (Missy) LeHand as his executive secretary. She now came to the house every day and played an important role in his psychological recovery. As Franklin felt better, he continued to conduct most of his business from home. (Even over the next few years, when Franklin was well enough to go into the office, he could not handle the firm's high, narrow front steps. Occasionally, though, he would report in to Fidelity & Deposit, which had a more accessible entrance.)

Sara was terribly proud of the grit and grace of both her son and Eleanor. "Eleanor was magnificent throughout," Sara said. "From the beginning she had realized the importance of keeping up Franklin's morale, and was always cheerful. She had said to me at once, 'You know, Mummy, you must not let Franklin know we are worried,' and through all the weary, worrying months that followed, I never saw her depressed."

Sara adopted Eleanor's tone, and Eleanor, in turn, wrote of her mother-in-law's strength: "I am sure that, out of sight, she wept many hours, but with all of us she was very cheerful." A friend noted that Sara was "wonderfully courageous and plucky, but it's a bitter blow."

The year 1922 brought new adjustments to the household, and everyone felt the tension. Despite Eleanor's outward courage, she later wrote that "in many ways this was the most trying winter of my entire life." Franklin's paralysis was not ebbing, as they had hoped, so the family's focal point increasingly became Franklin's health. The children became afterthoughts. Eleanor and Franklin's youngest son, John, was only five years old at the time. John's daughter Nina Roosevelt Gibson said that her father told her that after the polio struck, "from then on, I had no parents."

Still, Franklin was concerned that his children not be afraid of his paralysis. He demonstrated for them the trapeze arrangement that hung from his ceiling, showing them how he could exercise his arms and upper body and pull himself from his bed into a wheelchair. He'd also point out the muscles he was exercising so that they would not be shocked as his legs atrophied. By the beginning of 1922, he was able to get down on the floor to roughhouse with the boys, and he boasted about his growing upper-body strength. He was deeply grateful that none of the children had caught the disease he had brought home—from where, he wondered: Washington? the Boy Scout camp? the icy bay?—and that knowledge alone seemed to console him.

Nevertheless, the children naturally were hurt and confused by their parents' optimism and silence in the face of their own suppressed panic. The adults in their life, including Sara, did not express fear and thought that by not doing so they were protecting the youngsters. Of course, the children themselves knew that their father was terribly ill and in great pain. At the same time, they were told not to discuss his health with anyone, which must have made them feel as if they were keeping a guilty secret. They saw their household being turned topsy-turvy, yet their parents acted as if everything was fine. The children's own emotions were secondary. The Roosevelts were not purposely insensitive; instead, their attitude was typical of the time and place. The end result, however, was that the boys had no way to cope with their trauma: only teenage Anna was capable of lashing out with the hurt and anger that they all felt.

Eleanor, too, was under tremendous pressure and believed that her first duty was to Franklin. She was not an intuitive mother, and under stress, she needed no additional motivation to find reasons to take her from her children. Sara must have recognized that her grandchildren's inattentive parents had become even more lax. She took on even more child care—at age sixty-eight—and made their happiness her concern. She must have resented some of this responsibility, yet would have found it disloyal to place blame on her own son and daughter-in-law—especially now. Instead, she accused Howe, the only outsider in her midst, of causing disruptions. To a woman who had been raised in a world where kinship and friendship were synonymous, Howe was a constant irritant.

Howe was a strategic genius but was a physically unattractive man, made more so by his failure to bathe, his disheveled and often soiled clothes, his constant cigarette smoking (and complete disregard for ashtrays), and his asthmatic coughing (sometimes without covering his mouth). Few people would welcome him as a permanent houseguest, and certainly he annoyed Sara when she saw him. She uncharacteristically lost her temper in front of Franklin and called Howe "that ugly, dirty little man." She was factually correct but cruel to use such words to describe the man who would devote his life to her son. In any case, her spite only enraged Franklin. Later James said it best: "Louis was ugly and untidy, but his unwavering loyalty to Father was clean and beautiful." However, to explain his grandmother's distaste for the man, he also noted that "most well-bred people" initially disliked Howe.

Anna, too, saw Howe as emblematic of her problems in a household that was emotionally unsupportive of her needs. In the fall, when Franklin had entered the hospital, Eleanor had enrolled sixteen-year-old Anna in Miss Chapin's School. Eleanor paid only a short visit to Miss Chapin and thought she saw a personality resemblance between the headmistress and her beloved Mlle. Souvestre. However, Eleanor did not look very deep into the philosophy of the school and its practices, or she would have seen that the institution was very traditional and, in truth, everything she was coming to stand against. But she was hopeful that here Anna would blossom.

Unfortunately, it was not a time in Anna's life for adapting to yet another new situation. She was unused to the school's teaching techniques; she entered late, after the other girls had formed their own groups; and she found no teacher who paid her any particular attention. "I hated it," she said succinctly. Her grades fell and she made no friends. When she returned home in the afternoon, even her beloved—and somewhat idolized—father was no longer available to her, and sometimes his frustration with a needy adolescent sent her reeling from the room in tears.

On top of the dramatic changes in Anna's life, Eleanor decided—without speaking to Anna first—to give her bedroom to Howe. Anna would have to give up a large sunny third-floor room with private bath and move to a tiny bedroom with a shared bath on the servant's fourth floor. Now the self-absorbed teenager saw her only private space being invaded by a man who would pollute her room with his cigarette smoke and the heavy incense he burned in a futile attempt to disguise the tobacco odor. She felt banished from the family. Anna was also envious of Eleanor's closeness to Howe. She said, "So it was a year of complete withdrawal on my part from Mother, and Granny was feeling very excluded, too." No wonder Anna and Sara became confidantes.

Sara questioned—"with a good insight into my adolescent nature," remembered Anna—why her granddaughter had to move to accommodate Howe and encouraged Anna to protest Eleanor's decision. Sara may have been motivated by her dislike of Howe—or even by feelings of proprietary rights, because she had paid for the house—but it was typical of her strong family feelings to stand up for an unhappy granddaughter. It was at best unthoughtful for Eleanor to dictate that a teenager with so much on her narrow shoulders move to oblige her father's political adviser.

Because Franklin's live-in nurse needed to sleep near him, she took Eleanor's bedroom. Eleanor herself slept on a cot in the youngest boys' room, but as unpleasant as it must have been for her and her sons, it was her own choice. Self-sacrifice was natural to Eleanor, whereas for her teenage daughter it was not. In fact, Eleanor's decision was in keeping with her constant choice of taking physically decumbent positions, always seeking out the lowest position in the room. Sara, however, has been criticized for having sympathized with her granddaughter and indeed may have provoked Anna's running from her parents, weeping, as if much stimulus is needed for a teenage girl's eyes to tear up. Eleanor's unbending reaction to her daughter's pain—she refused to even discuss the issue with Anna—may have exacerbated Anna's anger as much as any encouragement Sara could have given her. It certainly seemed that Eleanor was behaving in the same manner—rigid and authoritarian—Sara has often been accused of. (Later Eleanor did admit that her treatment of Anna was "wrong," but of course her priority was Franklin's health.)

James has noted that by this time, his mother "had failed as a wife and mother, failed to find pleasure in life, failed to make any mark as an independent woman." Of course, she had not "failed," as her eldest son said, but was under intense stress to help Franklin while running a household with five children and a mother-in-law next door. Little wonder that she was at her wit's end. Eleanor was bearing an extraordinary amount of pressure and, in the spring, broke down sobbing as she read to her two youngest boys. She, too, was an afterthought in the family: both Sara's and Howe's primary concern was for Franklin, the children could hardly be expected to be supportive of her, and she had no female friends in whom she confided.

Her husband's goal was to renew his body and his political career, and he typically thought of himself first. In fact, at one point Franklin wanted to discharge both his private nurse and his physiotherapist and have Eleanor do their work. Dr. Draper firmly told him it was an "impossible plan": he thought it was wrong for Franklin to ask his wife, who "is pretty much at the end of her tether with the long hard strain she has been through and I feel that if she had to take on this activity, that the whole situation would collapse." It is a wonder that Eleanor crumbled only once.

With the spring, and Franklin now wearing leg braces, they all—even Eleanor—looked forward to their summer break in Hyde Park.

33

"Eleanor's Work Among the Women"

E leanor sent the children to Sara at Hyde Park as soon as school was out
in late spring 1922. She remained in the city for a few more weeks
while Franklin went to Boston to begin the first of many trips there for
therapy. With five children in the house, Sara had her hands full when Anna
came down first with the measles and then, immediately after, the mumps.
Sara put the girl into bed in her own room and engaged a private nurse to
make sure she was comfortable.

Late one morning on June 6, Eleanor arrived at Hyde Park for a quick
visit to host a luncheon for fifty mayors' wives. Sara made all the arrangements for the luncheon, which she set under the trees to take advantage of
the wonderful weather. Sara wrote Franklin of Eleanor's luncheon visit: "It
was lovely to have her for a few hours." Unfortunately, the children, who
had not seen their mother in days, behaved badly. Sara commented on this,
too: "I fear they were not very good yesterday when poor Eleanor was here.
They do stand a little in awe of me."

Sara was preparing to take Anna and James, sixteen and fifteen years old,
respectively, to France, Switzerland, and England in July. This would be the
elder children's first trip to Europe and their grandmother's special treat to
them. Before the voyage, Eleanor confided in Anna that it had always been

her dream to show Europe to her children herself, but now she could not afford the trip because of Franklin's illness. She did not discuss her feelings with Sara but rather confided in her teenage daughter her disappointment. Anna became more empathetic to her mother—which was a positive step for both of them—but Eleanor echoed her lifelong approach of making complaints *about* Sara, but rarely to Sara.

Franklin arrived in Hyde Park in July. With Sara and the elder children gone, he and Eleanor could spend time with Elliott, Franklin Jr., and John. Franklin was eager to show the boys his new crutches, and he demonstrated the specially devised parallel bars that Sara had installed for him in the back of the house. She had also put in a ramp that enabled him to reach his bedroom above the library, had left him his father's old-style wheelchair with its wicker back, and had tested the house's small trunk elevator for Franklin's weight so that he could lift himself upstairs hauling on its ropes. Vincent Astor, his neighbor to the north in Rhinebeck, told Franklin to use his heated pool whenever he liked.

Summer at Hyde Park gave Franklin and Eleanor a much-needed rest, although Franklin kept busy with at least two hours of daily exercise as well as a heavy load of correspondence. He and Howe had gone through the list of Franklin's numerous organizations and removed his name from active participation in many, keeping only those most important. He retained the presidency of the Boy Scout Foundation of Greater New York, for example, and his first public statement since his hospitalization called for more volunteer scoutmasters. When Franklin wrote about his work to an old friend who was now part of the postwar group of American expatriates in Europe, he was startled to receive the man's guidance that he should try to limit Boy Scout membership to those of "Nordic stock."

Franklin fired back: "If you were familiar with the Boys Scouts you would realize that thousands of Scouts are of Jewish origins. . . . I want to suggest that you come back home and spend the next few years in getting to know your own country."

His lack of parochialism is further illustrated by the fund-raising he and Rosy did for the construction of Manhattan's Cathedral of St. John the Divine, which was chartered as a house of prayer for all people. Franklin carefully stated, "There need never be fear that the Cathedral will represent a narrow or blind doctrine." Franklin also continued certain political activities, including chairing the Woodrow Wilson Foundation.

Still, Franklin subtly adopted Sara's perspective that his health should come first, and he spent the next several years either in therapy or vacationing in warm climates, still in the hope of a full recovery. He did not give up politics but rather deferred his ambitions, passing up repeated informal overtures to run as New York's Democratic gubernatorial or Senate candidate.

Sara revealed her own political interests in letters to Eleanor and Franklin discussing the New York political scene. Her correspondence makes it clear that she supported the auxiliary work Eleanor was doing on Franklin's behalf, which she had demonstrated more tangibly in June by opening her house to the mayors' wives. On August 28 Sara wrote from London: "I am so pleased to get a clipping from Aunt Annie saying that Mr. Al Smith will accept the nomination for governor, giving his letter to 'Frank.' It will save us from [New York publisher William Randolph] Hearst who is a truly great danger, and I hope he will be nominated and elected.

"Eleanor's work among the women, will, I trust, bear fruit."

Not only did Eleanor's work produce dividends for Franklin, but her efforts turned her into a pacesetting political wife. Howe talked to her constantly about her role in Franklin's future, and she realized that Howe could be her lifeline as well as Franklin's. Because Howe believed in Eleanor—and, more important, needed her support for Franklin—he urged her to get out into the public eye. Franklin backed him up, although Eleanor never found her unfamiliar tasks congenial. Each day was difficult; she could barely tolerate the thought of going to new places by herself to speak at civic and political meetings for the purpose of making friends for Franklin or just reminding people that he was in the wings.

Gradually, Howe's persuasion and Franklin's cajoling had their effect. She later commented that "my husband was skilled in using people and, even though I was his wife, I think he used me in his career as he used other people." Without Franklin's illness and Howe's encouragement, Eleanor might never have found a public role for herself. Her transformation into a political figure in her own right would take a decade to develop, but she was well on her way.

Howe sat down with Eleanor to work out her schedule. The plan was for her to stump for Al Smith in his 1922 race for governor (he had been defeated two years earlier in the Republican tidal wave of 1920), and she started by practicing the short talks she would give in Dutchess County. She repeated her speeches perhaps as many as one hundred times before she was comfortable with her presentation. Together, she and Howe calmed her nervous laugh and lowered her high-pitched voice. Eleanor was undergoing a stunning metamorphosis and made small gains every week. She had great potential, but it took dedication and hard work for her to realize it.

Rosy took his usual tongue-in-cheek attitude toward her activities. He warned Franklin: "It's only the beginning. Once they mount the soapbox, mark my words, they never get off."

That summer Eleanor drove to her campaign stops. She was a poor driver and had no license: driver's licenses were not yet required. Coming home one summer day, she turned the car awkwardly into Sara's long driveway and slammed into one of the brown gateposts that had originally been brought from Mount Hope. She wrote Sara, still in Europe with Anna and James, a letter of abject apology. Sara lightly sent word back: "Your running into our gate post was all right, so long as you were not hurt. I am sure after this you are becoming an expert chauffeur. It is the only thing to do now, and if I were not 100 years old I would learn!" (Sara was actually sixty-eight.)

The accident forgotten, Eleanor shouldered Franklin's burden and stumped for Smith throughout Dutchess County. Although Smith lost this traditionally Republican enclave, he carried the state and was indebted to Eleanor—and, more important, Franklin. Franklin's legs may have been paralyzed, but with Smith's election, it was clear that his political muscle was still strong. So was Eleanor's: no less than *The New York Times* referred to her sophisticated politicking.

Now Eleanor began to resume some of the interests she had taken up pre-polio and had given up abruptly when her life was put on hold. She took typing and shorthand lessons, wrote legislative reports for the New York State League of Women Voters, and became finance chair of the women's committee of the state Democratic party. For the first time, she made women friends who were outside her family circle, although not necessarily outside her social realm.

A woman with the unlikely name of Narcissa Cox Vanderlip took Eleanor under her wing. Vanderlip had attended the University of Chicago and, when Eleanor met her, was married with six children and still had time to head the state League of Women Voters. She persuaded Eleanor to join, for there was much overlap between the social reforms supported by the league and those promulgated earlier in the century by tenement social workers. Most prominent were child labor, pure milk and food regulations (mostly an urban issue), and, of course, the need for women to vote and vote wisely. Vanderlip was herself a Republican but was convinced that women had common causes, no matter what their party.

A few months before Franklin's polio struck, Eleanor had attended a fiery league convention at which Carrie Chapman Catt—the sixty-one-year-old woman who deserves credit for passage of the women's suffrage amendment—gave a strongly worded speech calling for women of peaceful interests to unite. Eleanor had duly noted the speech to Franklin but ended her letter with "Much, much love dear and I prefer doing my politics with you."

Now she had no choice: she would have to make a place for herself in the league as well as represent Franklin's interests in the Democratic party. Eleanor, like most women, had less formal education than a number of the league's officers, who were college educated or even possessed graduate or professional degrees. Eleanor wrote her legislative reports, for example, under the guidance of Elizabeth Read, an attorney who had earned her law degree at the University of Pennsylvania. Read's partner was Esther Lape, who had taught college for a number of years and now worked as a reporter and publicist for women's causes.

Eleanor's new friends included Marion Dickerman and her partner, Nancy Cook. Dickerman was a college dean who had actually run for office but was defeated, not surprising in an era when women had just received the vote. Cook headed the women's division of the Democratic party. In this brilliant crowd, Eleanor was not a luminary, but she was a hard worker who was willing to learn.

While Eleanor toiled, Franklin concentrated on his health, taking four lengthy Florida houseboat trips, which removed him from both Eleanor and the children for long periods in the years 1923 to 1926. His first trip began in March 1923 on a rented houseboat. With half a dozen companions, he enjoyed a lengthy fishing cruise along the Florida coast, believing that the waters brought him more progress than exercising on bars at home, perhaps because he was able to concentrate solely on the activity. In Florida he could also escape his wife's constant reminders about doing his exercises, which often had the opposite effect of what she wished. He swam for hours and proclaimed to whoever was around, "The water put me where I am, and the water has to bring me back."

Eleanor accompanied him for a few days on this first Florida trip. She did not enjoy fishing and was bored. When one man caught a jewfish (a kind of tarpon), she quipped, "I thought we left New York to get *away* from Jews." Over the next few years, Eleanor visited Franklin occasionally on his boating trips—often to celebrate their March 17 anniversary—but she actually preferred her work in New York. The houseboat was not her favorite form of relaxation: lazy days in the sun with cool rum drinks held little appeal to this serious-minded woman, and she disliked Florida's mosquitoes and its nighttime coastal winds. However, she did enjoy bringing her new women friends down to Florida for long, intense conversations.

Sara and Eleanor hoped that his trips would contribute to his recovery. When Franklin returned to Hyde Park after his first Florida voyage, Sara burst into tears when she caught sight of his new long sideburns, now gone gray. The muttonchops caused him to bear an uncanny likeness to his father, and Sara found this resemblance too hard to take. She begged him to shave immediately.

In early 1924 Franklin took his first cruise on a new houseboat that he had bought with his friend John Lawrence, who was also partially paralyzed below the waist. They named it *Larooco* (*Lawrence, Roosevelt and Company*). Eleanor did not accompany Franklin on his three-month cruise on February 2. Instead, a group of friends, including Louis Howe, would come and go as the houseboat cruised from St. Augustine down to the Florida Keys.

Missy LeHand served as hostess and assisted Franklin with a small amount of office work. *Larooco's* crew included a valet to assist Franklin, as well as a captain whose wife served as chef. Except for Franklin's exercise time, every day was a party day according to his log: "Gave all hands opportunity to go to Church. No takers." Franklin was partly play-acting: there were many days when "it was noon before he could pull himself out of depression and greet his guests wearing his lighthearted facade," remembered Missy.

Despite the outwardly festive atmosphere and months of close companionship, it is unlikely that Franklin's relationship with Missy went beyond a warm friendship. His health aside, there could be no secrets on a small houseboat, and surely one of Franklin's many guests would have commented, in the intervening years, on any nighttime giggles or stateroom-hopping. He was also a paternal figure to her (her own father had deserted his family), which Franklin recognized, sometimes signing his notes to her, "Father." In addition, Franklin could not have forgotten that Sara came precariously close to cutting off his financial lifeline a few years earlier; surely when he needed his mother's money more than ever, he would not risk being cast adrift.

In fact, Missy was exactly what was worrying Sara: she did not like Franklin's having an attractive single woman as his sunny companion for three months. Sara later commented that it was unfortunate that men could become "completely dependent on a nurse or a secretary" and said that her own husband had thought it judicious to avoid keeping a particular nurse "longer than a few days." Eleanor joked to her husband, "I haven't told Mama that Missy is back [on the houseboat] because I think she has more peace of mind when she doesn't know such things!"

Life north of Florida took its usual rhythm. Sara wrote Franklin: "This week the Flower Show is on and I feel a little hurried and busy, as I like a quiet life and yet hate to miss things, a sad contradiction!" Yet when James was confirmed in the Episcopal Church, Sara represented his parents at the ritual.

James now enjoyed having Elliott as his schoolmate at Groton. The younger boy's transition to boarding school was less traumatic than James's had been by virtue of Elliott's having an elder brother to show him the ropes.

However, Elliott was unhappy at Groton and asked permission to live with his grandmother and attend Hyde Park's high school. Eleanor deferred the decision to Franklin, who forbade it—long-distance, from the Florida houseboat.

"Looking back on this period," James said, "I must say in all honesty that neither Anna, nor my brothers, nor I had the guidance and training that I think Father would have given us had he not been involved in his own struggle to re-establish a useful life for himself."

Immediately after visiting James and Elliott at Groton, Sara entertained thirty-five of Eleanor's colleagues from the Women's Trade Union League. The next day Sara wrote Franklin, as frustrated as Eleanor had been about the poor turnout: "Eleanor and I had a WTU tea yesterday, 600 invitations sent out about 30 came!! Hardly worth while was it?"

Sara hosted a luncheon Eleanor was giving for thirty-five representatives of the National Council of Women at East Sixty-fifth Street. Among the women was Mary McLeod Bethune, president of the National Association of Colored Women. Bethune remembered:

> I can still see the twinkle in Mrs. James Roosevelt's eyes as she noted the apprehensive glances cast my way by the Southern women who had come to the affair. Then she did a remarkable thing. Very deliberately, she took my arm and seated me to the right of Eleanor Roosevelt, the guest of honor! I can remember, too, how the faces of the Negro servants lit up with pride. . . .
>
> From that moment, my heart went out to Mrs. James Roosevelt . . . and our friendship became one of the most treasured relationships of my life.

Besides Sara's continuing support of Eleanor's political and civic activities, nearly every weekend she had Anna (who did not go away to school and was still suffering at Miss Chapin's), Franklin Jr., and John with her at Hyde Park. "Little Franklin," Sara wrote her son, "says he will not farm, or become a lawyer, but just be President of the United States."

In the spring Anna graduated from Miss Chapin's, although her pleasure at getting out of school dissipated when she was forced into a Newport debut during its annual Tennis Week. As Anna related, "I was informed that I had to come out in society, and I died. And I wasn't going to come out. And Granny said, 'You are.' And I went to Mother, and she said, 'Yes, you must!'" She added, "I couldn't go to Father. . . . He would never give me the time of day." Sara, of course, bought her gown and other necessary outfits.

Perhaps Franklin had a reason not to attend his daughter's coming-out, but Eleanor—who made Anna go through the same ritual she had hated—

did not even attend her own daughter's debut. Instead, she relied on Susie Parish to chaperone her. Maybe Susie resented having to take care of another generation of Roosevelts and did not approve of Eleanor's shuttling her daughter off for the week. She may also have felt burdened by having to take on the myriad duties, including chaperoning this young slim beauty with long, wavy blond hair, that are part of a parent's responsibility. In any case, Susie maliciously used the opportunity to tell Anna of her father's love for Miss Mercer. The only good that came out of this gossip was that Anna—a deeply sensitive young woman—empathized with her mother's plight. "I felt very strongly on Mother's side."

As a reward for enduring the debut, Sara again took Anna to Europe. Anna wondered why her grandmother "should . . . have planned (before we left the U.S.) for us to have an audience with the Pope at the Vatican? She had grown up a Unitarian and became a low church Episcopalian only when she married my grandfather." Of course, Sara had always been curious about other religions and believed that all should be respected. Anna—who was aware of how young Italian men "liked my blue eyes and very blond hair"— also disliked having to accompany Sara to a formal meeting with Benito Mussolini, who at the time was at the height of popularity. Anna confided to her diary: "Granny and I have been bickering all day. And it's been my fault all the time. . . . Oh! Damn."

In June 1924 Franklin made his first important post-polio public appearance when he nominated Al Smith, a Roman Catholic, to be the Democratic presidential candidate. James, sixteen, served as Franklin's liege man to hand him his crutches and act as his father's emergency support. Franklin swung from his hips to walk the short distance to the podium and stood for thirty minutes as he gave his talk. A Hunter College undergraduate later characterized how he moved:

> [He] got to his feet with the help of James and his cane. . . . We held our breath as Roosevelt started to walk the eight steps to the podium. For a moment, he did not move at all, as if his feet were fixed to the ground. Then, overcoming the inertia of his large frame, he dragged his right leg sideways and forward and rolled his body after it, leaning on James to keep him from falling. Meanwhile, he started rolling his left leg forward to take a step on the other side. In this way, rolling from side to side, he moved ahead.

Franklin's appearance to nominate Smith (who lost the Democratic nomination to John W. Davis) would be, nearly three decades later, dramatized in the 1958 play (and 1960 movie) *Sunrise at Campobello*, written by Dore Schary. Franklin's nomination of Smith is the drama's final scene and enacts Franklin's full return to politics. However, Franklin's nomination speech was more symbol than reality: he would not become completely active for several more years.

Earlier in 1924 Franklin heard about amazing improvements in polio patients at Warm Spings, Georgia. In October, Franklin traveled to Warm Springs with Eleanor and LeHand to see if exercise in its warm mineralized waters could improve his walking gait. He moved into his own cabin and engaged a cook. He wrote Sara: "The pool is very effective as a Tonic after illness." He added that his nurse was "very keen about my muscle improvement. They are *all* stronger & this daily work in the pool is just what they need." Eleanor left him after he settled in, and he returned to New York six weeks later. A few months later, in February 1925, he took his second trip on the *Larooco* with LeHand and others. The elder children—Anna, James, and Elliott—had started to make visits to the houseboat. Eleanor went down in March for their anniversary, nursing an unspoken but legitimate grudge. She had been hospitalized in New York for a gynecological procedure, a dilation and curettage. Franklin had not called, sent flowers, or even written to her in the hospital or at home. After all that she had done for him, it seemed unthinkable that he would be so self-centered, but she did not broach the topic with him directly; instead, she merely asked him if he had received her letter about the hospitalization.

The 1925 houseboat trip ended in April, and Franklin returned to Warm Springs for more rehabilitation. He wrote Sara of an amazing coincidence that occurred when he was traveling in Atlanta:

> In the afternoon an old gray-headed negro came in—I recognized his face but could not place him. He looked at me hard & then said, "Yes, it certainly is Mr. James Roosevelt's boy!"
>
> It was William Yapp of Car 500! [The former porter of the Roosevelts' private Delaware and Hudson railcar.] I told him all about you—& he was thrilled—I think it would be nice if you would send him a line.

Franklin's life was falling into an easy routine: cruising in Florida at the beginning of each year and then going to Warm Springs. Franklin and Eleanor stopped joining the Delano family in Fairhaven for Thanksgiving and instead celebrated it at Warm Springs. They spent Christmas at Hyde Park and their March 17 anniversary on the Florida houseboat. Sara had injured her knee during her European trip with the children three years earlier and was now feeling the effects of arthritis. She reduced her number of short trips, and although she would go to Warm Springs, she refused to visit Franklin's semi-bachelor houseboat.

Sara faithfully wrote him of the work taking place on his behalf. On July 27 she sent him a note from Hyde Park: "Just a line to say that your Democratic gathering went off very well, I think 200 people came. Eleanor presided and made several excellent little remarks in her charming way." She also mentioned that she had lunched with friends and met Bishop Manning (the celebrated Episcopal bishop of the Cathedral of St. John the Divine),* who said that he was praying for Franklin's recovery. "He is very nice and very open-minded and liberal and I think, not narrow in anyway. As Bishop, he has to uphold the church laws, and certainly he had had especially difficult questions to cope with."

That summer Anna began studying agriculture, eventually taking courses at Cornell University. Oddly, Eleanor did not encourage Anna to earn a degree. "College for me was never even discussed that I remember," Anna said, so the classes she took were not part of a degree program. Sara, too, was against higher education for her granddaughter. At this point Sara feared that Anna would turn into a "bookworm," she said, or a bluestocking—or perhaps something *worse,* now that Sara had seen Eleanor's new college-educated friends who were so "mannish."

In any case, Anna went off to school resenting Eleanor's inadequate mothering. James said that "Anna accused him [Howe] of stealing mother's attentions from her. He did. And he did not care. He felt mother was needed more in public than her private life, that she had a higher destiny than merely being a mother. Anna was sacrificed to the cause, as we all were in a way. Anna argued bitterly with her mother about her sacrifice, and when she got to college she refused to answer mother's letters."

In August, Franklin found a new doctor who offered a different approach to polio. "I can think of you there and beginning the treatment," Sara wrote. "I feel so hopeful and confident! Once able to move about with crutches and without braces, strength will come and now for the first time in more than a year I feel that *work* is to be done for *you,* my dearest."

Franklin maintained his own optimism. In November he wrote his mother: "I find each day very fully occupied and everything is going well." Franklin had become enamored of Warm Springs's potential and was determined to buy it and run it as he wished. In February 1926 he left for Florida with Eleanor,

*Manning is mentioned in social references of the period from ski lodge guest lists to the Cole Porter lyrics in "You're the Top": "You're a Nathan panning, you're Bishop Manning, you're broccoli."

writing Sara that it would be his "last year in Florida waters if I can buy Warm Springs." Later in the month a representative of the center met with Franklin on the *Larooco* to negotiate the sale. Of course, to run it as he wished, Franklin would need investors. That month he wrote Sara that "it looks as if I had bought Warm Springs. If so, I want you to take a great interest in it, for I feel you can help me with many suggestions, and the place, properly run, will not only do a great deal of good, but will prove financially successful."

At the end of March, Franklin left the *Larooco* to sell the houseboat to raise funds for Warm Springs. By the end of April, he had acquired the entire property by transferring about $200,000 from his trust, more than two-thirds of his net worth.

Eleanor's concern over Franklin's committing so much of his personal fortune to a health center for polio patients was set aside in March. Sara's beloved elder sister Annie Hitch, age seventy-seven, died at her home in Algonac. It was nearly ten years to the day since Algonac had burned down. The Delanos were comforted by the knowledge that Dora had been living with Annie at the time of her death. (In 1921, when Dora's second husband, Paul Forbes, had died, Dora had left Paris and moved into Algonac with Annie.) Their brother Frederick had just left for Persia and could not return for the funeral, but three of the four remaining siblings were there.

Franklin received his mother's telegram on his houseboat at Long Key and prepared to take a train home. He wrote her: "Still I know it is as dear Aunt Annie would have wished it, active up to the last. It is no wonder people in every walk of life in Newburgh loved her. I shall always be glad that she and Aunt Doe [Dora] spent the last Christmas with us at Hyde Park."

Franklin attended Annie's funeral in Newburgh but remained in Hyde Park while the family left for her burial in Fairhaven. He returned to Warm Springs with Elliott while James went from Groton to attend Annie's memorial service with Sara, who wrote, as she so often did, that "Eleanor has been lovely and sympathetic and sweet to me."

Although Sara typified the Delano family's hands-on philanthropy and their generous donations to many just causes, Annie's charitable work on behalf of the people of Newburgh was extraordinary. Out of appreciation, the city lowered its flags to half-mast, and all stores closed for her funeral.

34

Splintered

By 1926 the Roosevelt family had splintered. Franklin was in Warm Springs for much of each year, and Eleanor was with her friends in Manhattan or at Val-Kill, the house that she was building at Hyde Park. Anna was engaged to be married, James and Elliott were at Harvard, Franklin Jr. was at Groton, and only John remained at school in Manhattan, supervised by his governess. Sara remained a constant at Hyde Park: always willing and able to assume a supportive role in her son's recovery as well as his political future, to assist Eleanor in her work with women's groups, and to help with the grandchildren. Sara's 1915 house expansion was proving useful, as the grandchildren were now also bringing their friends to her house. Sister Dora remained at Algonac with Frederick and his wife, who had moved in after Annie's death.

Eleanor had found a material way to express her need for separation from her family and Sara, finally achieving physical and emotional distance. Even when Sara was in Europe, Hyde Park made Eleanor uncomfortable because she felt unable to escape Sara's presence. She wrote Franklin that "there is no doubt in my mind but houses reflect the central spirit and are just empty shells without them!"

Eleanor began to put physical barriers between herself and Sara. In Man-

hattan she moved a large breakfront to block the opening between her dining room and Sara's because she was tired of Sara sliding the doors open to
check on Eleanor's table before guests arrived. Eleanor also wanted locks
installed on the other connecting doors to block her mother-in-law's casual
entrances. Now she needed to separate herself from Sara when they were at
Hyde Park, which was more difficult since the house did not belong to
Eleanor.

One late autumn day Eleanor and her friends Cook and Dickerman
lamented that they would no longer be able to visit their favorite picnic
spot along Fallkill Creek, on Franklin's piece of property abutting Sara's
land. Sara planned to close up Hyde Park until the Christmas holidays, and
the women would have no place to get together in the country. Franklin,
who had accompanied them on the picnic, brightly suggested that the
three women build a small residence on that particular site, about a mile and
a half east of Sara's house, to use just for themselves, year-round. One of
Franklin's delightful personality traits was his openness to others, including
his wife's new friends. He also liked nothing better than a project, so he
drew up the necessary papers, hired an architect, and put himself in charge
of the construction, which was completed in 1926.

The house became known as Val-Kill, picking up on the old Dutch word
for the location. Franklin must have homed in on the name, for he loved
local history and emphasized (in fact, exaggerated) his Dutch roots whenever possible. He threw himself into the plans and masterminded the project. He told the architect that the building must be stone to recall a Dutch
colonial farmhouse—albeit with conveniences that included an outdoor
swimming pool, a rarity in private houses of the time.

Franklin may have intuited that the stress of his polio on Eleanor would
be eased by her friendship with her chums. Val-Kill became if not Eleanor's
fortress, then her buffer against the rest of her troublesome world. There,
she could escape both her mother-in-law and her children, for they usually
stayed in the Big House—as Sara's house was beginning to be called to differentiate it from Eleanor's house—with their grandmother, leaving Eleanor
her freedom. Eleanor did not want to emphasize the distance between herself and Franklin; his opinion was crucial to Eleanor's independence as well
as her friends' ventures. "We always tried to help her in every way we could
and also to build bridges back to him," Dickerman remembered.

Val-Kill was a lovely place with great charm, but it seemed odd to Sara
that Eleanor needed another residence for herself and her friends, who were
always welcome in Sara's house. "Can you tell me why Eleanor wants to go
over to the Val-Kill cottage to sleep every night?" Sara would ask Florence
Stewart Kerr, another friend of Eleanor's. "Why doesn't she sleep here? This

is her home. This is her house. Why does she—she waits until late evening, and then gets in her car and goes over there to sleep and we don't see her until the next morning."

As Kerr recalled, "I thought I knew why, but I said, 'Don't you suppose that maybe it's quieter? And there's a lovely pool over there, maybe she swims.'"

Sara responded, "Well, I think she belongs here, and I don't know why she goes over there every night. If she wants to swim, she can go sometime during the day."

Kerr realized that Sara wasn't so much complaining as she was trying to understand the situation. "Puzzled, puzzled" was how Kerr described Sara. However, Sara saw that the house was important to Eleanor—and perceived, too, that Franklin wanted it for his wife. This must have perplexed Sara, for Franklin was certainly an atypical husband to suggest that his wife build a separate dwelling. Moreover, the three women received housewarming gifts from friends that resembled wedding gifts, bearing the combined initials E.M.N. (Eleanor Roosevelt, Marion Dickerman, and Nancy Cook). Val-Kill was an adult version of a "no boys allowed" tree house—one designed by a husband.

Despite Sara's puzzlement, she played hostess to both Eleanor's and Franklin's friends as if they were her own. "She was gracious to all of them, of course," wrote Franklin's biographer Geoffrey Ward. In fact, she showed real affection by suggesting to Cook and Dickerman that they call her "Granny" rather than "Mrs. Roosevelt." For a woman of Sara's era, when one always addressed others outside the family, particularly one's elders, by their last names, she showed a fond acceptance of her daughter-in-law's friends and all they represented. Her adaptability was amazing: soon she was writing Franklin that "Eleanor is so happy over there [at Val-Kill] that she looks well and plump, don't tell her so, it is very becoming."

Sara quietly supported the women's social reforms, even when they conflicted with her own interests. Earlier, during a strike by the United Mine Workers, Marion Dickerman had gone to West Virginia and western Pennsylvania to see conditions for herself. It was depressing: the striking miners had been dispossessed of their company houses and were living in tents pitched on muddy ground with their wives and children. If that wasn't enough, the owners would then buy the fields the tents occupied and throw the miners' families off that land, too. After seeing this, Dickerman said she "went over to the Vittondale Mine, where the men were not on strike. It was very different. The houses were much nicer. There were blue morning glories growing on the terraces. But no unionist was allowed—if he set foot in, he was arrested." When she asked the men why they weren't supporting the nearby strikers, they told Dickerman, "We feel our loyalty is first to our families."

"It was a very, very disturbing experience, and shortly after I was back they called me from Hyde Park and asked me to come up for a weekend. I went up, and I was so full of what I had been through that it was hard to talk about anything else. At dinner, I said quite a bit, and I mentioned this mine at Vittondale. I noticed there was silence, but I thought they were just getting bored."

When it was time to retire, Franklin asked Dickerman to talk with him a little longer, by themselves. "Did you know that the Vittondale mine was a Delano mine?" he asked her.

"I then understood why Granny had been a little cool at dinner."

Dickerman was speechless, but Franklin assured her that "Uncle Fred is in charge of that. I'm going to call him and ask him to come over and talk to us."

With Sara's full knowledge and understanding—for she had a stake in the mine left to her by James—Frederick came the next day from Algonac and had a long talk with Franklin and Dickerman about the conditions she had seen. Franklin told him, "You know, Uncle Fred, as long as those conditions exist, my family does not want any of the income from that mine. And I'll appreciate your seeing to it."

Although Franklin and Howe were friends with Eleanor's women friends—indeed, Franklin would be hurt if left out of any of their festivities—they reverted to adolescent behavior when they poked fun at Cook, Dickerman, and others behind their backs—"he-shes," they called them, as Eleanor's granddaughter Ellie Roosevelt Seagraves remembered. Alice Roosevelt termed the women "female impersonators." Rosy joked, ironically as always, to Franklin, "Hope your Parlour Socialists are not living too much on the fat of the land with you, against their principles!!" Sara may have been puzzled by Eleanor's desire for independence, but she was never mean and never joined in the name-calling.

Eleanor was proud of her house and had "Val-Kill Cottage" stationery printed. She also used Val-Kill as an experiment in progressive labor. By the time the residence was ready, Eleanor, Cook, Dickerman, and a fourth friend, Caroline O'Day, who had worked for suffrage and was an organizer of Democratic women, had founded the Val-Kill Furniture Factory. They hired skilled local men to construct early-American-style furniture. The group began working from the house and eventually expanded to a two-story structure built nearby—this one, however, made of functional cinder block and without charm. Now their residence was dubbed Stone Cottage, a term used to differentiate the home from the Val-Kill manufacturing site. The first pieces of furniture were sent to Warm Springs to decorate Franklin's cottage and served as a material link between the couple, who lacked a physical connection.

Although Eleanor took pride in the work of Val-Kill Industries, she still felt less competent than the women professionals whose circle she inhabited. Her self-esteem was still so low that she had said, "If I had to go out and earn my living, I doubt that I'd even make a very good cleaning woman." Marion Dickerman was teaching at Todhunter School in Manhattan, a progressive school that emphasized the arts: a school Anna might have preferred over Miss Chapin's. Winifred Todhunter, its owner, wished to retire to England and needed a buyer. Together, Eleanor and Dickerman purchased the school, and Eleanor—although she lacked a college degree—began teaching classes in American history, American literature, and English. She patterned herself after Mlle. Souvestre and, with Dickerman, admitted Jewish children to the school, though "not too large a proportion," said Eleanor's biographer Blanche Wiesen Cook.

Being Eleanor, she initially felt that she was not a talented teacher. Eventually she hit her stride and included modern social issues in her curriculum. She found her old notebooks from her London schooldays and used them to guide her as she took students on field trips to such events as police lineups. "Teaching gave her some of the happiest moments in her life," Dickerman noted.

Her own children were more problematic. Anna's beauty and kindness attracted men, and the nineteen-year-old began dating a twenty-nine-year-old suitor, Curtis B. Dall, a New York stockbroker. Anna soon dropped out of school to prepare for her June 1926 wedding to Curtis, whom she adored (although her younger brothers thought him pompous). Dall could be charming to adults, and he used this guile to win over Sara. The young couple were thrilled when she offered to purchase a swank Manhattan apartment for them as a wedding gift.

As with most of her gifts to the grandchildren, she did not inform Eleanor and Franklin beforehand; she felt that her presents were her decision and that they should not be subject to approval or veto. This time, anticipating trouble, Sara explicitly told Anna not to tell her mother, because Eleanor might want them to refuse such an extravagant gift. Still, Anna let the secret out, and Eleanor's fury in turn angered Sara so much that she said she would not go through with her plans if Eleanor disapproved.

Now Anna and Curtis were upset. Eleanor wrote Franklin in Florida: "It is all I can do to be decent. . . . I've reached a state of such constant self-control I'm afraid of what will happen if it ever breaks."

Sara explained her feelings in a letter to Franklin. "I am sorry I could not consult with you and Eleanor, but as it is my wedding present, I felt I should do it alone, also two other people had options on it."

Eleanor feared that the luxurious apartment would mean unanticipated expenses for a young couple and that such an address would imply wealth they did not actually enjoy. She may also have realized that the couple would need to rely on Sara to staff the large home and keep up with its costs. Eleanor may have wanted to shield Anna from being as dependent on Sara's largesse as she and Franklin continued to be. Eleanor knew by now the emotional strings attached to financial dependency.

Eleanor had progressed enough emotionally that she could write to Sara about her displeasure. Sara apologized, responding candidly:

Eleanor, dear, I am very sorry that I hurt you—twice, first by not letting Anna tell you before it was decided & then by saying I would not give it to them. I certainly am old enough not to make mistakes & I can only say how much I regret—I did not think I *could* be nasty *or* mean, & I fear I had too good an opinion of myself. Also, I love you dear too much to ever want to hurt you. I *was hasty*, & of course I shall give them the apartment. I only wanted them to decide for themselves & surprise you & Franklin—No doubt he will also be angry with me—Well, I must just bear it.

Eleanor tried to rouse Franklin from his Florida repose by forwarding Sara's letter to him and adding a note that contradicted her earlier angry letter: "I've been thoroughly nasty, but I'll try to behave again now for a time." Franklin would not be brought into the apartment dispute, perhaps realizing the hypocrisy of protest, given that his own family's New York town house was a gift from Sara. Rather than being frustrated by her husband's passivity toward his mother, Eleanor saw his attitude as a sign of a noble nature. Eleanor wrote Franklin that she had told Sara that he was not angry, because he "never demeaned" himself "by getting angry over little things."

The younger children generated less controversy. James was at Harvard and so was Elliott, even though Elliott had wanted to attend Princeton (gasp) rather than the alma mater of his father and Uncle Rosy. However, Franklin gave him no choice and Eleanor would not intervene. The elder children's rites of passage made Eleanor realize that her offspring were growing up and that she had missed their childhood through her reliance on Sara and the governesses. Elliott later wrote of Eleanor: "She felt that she had not personally done enough with Sis, Jimmy and me. Consequently, we were too close to Granny and not close enough to her. She was determined that things would be different with Franklin Jr. and Johnny."

Eleanor tried to start over by taking the younger boys on a camping trip. But this was not to be a family event—she also brought Cook and Dickerman, who "became irritated by my rowdy brothers," said Elliott, "and proceeded to show it." The group planned to stop along the road and camp at various farms, which was customary during a time without strict camping-permit requirements or many state or national park sites.

One day the entourage received a hostile reception. When Eleanor asked permission to spend the night on the property of a farm, the farmer took a long look at Cook and Dickerman, and their man-styled trousers and ties. He did not like what he saw. "Where are your husbands?" he queried.

Eleanor responded, "Mine is not with me, and the others do not have husbands."

"I don't want women of that kind," he said.

The troupe had to return to the car and look for another site. All in all, the trip was a disaster. Eleanor was exhausted by watching the three boys (Franklin Jr. and John were allowed to bring a friend with them), and the boys showed outright hostility toward her new friends. Elliott summed it up: "Mother's year-round schedule of keeping busy meant that she had limited time for her family, and she had been disillusioned about togetherness with her children after the horrendous camping trip; it was the first and last of its kind."

Franklin had never enjoyed the practice of law and had resigned from Emmet and Marvin in 1924, keeping his position with Fidelity. The next year he opened a firm named Roosevelt and O'Connor, although in actuality he did little work for it. Franklin still hoped to walk and considered therapy his primary job.* Therefore, his income suffered. At the same time, Eleanor was taking a larger role in the outside world and realized that she had the ability to earn money. Although working for income was unusual for a woman of her class, she enjoyed the tangible rewards of a paycheck, whether it was from teaching at Todhunter or her first published article in *Success* magazine, "What I Want Most Out of Life." Her sons were hostile toward their mother's activities. The next year Eleanor wrote Franklin:

---

*"Walking" to Franklin and his doctors meant being mobile with the use of canes or crutches and leg braces. By 1927 he had realized that he would always need auxiliary aids to walk.

"James will tell me he would not write for such a magazine, as he did about the *Redbook*. But I am glad of the chance!" On the other hand, Anna supported her mother's efforts and eventually went into journalism herself.

Eleanor began to enjoy her public recognition: in fact, in 1927 she authorized magazine ads for Simmons mattresses. The advertisement shows her maid in a bedroom on East Sixty-fifth Street, standing near a stripped bed displaying a Simmons mattress and bedsprings. Eleanor's photograph is prominently framed on the page. The ad is headed "Mrs. Franklin D. Roosevelt says, 'I've never known such comfort.'" Eleanor had come a long way from her days in Albany, when she was horrified when strangers recognized her.

To an outsider, the Franklin D. Roosevelt family may have appeared wealthy, but with such a large clan living in so many different locations, there were financial strains. A secretive Franklin kept Eleanor in the dark about their finances, which added to her stress. "I had no idea how much personal income he had," Eleanor admitted. As Elliott remembered, "from their wedding day until he died, Father's financial affairs were a closed book to Mother. Granny never told him just how much money she had or what her income amounted to. In the same tradition, he told Mother no more about the ups and downs of his finances than he did about his plans in business or politics." Not having access to the checkbook was naturally frustrating for Eleanor. She needed to write, rewrite, and even telegraph Franklin about bills that were overdue and allowances needed by the children. The couple continued to give Anna an allowance after her marriage, and Sara provided her with an independent income, too. Franklin was less generous with James, as he would be with all his boys, and suggested that he find a job on campus to help augment his annual allowance of $1,600 and to help pay Harvard's $300 tuition.

Franklin also gave Eleanor a monthly allowance; he was the sole signatory on the checking account. He would write her a check for $300 for household expenses, which she would cash and use to pay the staff's salaries. In fact, Franklin suggested that she let one servant go because he was in the house so seldom. She would not do so, seeing it as a false economy that would cause more work for the remaining help.

Eleanor had some money of her own and used its income for her own projects, paying for her investments in Todhunter School and Val-Kill Industries. Given her general insecurities, not knowing the details of Franklin's finances was troublesome, especially when he began speculating in such financial schemes as oil wells. Many of his investments lost money. Still, in the boom days of the late twenties, he was also able to make small profits, although never enough.

Perhaps if Eleanor had had a clearer idea of the family's finances, she would have felt more confident about Franklin's plan to buy Warm Springs. Then again, perhaps not—as the family's expenses always outpaced its income. The only person enamored of the Warm Springs purchase was Franklin himself. Eleanor, Sara, and Howe united in their opposition to his spending so much money on what then was a rickety unproved hotel and spa. In fact, despite Franklin's optimistic letter to his mother—"you needn't worry about my losing a fortune for every step is being planned either to pay for itself or to make a profit on"—Sara spent only three thousand dollars, enough to build one guesthouse that she rarely used and rented out instead. She also criticized the Warm Springs brochure Franklin wrote because she thought he was unfairly hyping his new venture by saying that none of his prior polio treatments had helped him. She thought this untrue and was angry that he twisted the truth for financial gain. She would, however, hold benefits and teas for Warm Springs over the years, including a meeting in the wealthy town of Tuxedo Park (Kassie's home) that raised tens of thousands of dollars.

In fact, Sara had her own institutions to fund, and now she decided that she would found Hyde Park's first library. In 1926 she purchased a lot on the town's main street and began building a two-story building. She endowed the library in her husband's name, and to this day the main room of the Hyde Park Free Library features an oil portrait of James Roosevelt. (The library's former name was the James Roosevelt Memorial Library.)

Franklin thought that his mother was too generous and that the town or school district taxes should pay for any library. "I have several times explained the question involved in *maintaining* the library. You know as well as I do that this is wholly impossible in Hyde Park. If the Rogers[es], Newbolds, Betty [Rosy's widow] and Mr. Vanderbilt and Eleanor and I each gave $100, how much more could you raise in the village. Possibly $200 by a food sale or dances! The money *won't* be *given*." Sara decided that she wanted the town to have a library and ignored Franklin's concerns. She continued to fund the library's expenses for the rest of her life.* (Franklin and his estate paid the costs for about six years after her death, and the library was purchased by the town only in 1947, twenty-one years after its establishment.)

Franklin's dream to turn Warm Springs into a major health center threatened his remaining trust principal and endangered his family's economic stability. By 1925, the last year for which detailed accounts are available,

---

*Most biographies state that Sara's husband, James, built this library, but its existence is due to Sara, who founded it nearly a quarter of a century after his death.

the family spent about $21,000 more than its income. Eleanor feared that they would not be able to afford college for the younger boys, to which Elliott remarked, "A fate which I, for one, was more than ready to face." Franklin reassured his wife that "Ma will always see the children through."

Howe had a sole concern: he wanted Franklin to keep his money for future political campaigns—in fact, Franklin had just cast an absentee ballot for Al Smith in the 1926 gubernatorial race. In addition, Howe's own finances were precarious since he received only a small salary from Fidelity as Franklin's secretary and had to scrounge for other income. Howe wrote Franklin: "I may remark that your check arrived in the nick of time, as I was busted. I hate like hell to take a cent from you when you need so much for W.S."

Adding to Eleanor's concern over the monetary fallout of Franklin's purchase was that "she was out of sympathy with her absentee husband's pursuit of the rainbow that would enable him to walk," as Elliott later wrote. Her income-producing work, coupled with Franklin's continued absence from his home, may have embarrassed Sara; Eleanor would be the first woman in three hundred years of Delano history to draw a salary. Eleanor later said that Sara felt "real grief" when she began to earn money. No evidence exists other than Eleanor's word, but her characterization seems likely. However, Sara was adaptable and eventually recognized that Eleanor was a modern woman doing good work.

On March 25, 1927, Anna gave Eleanor and Franklin their first grandchild and Sara her first great-grandchild. Following family tradition, she named the baby Eleanor Anna. (The public would know her as "Sistie.") And, again following family tradition, Anna allowed Eleanor to pay for the nurse and Franklin the medical bills and other expenses. Here Sara nudged him: "Dearest Son, Would you please send to Anna a cheque for $1,000 with a personal letter telling her that you want to pay her doctor's bill? I would give it, but I want it to come from you."

Sara was once more disappointed that her son had stayed in Warm Springs rather than near his daughter for the birth. She admonished him that she was "sorry the young grandfather could not be here for the great event."

Franklin was also absent for his half brother's last days. Rosy's respiratory problems had affected his health for years, and on May 7, 1927, he died of bronchitis. He took his last labored breath in his bed at Red House, with Sara and Betty by his side. Sara was only six months younger than her seventy-three-year-old stepson, and his death must have given her pause. As for Franklin, Rosy had left him a nice sum of $100,000 in securities. His two hundred acres of Hyde Park land went to Franklin under the provisions of their father's will, although Franklin gave it to Betty for her lifetime use. More important, Rosy willed his hunting and fishing equipment to Franklin, an affirmation that he would walk again. Franklin wrote: "It is very hard to realize when I am at Hyde Park that he is no longer there and in so many more ways than I had realized, I depended on his companionship and on his judgment."

35

"If He Does, I Hope He Wins"

By 1928 Franklin had spent seven years away from his family regaining his health. He realized that he would never fully recover his ability to walk but was satisfied, if not content, with his progress. He was circling around politics as a strategist rather than a candidate, yet he yearned to plunge back into the maelstrom.

At first, 1928 did not look as though it would float his political boat. As in the 1924 gubernatorial race, Franklin managed Al Smith's presidential campaign, and at the June 1928 Democratic convention in Houston he gave a nomination speech to thunderous applause that put Smith over the top. The cheers were for Franklin rather than for Smith, and the Democratic politicos sat up and took note of the delegates' wave of enthusiasm. Eleanor had vacillated about accompanying him, eventually deciding against it. When she heard of the crowd's outburst, she regretted that she was absent at this great moment.

Franklin had made careful preparations before his momentous appearance. Elliott was his support this time; James, who would soon enter his junior year at Harvard, was in Europe with Sara. Franklin and Elliott practiced, repeatedly, his walk to the lectern. Franklin wanted more than anything to demonstrate physical prowess. His aim was to appear as unaffected by polio as possible. Four years earlier he had been dependent on crutches: now, he would "walk" with a cane, unobtrusively gripping Elliott, who supported much of his father's weight. Franklin would accept being thought lame, but never crippled.

As he began his speech, he leaned on the podium with one hand and used the other to gesture. Franklin held his chiseled head high and spoke clearly to the audience of 15,000 who faced him and by those 15 million who listened over the radio.

Smith's hope was that if he won the nomination for president, Franklin would succeed him as New York's governor. The governorship had always been Franklin's goal; he had said for years that "anyone who is governor of New York has a good chance to be President with luck." Nevertheless, following his nomination of Smith, while the state convention met in Rochester in September, Franklin played a cat-and-mouse game with the Democrats who wanted him for the office. He returned to Warm Springs and purposely kept out of telephone reach.

Sara was still with James in Europe. One day James had safely returned to the ship while Sara, touring Cherbourg with Dora, missed the tender. She quickly chartered a tug to return to the ship, the sailors threw a ladder down to her, and the amazed passengers watched the seventy-four-year-old woman clamber nimbly up. Now she wrote Franklin from France: "Last evening, Mr. [Bernard] Baruch told me he had seen by a paper that they were trying to draft you Franklin for Governor. He says he is drafted to go home and help in the campaign." She added no opinion of her own but returned to the United States and journeyed down in September to see her son in Warm Springs.

A small delegation from Franklin's home state, including politico Eddie Dowling, went to Warm Springs to persuade Franklin to run. They found that Sara was also in town, in her cottage. Sara thought Franklin's consideration of the office still premature. Although she felt that he had let his family down after his polio by fleeing to Florida and Georgia, her essential concern remained his health. That she was in town did not encourage the coalition from New York.

Sara also knew that Franklin had already called his physician about running for governor and had been advised against it. The doctor told him that he needed more therapy in Warm Springs, that Albany's cold weather would harm his health. Franklin's response was a laconic "Well, you're the doctor." Then he hung up and did precisely what he had intended all along.

The New York group sought out Franklin, who was sitting by the side of the pool. "Well, gentlemen," Franklin concluded after their conversation, "you go back and you tell Al I'll run for anything to help him.

"But don't let my mother know about this."

Dowling recalled that "Mrs. James found out, and she nailed us before we left. She said, 'First of all, I don't know what anybody wants these things for. But if this costs me my son, I shall never forgive you.'

"'I will hold you all responsible for the death of my son.'"

Yet once Franklin made up his mind, Sara trimmed her sails to the course Franklin had chosen. As rumors of his candidacy began to circulate, she said, "I don't want my boy to run for office—but if he does, I hope he wins." She responded to a friend's note of congratulations by writing: "Thank you for your kind interest. I so hope my son will be elected."

Moreover, she put her best efforts into seeing that he was successful. She contributed $2,000 ($22,000 today) to his campaign, bought Hyde Park's first radio so she could follow the election news, and took a large worry off his shoulders: "Now what follows is *really private*. In case of your election, I know your salary is smaller than the one you get now. I am prepared to make the difference up to you." Although Sara had made it her business to know Franklin's, his wife did not learn that Franklin had accepted the nomination until she read it in the New York newspapers.

Eleanor sent him a cool telegram: REGRET THAT YOU HAVE TO ACCEPT BUT KNOW THAT YOU FEEL IT OBLIGATORY. Sara wrote more kindly: "Yet if you run I do not want you to be defeated! However, all will be well whatever happens." Eleanor bowed out of accompanying her husband on his first statewide campaign. She had been working in the New York office to elect Smith president, and she and Franklin decided she needed to continue there. She learned political tactics that would serve Franklin well four years later, and she grew in character as she saw the vitriolic prejudice hurled at Smith, a Roman Catholic. That he would take orders from Rome was one of the least offensive charges. Eleanor responded by quoting two letters written by Uncle Teddy while he was president, in which Teddy wrote that he hoped that a Jew or Catholic would someday be elected president.

Early on election night, it became clear that Smith had fallen badly behind Herbert Hoover. (In fact, Smith's defeat ended up being the worst the Democrats had suffered since Abraham Lincoln's second election.) "People were crying everywhere," remembered Frances Perkins, a member of the state's industrial commission. "It was his assumption, and everybody's assumption, that Roosevelt had gone down too."

Perkins returned to the Roosevelt campaign headquarters. "The number of people present became really small," she said. Franklin and Eleanor stayed in Hyde Park. Sara was with the campaign workers, "and she wouldn't quit," said Perkins. "The time went on and practically everybody had gone. I don't believe there were a dozen people left outside of those who were in the room where the returns were coming in. They had turned out the lights in the ballroom. The few of us who were there were sitting in one of the corridors.

"Only one other person seemed to have the idea [that Franklin could still win]—Sara Delano Roosevelt. Almost everyone else went home, except the telephone operators and the tally men."

Perkins said, "She wasn't going to desert her boy. He was up at Hyde Park, but she wasn't going to desert his headquarters."

The early-morning edition of the papers came in at about two A.M. They reported on Smith's concession and said that Roosevelt "was badly defeated." Still, Sara hung on.

An hour or so later, the reports started to look more optimistic. The tallies were giving Franklin very tiny leads—winning by six votes in Cattaraugus County, for example. Perkins said, "I think it was three or four o'clock in the morning when . . . some other people said, 'Roosevelt is elected!'"

Sara was the only family member at headquarters to hear the tally counter announce Franklin's victory. "Mrs. Sara Roosevelt and I," Perkins said, "had a very private little celebration. . . . She, of course, was ecstatic. I think she telephoned to Hyde Park and talked to him. They knew it up there. She knew it and we knew it, but very few others knew it" for much of the day because all the morning papers had announced Franklin's defeat.

Perkins said, "Only after that [did I take] her home to her house, said good night to her and went home."

Franklin squeaked home by a narrow margin and dubbed himself the "one half of one percent governor." Despite his self-deprecating tone, he knew that Smith's sinking left him at the head of the fleet as the most attractive Democratic presidential candidate for 1932.

Although Sara has been identified as the woman in Franklin's life who did not want him to run for office, she at least threw herself into his campaign once he was nominated. Eleanor had worked hard for Smith and was bitter—at her husband's expense—that Smith had not been elected. "If the rest of the ticket didn't get it, what does it [Franklin's governorship] matter?" and "No, I am not excited about my husband's election. I don't care. What difference can it make to me?"

Eleanor's high profile as chairman of the women's division of the party made her one of the most influential Democrats in the region. Of course, a woman with so much political experience was a threat, and whispers grew that she would tell Franklin how to govern. Also working against her were those who thought a woman's place was in the home and the many influential articles she had published—not just on women's tactics (*Redbook's* "Women Must Learn to Play the Game as Men Do") but also on solid political thought (*North American Review's* "Why Democrats Favor Smith: As a Political Idealist"). Eleanor had to issue a statement downplaying any influence over her husband. As it turned out, her protestation was more prescient than she had thought it would be.

Now it was time for the couple to return to Albany—as New York's governor and First Lady. The inauguration was held on New Year's Day 1929. Sara was seated on the platform near Eleanor and Franklin. Al Smith spoke, and as he acknowledged the important people present, he turned in Sara's direction. With "touching tenderness," she remembered, he said, "I congratulate the mother. It is a great day for her. I remember my mother. My mother was on the platform with me for two inaugurations. I know how she enjoyed it and how she felt about it."

Sara brushed away tears and Mrs. Smith openly wept at the memory of her mother-in-law. Sara was deeply moved at his kindness and his appreciation of the significant role she had played in her son's life. Then she watched Franklin take the oath of office with a hand on the carefully preserved Bible that had originally belonged to Claes Martenszen Van Rosenvelt. The volume was not the only reminder to Franklin of family history: Franklin's inauguration as New York governor took place thirty years to the day after Teddy's. That night at the inaugural ball, Sara wore a black satin dress decorated with the same piece of her mother's lace that had graced her gown at Franklin and Eleanor's wedding.

Sara was free of child-care responsibilities for nearly the first time since Franklin's birth forty-six years earlier. Eleanor had enrolled John in Groton the previous September (a bittersweet farewell, as he was the youngest child), which meant that all four boys were away at school. Anna had a home of her own, with a husband and daughter. Sara, having greater freedom, stepped up her entertaining. Her guests had changed over the years, though: rather than being primarily family, relatives, and small groups of friends punctuated by occasional large gatherings of Franklin's constituents or Eleanor's women's groups, the composition of the gatherings was reversed. Now Sara rarely had a quiet dinner with her family. Eleanor and Franklin brought a political entourage with them every time they went to Hyde Park.

A party official who was present at one dinner related that "the Governor's mother, Mrs. James Roosevelt . . . presides at the far other end of the table, giving occasional directions in French to the butler." Others present, he pointed out, were "a secretary and a handsome, husky sergeant detailed from the State Troopers," the American wife of an English peer, the novelist

Fanny Hurst, Anna and her husband, and a stenographer and an assembly-man from Albany. The table also included the head of the Women's Labor Union, who whispered to "the bob-haired" Nancy Cook, and "knickerbock-ered friends from Hyde Park manors and fox hunting friends from Staats-burg."

In fact, one time when they were out of earshot of Earl Miller (the state trooper assigned to Franklin), Sara gently joked to Dickerman: "He used to be Sergeant and ate in the kitchen, but now he is Earl and eats with the family."

Sara's own friends and relatives were getting older and going out less; in fact, many of her husband's friends already had died, as they had been con-siderably older than Sara. She enjoyed the opportunity of having younger guests and welcomed them to her house, realizing that the world would have to come to Franklin since he could not go to the world.

Franklin worked from the house a great deal in his modest old study, not in his more sumptuous library. In fact, Sara told Perkins, "I do wish he'd let me fix him up a nice study, now that he has grown up and is the Governor." However, he preferred to keep things as they were.

Perkins enjoyed going down from Albany to Hyde Park, especially in the summer. She described one moment:

> I approached through the library and saw through the open door an unfor-gettable picture. Mrs. Sara Roosevelt, in a soft, light summery dress with ruf-fles, her hair charmingly curled, sitting in a wicker chair and reading; Mrs. Roosevelt, in a white dress and white tennis shoes with a velvet band around her head to keep the hair from blowing, sitting with her long-legged, grace-ful posture in a low chair and knitting, always knitting; Roosevelt looking off down the river at the view he admired, with a book, often unopened, in one hand, and a walking stick in the other; dogs playing nearby, and chil-dren romping a little farther down the lawn. The scene was like a Currier and Ives print of "Life Along the Hudson."

Although Franklin kept to the same rooms in the house, Sara found it necessary to leave her beloved bedroom. Franklin needed to receive many evening visitors sitting in his bed, because his back would ache if his legs remained in a seated position. Sara all too often would be unable to sleep because of the noise and smoke coming from meetings in Franklin's room, which was close to hers. Headed down the hall to the bathroom in her robe and slippers, she might bump into a visitor leaving her son's room. Sara finally moved to the end of the hall to the couple's east sitting room, which they were no longer using. It was quiet and more private and included an adjoining bathroom. (Since the house has become a National Park Service site, public visitors have been told different stories over the years about the relocation of Sara's and Eleanor's bedrooms. Several decades ago, tourists were told that Eleanor's sitting room was used by Sara as her own bedroom, which places Sara in a room with an adjoining door to the couple's master bedroom. Visitors mistakenly assumed that Sara chose that room so she could walk into the couple's bedroom at will. Now tourists are told that Eleanor left the master bedroom after Franklin contracted polio and that Sara also then moved to the east sitting room to be closer to Franklin. Most likely, Eleanor moved bedrooms after learning of the Mercer romance, and Sara, whose original bedroom was actually close to the couple's master bedroom, changed locations to preserve her privacy. The exact years the women moved bedrooms remains undocumented.)

Where Sara slept in Hyde Park was of no interest outside the family at the time. However, the sleeping arrangements in Albany caused some concern. Franklin had renovated the mansion, adding an elevator, ramps, and a swimming pool. When they moved in, Eleanor had assigned Missy LeHand to the bedroom that traditionally belonged to the governor's wife. People may have been quizzical, but Eleanor did not care about their opinions.

Eleanor's cup was overflowing. For one thing, she had enjoyed teaching so much that she continued her classes and commuted from Albany to Manhattan, staying in the city for a few days each week. In her role as the state's First Lady, she also visited many schools, prisons, hospitals, and other institutions. Before the days of accessible public buildings, Franklin was often unable to get around such places, so Eleanor became his eyes and ears and would tell him what she learned. Franklin was a better editor than she was a reporter: she would recite the items listed on the institution's menu, and he would ask if she had looked inside the pots and pans to see what was actually being served. Eventually she learned to give him the facts and not the facade.

Whenever Eleanor could not carry out the numerous duties of the governor's wife, Franklin named his mother acting First Lady of the state and she would assume Eleanor's place. Sara and Franklin, for example, went to the capital to receive Admiral Richard Byrd, a New Yorker who had just returned from the North Pole. Franklin even sent his mother a questionnaire from the *National Cyclopedia of American Biography* and asked her to fill it out and submit it for him. Sara enjoyed socializing but demurred at seeing her photograph in the newspaper, preferring to see Franklin highlighted instead.

She wrote a new acquaintance, the writer Rita Halle Kleeman, who wanted to profile her for a magazine. "How sweet it is of you to be interested in my rather old world stories. I am sure you would write something very charming, but I fear *I* could not have anything published about my life while I am still here! (on earth!)

"When I get to town we will have a talk about it, but I think I like to remain out of the picture, even when my beloved son is to be our forerunner." Then she added somewhat coquettishly, "It is rather amusing your suggesting this, as only about six weeks ago, I was talking with friends . . . & *they* begged me to write my memoirs—!"

Hyde Park, too, was in the swim, becoming "almost like a public recreation ground," said Perkins. Sara "proved herself up to the demands. Her devotion to her son in his—to her—almost incomprehensible taste for politics was sufficient to take her over the hurdles. She remained completely maternal in her attitude and once told me, 'I have always believed that a mother should be friends with her children's friends.'"

Eleanor was planning a huge celebration for the New York Federation of Labor and the Women's Trade Union League at the latter's clubhouse. Sara sent her a telegram suggesting that she hold the huge rally at roomier Hyde Park instead. Eleanor took her up on the idea, and on June 8, 1929, long buses belching black exhaust lined up on Albany Post Road to deposit thousands of visitors at the driveway. Entertainment was included in the day's events, and Sara, with Franklin and Eleanor, watched the pièce de résistance: a pageant reenacting important labor strikes. The volunteers took the roles of strikers, employers, and police while a trumpeter blasted like Joshua at Jericho during the dramatic clashes. For a woman whose own life for her first forty-six years was limited to those within her own set, Sara's transformation was amazing.

Although Eleanor said little about her mother-in-law, Sara expressed only admiration for her daughter-in-law: "My generation did not do those things, but Eleanor and the women of her generation are doing useful work in their different way. I think they are splendid!"

The two years of Franklin's governorship went by quickly. Sara was pleased when James, who graduated from Harvard in 1930, asked Betsey Cushing, whom he had dated for two years, to marry him. She was the daughter of Dr. Harvey Cushing, a famous neurosurgeon. Miss Cushing's reputation was for her beauty, and she and her two sisters—Babe Cushing Mortimer Paley and Minnie Cushing Astor Forsburgh—were known as the glamorous Cushing daughters of Boston. Sara gave James a wedding check for three thousand dollars and promised him an allowance while he was at Boston University School of Law. James had already borrowed money from his grandmother—without consulting his parents—and Franklin was furious at him for his poor money management.

The disagreements between Eleanor and Sara over her gifts to her grandchildren continued. A year or so earlier James—at his parent's insistence—had saved enough money to buy a car to keep in Cambridge. One winter the secondhand Ford slid off the snowy road. It was not drivable, and James could not afford another. Eleanor thought the accident was his fault and refused to pay for a replacement. A short time later, at Christmas, Sara presented James with a new Chrysler runabout. (Sara did the same thing again when Franklin Jr. wrecked his car, which had been a high school graduation present from his parents.)

When Sara told James of his Christmas gift, Eleanor went to Franklin to demand that he tell his mother to send the car back. Elliott later interpreted his father's refusal as follows: "He wanted no argument with the woman whose money made his career possible. He never did raise the subject with Granny, but she and Mother feuded for weeks over this thwarting of control over my brother." (Privately, Franklin bemoaned his position to a friend: "Now what am I going to do?")

However, when the couple's bills piled up in 1929, the year Eleanor hoped to take Franklin Jr. and John and several of her own women friends to Europe, Eleanor was delighted that Sara sent a large check to Franklin. "I am glad Mama is giving you a present because now I hope we will be able to pay all our many demands."

Although Eleanor criticized Sara for interfering, she involved herself in James's financial affairs. In late summer 1929 Sara had given James a thousand dollars for a European trip the following summer with Betsey. James, rather than banking the money, saw a booming 1929 stock market and decided to invest the money through his brother-in-law, Curtis Dall, in blue-chip stocks. Curtis followed James's instructions, but the October crash swamped even these safe investments. Their value was negligible.

At breakfast not long after, Eleanor told Curtis that James had mentioned his stock loss, phrasing it as "You have lost his $1,000 for him." Curtis said, "Yes, he has about lost it. Much to my regret, and the market is still moving lower. I bought a few shares of two leading common stocks for him, on margin, and the panic has put his account in bad shape."

Eleanor told him, "I think you ought to return his money to him."

Curtis was astounded but agreed to follow his mother-in-law's wishes. Fortunately, James—who was both surprised and annoyed at Eleanor's interference—refused reimbursement, saying that the decision to invest had been his own.

Sara felt less affected by the crash than other people. She was a very wealthy woman from her initial Delano inheritance, swelled by the legacy from Annie, who, dying childless, had divided her fortune among her philanthropies and her siblings. In today's dollars, Sara was worth about $50 million, which she conservatively invested, by the time Franklin finished the governorship. She felt no jolt from the foundering economy.

Eleanor was looking forward to her own European trip with the two younger boys. Sara was shocked to learn that Eleanor planned to be the caravan driver. She thought that undignified for the wife of a governor to travel in such a Gypsy fashion, looking for lodgings along the road, and expressed her feelings about Eleanor at the wheel in no uncertain terms. Franklin Jr. innocently chimed in, "Mama will probably land us in the first ditch," and then sweetly added, "but we'll be all right."

Eleanor was infuriated and snapped at her mother-in-law, "Very well. I will take your grandsons in a manner consistent with what you think their positions ought to be." She left the table and strode from the room. Franklin was angry with his son and told him to go after his mother and apologize. However, Franklin said nothing to Sara.

Eleanor stayed stormy. She told the group she needed to change her plans, and she and the boys—who were told to wear suits and ties—were driven by liveried chauffeurs while Dickerman and Cook traveled ahead in casual clothes, driving their own convertible. Eleanor made Franklin Jr. quite miserable by letting him imagine that it was all his fault for his mistimed remark. Dickerman later said that Franklin Jr. "paid very dearly for that remark. Eleanor could be very hard." Eleanor, who did not take day-to-day care of her children, said she had forgotten the "constant care & supervision" that teenagers need and found the trip "rather wearing." Just like Eleanor's camping trip a few years earlier, this one also was a failure. She said it would be the last trip she would take with her children.

Dickerman, who was present during the initial blowup, pointed out that "Eleanor never forgot. She never forgot a hurt, never."

Not that Dickerman was completely uncritical of Sara. "Oh, sometimes, her remarks weren't always kind, but I can remember Eleanor being quite unkind about certain things with Granny, getting up and leaving the table when things didn't suit her.

"So it wasn't all one-sided. . . ."

As 1930 began, Sara kept up her hectic schedule. For example, on Wednesday, January 1, she took an 8:30 A.M. train to Albany, where she joined the family at the state capitol "and heard Franklin read his fine message to the legislature." She returned to the mansion for lunch and left on the 3:12 P.M.

train for Manhattan with James and Betsey. "Betsey stays with me at 47 [East Sixty-fifth]," she wrote, while James remained at 49. Sara then had a large crew of people to dinner.

The next day she had Dora and six others to lunch at her house and joined Kassie at Sherry's for dinner and saw *Don Giovanni* from Kassie's opera box. On Friday she went to a daytime concert, then took the train to Hyde Park in time to greet her two youngest grandsons, down from Albany for the weekend. On Saturday, Franklin and LeHand joined them while guests "skated and rode—a lovely day," Sara wrote in her journal. There were only seven for lunch.

On Sunday she went to church, had another lunch party, took the boys to Manhattan on the train, and paid a visit to a friend. On Monday she walked, went to a meeting, visited friends, and had a group at 47 to dine before seeing a musical comedy. Tuesday she got the boys to the train and saw them off to Groton, lunched with Anna, and shopped with her in the afternoon. Wednesday her lunch club came over to discuss Edith Wharton's *Hudson River Bracketed*, about two lovers who meet and live in a fictitious town along the Hudson. (The title refers to a local architectural style that literally is named "Hudson River bracketed.") On Thursday, Sara had a Babies Ward meeting at the Laura Franklin Hospital, lunched at the Plaza, heard a concert, and had another large group for dinner. On Saturday she wrote in her journal, "Rather tired so I stay in bed all day & have a good rest."

Franklin took the governorship again in fall 1930. The race was nearly anti-climactic after the election of 1928. Franklin won the largest vote of any New York gubernatorial Democrat until that time. The trickle of "Roosevelt for President" was turning into a groundswell.

On the rising tide of his popularity came flotsam of the sleaziest nature. The cheapest remarks involved his lack of mobility. Smith rejoined, "We do not elect [a governor] for his ability to do a double back-flip or a hand-spring. The work of the Governorship is brainwork." Soon the opposition noticed that statement; Dr. Draper had to issue a statement correcting those who claimed that polio eventually attacked the mind.

Eleanor and Franklin had an unpleasant encounter at the Hoover White House during his campaign. They became suspicious when they waited at the mansion's party for President and Mrs. Hoover, and were kept standing for thirty minutes. Eleanor whispered to Franklin to sit down, rather than remain leaning on his cane, when it became apparent that the First Couple was not entering the room as announced. However, Franklin feared that sitting when others still stood would show weakness, and instead he skillfully masked his pain.

Another malicious undercurrent concerned Sara. Allegedly, she was accepting money from the state government for the numerous functions she held for Franklin and Eleanor at Hyde Park. "She was proud of her home," said Eleanor, "and extremely happy when her son and his family and friends could be with her, and nothing would have induced her to accept money from any source." Sara reacted to tawdry scuttlebutt with a good old-fashioned sense of ethical outrage. The rumors did not stick.

The day after Franklin's overwhelming 1930 reelection as governor, Democratic leader Jim Farley made an important statement indicating Franklin's future. "The Democrats in the nation naturally want as their candidate for President the man who has shown himself capable of carrying the most important state in the country by a record-breaking majority. I do not see how Mr. Roosevelt can escape becoming the next presidential nominee for President of his party, even if no one should raise a finger to bring it about."

36

~~~

Happy Days

As Franklin entered his second term as governor, he began to drop the masquerade of being solely New York's chief executive and confidently assumed the role of presidential front-runner. Still, he knew that Al Smith would be his competition; despite Smith's astounding loss to Hoover in 1928, the man had deep support among conservative Democrats.

With this ripple of worry trailing behind him, Franklin surged ahead to firmly govern the state and barely deviated from his course when he traveled to Warm Springs for therapy every spring as usual. Eleanor did not like to go, so he took Missy LeHand instead. Before Franklin's 1931 trip, Anna implored her mother to accompany Franklin to Warm Springs, writing her that "Father's letter to me was mostly about trying to persuade you to go to Warm Springs for a week with him. . . . Do go. Pa seems to want you there so badly." Eleanor refused, giving the trip's conflict with her teaching schedule as her reason.

However, Franklin's journey did not start as planned. Sara was taking her own annual spring tour of Europe—she called it "running over to Europe"—when Franklin received word from Dora in Albany that Sara had been hospitalized with pneumonia at the American Hospital in Paris. Sara had never been hospitalized in her life, and this illness was grave. Franklin postponed his Georgia trip and journeyed to France with Elliott and his valet.

The New York Times determined that Sara's illness deserved front-page treatment: "The Governor, an only son, and his mother are deeply attached and Mr. Roosevelt showed yesterday his distress at the news of her illness." The following day, in another front-page article, Franklin was optimistic about her recovery. Still, he cautiously added: "But my mother is 76 years old and her sister, Mrs. D. D. Forbes, who is with her, is 81. I might be helpful to them in some way by going over." Franklin had not been abroad since his 1919 navy voyage and was embarrassed to find that his passport had expired. The governor put in a rush request for a new one.

Sara knew that her son was on his way, and rather than gaze out her window at the leaf-green spring scenery that she treasured, she watched her hospital door. "When it opened and that handsome son of mine stood there with his arm around his own tall son, I am afraid I was very *émotionnelle*." She added, as if to excuse a lapse in decorum, "I was still very weak."

The French, too, had got wind of Franklin's glowing future. Although Sara was a good friend to quite a few statesmen, even more national leaders stopped by to pay their respects to both Sara and her son. General Ferdinand Foch, Allied supreme commander for the western front in 1918, was merely one of many at Sara's bedside. The *Times* reported of Franklin: "His visit has caused much comment in French circles, where he is regarded as the probable Democratic nominee for President in the 1932 election."

After Sara was released and resting in her suite at the Hotel George V, Franklin thanked the American Hospital in a French radio broadcast, toured a French reconstruction of Mount Vernon, and paid homage at various French battlefields. On June 15, 1931, Sara returned from France and was greeted by Franklin and Eleanor at the dock, though Franklin waited in his limousine, out of the bad weather.

Fully recovered by August, Sara journeyed to Farmington to visit an ailing Bamie. Bamie was using a wheelchair and was nearly deaf: for several years she had needed her friends to shout into an Acousticon box to amplify their speech. Although she was only seventy-six, her poor health during her lifetime had caught up with her. She was in great pain but would not let Sara feel sorry for her: "Never mind, it's *all* right," she whispered before slipping into a coma. Her words to Sara were her very last. Corinne, Teddy's youngest sibling, was now the only one left.

Bamie's death was widely noted, but political life went on as the struggling nation watched the approach of the next presidential election. It seemed that the rise of the Hyde Park Roosevelts nearly coincided with the ebb of the Oyster Bay relatives. The next summer, however, Teddy's elderly widow, Edith, attempted to stem the tide by appearing in mourning garb (a full quarter of a century after her husband's death) to introduce Herbert Hoover at the Republican convention in Chicago.

But Louis Howe hoped to use Sara's motherly affection for political gain. At his behest, Sara agreed to be interviewed for a series of three articles in *Good Housekeeping*. When the first issue appeared, trucks delivering the magazines blazoned "MY BOY FRANKLIN" BY SARA DELANO ROOSEVELT on their sides. Sara was horrified that her name decorated the sides of trucks, and she refused to complete the interviews. Franklin had to provide the rest of the information and anecdotes needed by the writers, something that never was acknowledged in the articles' text.

While the Republicans were still gathered in Chicago, in late June 1932 Franklin's men Howe and Farley traveled there in advance of the Democratic convention's start. Waiting for them were Anna, James, and Franklin Jr. In Albany were Eleanor and Sara, glued to the radio. Franklin was with them, within arm's reach of the telephone. He smoked one cigarette after another, sitting in his shirtsleeves while Eleanor's knitting needles clicked and flashed. The process was longer than usual because of the ferocity with which Smith fought for the nomination. The Democrats knew that Hoover was adrift in leading the country out of the depression that had struck two years earlier, and the party would take advantage of the situation by putting a new man—a Democrat—at the helm. Sara found the suspense unbearable and returned to Hyde Park.

Franklin was wound tight sitting in Albany, but he smiled when he heard his choice of campaign music, "Anchors Aweigh," coming from the convention hall. Howe, who was inside, thought the song sophomoric and not a crowd-rouser. Frustrated, he countermanded his boss's orders and demanded that the band play his own bright choice, "Happy Days Are Here Again." The change of lyrics and melody seemed to capture the mood: on July 1 Franklin became the Democratic presidential nominee.

The next morning Eleanor and Franklin went out onto the mansion's grounds for photographs. "Mrs. Roosevelt, are you thrilled at the idea of being in the White House?" shouted a reporter. Journalist Lorena A. Hickok caught Eleanor's glare, which ended all further questioning along that line. Eleanor's mood did not improve. The couple then left for Hyde Park, where Sara welcomed Franklin at the door, "weeping with pride and an overwhelming sense of fulfillment," said Elliott. Mother and son embraced.

Corinne Alsop, who disliked both Sara and Eleanor, told Alice Roosevelt that after the election returns came in, Eleanor was crying in a corner saying, "Now I will have no identity. I'll only be the wife of the president."

A disaffected Eleanor kept out of the limelight while Sara stepped into it. *The New York Times* interviewed the delighted mother, who the writer said was seventy years old (she was actually seventy-eight). The paper quoted Sara as saying, "My son called me up to tell me he had been nominated, but I had already heard it over the radio in my own home. Of course, I am glad he got the nomination, glad he got it by such a large majority. But I was not very much surprised."

Before 1932 the custom was for the winner to accept his nomination in his hometown a week or so after the convention. However, Franklin wanted to keep his momentum going. Exploring uncharted political waters, Franklin and Eleanor flew against heavy winds to Chicago so he could give his acceptance speech at the convention. His presence electrified the crowd, and he pledged that he would regenerate the social and economic progress of the country, promising to remember—using for the first time his unforgettable phrases—"the forgotten man" as he ensured every citizen a "new deal."

Now it was Eleanor's turn to worry—not for the country or for Franklin but for herself. Years later she bluntly wrote: "I did not want my husband to be president . . . It was pure selfishness on my part, and I never mentioned my feelings on the subject to him." Rather than viewing his presidency as an opportunity to promote her own agenda, she feared she would suffocate in the White House. She reflected on this during the campaign, when she talked about the positive effects of turning forty-eight, "You don't take it so hard when things happen to you that you don't like." Only a few women reporters took note of her odd reaction.

Eleanor's sour attitude was not mere personal grumpiness. She had been disheartened when Franklin, as governor, had not acquiesced to her proposals. Now as the presidential nominee, he had already embarrassed her by trading idealism for practicality, repudiating the League of Nations in a calculated move to win wider support.

Sara, on the other hand, actually welcomed the idea of Franklin becoming president, having adapted smoothly since 1928, when she wrote *Eleanor and Franklin*: "I had two charming old ladies to tea . . . both longing to vote for you! (of course for President). I said 'When that happens, I shall vote and then emigrate to foreign lands!' (I suppose that sounds cowardly.)" By the time of his nomination, Sara had seen how he had skillfully integrated his physical therapy into his work as governor, and how he had suffered no health crisis in the past four years. Now Franklin sought the nation's leadership, and if he wanted it, so did she. Sara had also overcome her aversion to being in the public eye during Franklin's years as governor and privately admitted that, like her son, she enjoyed her role as "first mother" of New York.

In September 1932 Eleanor Patterson, the publisher of the *Washington Herald*, profiled Sara. She wrote what would be the foundation of Sara's public image throughout Franklin's presidency, heading her story ROOSEVELT REFLECTS GREATNESS: FAMILY'S LIFE ROOTED IN FINE U.S. TRADITION. She began floridly:

> Mrs. Roosevelt is Governor Roosevelt's mother. And as men, especially great men, nearly always "take after" a great mother, I would like particularly to tell you about the elder Mrs. Roosevelt.
>
> A proud, tall woman, the Governor's mother, with a fearless lift to her head—a gift of nature passed on to her boy, Franklin. . . . You look at this tall, broad-shouldered, gallant lady, and you know that she will no more bow her head and submit to old age than Franklin, her son, submitted to the illness which once threatened his whole future.

Sara was an outspoken interviewee. She received Patterson in Hyde Park's library, and when Patterson asked her about the house and farm, she responded that the estate was hers but would go to her son upon her death. At the present time, Sara explained, "Franklin couldn't afford to run it by himself."

Illustrating the feature was a two-column photo of Sara. Across the top was the designation A REAL AMERICAN MOTHER, and under the photo it read: "INSPIRATION—Mrs. James Roosevelt, mother of the Democratic nominee for President, whose fearless Americanism, says Eleanor Patterson, is reflected in her son, Franklin."

The syndicated story ended with "Beautiful American countryside. Beautiful American home, deep rooted in American soil. Deep rooted in American tradition."

Satisfying political bedfellows was a less attractive tradition, deep-rooted in a less salubrious soil, but still a practical necessity. Franklin needed to court politicos whose only interest was anchored in gold. Huey Long was one such treasure seeker. He had been elected in 1930 as U.S. senator of Louisiana, having previously been its state governor, entering office after trouncing the state's Democratic machine. (In fact, he embroiled himself so completely in Louisiana's affairs that he did not bother going to Washington to take his oath of office until 1932.) As governor, Long had been impeached by the state's lower legislature for bribery and gross misconduct but had oozed past a conviction. He was considered a nominal Democrat and a dangerous politician who gave himself the nickname "Kingfish" to reflect his importance to Louisianians. However, as the 1932 presidential election approached, he persuaded Democratic leader Farley that Franklin would need his support to win the office. Farley arranged for their first meeting at Hyde Park.

Sara was adept at making her guests feel comfortable, no matter what their background. Once a guest unknowingly placed the ice cream in his finger bowl. Sara immediately followed suit. But at this lunch, she anticipated Long's behavior. He despised the rich but coveted their wealth. He had been well briefed on Franklin's aristocratic family tree. For this lunch meeting he intentionally showed his disrespect—for he did not usually dress vulgarly—by appearing at Sara's door wearing a loud blue pongee suit with an orchid-colored shirt punctuated by a strawberry-pink tie. He talked loudly and crudely, and his first comments were cheap flattery directed at Eleanor's appearance. His dress and speech were carefully calculated to show his hosts that he was not impressed by them.

Franklin seated Long on his right, the place of honor. Sara was at the opposite end of the table and could barely stand to see her fine son truckling to this man. Long was haranguing Franklin with his ill-conceived notion of making whistle-stops around the country to support him. The last thing that the Roosevelt campaign wanted was an association with this sleazy politician.

Sara pounced during a short pause in Long's lecture to send a warning to Franklin. "Eleanor, who is that man?" Eleanor tried to ignore her. Sara began again. "Who is that man?" she stage-whispered to Eleanor and the guests. "I don't like him."

The story traveled far and fast, for she had said what so many people were afraid to. Unfortunately, her question was later used by those who wished to show Sara's alleged class-consciousness (forgetting that they, too, would have despised the Kingfish). Sara was not unintentionally rude: rather, it was her way of giving Franklin notice. Whether Long was frustrated because Sara saw through him or because Eleanor was not fooled by his honeyed words, this man who came from nowhere proclaimed, "By God, I feel sorry for him. He's got more sonofabitches in his family than I got in mine." Franklin's response was "That is a man totally without principle." However, Franklin did use Long in a reduced role to his own advantage.

Franklin made his traditional last campaign stop at Hyde Park, whose portico Sara had festooned with red, white, and blue bunting. Sara was elated, knowing that if her son won, she would be the first mother in American history to have voted for her son as president of the United States. Following election night, she told a writer of her presence at campaign headquarters: "Instead of remaining quietly in a chair receiving congratulations, as I suppose I should have, I fluttered up and down the crowded corridors part and parcel of the excitement engendered by Franklin's victory." His November triumph ran deep, carrying all but six states, and swept in a Democratic Congress. The country would be his oyster.

Sara wrote that she had "but one devout wish—a wish that amounted to a prayer—that as President of the United States he be a good one!" She began her ceremonial role as the president-elect's mother immediately. Eleanor disliked traditional First Lady activities, so Sara relieved her by taking on such duties as shopping at a sale to benefit the blind and distributing Christmas trees to the poor. The two women operated separately, each helping Franklin and their country through their respective roles: Sara as the traditionalist whose image comforted an uneasy America, and Eleanor as the president's eyes and ears, a catalyst for change. Despite their different outlooks and styles, both women were prods to Franklin's conscience.

In February 1933 Sara published *My Boy Franklin*, "as told by Mrs. James Roosevelt to Isabel Leighton and Gabrielle Forbush." The writers had interviewed Sara (and Franklin) earlier for a lengthy magazine series about her son and turned the pieces into a sweet book about Franklin's wonderful childhood. "The boy is father to the man," began a brief commentary in *The New York Times Book Review*; so the story of her son cast an image of a man firmly based on a solid past.

Isabel Leighton also published a portrait of Eleanor with her favorite recipe for boiled whitefish in the March edition of *Ladies' Home Journal*, although the light story did give Eleanor a chance to articulate, "If there is any one thing I want, it is for every human being in the world to have the opportunity of leading his own life according to his own lights."

37

❧

First Mother

Franklin's presidential inauguration took place on March 4, and it was one of the most closely guarded in years. Not only was the country in deep unrest—thirty-eight states had closed their banks, millions were unemployed, farmers' commodities prices had never been lower, and some towns had replaced U.S. cash with scrip—but an anarchist had shot at Franklin at a parade in Miami and had fatally wounded Chicago mayor Anton J. Cermak. (Sara was the family member who greeted Franklin when he arrived home at Hyde Park from the Miami campaign, and showed him the bulletproof lectern sent him by CBS.) The situation in Europe was worrisome, too: in January an Austrian demagogue was elected Germany's chancellor. Franklin was taking over "the biggest job in the nation at the hardest period in its history," according to *Time* magazine.

As the day itself approached, Franklin was shocked when Eleanor said she would not be with the family on the special train car that would take them from Hyde Park to Washington. She wanted to drive down with her luggage, the dogs, and Lenora Hickok instead. But in the wake of Franklin's wrathful reaction, she consented to be part of the family group. Anna was already in Washington, so the party included the soon-to-be First Couple, Sara and her sister Dora, Elliott and James and their wives, and Franklin Jr.

and John, who were still Groton students. (Sara had just returned from Paris, where she had gone to accompany her sister back for the inauguration.)

Of course, both Franklin's and Eleanor's colleagues were on the train. Farley talked with Sara and mentioned the seriousness of the issues that would immediately face Franklin after he took the oath of office. Sara dismissed his concerns: "I am not the least worried about Franklin. His disposition is such that he can accept responsibilities and not let them wear him down."

Henry Luce, the publisher of *Time* magazine, refused to put the president-elect on *Time's* cover during inaugural week. Instead, Luce decided to use the portrait of someone more palatable: Sara Delano Roosevelt. The president's mother made the cover of the nation's most influential weekly magazine before Franklin or Eleanor. The accompanying story mentioned that there would be 250,000 spectators at Franklin's inauguration. "But in all the crowd no heart will pound with such pride as that of an erect, white-haired, hazel-eyed lady sitting close to the new President as he takes the oath before the Capitol, looking over his shoulder on the reviewing stand."

Franklin had arranged to take his oath on the Roosevelt Bible. "I will swear to the oath of office, and I think it is best that my three names be used. I expect to bring with me from here our old family Bible in Dutch on which I have twice taken the oath as Governor of New York. This book is a very large and heavy folio."

As Sara and Eleanor took their seats on the reviewing stand opposite Mrs. Hoover, Franklin took James's arm and walked up a ramp inside the Capitol. From there, out of view, he moved in a wheelchair to the door leading to the stand. Again, he took his eldest son's arm as he swung down the burgundy carpet to the rostrum.

After Franklin was sworn in, Eleanor returned to the White House in her pinstripe suit to receive in the Blue Room. Franklin's cousin Daisy Suckley jotted down notes of the evening: "Delanos & Roosevelts in large numbers. Mrs. James Roosevelt came, looking tired but 'game' and said she was of course 'just waiting around to see Franklin.'"

However, by evening, Sara was radiant. "Her spine was as straight, her jaw was as strong, and her commanding hazel eyes as bright as ever," remembered Elliott. "She took special pains with her *toilette* this evening, with every gleaming hair arranged in place in her pompadour, resplendent in a long gown fitted snugly to her majestic frame, with her magnificent pearls looped on the pale skin of her imposing bosom."

The Delanos were there in full force, including sisters Dora and Kassie, with her second husband, Hiram Price Collier. Also present were Frederick, now a widower, with his two daughters. Betty Roosevelt, Rosy's widow, was present, as was her stepdaughter Helen Roosevelt Robinson. Eleanor's aunt Corinne was at the dinner along with cousin Alice, who helpfully told Eleanor that she would teach her the First Lady's duties. Sara would write Anna: "Aunt Kassie loved it and I hear of her singing praises of your Mother, which pleases me above all, as I like to see the family appreciate her & they *do.*" Franklin's legitimate ambition also glowed that night. He had color, force, and splendor.

On that same evening, in her room at the White House, Sara wrote out a message to the nation in her own hand on her Hyde Park stationery: "I shall leave my son in Washington, confident that he will give all that is in him, to help his country, & I shall be glad if every mother will pray to help and preserve him." She signed the message, "Mrs. James Roosevelt."

This was only the first of her visits to the White House during Franklin's occupancy; including Inauguration Day and Christmas, she would come here for a total of fifteen days in 1933. In fact, she sat by Franklin's side on March 7, a reassuring presence to the nation, when her son held the first of his Fireside Chats. Before he made any decision about the nation's banking crisis, Sara had called him: "Franklin, I am bringing two banking friends of mine in to see you at eleven tomorrow morning." At her insistence, he met with the heads of Chase Bank (Tom Lamont, who had once rented 49 East Sixty-fifth) and National City Bank of New York (James Perkins). "The bank holiday of March, 1933, was their idea; Father dictated cooperation with bankers as an ingredient of the New Deal," said Elliott.

Eleanor held her first "at home," receiving one hundred officials on March 17, coincidentally the couple's twenty-eighth anniversary. Franklin told her to pick out a gift for herself: "After a fruitless week of thinking and lying awake to find whether you need or want undies, dresses, hats, shoes, sheets, towels, rouge, soup plates, candy, flowers, lamps, laxation pills, whisky, beer, etchings or caviar . . . I GIVE IT UP!"

Sara continued to hold the nation's attention. Awards and honors came to her from across the nation within weeks of Franklin's inauguration. The Huguenot Society, of which she was a member, bestowed its Huguenot Cross, after which she gave a brief thanks and mentioned Philippe de Lannoy, her Delano ancestor. Everyone was interested in Franklin's family. The president received a message from the assistant secretary of the navy, Henry Latrobe Roosevelt, who happened to be his fifth cousin.* "[A colleague] asks if Sistie is too small to christen one of the submarines." Anna's daughter

---

*Five Roosevelts served as assistant secretary of the navy. The first was Teddy; then came Franklin, then Ted Jr. (who served under Harding and Collidge), then Theodore Douglas Robinson (Corinne's son and Teddy's nephew, who served under Coolidge), and, last, Henry Roosevelt.

was not yet six. Franklin replied, "Yes, I think Sistie is too young to do a christening for about two years. I have no other candidates!"

Eleanor rejected the title "First Lady," preferring "Mrs. Roosevelt"—just as another Democratic wife, Jacqueline Bouvier Kennedy, would do nearly thirty years later—but Sara enjoyed being thought of as First Mother. Naturally, as Mother's Day approached on May 14, the only living mother of a president was tops on the celebration list.

Mother's Day, declared by Congress in 1914, was initially established as a part of the Mother's Day Work Club, which improved unsanitary living conditions that contributed to childhood disease. Anna Reeves Jarvis, who had lost eight of her ten children to disease, began the club in the 1800s. On May 14 1933 (Mother's Day), Sara was named Mother of the Year and broadcast a carefully crafted message over NBC that reflected her son's vision:

> At last Mother's Day has a real significance for me since my son, the President, has issue a Proclamation which lifts this day somewhat above the largely sentimental expressions of other years. It suggests a "new deal" for "forgotten mothers" and neglected children. Millions are unemployed and myriad of destitute mothers with dependent children are praying, not for flowers but for flour; not for candy but for bread; not for greeting cards and telegrams but for food, clothes, medicines and the practical things of life.

A phonograph record was made of her address, and Sara sent one to her son.

In counterpoint, Eleanor's uncommon activities perplexed the American public, many of whom were horrified—not so much at her causes but at the fact that she carried them out independent of her husband. Eleanor had hoped to ground her work in the East Wing. Vice President Jack Garner's wife, Ettie, continued to be her husband's secretary, so Eleanor asked Franklin if she could handle some of his mail. He firmly turned her down, giving the reason that it would upset LeHand. Of course, her exclusion from the Oval Office gave her a great opportunity to dedicate herself to her own national interests—but at the time, she was hurt by Franklin's dismissal.

Marion Dickerman said that Eleanor "wanted him to confide in her his ambitions, his plans, his ideas. And yet as he approached the presidency, he seemed more and more to withdraw, and when he did become president and Eleanor asked to be his secretary and he refused, I think it was a factor that drew her more completely into a desire to be a person herself and to continue with her writings."

Neither Eleanor nor Franklin wanted the lives of her friends to be the object of speculation, so Eleanor put a spin on the past. Hickok, now providentially assigned by the AP to full-time coverage of Eleanor, wrote: "She built a cottage near the furniture factory in order that the children might learn to live without servants." That the cottage was built for her and two women companions, and had nothing to do with her children, never saw print.

Sara, on the other hand, epitomized tradition, but to family members and friends she had already shown her incredible adaptability to circumstances that are still seen by many Americans as outside the norm. For example, she forged a close relationship with Eleanor's friends Marion Dickerman and her partner, Nancy Cook. A number of biographers have stated that Sara was cool to Eleanor's friends. Yet in July she left with her grandson John on a trip to Europe, and the first letter she wrote on board was to Dickerman. The news Sara imparts is not of great interest, but rather its importance is more subtle—it lies in the warm feeling she shows for Dickerman and her acceptance of Dickerman's relationship with Cook and, in turn, their relationship with Eleanor.

"My dear Marion," she wrote. "Your peppermints are welcome & delicious & better still, your kind thoughts of me. . . . The first 24 hours are past & the sea is absolutely smooth & the sun shines. My two windows are open & I am not tempted to go on deck. It is lovely here with books and flowers—Hope you will have a peaceful happy summer & take a rest after your strenuous work in New York—& try to take care of my dear Eleanor—Give my love to Nancy and believe me affectionately yours. . . ."

Later that month Franklin and Eleanor returned to Hyde Park for a quick break. Again, Sara made headlines: MOTHER WELCOMES ROOSEVELT HOME. Franklin had urged the newspapers to refer to his family homestead not as Hyde Park but as Krum Elbow, making use of the old Dutch word for the crooked part of the river on which it sits. *The New York Times* quickly ran a story on its front page, PRESIDENT IS OVERRULED BY MOTHER ON KRUM ELBOW. It said: "Both the President and reporters were rather firmly corrected today by the only one with authority to overrule the President, Mrs. Sara Delano Roosevelt, his mother and owner of the property. His mother said that her husband disliked the name Springwood, which was the estate's proper name, and had changed it to Hyde Park. 'This is one time,' said Mrs. Roosevelt, 'when I can correct the President.'"

In August news of Sara was placed under the *New York Times* masthead directly in the center of the paper. She and Rosy's widow both signed a National Recovery Association agreement applying to the wages and hours of Sara's sixteen Hyde Park staff and farm employees and Betty's nine. In

October, Sara and Franklin motored to Leesburg, Virginia, to see friends. In November she presided at an emergency fund meeting of the Visiting Nurse Service of the Henry Street Settlement, to which she had been a contributor. In her comments at 47 East Sixty-fifth, where she gathered her committee, she praised the work of her friend Lillian Wald, the settlement's director, in leading nurses to pay a total of 8 million free visits to the sick throughout the city's boroughs. Sara used her connections on behalf of one of the world's greatest centers for nursing education, which heeded its slogan of "never refusing a call." At one anniversary benefit, Sara assisted in reeling in George Gershwin and George M. Cohan as entertainers.

More gravely, Sara vehemently opposed recognition of the Soviet Union by the United States. When Franklin sought improved relations with that country, Sara "felt this would be a disastrous move and widely misunderstood by the great majority of their friends," remembered Eleanor. Franklin was amused and admitted that it probably would shock some old friends, but the Communist country would nonetheless be recognized. Sara was peeved and declared that she would never visit the White House again.

It took her two weeks to relent.

38

⁂

"The Duchess"

As 1934 began, Sara realized that she needed a secretary to navigate waves of press demands and a steady current of correspondence, for she was awash in more letters and requests than any other previous president's mother. Although many wealthy women had social secretaries, Sara had always preferred to respond to her letters, pay her bills, and keep her calendar herself. Since 1900, the year of James's death, Sara had managed Hyde Park, its estates and its farm, alone. She now realized that Franklin's need for a ceremonial figure—Eleanor was not happy in such a role—was displacing the comfortable activities of her past. Although she had never before delegated the responsibilities she deemed her own, given her son's presidency, she agreed to have a personal secretary assist her.

Sara was more popular and better known than any president's mother heretofore. The American public, in the uncertain Depression, looked to Sara for steadiness and sensibility, traits she exemplified. Her graciousness, her exquisite manners, and her image as the family figurehead garnered her the White House nickname "the Duchess." As Great Britain turned to King George V and Queen Mary for stability as the Depression continued, America looked to Sara Delano Roosevelt. "No member of the President's family is more popular than this energetic woman who wears her years so lightly," said one publication. *News-Week*, which put Sara on its cover in September, stated that "she is the closest to a Dowager Queen this delighted country has ever known."

By the middle of Franklin's first term, the common man was steadfastly behind Franklin, even if big business was not. His mother was becoming an icon. It would have been hard to escape her image in the 1930s. Movies, for example, were popular as an inexpensive escape from hard times, and selected shorts, shown before the feature, offered Sara as light relief from grim newsreels. *Literary Digest* noted that "when she smiles she looks so much like the President that motion-picture audiences break into delighted applause."

Eleanor's picture did not draw the same delight: she was highly praised by many; she was vilified by some. For one thing, Eleanor was deeply involved in her own work for social justice. "She is, by being herself, a good deal of the New Deal," said *News-Week*, which also stated that Eleanor, compared with Franklin, "is undoubtedly more radical than he is in his public utterances."

The year before, Eleanor had been the driving force behind a model resettlement community for the poor in Arthurdale, West Virginia. She was also focusing on civil rights for African Americans and had invited Mary McLeod Bethune to the White House a number of times. Having seen Sara tactfully smooth over an embarrassing moment during their 1924 luncheon with Bethune, Eleanor watched for Bethune's entrance up the White House walkway so she could run and take her arm to prevent her from being quizzed by ignorant guards. (One time a White House guard addressed Bethune as "Auntie.")

Eleanor disliked ceremonial activities and gladly left them to Sara, especially those in the New York area. One paper said that "New York City has called upon her to represent her son and daughter-in-law at various functions since they entered the White House." Another opined: "No public function in this city is complete without her, and as titular head of her family she represents her son at a ceaseless round of functions, public, private and philanthropic." It seemed almost as if Eleanor and her husband had planned the timing of the White House years: now that their children were grown, Sara could focus her attention on filling in for Eleanor and making Eleanor's absence from Franklin's side less noticeable.

One of the most important of these events was the January 30, 1934, birthday party held in Franklin's honor to benefit the Warm Springs Foundation. The nation was wildly enthusiastic. Preparation for fund-raising galas across the nation had begun the previous year. Forty events were cele-brated in New York City alone. Many places outside the country also joined in the festivities; possibly the most surprising location for a virtual birthday party was Admiral Byrd's base camp Little America in the Antarctic on the Bay of Whales.

At the White House, Franklin received a birthday message signed by forty thousand names that took forty-eight hours for Western Union to transmit over four wires. Eleanor herself attended three charity balls in Washington. Public school teachers throughout the country gave talks to students "emphasizing the courage and heroism of the President, especially in his overcoming of physical handicaps," according to *The New York Times*.

On the great day itself, Sara called Franklin first thing in the morning from East Sixty-fifth Street to wish him a happy birthday. Franklin teased her, "I see by the papers that you have planned a very busy day for your-self." Sara first went to a luncheon engagement. From there, she appeared at a tea and fashion show held to benefit the Warm Springs Foundation on the liner *Queen of Bermuda*, which was docked in New York Harbor. From the ship, Sara gave her second national radio address: "It pleases me immeasurably to know that Great Britain, through one of her colonies, is honoring my son the President and taking this interest in Georgia's Warm Springs."

Sara was driven home to change for the evening. When she left her house again, she was accompanied by a motorcycle escort and a car with three Secret Service agents, including a man who still carried lead splinters above his eye from a bullet fired in the Miami assassination attempt on her son.

The pomp was just beginning. At the Astor Hotel (on Broadway in the mid-Forties), the Seventy-first Regiment of the New York National Guard—who were wearing full-dress uniform of white trousers, gray jack-ets, and tall black shakos (a cylindrical military hat with a peak and a plume)—presented arms as Sara entered the ballroom lobby. *Literary Digest* said that "America has never seen anything any more like a queen mother than the picture she made as she swept through the line of saluting soldiery at the President's birthday ball in New York."

Sara was shadowed—as she had been all day—by women reporters. At dinner she received so many corsages that she offered all but the white orchids that she selected to complement her black gown to the contingent of female journalists, saying, "They are so beautiful they should not go to waste." After dinner she spoke: "What gives the greatest happiness to me is the realization that my son, the President, is receiving such a wonderful tribute of affection. It is that which means most to us."

From the Astor Hotel, her motorcycle escort led her car to the Waldorf

Hotel. When Sara entered the ballroom, five thousand people rose in her honor "as a fanfare of trumpets heralded her arrival" and George M. Cohan waved a huge American flag from the stage. She walked to box number one, where Bernard Baruch awaited her. At eleven P.M. Sara cut a giant birthday cake and then Franklin's voice entered the ballroom from his radio broadcast at the White House, saying that he represented "the hundreds of thousands of crippled children in our country." Sara, who was seventy-nine years old, left after the entertainment ended sometime past midnight.

When Sara returned to Hyde Park, she continued the theme that she had begun with Franklin's presidency, which was to mention her husband, James, often and give him credit for Franklin's success. She frequently told her friends that her only sorrow was that James had not lived to see his son become president, although she thought that *somehow* he knew what Franklin had achieved. "He would have been very happy with the developments of the years," she said modestly. Now she told reporters that never "in her wildest dreams" did she think her son would be president and that her only ambition was that he "grow to be like his father, straight and honorable, just and kind, an upstanding American."

A few weeks later she was off to Canada for a wedding and again said that her son's sense of justice, which she thought was his most outstanding characteristic, "was an inheritance from his father." Later Sara added that she was "glad he has such a marvelous fund of knowledge—he got that from his father—and such a wonderful disposition." She did admit that "he belongs to an energetic family." After the wedding Sara made a special trip to Hamilton, Ontario, to visit Franklin's beloved nanny, Mamie. Later that month Sara was again quoted as saying that her only wish for her son was that he "grow up to be like his father . . . whom he worshipped."

The esteem in which Sara was held sometimes inadvertently embroiled her in conflicts from which there was no easy retreat.

In March, while Eleanor was traveling to Puerto Rico with Hickok to measure the Depression's impact there, Manhattan's Lower East Side aldermen voted to establish an eight-acre park that stretched seven blocks long, from Canal to East Houston Streets, and one block wide, from Chrystie to Forsythe Streets. It was the largest park project in the area in a hundred years, big enough to accommodate seven playgrounds. (The majority of the playgrounds were restricted to being for either just boys or just girls, with the best equipment reserved for boys.) Five thousand children could play at one time. Two pools allowed wading in the summer and ice-skating in the winter, and a roller-skating rink operated year-round. The park was to be ringed with trees and benches. There would be a band shell, and floodlights would make the park available for use until 10:30 P.M.

Landscape architects from Franklin's Civil Works Administration planned the park, which was "a prototypic urban renewal project of New York Parks Commissioner Robert Moses," according to a neighborhood newspaper. (The wire trash cans planned for the park were the first ever designed and put into use in the city.) Parkland was available because the city had condemned residences and cleared slum areas from the Manhattan Bridge to Canal Street. Since the neighborhood was crammed with tenement houses filled with immigrant families, the park would serve a real need. *The New York Times* reported in a front-page story the day the park opened that before, neighborhood children had no choice except to play in the street: because of the park's sunny expanse, "many of them got the first coat of tan they ever had in their lives." No one doubted the necessity of this green space. However, given that it was New York City, a political controversy arose over its dedication.

As soon as Sara was proposed as the honoree, another faction developed in favor of naming the park after Charles B. Stover, the late city parks commissioner. A reporter from the *New York Daily News* called the aldermen's committee meeting "a cat-and-dog fight." Apparently when Sara got wind of the dispute, she sent two telegrams that said she "was not entitled to the honor" and suggested that the park be named either for the former parks commissioner or for Lillian D. Wald, founder of the nearby Henry Street Settlement and, in 1893, the Henry Street Visiting Nurse Service (later, just the Visiting Nurse Service).

The committee member who proposed Sara's name was indignant that she had learned of the aldermen's disagreement. "How did Mrs. Roosevelt happen to send those telegrams withdrawing her name and endorsing the name of Stover?" he demanded. Someone on the dissident side confessed that he had written Sara to tell her of the fracas.

The East Side alderman "snorted," according to the *Daily News,* and asked, "What did you expect that this noble woman would reply to a letter of that kind?"

Nonetheless, in mid-March the Sara Delano Roosevelt Park was officially named and was dedicated in mid-September. Mindful of the hard feelings that the naming dispute had caused, Sara wrote her friend Rita Kleeman: "Please dear Rita do me a great favor. *Call up* Mr. Moses. . . . I am unable to be in New York and am very sorry I cannot be at the opening of the park—it is impossible for me to leave home." She did, however, listen to the radio dedication and heard a speaker orate, "Mother Roosevelt . . . symbolizes the ideal mother and, indeed, glorifies American motherhood."

~

Sara made only half a dozen trips to the White House in 1934, staying for a total of eleven days. The chief usher, J. B. White, recalled that when she visited, "the staff snapped to attention, and the service was as formal as if a queen were being entertained." Sara usually traveled with her own tea, as the Delano private stock was so much finer than anything that could be bought commercially. Still, the White House staff joked that Sara was not getting her money's worth, for she was subsidizing her son's White House and family expenses to the tune of $100,000 a year ($1.4 million today). "We used to say Sara had as much right to be at the White House as anyone—she was paying for the privilege," said Lillian Rogers Parks, a maid at the residence. Grandson Elliott said that Sara regarded her contribution as "her duty to him [Franklin] and to her country." Sara was already earning fewer dividends because Franklin had put her portfolio under the same strict scrutiny as his own. Long before blind trusts were required of presidents, Franklin had sold any stocks whose companies competed for government contracts, as well as mining stocks, for ethical reasons. Sara did the same at his request.

Franklin and Eleanor would join Sara at Hyde Park whenever they could, and in the first year of his presidency, Hyde Park had begun to be called the summer White House. Grace Tully, Franklin's private secretary (his longtime secretary Missy LeHand was in failing health), noted that Sara "never quite knew who would be roaming around her home or how many would be occupying her rooms—she accepted these changes in her otherwise peaceful life as necessary to her son's carrying out his official duties, and never complained."

To Eleanor's amusement, at one lunch a Vassar student asked Sara, "Mrs. Roosevelt, what is the president going to do about the budget?" Sara, whose attention was elsewhere, heard the word *budget* and said, "Budget? Budget? What does the child mean? Franklin knows nothing about the budget. I always make the budget."

In time she realized that the national budget was a very heavy load on her son and wanted to understand it. Sara often hosted Franklin's friends and political appointees when they came to the area, even when Franklin was not in Hyde Park. Lewis Douglas, an economist who was an adviser to the Treasury Department, told a story about lunching at Hyde Park. "Of course, Mrs. Roosevelt Sr. presided. I sat on her left. She said to me, 'They tell me you're an expert on the budget. Some of my friends tell me that my son, Franklin, is doing very funny things about the budget. Will you explain it to me?'"

Sara asked even her own help to assist her in understanding her son's policies. "One day at Hyde Park," said Lizzie McDuffie, a White House maid and the wife of Franklin's valet, "she even called me out on the front porch and had me sit down and discuss the theory of pensions with her.

"'Don't you think I take good care of my help on this place?' she asked me. 'Shouldn't they be able to save money for their old age, and not expect pensions?'

"That was a hard one to answer!" the housemaid remembered.

In April, Eleanor agreed to join Sara for a public visit to the Museum of the City of New York to view a portrait of Franklin. In honor of the unveiling, Sara had lent the museum Isaac the Patriot's silver tankard. Before they approached the display, Sara explained its history: "During the Revolution, when the British, or the Hessians—I prefer to think it was the Hessians—looted some of the houses, they broke into the Isaac Roosevelt house and took the family silver. But this piece was on the hob [a shelf in the fireplace] and was blackened by smoke from the fire and they didn't know what it was."

Sara continued with a laugh, "One of them kicked it and there's been a dent in it ever since!" By now the group had arrived at the tankard. The reporters, along with Sara and Eleanor, leaned forward to study the beautifully polished piece for the flaw—which seemed to be missing. Apparently, a zealous museum staff member had decided to have the historic dent repaired. There was an embarrassed silence, and the group walked to the next display and feigned great interest in it.

After the trip to the museum, Eleanor lunched at Sara's house, along with the Monday Sewing Society, to which Sara—but not Eleanor—still belonged. Eleanor had entertained Sara and the club at the White House the year before and was grateful for a complimentary note sent her afterward, to which she responded thankfully that she had worried that "the old crowd might disapprove of many things which I did."

That afternoon Sara remained at home after the meeting, while an energetic Eleanor visited a benefit exhibit at an art gallery, paid a call at Todhunter School, and received a committee of the New York Newspaper Women's Club at her own house. A reporter summarized Eleanor's activities with no sense of irony: "Mrs. Roosevelt had a busy day, with not even time to go shopping."

A few days later Sara dedicated trees in the Shakespeare Garden in Central Park and scattered rose petals from her Hyde Park garden on the ground. As she was getting into her car on Fifth Avenue, an eleven-year-old girl who had heard that the president's mother was in the park roller-skated up to the car and jumped into the open vehicle to look for Sara's son. The child was dismayed when she saw for herself that the president was not with his mother. As a consolation, an unfazed Sara gave her the bouquet she had just received.

Again on Mother's Day, Sara was feted in Manhattan. She used her role with great authority and influence, first accepting traditional wishes from her daughter-in-law and son and from the wives and widows of past presidents, including Eleanor's aunt Edith. She also accepted greetings from the mother of Charles Lindbergh, who was still the nation's hero (although he would not be for long). Sara then gave a nationally broadcast radio talk to announce that the federal government would be disbursing hundreds of millions of dollars to recondition the dwellings of the poor. She also asked for contributions for the American Friends Service Committee to be used as relief for West Virginia miners and their families.

In mid-June, Eleanor and James saw Sara off on a two-month trip to Europe as Franklin's goodwill ambassador and as his covert diplomat. (Eleanor was about to leave for the western states on a vacation to national parks with Hickok.) In London, Sara stayed at the American embassy with Ambassador Bingham (the post was not yet Ambassador Kennedy's). The ambassador soon received a friendly note from Buckingham Palace asking if Mrs. Roosevelt was available for tea. Sara responded "without ado" that she could go immediately, and her driver was directed through the palace's garden entrance, reserved for family and other royalty. She had a friendly private chat with Queen Mary and King George V and sipped tea in their majesties' private apartments.

Sara claimed that King George V said little but expressed "friendliness and frankness and a common sense view of the world." However, she took some private messages from them back to Franklin. Sara was asked to stay for dinner but had another engagement, although she returned for a garden party on another day, at which both French and British leaders also entrusted her with messages for her son. At a luncheon given for Sara by England's prime minister, Ramsay MacDonald, the two discussed Great Britain's increase in naval warship construction and its impact on the upcoming world naval conference. Also lending importance to this informal discussion were a number of arms experts. She brought everything she heard to her son after returning home.

When Sara was in Europe, Eleanor was on a trip to the Caribbean with Franklin and their elder sons James and Elliott. Franklin wrote his mother:

"How thrilling is the news about your visit to Buckingham Palace. The papers here say you were the 'best Ambassador the American people have ever sent to England!'" He added: "My only worry is Europe! I am glad you are not in Germany."

Sara spent three weeks in England and in Scotland, where she bought some tweed for a suit for Franklin. Then she left for Paris, where she visited Dora and again stayed at an American embassy. There she conversed in French and made a short radio address in both languages at a luncheon in her honor. The American papers reported that Sara had "made the biggest hit in Paris since Lindbergh." When told this, she responded innocently, "Isn't that complimentary. Depend on the newspapers to say beautiful things."

The Europeans deemed her a "wonder woman" to keep her schedule. As she moved bilingually from one event to another, she answered reporters' questions—"Am I tired? No indeed." She was the last person to board the ship home because she tried to squeeze in some final moments at the Rouen Cathedral. Arriving in New York, she politely refused to see the custom-officials who came on board in deference to her status and instead stood on the pier in chilly weather to wait in line under the sign "R." Her granddaughter Anna, and the inevitable reporters, waited for her. Sara told them that everyone in Europe was for her son, adding, "Those who didn't feel that way I probably didn't meet." Then she left for lunch at Sherry's with Anna and Sara's siblings Fred and Kassie.

Soon after Sara returned, *News-Week* magazine put Sara on its cover with the head THE PRESIDENT'S MOTHER. In this candid photo taken at an evening event, she wore a cascade of orchids, two strings of pearls, and long white gloves. Her hair was silver and her figure obviously thicker than when Franklin had first taken state office more than a decade earlier. The story, "Sara Roosevelt, Matriarch of an American Clan," talked of her as being America's aristocracy, representing breeding, intelligence, virtue, and wealth. As the nation saw a spate of change rushing through in the guise of various alphabet-soup agencies, Sara remained as steady as Plymouth Rock.

Eleanor planned a huge eightieth-birthday party for Sara on September 21, which was allegedly a surprise party, albeit one with reporters present. As she planned the party, Eleanor wrote Hickok: "I've been such an unsatisfactory daughter-in-law." Yet she made sure to invite every family member, about sixty in all. Informal invitations were sent and no one was sure exactly how many were coming, so the Hyde Park staff prepared food in abundance. The kitchen had been well prepared by Franklin's frequent trips from

Albany, when he brought home any number of people as guests. Sara's habit was to have extra places put at her table. "It is so much pleasanter and easier to remove places if no guests come than to add them hurriedly for unexpected people, and so make everyone crowded and uncomfortable." Three manservants who had served Sara at the governor's residence in Albany asked for the privilege of serving at her luncheon. The party was also to celebrate Elliott's birthday, which was the day before Sara's, as well as Franklin Jr.'s August birthday.

The White House staff sent a telegram: "Those of us who are working temporarily in 'The President's House' here in Washington join today with those who gather at 'His Mother's House' in Hyde Park to celebrate the triple birthday anniversaries." Franklin had left the White House to watch the America's Cup races in Long Island Sound from Vincent Astor's yacht and then went on to Hyde Park.

Although Dora stayed in Paris, Frederick and Kassie helped their sister celebrate her day. Frederick seemed uncomfortable with photographers present, and when he wished his sister a happy eightieth, he shook her hand. Sara wore a white crepe dress, a change from her usual black or gray, with an amethyst necklace and an orchid corsage that matched the shade of the stones.

The New York Times described the event: "This was no party for a quiet, house-bound old lady; it was a lively and energetic celebration of the anniversary of a woman who in recent weeks toured Europe and who exercised full and active supervision over the estate to which she came as the bride of James Roosevelt, long since dead."

Franklin rose and with a glass of vintage sauterne toasted her simply: "The best mother in the land." Her grandchildren gave her a scroll that read, in part, "On this 80th birthday, we, your five grandchildren, want you to know that there is nothing we can give you which can really express the feeling of all of us in terms of love and affection."

Sara responded, "I believe this is the happiest birthday of my eighty years. It is so nice to be here with my son, the family and my old friends and neighbors. It seems especially nice to celebrate here in my own dear home, which has always been the sweetest and most beautiful place in the whole world to me.

"Of course, that is what a home should mean to everyone, and I believe the thing I am proudest of in what my son is trying to do, is the movement to enable so many people to brighten and beautify their homes. Where and how we live has so much to do with our happiness, that this is bound to bring about a more prosperous and a happier country."

She then cut the cake and gave Franklin the first piece. The next day she wrote Franklin: "You all gave me a wonderful birthday. Eleanor was too *lovely*. Your loving Mummy. I miss you all but I seem busy in my lazy way."

The celebratory mood of the birthday bash masked the younger genera-tion's many problems. Elliott had made a precipitous first marriage and then abandoned his wife and young child. At age twenty-four, he was already divorced and remarried. Eleanor always had a soft spot for him—he was the child born after the death of the first Franklin Jr.—and sent him money so as not "to give the impression to others that we won't give him anything." Anna had fallen in love with John Boettiger, a journalist, and would divorce Curtis Dall. Rumors about James and his other women swirled around him, while his wife, Betsey, did her best to ignore the gossip.

Sara knew about these problems and, although she was dismayed, did not take sides. She wrote in a very shaky hand to Anna, who had left New York to obtain residency in Lake Tahoe, pending a Nevada divorce. "Dar-ling little Anna, I am glad you wrote poor old Granny, as the news is in all the papers this morning." She was extremely sympathetic, though she admitted that "the thought of Reno gives me a sinking feeling in my heart!" and invited Anna and her two children to settle at Hyde Park. To Eleanor, she commented sadly: "So the news of our family is out." Eleanor responded similarly to Hickok, writing: "One cannot hide things in this world, can one?"

Eleanor said that the children's marriages were unstable—there ulti-mately would be nineteen marriages among the five children—because they "were not really rooted in any particular home," and lived a nomadic exis-tence, which she once blamed on Franklin for not breaking from his mother. Eleanor apparently could not understand the children's deep love for Hyde Park, as attested to by their many statements and the scroll they had just given Sara, which read, "Hyde Park has been, and always will be, our real home, and Hyde Park means you and all the fun you gave us there."

Sara, on the other hand, thought Eleanor should be more outspoken with her children about personal ethics. "She often got angry with me because I seldom told them what was right or wrong," Eleanor later wrote. "The reason I didn't was that I was never sure." Things were black or white to Sara, whereas Eleanor saw shades of gray.

Eleanor took some responsibility for the continued unhappiness of her children, telling Elliott that "none of you older children experienced secu-rity. You could never count on advice of a father and a mother." This state-ment echoes Sara's comment about the necessity of teaching right from wrong. Eleanor always felt that she was a better mother to the younger children than the elder ones, yet it was the youngest, John, who said he no longer had parents after the onset of Franklin's polio. Eleanor ultimately took a pragmatic approach to her children's divorces, saying that when there is no possibility of marital harmony, "it seems to me that there is nothing to do but to resort to a divorce."

Sara was a little more pointed in her opinion. Earlier in the year she had agreed to be interviewed for a biography, written by the journalist Rita Kleeman. (Kleeman met Sara when they were passengers on the same ship sailing from France. Her first glimpse of Sara was as she boarded the ship from a tugboat, climbing up the ladder thrown down to her; Kleeman became an immediate admirer.) Sara put her finger on the causes of her grandchildren's divorces: "But after all, they are the natural result of their upbringing." Her statement was a zinger, but no one paid heed.

Sara's indulgence had run its course, and she was displeased when the grandchildren took advantage of her. One time James stopped by "without notice" to ask his grandmother for money while she was entertaining Amelia Earhart and Lord and Lady Astor. She commented to her guests, "I always like having the children, but . . . they never bother to telephone. . . . But of course they have had no bringing up."

Unstated was that the Roosevelt children lacked any model of a happy marriage. Of their grandparents, James had died before they were born, as had both their maternal grandparents, following a miserable marriage. Despite Sara's efforts to have Franklin and Eleanor spend time with their children, the ill-suited couple preferred to remain the stars of their own galaxies. Franklin focused on his health and political ambition, and Eleanor's many causes took her far afield.

Eleanor later admitted to Elliott that she "spent so much time away. You never knew what home could be. It was selfishness on my part." Her sentiment was seconded by James: "Mother was so busy she had little time for any of us."

After the Mercer situation, the children noticed that if Franklin held out his arms to Eleanor, their mother would just walk past. As the children grew, vicious caregivers paid them punishing attention, mitigated only when they visited Sara, who overcompensated by indulging them. Back home they had to share their house with various so-called he-shes and Louis Howe, who ignored his *own* family. This was not a model of a happy home from which strong marriages would naturally evolve.

Sara wanted to dissociate herself from the situation. She pointed out that "they are Franklin's children—not mine. Of course I love them, but Franklin stands alone!" Sara was never a worrier, and she held her head up during her grandchildren's divorces. "You know, a little philosophy helps a great deal," she would say. Her grandchildren noticed how well she responded to their marital woes. Anna said, "I've always been quite amazed at the fact that Granny was able to accept the divorces without seemingly getting upset."

The yet-unmarried children were having a few adjustment problems, too. John had just graduated from Groton and Franklin spoke at the graduation, which pleased everyone but his son. Neither John nor Franklin Jr. liked the attention their father's presidency brought, and they often refused to let photographers take their pictures. Sara commented with her usual sense of perspective: "They don't like having their father President. They consider it a definite handicap but I tell my grandsons that it is something for them to live up to."

Still, both Eleanor and Sara realized that the divorces were inevitable and smoothed over their differences. As 1934 came to a close, Sara and Eleanor left together on a campaign tour to stump for Caroline O'Day, a woman running for the congressman-at-large seat (that no longer exists) from New York. Sara and her daughter-in-law had actually become a remarkably effective political odd couple.

39

Gracious Lady, Modern Woman

By the third year of Franklin's presidency, Sara and Eleanor had settled into their respective roles. Although Sara's activities were less controversial than Eleanor's, she made sure that her appearances, no matter how ceremonial, dovetailed with Eleanor's interests and with those of Franklin. She carefully directed her energies toward disadvantaged women and children, as well as health and education.

In 1935, for example, eighty-year-old Sara attended meetings of the New York Kindergarten Association and of the United Parents Association, an advocacy group for children's education. She also lent public support to the Psychiatric and Dependent Children Institutions of the Girls Service League and to the first City Parks and Recreation Department program for "fifty-three helpless eastside tenement tots, victims of infantile paralysis representing twenty-two nationalities," as described by *The New York Times*. Sara generated interest in Children's Village, a juvenile correctional facility near Dobbs Ferry, and in New York City she helped celebrate both Hospital Day and Florence Nightingale's birthday.

During the Depression's national housing crisis, Sara opened an exhibition of prefabricated houses and spoke of her hope that "women of America will more and more have good homes, well planned, such as this." By such actions, she brought media attention to social problems that desperately needed resolution.

As Eleanor would also do, Sara used her fame to raise the fortunes of her own favorite causes. For a decade she had been president of the New York Produce and Flower Guild (formerly Plant, Fruit and Flower, the group that had Teddy as its president). Ever since her son entered the White House, Sara had used her own presidency to draw national attention to the guild's encouragement of child gardeners. She also continued attending Henry Street Settlement meetings.

Most of Sara's events involved serious thought and discussion. In April, though, her dedication of the fairy castle dollhouse given by the actress Colleen Moore to raise funds for crippled children's hospitals must have been pure delight. The fairy castle was so large, and had so many chambers, that it needed its own room to hold it. Moore had spared no expense in its construction: by the time it was finished, more than seven hundred specialized craftsmen had contributed to its whimsical beauty. The fairy castle raised $650,000 on its national tour launched on the toy floor of Macy's by Sara, who said, "The work of our hospitals for crippled children is very dear to my heart." (The fairy castle remains one of the most popular permanent exhibits at the Museum of Science and Industry on Chicago's South Side.)

Franklin's birthday celebration was held at the end of January. The recipient of the 1935 funds was an infantile paralysis research organization (now March of Dimes). The event was larger than the year before: now 7,500 communities (1,173 more than in 1934) held at least one function, not counting numerous parties given at private homes. More than two hundred public festivities took place in New York City. Before the big day Sara accepted the official poster for the birthday celebration drawn by Howard Chandler Christy, who also would be the illustrator of the acclaimed "I Want You" Uncle Sam poster. (His mural *The Signing of the Constitution* hangs in the rotunda of the U.S. Capitol.)

In deference to Sara's age, the New York officials asked her to attend only two events. The first was at the Waldorf-Astoria, where chairman Frank Vanderlip Jr., the son of Eleanor's friend Narcissa, and an honor guard escorted her to her box. Sara later left the party to cut a cake at the Plaza Hotel, which held the only benefit for the Warm Springs Foundation. Franklin made an appearance at the Washington ball at the Shoreham Hotel, where he spoke through a nationwide radio hookup.

Each year Franklin's cabinet gave a gala dinner in his honor, and its esteemed guests included Eleanor and Sara. This year the party was held in March at Washington's Mayflower Hotel. Harold Ickes, secretary of the interior, noted in his diary that the group missed Louis Howe, who was "too ill to be there." Howe was deteriorating rapidly from respiratory disorders and would soon be moved by ambulance from the White House, where he had been living in the Lincoln Bedroom and advising Franklin as his secretary, to the Navy Hospital.

Despite her many functions that took her up and down the East Coast, Sara learned to pace herself. She would drop by a movie house every week or so, not to catch the feature but to watch the newsreel that inevitably included her son. As soon as it ended, she would go about her business. In March she unveiled a portrait of Franklin that was commissioned by the New York Genealogical and Biographical Society. Although she admitted, "I have always had a weakness for genealogy," she also told a reporter that "tracing relationship to princely background is a foolish pastime. We all spring from Adam, it is to be supposed—or at least from Noah!" A squall arose among artists because the society had selected a British painter—until the society pointed out that an American artist had painted the coronation portrait of King George VI.

As the Depression wore on, maternal deaths in childbirth increased exponentially, mostly in those many families who could no longer afford full health care and assumed that mothers should come last. In honor of Mother's Day, the U.S. Senate passed a proclamation that included a message on cutting such deaths in childbearing. Sara gave a nationally broadcast talk discussing the work she was doing with the National Association of Maternity Centers "to call attention to the awful and needless sacrifice of lives of mothers and children through lack of proper maternity service." Prizefighter Jack Dempsey spoke at the ceremony, saying that women should train for childbirth in the same way he prepared for a fight. In May and June citizens were pasting decorative stamps on the envelopes they mailed. The stamp had an image of Sara's face framed in an oval, surrounded by the words "Honor Your Mother by Helping Other Mothers."

Now that so many of Sara's older friends were gone, she decided to include more people in her inner circle. One was the esteemed Colonel Edward M. House, who had been a private diplomatic adviser to President Wilson. He and Mrs. House would visit Sara frequently at Hyde Park, and in the summer she would stop at their house in Manchester, Massachusetts, as she journeyed home from Campobello.

Another friend was New York's Judge Benjamin Greenspan,* who told Sara that when one of his daughters was seriously ill, he promised God he would be "a good Jew and devote time and money to good causes." Ever-curious Sara asked a favor of him: she had never been to an Orthodox service on Friday night—could she attend with his family (which included four children)? She went and was "so thrilled and talked and talked about it, and the sincere piety shown by the children."

Sara used her influence on Franklin just as Eleanor did. She maintained the Delano interest in African-American education and believed people of color should be accorded the same privileges as the rest of the population. In March she asked Franklin and Eleanor if they would allow their names to head a list of patrons for a town hall concert to benefit the Palmer Memorial Institute in North Carolina. Missy LeHand wrote a note to Franklin explaining that "it is the colored school of North Carolina, and Mrs. James Roosevelt is very interested in helping Mrs. Charlotte Hawkins Brown with this concert."

That was an easy choice. Weighing more heavily on Franklin was the incidence of the heinous crime of lynching, which increased in the South as the effects of the Depression deepened. In the 1920s federal legislation condemning lynching had been defeated. In 1930 Bethune suggested calling on white southern women to come out against lynching. The idea was praised by African-American men who recognized what a powerful force women had been a decade earlier for suffrage. Consequently, a number of women traveled to Tuskegee Institute to meet with Booker T. Washington's widow to see how they could help. The meetings continued: in Memphis, as four black women delegates entered the auditorium, the one hundred white women already seated rose to their feet in respect. It was an unprecedented action that made the civil rights leaders hopeful. The Association of Southern Women for the Prevention of Lynching (ASWPL) was formed and organized in such states as Florida, Georgia, Mississippi, and Texas.

By the time lynching incidents peaked in 1933, the issue was being revisited by Walter White, the NAACP's executive secretary. White also saw the problem as a good test of the New Deal's civil rights commitment. In December 1933 Franklin gave a national radio address to speak against the "pagan ethics" of lynching.

White's strategy paid off when two senators, including Robert F. Wagner

---

*Judge Greenspan allowed Erskine Caldwell's God's Little Acre to be distributed by Viking Press in 1933. His decision—"The Court may not require the author to put refined language in the mouths of primitive people"—was a milestone against censorship.

of New York, and Harlem congressman Joseph A. Gavagan introduced the Costigan-Wagner Act. The bill would criminalize the acts of local law officers who failed to protect a prisoner or prosecute racial crimes. The ASWPL, however, did not support the bill because its members felt it did not respect regional efforts. Still, the recent passage of federal kidnapping laws following the infamous 1932 Lindbergh kidnapping, and laws against Mafia crime made citizens understand why federal intervention in state crime might be necessary.

Although the bill sailed through the House, filibusters kept it from coming to a vote on the Senate floor. One fierce opponent, Senator Theodore Bilbo of Mississippi, advocated sending all African Americans to Liberia and suggested that Eleanor go with them, to be made "queen of the Negro nation." A rumor floated that "Eleanor clubs" were being formed throughout the South to encourage African-American women to walk out of their jobs as housekeepers and nannies.

Walter White was desperate to meet with Franklin and get the support of the White House behind the bill. Franklin kept dodging him. He knew that this bill would be unpopular in southern states, and he had his first reelection campaign coming up soon. The most significant gesture Franklin had made for African Americans was ensuring that they could be included in federal jobs, but even there he permitted segregation to continue.

White appealed to Eleanor, and she in turn enlisted Sara's support. Both women met him on the White House portico one Sunday afternoon in May. The three cooled their heels there while Franklin, out on a sail, kept them waiting. When he finally joined them, he was in a jovial mood and began to spin a number of amusing anecdotes. However, Franklin could not divert his mother, his wife, and White from their mission.

Finally, the little gathering faced the issue at hand. White presented carefully prepared arguments to back up why the Costigan-Wagner bill should be passed. "Somebody's been priming you," interrupted Franklin, as if White himself was not capable of putting together a cogent argument. "Was it Eleanor?"

When he denied this, Franklin turned to his mother. "Well, at least I know you'll be on my side." Sara "shook her head" and told him absolutely not—she agreed with Mr. White. Franklin laughed at being caught between the two strong-willed women in his life but maintained that he could not afford to alienate the southern leadership of the Senate and House committees.

Without the president behind the bill, support for it evaporated. Throughout the bill's seven-day filibuster, Eleanor sat in the Senate gallery to show her support. Franklin disappointed both women by his choice of political expediency over morality.

~

Sara quickly returned to Hyde Park and left for Campobello the next month. She offered the Hyde Park house to Anna, who moved in with her two children. In July, Sara returned to the Hudson Valley via Fairhaven but had to leave before Eleanor arrived for her own visit. Sara wrote Anna: "I hate missing Mother—she gets here Saturday. . . . I put in wood & coal—I hope Mother will really stay & have a rest."

Sara herself was beginning to feel her age, and the summer heat bothered her terribly. "I find in this hot weather the weakest iced tea with lemon and sometimes mint refreshing and cooling," she wrote her son, "and I only have a little fruit or toast for my evening meal and really feel very well."

The heat did not keep her from entertaining her great-grandchildren, though. Sistie and Buzzy—who "does not wish to be called Buzzy . . . but prefers *Curtis*," she wrote Franklin—were still in Hyde Park and visited "Granny" each morning as she was eating breakfast in bed. "She was very sweet to us," said Ellie Roosevelt Seagraves (Sistie). "We'd climb into her big bed after breakfast and she would read the Katzenjammer Kids and other popular comics until we got restless." (Sara had put on weight and her little great-granddaughter innocently asked Anna why she felt smothered by her nightgown-clad granny's morning hugs.)

That same month Franklin had sent her a newspaper clipping that opined he was "the most consummate socialistic demagogue in our history. He has neither depth nor intellectual honesty in his make-up. He is a rich socialist—the most dangerous man in public life."

Franklin attached what he thought was a whimsical note to his mother: "It's only a very wonderful Mother that can set a wayward son straight again. It's worth trying." Sara was not amused and returned the clip *and* his handwritten addition. "Enclosed seems to me a strange note to send to me, darling son."

Both enjoyed, however, a letter Franklin received from a distant and unknown Delano relative who said she was raising her sons to live up to the "Delano Standards." Franklin wrote back, saying that he liked the expression "Delano Standards," and shared it with Sara.

In August, Franklin and Eleanor arrived at the summer White House, and he reveled in the familiar surroundings. Sara erected a luxurious playhouse called Swan Cottage for the great-grandchildren, complete with windows and front portico. It was designed by an architect to resemble the main entrance to Hyde Park, gray trimmed in white. He modeled the little building after a central-hall colonial house, with ivy climbing up its walls.

Inside, there was one single room, twelve by fifteen feet. There were four windows, two facing front and two facing the Hudson River in the back. The walls were painted blue, and it was outfitted with blue and white curtains and a blue rug. Sara decided to have electricity installed to make it a more realistic home, so there was a kitchen area with an electric stove and small white sink with running hot and cold water. She supplied it with a blue and white child-size tea set, and a set of small red dishes. The living area had comfortable chairs, a round table, and several bookcases. She showed the cottage to a reporter and said—despite her household's many servants—that its purpose was to teach children courtesy and housekeeping skills that are appropriate to learn at *home*. Then she shrugged and noted that nobody seemed to agree with her values anymore. The house was rarely used by the great-grandchildren. Instead, its front portico was the site of spirituals sung for the family by Sara's maid, who had been a professional singer.

To coincide with Sara's birthday, her authorized biography, *Gracious Lady*, written by Rita Kleeman, was published. Kleeman was the author of a number of magazine features and in 1928 had published the country's first college guide after recognizing (through her own experience) that parents needed help in selecting colleges for their children.

Sara had been unsure about having her story told, yet Eleanor encouraged her. "I think you should do it, Mama." Kleeman dug through the Delano journals that survived the Algonac fire, and Sara found various diaries of her own in Hyde Park's attics.

Any writer would feel sorry for what Kleeman was put through before her manuscript could be sent to the publisher. Sara and Franklin reviewed it, as did each of the five grandchildren. "Dear Rita," begins one letter from Sara, "Anna & Johnny do not like a paragraph in your book, in which you say that I show 'great democratic feeling.' . . . I think it better to say in my later years I had been more 'widely interested in modern thought.'"

The edits made by Franklin are interesting, though. He made a few tiny changes here and there and expunged the paragraph about how Sara "could see no use for a woman's club." He crossed out the entire reference to the Colony Club, as he did the accurate statement that Sara had not originally thought that women should have the vote.

He also added a phrase (given here in italics) to Kleeman's description of Sara's occasional official escorts: "a police escort was given her—*though she disliked it*—and her car was preceded by motorcycle policemen while shrieking sirens cleared her way."

He also edited out part of the reference to his handicap. Kleeman had written that Franklin had "recovered the use of the upper part of his body and the paralysis persisted only in his legs from above the knees." Franklin excised the middle material so it read that he had *"partially* recovered the use of his legs from above the knees."

The only immediate family member who said she did not have time to look at the manuscript was Eleanor.

Gracious Lady was widely and favorably reviewed and added to Sara's stature. *The New York Times* wrote: "In 1900 she was, quite distinctly, a mid-Victorian lady almost 50 years old; in 1935, at 81, she is a modern woman."

One fall day Sara expected several guests Franklin had sent to her house, including the president of General Foods, Clarence Francis. At lunch she turned to him and said, "I get one of these Christmas boxes from your company every year. How can I get twelve?" He told her he'd send the twelve she wanted and added that they would cost $3.75 each.

"That's fine," said Sara. "Send six to New York and six up here."

Francis said that after they left, one of the lunch guests asked him, "You're not going to charge her, are you?" He replied, "You bet I am. That son of hers has taken a lot of money from me. This is the first chance I've ever had to take some from him."

When he returned to the office, the public relations director of General Foods went to see him. He had heard about the charges for the Christmas boxes and objected vehemently to the company's sending a bill to the president's mother. After some discussion, Francis wrote her saying all twelve boxes would be a gift.

Sara responded, "I insist upon you charging me for eleven. I will be very glad to accept one from you to me, for Christmas."

A short time later Francis had a meeting with the president and was unavoidably late. "Don't apologize," Franklin said. "I know where you were—Mother got hold of you."

Rita Kleeman was not the only woman in Sara's life who was a writer. Eleanor was publishing widely. For two years she had been writing a monthly column and now signed for a five-hundred-word column, "My Day," to be syndicated to newspapers five days a week by United Features. Unfortunately, her cousin Alice Roosevelt had a bad case of envy. Alice had undertaken a regular column for McNaught, another top syndicate. The columns of the two vying cousins were placed next to each other. Everyone knew that one writer was a New Dealer and the other a Republican. The columns took completely different viewpoints.

United Features editors were pleased with Eleanor's work, but at McNaught the editors were unhappy that Alice's pen was duller than her tongue. One editor said, "Why the hell do I roar hilariously when I'm with her and then only smile when her copy comes through?" Then he added, protectively, "Still, it's better to smile than read about Eleanor going from Pittsburgh to Cleveland to a CCC camp in Kentucky."

Eleanor often used her columns to fly Franklin's ideas and gauge the reaction; this way, she could also test her own opinions. Alice took potshots at Eleanor's notions and also made snide comments about her children's divorces. (Alice's daughter, a single child, ultimately committed suicide.)

Eleanor was stung by Alice's barbs, which were sharpening now that Eleanor's importance—however controversial—was recognized on a level that Alice never even tried to achieve. Elliott noted that "Alice was the only person whom I have ever known who could make my mother break down and cry." Despite the hostility, Eleanor dutifully invited Alice to the White House. (In fact, in 1933 when Franklin declared the country off the gold standard, Alice showed up at a White House dinner bedecked in gold jewelry to flaunt her opposition to the move.)

Sara did not return to the White House after her sortie on behalf of the failed anti-lynching bill until her traditional Christmas visit. The family, with great-grandchildren, was easier to host at the residence with its large and accommodating staff. There was something magical about spending Christmas at the White House, even if the grounds were so rarely white. Sara brought Betty with her, and because the woman was so much younger than she, Sara began referring to her as "my daughter-in-law."

Christmas Eve afternoon, White House staff stopped by to shake hands with the president and Eleanor and receive a remembrance. Then Eleanor was off to light the tree on the Mall, which she especially enjoyed because of the Marine Corps band. While the younger children ate their supper, the elder ones decorated the tall silver and white Christmas tree on the family floor. Franklin directed their efforts with firm opinions on what ornament was appropriate for what branch. Despite his fear of fire—and the tree's placement between priceless portraits of George and Martha Washington— he insisted on having lit candles. Franklin, of course, would read *A Christmas Carol* while Eleanor put little parcels of toothbrushes and soap (and fun items, too) in the stockings that hung in Franklin's bedroom. When the children were put to bed, she went to Christmas services.

The next morning everyone, including Sara and Betty, congregated in Franklin's room to open their stocking gifts. The family went downstairs for a big breakfast while Franklin ate in bed and read the papers. They all attended the Foundry Methodist Episcopal Church (more recently known for the Clinton family's membership) and returned home for lunch. In the afternoon the upstairs tree was lit. The president worked, the children played, and Eleanor went to "the Alleys" of Washington, poor slum areas throughout the city, to distribute toys to children. As she said, she would come back to the White House "with an added awareness of the inequality of our earthly blessings."

Then, about five P.M., the family's present-opening began. The children's gifts were laid out under the tree, while the adults' were placed on the mahogany tables. Eleanor handed each to Franklin, who then called out the name of the recipient, starting with the youngest and ending with Sara. He savored each gift while Eleanor would rush through hers, she said, because she was eager to get her thank-you notes off the next day. Then there would be dinner, followed by a movie. Some years Franklin would tell the entire family to gather for a train trip to Hyde Park, where his grandchildren would use White House cafeteria trays to slide down snowy slopes. This for him was the perfect climax to Christmas.

4 0

❦

"You Are My Life"

By 1936 Sara's grandchildren were nearly all adults with families of their own. Sara was eighty-one—at a time when the average woman lived to only sixty-one. Sara herself recognized that she was aging. Although her memory was sharp, her handwriting had started to deteriorate. She told one friend that she was using her "smallest note paper [so as] not to be tempted to write much." Jotting a message to Anna, Sara wrote: "Please destroy this, such terrible handwriting."

She now brought much of her remaining energy to bear on Franklin. As the year began, Sara told Franklin, "I can only repeat what you have always known, that you are my life." Daisy Suckley also took note of Sara's reaction to her son: "Mrs. James Roosevelt came to the reception at 4 & told us the news that her dear Franklin was arriving at the house at five & we must excuse her if she said anything queer! Her cheeks were pink and she looked better and handsomer than I have seen her look for a long time."

Franklin dominated her universe. No wonder Sara was stunned when Eleanor casually told her, "It would not break my heart if Franklin were not elected." Sara was aghast at what she saw as Eleanor's betrayal of her son. She reeled to face James, who was with them, and said, "Do you think

Mother will do anything to defeat Father? Is that why she stays in politics, just to hurt his chances of reelection?"

While Eleanor was deeply hurt by this rebuke, Sara did not see her reaction as inappropriate. Eleanor, again—just as when Franklin was governor—was indicating that she felt no personal satisfaction in Franklin's present or continued political success. Just why Eleanor was so ambivalent about her husband's presidency and about continuing the role she had shaped for herself remains a matter of conjecture. However, it certainly was an odd twist: in 1921, after Howe's pep talks, Eleanor had urged Franklin to return to the political arena. Sara was the one who initially had wanted him to stay close to home and hearth. But once Franklin had achieved his ultimate objective, Eleanor was able to express little pride in his accomplishments (or in her own).

In many ways the quick exchange between the two women was seminal. It went to the root of their different views—a difference that was at the core of much of their ongoing and unspoken interpersonal tension. Sara loved Franklin without reserve; his success in any endeavor is what gave her life meaning and joy. Eleanor's feelings toward her husband were different from his mother's. Moreover, Eleanor simply did not see her own happiness or self-fulfillment tied to Franklin's activities, except tangentially. From Eleanor's perspective, it did not really matter whether Franklin remained president, as she so bluntly informed Sara.

At the end of January, Franklin's birthday balls skyrocketed in number, and Sara again was the belle of the Waldorf-Astoria gala. Kassie's daughter, who was married and living in Bermuda, even gave a fund-raiser in Hamilton. (The next year's festivities were said to have 5 million attendees. The funds began to be split seventy–thirty, with the greatest share going to support community polio patients and the rest to research.)

Over the next several years, Sara continued to chair events for the philanthropies that both she and Eleanor supported: the Visiting Nurse Service, Children's Village, Child Welfare League, Chrystie Street House of Hospitality, and the Henry Street Settlement. Sara's own favorites included Lycée Français, Dutchess County Historical Society, Hyde Park Free Library, and the Musicians Emergency Fund (here, she worked with the wives of Jascha Heifetz and Efrem Zimbalist). Because tuberculosis was the leading killer of people ages fifteen to forty-five, she also backed homes for tuberculosis patients and publicized the Christmas Seals that benefited them. Franklin had asked her to go in his place to hammer a nail into a model house that would be distributed in great numbers throughout the country by the lumber industry, and she used the occasion to say, "Women's activities have become the world's activities."

As president of one of the nation's oldest flower guilds, she awarded ribbons to children for their gardens and planted more trees in Central Park—this time in honor of the coronation of King George VI. (She was especially happy to do so because she disdained the abdicated King Edward VIII, calling him "a little stick of a man." She was also ashamed that Wallis Warfield Simpson was American, although Franklin reacted tellingly: "Why shouldn't he marry the woman he loves?")

Sara's greatest contributions were to African-American education. She gave a fund-raising kickoff for her and Eleanor's friend Mary McLeod Bethune. The money was for the Bethune-Cookman Institute in Daytona. At the tea she threw for Bethune at East Sixty-fifth Street, Sara promised to raise $500,000. She knew she could draw an enthusiastic crowd because everyone savored the tea—a Delano necessity—that her sister Kassie imported directly from China and shared with Sara. Combining a good cause with fine pastries and strong tea enriched with fresh cream sent daily from Hyde Park pleased even Sara's sophisticated friends.

The next year the Palmer Memorial Institute in North Carolina, another traditionally African-American school, was able to turn Sara's generous financial donations into a plea for Eleanor and Franklin's support. Although the First Couple did not attend the school's anniversary ceremonies as invited, Franklin sent a message from the White House at Sara's request.

In February 1936 Franklin went home for a working visit. Stephen Early, Franklin's acting secretary (Howe was still gravely ill), sent a letter a day to Sara at Hyde Park before her son's arrival: "Will you please permit the broadcasting companies to install radio equipment?" She telegraphed back: VERY GLAD PRESIDENT WILL SPEAK PLEASE MAKE ARRANGE-MENTS. The night of the address, both Eleanor and Sara sat a few feet from Franklin.

When Sara was in Washington, Franklin would clear his schedule if she found herself available for lunch. David Brinkley said that he once saw Sara hand Franklin an envelope that his secretary told him enclosed a check—one of many she gave him to shore up his shaky finances and pay his additional White House expenses.

Sara herself was proud of being the president's mother but did not expect special treatment. One day she decided to visit a flower show. Coincidentally, the Herbert Hoovers had arrived a few hours earlier, causing consternation to the show's senior official, who offered to escort the Hoovers through the show. When Sara arrived, the doubly surprised official offered to accompany her, too, but she declined. As she peered at the flowers, someone interrupted to tell her she bore a remarkable resemblance to the president's mother. "I *am* rather like her, aren't I?" she replied.

Sara was eager to be the same beloved figure to her great-grandchildren that she had been to their parents. Anna's former husband had their two children for Easter, so Sara invited them to spend the holiday at Hyde Park. Such an invitation was unusually broad-minded for the time.

In April, Louis Howe's death at age sixty-five was a sad day for Eleanor and Franklin, and both dropped everything to arrange his funeral in the East Room of the White House. Now Stephen Early stepped up to the position of secretary to the president. It would be a busy year, with an upcoming nomination, campaign, and, presumably, successful election. Sara gave her astringent opinion: "I don't think my son should campaign this year. The people know whether they want him for another four years. If they don't, he'll get along well enough."

Sara's age was affecting her daily routine. One day she tripped on a six-inch doorsill and fell hard but dusted herself off and ignored the pain for nearly a week. Finally she admitted in a call to Franklin that she was "slightly handicapped" by the tumble. He sent a physician at once, who determined that she had cracked a protrusion of the thighbone. She was angry with herself. "I've always been afraid of breaking my hip. Every old person I know has at one time or another broken their hip, and I'm simply NOT going to have a broken hip. Imagine me with my leg up to the ceiling in a hammock!" Still, with a cane, she entertained hundreds from the Garden Club of America at Hyde Park.

By May, Elliott's second wife had given birth to a baby boy, Elliott Jr., and Sara decided to make the long train trip to Fort Worth, where they lived on a ranch. "She announced when she wrote and said she was coming that this was the first time that she had ever been west of Buffalo [not counting her 1884 train trip to Mexico]. Was El Paso close to my home?" Elliott remembered her asking. "She had no more concept—she came to Texas thinking that she was going to live in a teepee!" As for Sara, she said she felt that her grandchildren were actually her children and that she needed to visualize all of them in their settings.

Sara and her maid had a three-hour layover in St. Louis, so they went to a nearby hotel suite to freshen up and have tea. Photographers were downstairs, wanting to come up. "Why do you boys always want pictures?" she asked them. "Now in the case of the president and his wife, it's a different matter, but as for me . . ." She told them that she was going to visit her grandson Elliott: "spell it with two l's and two t's."

The next month, perhaps with some prescience of mortality, Sara offered up a number of household items at auction. Most were out-of-date jewelry or expensive silver that Eleanor and the grandchildren did not want. She garnered seventeen thousand dollars from the sale. However, a number of items were bought by relatives who did not want family pieces going to the public.

Although she was still using a cane, Sara went to Philadelphia for the Democratic convention, which she said she "wouldn't miss for anything." At the women's tea, she was joined by the first female cabinet member, Frances Perkins, secretary of labor. (Eleanor had pushed Franklin for Perkins's appointment.) One unusual item of business at the convention was a proposal by the National Federation of Business and Professional Women to support the repeal of a newly enacted federal law that forbade husbands and wives to hold government jobs concurrently. Consequently, more than six hundred wives had been fired.

Sara was asked by a reporter about her view of Franklin's being president for another four years. "I am eighty-one," she said, "and I know I will not see much more of him anyhow. I would love to have him more, but if it were not the White House, he would probably be called away somewhere else for this or that."

She stayed for the closing sessions to see Franklin renominated. All the children but Elliott were at his side. The papers reported that "a cheer went up from the crowd when Mrs. James Roosevelt, mother of the President, arrived and was escorted to a seat."

41

"Hyde Park and Me"

Sara was true to her word: she did not campaign. Instead, she went to Campobello in July and was joined by Eleanor and some of Eleanor's friends, including Cook and Dickerman. While at Campo she wrote Anna that "this place is a *refuge* & I love it & am very proud of this house & its associations."

Because Franklin was arriving, a telephone system needed to be set up—it would be the first telephone on Campobello Island. Making the installation more complicated was that security demanded the line be routed not through Canadian lines but directly to phone lines in Maine. It was completed before Franklin arrived, sailing in on a small schooner, heading into a southern wind and tacking between the small islands. This was an informal visit to his own house, but technically he was arriving in a foreign country and so was greeted at his private wharf by a silent salute from forty Royal Canadian Mounted Police in dress uniform.

Franklin enjoyed the crisp island breezes but learned that the townspeople of nearby Maine were distressed not to have caught a glimpse of him. (He hadn't been to Campo since 1933.) He knew how to cure their disappointment: he and Sara took her auto on the two-car ferry and went over for a leisurely drive through coastal towns. Soon after Franklin's arrival,

Eleanor left for Val-Kill with her cronies, or, as Sara wrote Anna: "Mother & her 'three' left yesterday morning."

In September four generations gathered to celebrate Sara's birthday. Elliott stayed in Texas, away from the family, and Eleanor was in Washington recovering from the grippe. It was Sara's eighty-second birthday and her fifty-sixth year as mistress of Hyde Park. She took great pleasure that day in arranging flowers in the same bowl that James had asked her to fill the first time she had visited his house.

The next month Franklin made a campaign speech in New Bedford. Then he crossed the river and traveled ten minutes to Fairhaven to have lunch at the Delano Homestead, which was still maintained by the family even though it was nearly always empty. The town of Fairhaven gave its children a school holiday so they might have the chance to see the president.

Only about fifty people, children included, were waiting in front of the Homestead for Franklin to appear. Preston W. Gifford Jr., who would have been in elementary school that day, remembered being lifted by his father onto his shoulders so he could see the president. Franklin arrived in an open car, waving his fedora as he turned past the house to park in back, where the Secret Service had put a wooden ramp over the building's rear steps. Then Eleanor came out the back door and around the side yard to accept flowers from the local Mother's Club president. Gifford recognized the tall lady instantly—her face was better known to him than was the president's.

Sara had stayed at the Homestead the night before so that she could be driven to a New Bedford hotel to watch Franklin's speech. She managed to get back to Fairhaven in time to greet her son and Eleanor for lunch, which was a complete surprise to them, as they had not expected her.

Franklin's staff was starting to make arrangements for election night. Early wired Sara, as he had done before: "The President plans to deliver radio address Monday evening from his study in your home. Morse telegraphic wire and press association printing machine he would like to have installed in the smoking room off the dining room. A private telephone wire connecting dining room where the President will work that evening also is to be installed so that he may have direct communication over telephone with Democratic Headquarters in New York. All of us will be deeply grateful if you will permit workmen to make these installations in study smoking room and dining room."

On election day at Hyde Park's town hall, the Roosevelt extended family cast nine votes. The total included Anna's husband, John Boettiger, who with Anna used Hyde Park as a legal residence. Also using Sara's address to vote were the White House residents Missy LeHand and Malvina "Tommy" Thompson, who was Eleanor's personal secretary. *The New York Times* reported that

> Mrs. Roosevelt drove her own coupe with Miss Nancy Cook, a close friend and resident of Val-Kill, the President's farm in the same district. . . .
>
> Already on hand and sure to be a chief figure in the gathering about the President was Mrs. Sara Delano Roosevelt, his mother. She accompanied her son to the voting booth this morning, entering directly behind him, to cast her ballot. She was enveloped in a royal purple cape resembling an Inverness, reaching almost to the hem of her dress. She wore her usual hat of black velvet.

Even Franklin Jr., a Harvard senior who had just turned twenty-one, was not able to escape press attention. He was supposed to show his diploma from Groton to prove literacy, but he couldn't find it. In order to cast his first vote, he was made to take a test. The embarrassed young man tried to be unobtrusive as he was directed—with much pointing—to the high school nearby to take an exam while the other members of his family voted. (Franklin Jr. answered multiple-choice questions after reading a paragraph about the Civilian Conservation Corps.)

Franklin, Sara, and Eleanor cast their ballots in that order. After voting, Franklin took Sara home while Eleanor went her own way and returned to Val-Kill with Cook. That night Franklin, with a doughnut on a plate in front of him, tallied the returns on his study desk. Sara thought he appeared less than presidential and said, "He looked like the clerk of a court." The first returns signaled a Democratic rout of the Republican candidate, Alf Landon. To cap the evening, Sara served a buffet supper at ten-thirty to the family and neighbors. Sara announced, "I wasn't worried a bit. I just felt he would be reelected."

Franklin returned to Washington and tried to concentrate on a pact between Japan and Germany, but his attention was diverted to matters that lay closer to home. A letter came from the White House to Mr. Plog, Sara's groundsman: "It has been reported that people are stealing [Hyde Park's Christmas] trees and [the president] asks that a State Trooper be assigned from the first of December to Christmas to try to protect these plantings. Says this is legitimate because the trees form an experimental station for the State College of Forestry."

Another holiday of sorts was approaching, the first anniversary of "My Day." Eleanor's column was gaining ground over Alice's, even though

Eleanor's writing was still a little too much a sketch of her daily appointments. It gained strength as she became more skilled at column writing. "My Day" helped personalize the New Deal and its achievements and gave Eleanor a forum through which she could shape her public image. Of course, its success rankled Alice, and in the December *Ladies' Home Journal*, she expressed her own thoughts on "The Ideal Qualifications for a President's Wife."

To an uninformed eye, her article appears supportive, but Alice certainly knew how to needle her cousin. She wrote: "Mr. Roosevelt does not appear very often in public, but Mrs. Roosevelt more than makes up for his comparative seclusion." Alice also slyly suggested that any First Lady "ought to screen well and have a good radio voice."

The depths of disaffection that lay between Oyster Bay and Hyde Park were demonstrated by the lack of communication between the families at Christmas, when they each kept to their own. This Christmas was different because Eleanor was in Cambridge, taking care of Franklin Jr., who was sick with sinus problems. Sara wrote Anna, who was also absent in order to house hunt in Seattle: "I miss Mother very much, but perhaps the rather quiet life in Boston will give her some rest."

Sara was doing a great deal for Anna: not only were Sistie and Buzzy in her care over the holidays, but she had also sent the Boettiger family a generous Christmas check of two hundred dollars. Soon after, she wrote them that she "just got an extra dividend of $1,000 a most *unusual* treat, so I am *dividing* it equally among my five grandchildren." Anna's husband replied, "We have had a grand Christmas, thanks largely to your generosity," and thanked Sara for taking care of "the swans."

Sara also gave them a few housewarming presents, including a heavy embroidered linen tablecloth and matching dinner napkins, a linen lunch set, a throw blanket, a set of towels and washclothes, a bath mat, and dish towels. She sent Anna a blue negligee and another check for $200 as well.

On Christmas morning Sara left the White House to breakfast with her brother Frederick, who had enjoyed a distinguished career and was now the chairman of the National Resources Planning Board. She was soon back in Hyde Park with Anna's children—"I love to look at their little intelligent faces"—and then returned to Washington for the inauguration. In Hyde Park once more, she received a note from Franklin: "Ever so many thanks for the check. It is far too much—so I will straighten it out when I get back."

The time between the election and the inauguration was shortened in 1937 by moving the latter's date from March to January, as members no longer needed weeks to travel by carriage or horseback to Washington. Sara returned to the capital city on New Year's Day to see her son take his oath of office on January 20. This was another precedent; no other mother had seen her son inaugurated president a second time. Sara wrote that "Kassie and I left for Washington as my blessed son is to have his second Inauguration as President of the United States. Inauguration very fine, very impressive, Franklin magnificent."

Sara maintained her constant schedule of dining with other people at both lunch and dinner. She and Eleanor had lunch with Mrs. Morgenthau, Sara's old friend and Eleanor's close friend—whose husband was now the secretary of the treasury. In Manhattan, Sara again was a guest at the house of "Judge Greenspan and his nice wife and four children. Very interesting & *really* Jewish." By this last comment, Sara meant to note that they were observant. A few of Eleanor's biographers have picked up this comment and taken it out of context—ignoring the fact that Sara had asked to be taken to an Orthodox service with the Greenspans—and interpreted it as anti-Semitic. As a matter of fact, Sara complained that several old acquaintances criticized her for "the type of people" she knew. Her answer was "Oh, dear, I suppose I should change my ways and learn to be a snob."

That same month the Roosevelts marked a milestone: John, their youngest son, turned twenty-one. Now all of the children were adults. As the boys became older, though, they seemed to grow away from Sara, and only Anna maintained the same close ties she had as a child. Elliott's two children from his first marriage rarely saw their grandmother or great-grandmother, even though Sara and Eleanor were on very friendly terms with the former daughter-in-law, who had sweetly suggested that she return to Eleanor a pearl necklace wedding gift. (Eleanor insisted that she keep it.)

Dora arrived in New York from Paris in the spring. Sara excused herself one day to go "to the Henry Street House to celebrate Miss Lillian Wald's seventieth birthday & I read Franklin's nice letter to her over the microphone." He praised Wald for her "unselfish labor to promote the happiness and well being of others." Sara's driver, Louis E. DePew, drove her in her Lincoln limousine (with its New York plate number 10) to the Sara Delano Roosevelt Park, her first visit to the "7 blocks given up to a fine playground." Two thousand children were there to cheer her.

Shortly after, DePew himself was in the papers. He was driving Sara's car (she was not a passenger) when he struck a pedestrian. The injured man was out of work and had a young family. Although he fully recovered from his injuries, he sued Sara for $50,000 and won $21,000. Sara was unhappy that he had been hurt but could not seem to understand how she could be sued when she felt she had nothing to do with the accident. However, she paid the large judgment promptly and did not appeal.

DePew does not seem to have been a skilled city driver. Driving in Manhattan a few months later, he suddenly braked, which threw Sara to the floor of the limousine. She broke an anklebone, and as she wrote in her journal, "Dr. Finkelstein put it in plaster!" She was laid up for two weeks, and her son took advantage of her unusual convalescence to tease her: "And as you have so often said to me, 'it will give you a rest in spite of yourself!'" He also made a trip to check on her at Hyde Park and attended St. James Episcopal Church in his role as senior warden. At the church someone had added a small sign to its exterior wall that read, "Church of the President." Franklin howled when he learned that another person had put up a second sign: "Formerly, God's."

Fortunately, Sara's accident happened shortly after she completed several scheduled events, including going to the Waldorf's roof restaurant to receive an "America's Beloved Mother" medal from the Daughters of Jacob. Mayor La Guardia presented it, intoning that the Daughters of Jacob were "the symbol of the ancient civilization of the East," whereas Sara represented wisdom and inspired teachings of the West. Sara saw the mayor again at the end of the month when she helped lay the cornerstone for the World's Fair in Flushing, to be held in 1939.

The award she had just received from the Jewish sororal group was the only public appearance she made to honor mothers. For the first time since Franklin's initial inauguration, she did not participate in any celebration on Mother's Day itself other than to give a radio address from East Sixty-fifth Street.

Sara was planning a trip to Europe with her grandson John, but she also longed to see Anna and her children. However, she felt better knowing that Eleanor would be traveling to Seattle to visit them. "You will very soon have Mother with you & how happy you will both be. I shall watch the papers for her daily progress of 'My Day.'"

The family gathered in Wilmington on July 1 for Franklin Jr.'s brilliant wedding to Ethel du Pont. As the president's motorcade approached the small private du Pont church, farmers from around the area perched on split-rail fences to gawk at the limousine motorcade. Servants of the bride's family peered down at the wedding from the choir loft, and the families of both the bride and groom tried for one day to put aside their bitter political differences.

The Roosevelts returned to Hyde Park the same day. Eleanor gave her weekly radio broadcast and oddly commented on her son's wedding: "I don't know whether to be happy or sad, but simply say prayers that fundamentally their lives may so develop that they may be useful lives and therefore happy ones."

By mid-July, Sara was off to Europe with John. This particular trip was significant because so many people, including Sara's own grandson James, have misinterpreted its events. When Sara and John arrived in Florence, she stepped off the train and was met by the city's prefect, who brought a bouquet with an enclosed message of respect from Italy's leader, Benito Mussolini. According to news accounts, she thanked the prefect and asked him to convey her appreciation to Mussolini.

John, however, with the two sons of the American ambassador to Italy, went on to a private meeting with Il Duce. The American news leads were "Duce Meets a Roosevelt." The Roosevelt was John, not Sara. However, James later wrote that Sara's acceptance of Mussolini's bouquet disturbed Franklin. This seems unlikely; Franklin knew that his mother would not have rudely tossed the flowers back to the prefect, even though she described herself "as Yankee as a piece off Plymouth Rock."

And if James is accurate about Franklin's dismay, why wouldn't his first concern be directed at his own ambassador for arranging a private meeting with Italy's dictator for John and the other young men? Sara did write Franklin that "all seems very flourishing & peaceful & the devotion to the 'Head of the Government' is general in all classes." Although it may not have been what Franklin wanted to hear, it was most likely an accurate description of what she saw.

One of Eleanor's biographers actually wrote that Sara "had tea with Mussolini, whom she considered a splendid leader." Although Sara once had tea with Mussolini in the 1920s, she came to despise the dictator and gave money to Italian refugee organizations. The biographer also mischaracterizes Sara's having been twice in the same room with the Duke and Duchess of Windsor and implies that she was awed by them. Over the summer the couple and Sara were both in the audience of the Salzburg music festival to see Arturo Toscanini direct Beethoven's *Fidelio*. Another time, together at a large tea, they were introduced. Eleanor knew that her mother-in-law despised the duke, having called him "a little stick of a man," and that she greatly admired the Queen Mother, with whom she had tea a few years earlier. Eleanor wrote Franklin: "Do you know Mama met the Duke and Duchess of Windsor at tea? I wonder how she will now feel about them!"

It was actually Franklin who was sympathetic to the abdication and would argue with his mother when the duke and duchess came to the United States. He talked about having them as guests at the White House. She retorted, "I won't have them in my house."

Franklin corrected her: "This is not your house, Mama." However, he did not invite them.

Another falsehood that spread after Sara's death about this trip is that when Sara arrived in France, a woman she had known for years asked her,

"What is your son doing these days?" She allegedly replied that he was busy in Washington. As the story goes, when Sara repeated this anecdote to someone else, she was challenged to name the premier of France. Allegedly, Sara—who on this same trip had lunch in Chantilly with Premier Chautemps—could not do so.

In fact, the ambassador to France in September wrote Franklin that "your mother is in tremendous form. You might as well have asked me to stop the flow of Niagara as to have asked me to see to it that she did not accept a vast number of invitations. . . . She is, of course, having an immense personal success. All the French love her and unlike the thirty-six Senators, Congressmen, and wives that are now with us, she speaks admirable French."

Cordell Hull, Franklin's secretary of state, also described Sara: "In my opinion, she was a remarkable woman who had consecrated her all to her son and country. She became my warm personal friend, and in our conversations exhibited at all times a wide intelligence and excellent understanding of international questions and conditions."

After Sara got back to Hyde Park in October, Franklin went for a visit. Sara was delighted that Eleanor arrived a day or so later, and they went for a picnic. However, as soon as her son and Eleanor returned to Washington, she felt let down. Europe had been exciting and now she was lonely. She wrote some plaintive letters to her favorite grandchild, Anna, alternately asking if she could visit Anna and the family in Seattle or if Anna would send Sistie and Buzzy to her and she would see to it that they were tutored (she added that she would send a check to cover their travel expenses) or if the entire family could come to Campo the next summer. She made it clear, however, that if John Boettiger could not get away from his newspaper, Anna's place was with him. Sara's frequent letters were augmented by calls engendering astonishingly heavy telephone bills. With her family spread across the country, her quarterly phone bill came to seventy-seven dollars.

Sara was still worried about her expenses—and the cost of maintaining Franklin's presidency—so she decided to profit from her renown by appearing in advertisements as Eleanor had done. Sara sponsored Royal Baking Powder, with a message to housewives that she signed near her photo. Not all the response was positive, though, especially because Sara was a wealthy woman. Letters came in to the White House saying that it "belittles the mother of the president to go into commerce in any manner." Another wrote: "We have always said that Mrs. Sara Delano Roosevelt was the only retiring and dignified member of the Roosevelt family, and we loved her, but now the Roosevelt earnings must go on and on. . . ."

As she had conferred with Franklin about the ads before agreeing to them, he was not concerned about the carping that, finally, Sara was getting. Franklin protected his mother by not sending these letters on to Hyde Park, and she remained relatively immune from the criticism.

As Christmas approached, Sara again wrote to Anna to tell her that she would send a check for her to come to the White House or for the children to visit. Instead, Eleanor decided to skip the family holiday and go to Seattle herself, for she and Anna were becoming close again. Sara was pleased for Anna but still longed for her. As the holiday drew near, she wrote: "I worry that Buzzy will forget Hyde Park and me," unconsciously placing the estate before herself.

42

"The Dowager Mrs. Roosevelt"

B y 1938 the tensions of the European situation dramatically juxtaposed with the tranquillity of Hyde Park. Sara began to turn down countless invitations, sponsorship requests, and attempted honors, shying away from even the 1938 birthday balls. She retained an interest in only a few causes, including the Bethune-Cookman Institute, and she once again hosted Bethune at a meeting at her house on East Sixty-fifth Street in March.

In April, Sara humbly accepted the Einstein Medal for Humanitarianism, given by the Jewish Forum in honor of her "broad sympathy and activities in alleviating the conditions of all people throughout the world who suffer from poverty, oppression and hatred." The speaker referred to the brutality that had "swept over many nations of the world" and said that Sara's "life-time of devoted service to every communal cause in the country" was the type of effort needed to ensure continued democracy. In the Waldorf-Astoria's ballroom, sixteen hundred people applauded Sara's short speech of thanks. All stops were pulled out for the program, which featured the singer Gladys Swarthout and the violinist Efrem Zimbalist.

Later, in October, Sara became active in the efforts to save German Jews. Women of the League for the Honor of Israel (not yet an independent country, of course) sent a message asking her to influence Franklin to allow more orphaned Jewish children into the United States. The league plaintively described the awful situation: "These unfortunate orphans, whose parents were murdered or imprisoned, rove about the streets of Germany, hungry, destitute and forlorn, with nobody to care for them."

Sara began to talk and write to Franklin about the tragedy. She also started receiving individual requests from Europe. She wrote her son in November, asking, "What can I do with very nice letters from Germany asking for help to get over here! It is all so awful for the Jews!" She petitioned him directly on behalf of relatives of her friends, describing, for example, the needs of a particular "Jewish family who have a shop" and could be self-supporting.

Aside from the catastrophic storm in Europe, the needs of Sara's family and property absorbed her time. She wrote Anna often. "I came up [to Hyde Park] on Thursday in order to hear your Mother speak on peace. . . . Your Mother spoke beautifully, looked lovely." Soon after, Franklin arrived for a short holiday and purchased more of Sara's land, to make his own property eight hundred acres. One newspaper breathlessly reported the implications of the additional property: "The President's old neighbors here in Dutchess County . . . insisted that [the increased acreage] must be taken as added proof that F.D.R. does not intend to seek another White House term after 1940."

On June 18 John was to marry Anne Lindsay Clark of Boston. The service was in Nahant, Massachusetts, at the Clarks' summer home. Eleanor arrived the day before to stand in for the bride at the rehearsal. Having arrived at the church hatless, Eleanor tied a handkerchief, which, according to the watching press, was "hastily and insecurely anchored," to cover her hair. Then she "promenaded solemnly throughout the role with a sheet tied about her waist to represent the bride's train."

All the Roosevelts, including Anna and her children from Seattle, came out the next day for the wedding. Ellie Roosevelt Seagraves remembered her eleven-year-old awe as she watched the marriage of her uncle, just ten years older than she. Sara arrived with Kassie, "two of the most handsome dowagers in society," according to the *New York Daily News*. Sara was termed "the dowager Mrs. Roosevelt" by *The New York Times*. Although Eleanor's dress was described in detail, no one pointed out that practical Sara wore the same dress she had to Franklin Jr.'s wedding the year before.

The town played host to five thousand uninvited spectators who turned out with lunch boxes, binoculars, and cameras. There were very few cheers, however, for the president from the residents of this old-guard ocean spot. After the wedding, Sara headed the reception line, with Eleanor next to her and Franklin farther down. Sara summed up the wedding and reception as "a fine shindig.'

For a number of years, Franklin had enjoyed a warm friendship with Daisy Suckley, whose family home was just north of Hyde Park, in Rhinebeck. A few years earlier he and Suckley had talked about building a getaway on Franklin's property, a modest lean-to shelter with a fireplace and kitchenette. Franklin explained his need for a separate house:

> I found that on my trips to Hyde Park from the White House, it was almost impossible to have any time to myself in the big house. These trips were intended primarily for a holiday—a chance to read, to sort my books, and to make plans for roads, tree plantings, etc. This was seemingly impossible because of: a) visitors in the house b) telephone c) visits from Dutchess County neighbors d) visits from various people who, knowing I was going to be in Hyde Park, thought it an opportune time to seek some interviews. Therefore, I began talking about building a small place to go to "escape the mob."

Franklin and Suckley enjoyed a particular spot they called "our hill," which was where the house—more elaborate than originally planned—was built in 1938. Franklin said it should be Dutch-style and built with fieldstone from old stone walls. Its design was accessible, too. Although steps rose to the house's front door, its porch—from which Franklin could see his beloved trees and river, and the Catskill Mountains beyond—was at ground level, and the interior had no thresholds to impede his wheelchair.

Top Cottage, as it was named, had two wings—the north wing with Franklin's double bedroom, and the south wing with two bedrooms for family members. Above the north wing were the living quarters for the caretaker. Top Cottage's central living/dining room had a curved cathedral ceiling and opened onto the porch.

Franklin was never so happy as when he had a plan; unfortunately, Sara did not cotton to this one. Perhaps she had adjusted to Eleanor spending the night in Val-Kill, when Franklin was not at Hyde Park, but it was difficult for her to understand why Franklin wanted his own place. Moreover, it did seem odd—husband and wife having separate houses, especially when the couple had never actually had their own house together. (Imagine the commentary these arrangements would provoke in a more modern news media.) Adding to Sara's worries was Franklin's flirtatious relationship with Suckley; the explanation that they were cousins did not hold much water in *this* family.

As construction began in 1938, Franklin promised Sara that whenever she was at Hyde Park, he would sleep at the Big House and not Top Cottage. When the residence was completed the following year, Franklin told reporters simply, "There isn't any telephone in the place because, you know, if there's a telephone, somebody is sure to use it."

Anna came to New York with her children for the month of June, leaving the youngsters with Sara at Hyde Park. They had another playmate: five-year-old Diana Hopkins, daughter of Harry Hopkins, Franklin's adviser. After Diana's mother died in 1937, Eleanor suggested that the father and daughter live in the White House. When summer arrived, Eleanor shipped little Diana to the Hudson Valley to be under Sara's watchful eye. Years later Diana Hopkins Halsted remembered the "interesting contrast between Sara and Eleanor—Sara was obviously the grande dame, but she still was much easier to relate to because of her warmth. It was much harder to relate to Eleanor, despite her kindnesses. She had difficulty with intimacy, while a child could respond to Sara."

Sara cared for Diana as well as Sistie and Buzzy and encouraged Anna to stay at the Colony Club while in the city even though, she wrote with disappointment, "your Mother resigned from the Club." After Anna returned home in July, Sara wrote her from Hyde Park that Franklin "left yesterday, & Mother moved over to her cottage."

With Franklin absent, Sara sought Campobello's cooler breezes in mid-July. On her trip the press waylaid her to ask if her son would seek reelection for a third term. "I don't know any more than you do," she told them. "I have never heard him mention it. He has never even hinted it."

Eleanor raised the same topic with Franklin the next month. She expressed her firm opposition to his seeking a third term in one of the memos that she almost nightly dropped off in the in-box she put by his bed: "I thought this most unwise. You know I do *not* believe in it."

Shortly after Sara returned to Hyde Park from Campo at the end of September, she left by train for the West Coast with her personal maid, Jennings. At each layover, Franklin had arranged an escort to take care of her arrangements and make sure she felt well. She sent a letter to Anna from one of her stops, warning her, "You will find me a very *dull* guest & I am not as strong in some ways as I have been."

She and Anna had a delightful week together and did not undertake any activities more arduous than shopping. While she was there, Anna received a sour note from her mother: "I hope Granny is feeling well and that she can refrain for the week she is there from trying to plan your lives! She seems to me to be aging fast but she still takes so much interest in us all that she would be glad to direct our actions even in the future!"

Anna, however, had no complaints about her grandmother's visit but was merely worried when she learned that Sara had become "woozy" after arriving in Chicago. Sara wrote that she felt better after being taken to Grant Park on Lake Michigan to breathe fresh air. Once she got back to Hyde Park, Sara felt herself again, writing in her journal: "A heavenly day. Every leaf golden or red & vivid."

Sara was pleased by an early-morning phone call she received from Franklin. As she strolled through her side grounds, she spotted her gardener up on a ladder. "Do you know what my son, Franklin, told me this morning?" she asked the startled landscaper. He replied that he did not. "When he dies, he wants to [be] buried right here in this rose garden!" Sara told him delightedly.

The beauty of the land contrasted with Eleanor's continued peevishness. Eleanor felt, accurately enough, that Sara was trying to get James interested in the working affairs of Hyde Park. Rather than let James and his grandmother sort out the arrangement for themselves, Eleanor stepped into Franklin's role. As she wrote Anna, "I told her I thought Father would want to be consulted and would not like her to ask any one else." She further wrote that when she told Sara this, she had "demurred and I think I know the reason, she is trying to tie someone in the next generation to the place while she is alive because she is so afraid it will not continue in the family."

For several years there had been no family gathering at Fairhaven to look forward to at Thanksgiving. In fact, hardly anyone gathered at Hyde Park, either. Sara commented on the inevitable: "What a family we are, dotted about from Hyde Park [Sara] to Warm Springs [Franklin], Charlottesville or Wilmington [Franklin Jr.], Brookline [John], New Haven [Eleanor], Texas [Elliott], California [James] & Seattle [Anna]."

At Christmas, though, Sara made an unusually long visit to the White House. Franklin Jr.'s son, named Franklin III, was being christened in Washington on January 7, 1939, and she decided to stay there and return to New York after the ceremony. She wrote to Anna that "Mother looks prettier than ever." Sara did not realize, as the New Year began, the illustrious visitors whom she would soon entertain at Hyde Park.

In August 1938 Franklin had written King George VI that the Canadian prime minister had confided that the king and queen might come to the dominion—and possibly the United States—for a visit the following summer. "My dear King George," he wrote, "If you should be here in June or

July, you might care to avoid the heat of Washington, and, in such a case, it would give us the greatest pleasure to have you and Her Majesty come to visit us at our country home at Hyde Park, which is on the Hudson River, about eighty miles north of New York and, therefore, on the direct route between New York and Canada.

"Also, it occurs to me that a Canadian trip would be crowded with formalities and that you both might like three or four days of very simple country life at Hyde Park—with no formal entertainments and an opportunity to get a bit of rest and relaxation."

In November, Franklin wrote again about a disturbing discussion he had had with an English emissary: "I say this to you quite frankly because he does not even refer to your coming to stay with Mrs. Roosevelt and me at Hyde Park.

"If you could stay with us at Hyde Park for two or three days, the simplicity and naturalness of such a visit would produce a most excellent effect—in addition to giving my wife and me the greatest pleasure in getting to know you both."

43

❧

"A World of Peace"

On May 1, 1939, Franklin opened the New York World's Fair and used the opportunity to serve notice to the world that the Western Hemisphere countries were united in their desire for peace. Eleanor and Sara were with him, making it Sara's third trip to the fair. Besides laying its cornerstone a few years earlier, in April she had unveiled a bust of FDR, cast in nickel silver, that was to be prominently displayed in the federal building. A few weeks after the opening ceremony, Eleanor wrote her thanks to Sara: "Everyone at the fair says you have been too wonderful."

Eleanor had just been featured on the cover of *Time*, which speculated on whether the upcoming June visit of Queen Elizabeth and King George VI would take place, given that England could find herself at war at any time. *Time* woefully underestimated Eleanor by saying that the visit of the royal family would "crown her career." Eleanor, of course, would go on as an international force until the day of her death. The woman who did not have much time left was eighty-four-year-old Sara.

Telephone calls and letters swirled around the arrangements for the king and queen, who were to visit the White House first and then travel to Hyde

Park. Initially, Sara told Franklin that she should leave Hyde Park before they arrived, in case there was a question of who was hostess. "But, Mama, you can't be away," he replied. "It is your party!" Sara was delighted to reciprocate the hospitality shown her when she was invited to the private quarters of the king's late father and his mother for tea.

Eleanor was pleased, too. At formal White House dinners, Sara had felt insignificant because protocol dictated that she sit below the salt. Just a few months earlier, during a visit from Sara, Eleanor wrote: "I've played rather a mean trick tonight, pleaded a headache & sent Mama down to sit as hostess at the Diplomatic dinner. . . . I thought this was a good way to put her at the top." She also wrote a similar note to Anna referring to the date when Sara was to return to Hyde Park: "I say a little prayer to live thro' the 11th."

The White House staff frequently overheard Eleanor criticize her mother-in-law. Lillian Parks recalled that "Eleanor ran down the houses she had been forced to live in, as if they were prisons. We servants thought Eleanor was lucky indeed that Sara had provided houses for them to live in and paid for part of their servant staff."

In preparation for the royal visit, Eleanor sent Sara a letter in which she mentioned her idea for a hot dog picnic: "I am hoping that your people will be able to make enough salad—lettuce and tomato—for seventy-five people. Do you think they could make chicken and ham sandwiches for that many? Also, will you have enough cream and butter for that many? The State Department is paying all the expenses, so please keep track of what you spend so I can give them an account. . . . My love to you, Eleanor."

Sara was managing the many press calls that were coming in to her house. The Associated Press wanted to take pictures of Hyde Park's grounds. She contacted Early, who checked with both American and British security and said yes as long as "no panorama scenes of the grounds be made." In response to another photographer's query, Early said that there could be no snaps of the bedrooms where the royals would sleep.

Eleanor also told Sara to keep her personal guest list short. "Franklin says family and *near* neighbors will be asked to picnic but no one below Fishkill or above Tarrytown or beyond Tuxedo! There are a terrible lot of disgruntled people here & I suppose there will be in H.P. I'll be thankful when this is over & never in my life will I get to meet any celebrity—!"

Franklin was as excited as a child over the visit; he dictated a two-page letter to Reverend Wilson of St. James Episcopal Church that laid out a detailed plan of seven points. Point number five was:

After the service is over, it is my thought that you and the Bishop would stand at the door and greet us as we come out. We would then step across the gravel to the edge of the grass and be photographed facing the highway. This would give the rest of the party and the parishioners in the church a chance to come out behind us and move off to the right and left so that they can see the King and Queen while we are all being photographed. Then the cars would move in behind us (between the grass and the church door) and we would get in and drive away.

Sara was a relaxed hostess, though, and harrumphed when asked if she was planning to redecorate her house for the visit. Of course not, she said. "They're coming to see *my* house, not a redecorated house!" Because of her age and involvement in the upcoming royal visit, she agreed to accept only one Mother's Day award, choosing to receive the honor from Hadassah, which donated the proceeds from a 1,500-person luncheon to planting trees in Palestine. Her family's long affiliation with China led her to accept also the honorary chairmanship of a committee to aid Chinese refugees fleeing the Japanese invasion. "I only regret," she said, "that I am no longer young or strong enough to give active service on the committee."

At the end of the month, *Life* underscored the importance of the royal couple's private visit to Hyde Park, which was to take place after their trip to the nation's capital. The article called Hyde Park "the nearest thing America has to a royal palace." It noted that "the president's mother is mistress there." Margaret Bourke-White was sent to photograph the estate, "an old shoe of a place—worn, scuffed and scratched, polished into shape, fitting the owner well." It contrasted Sara's crowded snuggery with Eleanor's "functional and neat" space. The story also illustrated the house's lack of pretension by pointing out every mended chair as well as the door of Franklin's night table, which "doesn't shut properly so it is jammed tight with cotton gauze."

Regardless of the homey character of Hyde Park, Sara Delano Roosevelt became the first woman in American history to entertain a British monarch in a private home. For twenty-four hours, Eleanor was hostess in the White House and then turned over that role to Sara when the king and queen retreated from humid Washington to the refreshing breezes of the Hudson Valley. Sara had been invited to the White House festivities but declined, the better to turn her attention to the upcoming events at Hyde Park. The plans for the next day began with a church service. Then there would be a picnic at Val-Kill, hosted by Eleanor, and the day would end with a formal dinner given by Sara. The king and queen had the afternoon to themselves for relaxation.

Eleanor and Franklin were greeted by Sara on the portico when they arrived from Washington on Saturday afternoon. The couple checked the provisions at Top Cottage for the following day's picnic, and Eleanor ordered the "perfectly awful" wooden crates (used to cart in refreshments) removed—until the couple learned that a mother robin had efficiently used her afternoon to build a nest and lay eggs in the packaging.

Early that evening, the operator of Hyde Park's two-way fire department radio received the call of his lifetime. Mayor La Guardia was on the line and commanded the man, "Call the President of the United State at Hyde Park. Tell him that Their Majesties, the King and Queen, have just left Columbia University [originally, King's College] for the President's home."

Two hundred thousand people lined Albany Post Road from Poughkeepsie to Hyde Park, and the crowds were kept from rushing the motorcade by one thousand National Guard sentries armed with steel bayonets. Eleanor and Franklin returned to the estate's portico to greet the king and queen, who arrived mid-evening, more than an hour later than expected. Sara had the long driveway sprinkled with water to keep the dust down before their motorcade drove in. The flags flying over Hyde Park were the royal standard, the Union Jack, the Stars and Stripes, and the presidential flag with its blue field. A crimson carpet was laid from the driveway up the house's front steps. The grounds and house were guarded by the Secret Service, New York state troopers, and West Point army regulars. At 9:45 P.M. Sara gave a relatively simple dinner—clear soup and cheese straws, halibut mousse served with a sauce of brandied lobster, filet of beef, ham, green beans, asparagus and mushrooms, assorted cheeses, ice cream with strawberries, and cake. Sara's Scottish cook was distraught at having to keep dinner an hour beyond its scheduled time, but the beef remained pink at the center. The men wore dinner jackets rather than white tails, to indicate the dinner's informality.

The next morning everyone moved on to Franklin's orchestrated church service. What he had not counted on was that Sara's hands were beginning to tremble with age, and she dropped her prayer book over and over again. Each time, Queen Elizabeth, who was sitting next to her, leaned over to pick up the book. Finally, it went over the pew, so Sara had to share the queen's book with her. The queen smiled during Bishop Henry St. George Tucker's homily when he reminded parishioners to return to church even when the royal couple were not guests.

Lunch was a Top Cottage picnic of hot dogs, as well as smoked and roasted turkey sandwiches, baked beans, and salad. (Sara had wanted to serve pork link sausages, but Eleanor insisted on the more American hot dogs.) Dessert was biscuits with strawberries and whipped cream, ginger-bread, cookies, and doughnuts. The king, Franklin, and Sara enjoyed a glass of beer. The royal couple ate at a table set up on the porch, and from time to time Sara wandered from her seat to mingle with the guests. Afterward the king and the president went to Val-Kill for a short swim in the pool and went boating out on the Hudson to get a better perspective on the growth of Franklin's new timber.

The choice of picnic lunch—sausage or hot dogs—has been exaggerated into a confrontation between Sara and Eleanor. They agreed on the casual outdoor lunch, and their different menu ideas were hardly miles apart. Though the women had agreed on the picnic idea, there was a disagreement about the dinner that evening. Sara wanted it served by her own servants; Eleanor wanted to bring the White House servants to augment Sara's staff. In our time, the controversy has centered on the fact that Sara's servants were white, whereas the White House waiters were black. Allegedly, Sara—who sometimes had black guests at her home—would not allow black staff in her kitchen. Sara's real concern, according to her two great-grandchildren Ellie Roosevelt Seagraves and Curtis Roosevelt, was that Hyde Park was *her* house and she thought that *her* servants were best prepared to serve. Sara's English butler, who was old enough to retire, was thrown into such a tizzy about the royal visit that he offered his resignation, stating that he was no longer at his peak and therefore not good enough to serve his king and queen. (Eleanor's biographers have turned his retirement into a refusal to work with black help, which would be odd since he served her black guests uncomplainingly.)

As it turned out, a White House waiter *did* stumble during the dinner. The staff had placed two sawhorses in the hallway on which they balanced a long board draped with linen napery. Then they laid an entire set of china for twenty-four people, as well as the accompanying serving pieces, on this jury-rigged table. The bone china had been a special gift to the United States from France.

During the dinner, White House waiters deposited a heavy stack of plates at one extreme end of the plank. All at once, the board tilted downward as hundreds of exquisite china pieces came sliding down the plank to crash resoundingly on the floor. Only the extreme composure of the guests kept them from jumping at the noise. The sole person who reacted was Betty, Rosy's widow, who had lent Sara a few serving pieces and commented, "I hope that was not my china!" (A few pieces survived the breakage and were divided evenly among the children.)

The rest of the guests concentrated on a meal of fish chowder (made from an old Delano Homestead recipe) with oyster crackers, sweetbreads with mushrooms in pastry baskets, in-season peas and asparagus, tongue in aspic, avocado and grapefruit salad, and ginger ice cream with cake. Thirty people were at the table, including Sara's closest neighbors. (Her friends the Rogerses quietly left town rather than embarrass her by their presence—they had become close friends with the controversial Duke and Duchess of Windsor.)

At length, dinner came to an end. Still in dinner clothes, Franklin, Eleanor, and Sara accompanied their visitors to the Hyde Park train station and found crowds gathered. The fear of war was on everyone's mind, and as the royal couple entered the train and walked out onto its rear platform, someone in the crowd began singing "Auld Lang Syne." Everyone joined in, including the three Roosevelts. The king turned solemn, and when the song ended, he saluted the crowd. The queen had tears in her eyes as she waved good-bye, perhaps knowing that when the seasons changed, England would be at war with Germany. The royal silver-and-blue standard floated on the breeze as the train pulled northward to Canada.

In 1937 Franklin began to plan for the first presidential library ever. His confidant was his friend and Sara's, Helen W. Reynolds of the Dutchess County Historical Society. He also confided in the Roosevelt attorney, Henry Hackett of Poughkeepsie, and sent him a letter that read:

> By the way, I wonder if you have heard grumbling about the proposed new library as being another piece of property taken off the assessment rolls when it is owned by the government.
>
> If anybody says anything, you might intimate that in all probability some kind of a fund will be set up to pay taxes equivalent to the present taxes. . . . That means that the Town will retain what it gets from the taxes today.

His library set a precedent that all presidents followed. "Future historians will curse as well as praise me," Franklin perceptively commented on his vast collection—on not merely what would be four terms' worth of presidential papers but also fifteen thousand books, twelve hundred prints, and countless other flotsam and jetsam of personal memorabilia.

In 1938 Franklin was to hold a press conference to announce the library and museum that was to be built on property that Sara owned near her house. Although Sara thought her son worthy of a library equal to Alexandria's, his plans to set it east of Sara's large rose garden—and to admit the public—would obviously disrupt the calm environment that was Hyde

Park. However, Franklin moved quickly to establish his plan and called for an enormous July press conference at Hyde Park. (He would justify the library's location by saying that the nearby city of Poughkeepsie "has good hotel and other accommodations," to the laughter of the reporters. Even Franklin could not keep a straight face after he saw their smiles.)

However, Sara had left for France to visit Dora without signing the necessary papers deeding the property to the federal government. A mere two hours before the press conference, Franklin was told that the deed was not in hand. There was no way the White House could put off the reporters without tremendous embarrassment to the president. Franklin decided to wing it: with the help of the Justice Department, he and Eleanor were filmed sitting under one of Sara's grand trees signing property that they did not own away to the U.S. government. The deed was worthless, but no one knew.

To try to make amends, an authentic deed was sent posthaste to France with a note to the ambassador. "I enclose a number of documents, together with an explanatory note to my Mother. Will you do the necessary about getting her signature to the deed and the proper acknowledgments, etc . . . ?" It was essential to have the correct papers because Congress was to issue a joint resolution for the library. It was one thing to pull the wool over reporters' eyes but quite another to trick the joint houses of Congress. Franklin received no reply from his mother, so he called the American ambassador's residence to charm her into signing away her property. She was delighted to receive his call and only then signed over the property.

When Sara sailed for France, reporters asked her if she feared war breaking out while she was there. She replied, "I don't know. I suppose so, but I'll live through it, and if not . . ." When she arrived, Franklin sent a telegram from the White House: DELIGHTED YOU ARE SAFELY WITH AUNT DORA . . . I SUGGEST PERHAPS BETTER NOT TO VISIT ITALY THIS SUMMER.

Eleanor and Franklin spent most of the summer at Hyde Park, because Eleanor wrote, they "always enjoyed being able to do." She had to make an emergency trip to Boston when John and Anne lost their first baby, which brought back her sorrow over losing her own son. Sara was a week or so short of her planned six-week visit when Nazi Germany and Soviet Russia signed a non-aggression pact and the American embassies in France and Germany issued an advisory to American citizens to return to the United States. Sara left Europe, telling the press as she boarded her ship, "I want to relieve my son of all unnecessary anxiety in this crisis." The *Washington* was the last large liner to leave Hamburg and its officers were relieved upon arriving in New York, for besides the president's mother, the ship carried more than $25 million in English gold that was to be held by U.S. banks. (Sara's grandson John and his wife were also on the ship, as was the actor Edward G. Robinson.)

Eleanor was at the dock to greet her son and mother-in-law. Sara, however, had not been able to persuade Dora to come back with her or to leave a few days later on the *Washington* when the liner sailed back immediately to Le Havre with five hundred extra cots to pick up stranded Americans.

On September 21, Sara's eighty-fifth birthday, reporters asked her about a third run for Franklin. Although she said her son could "stand another term very well" because his health was "excellent," she also asserted that "he is thinking only about the war. He is trying to do all he can for peace." She added a few wishful thoughts of her own, which were that "I don't think my son has the slightest wish" for another term, and suggested that "he would like to retire to Hyde Park to write."

Despite her public statements about Franklin's health, Sara was concerned about the White House draining his energy. She wrote a friend in late October: "My son is here for three nights. He looks worn out when he comes and when he leaves after home and good air, he is a different man."

Alf Landon, the Republican front-runner, challenged Franklin to announce whether he would run. When reporters brought his message to Hyde Park, Franklin merely smiled enigmatically and said he would not comment. Sara was as frustrated as the newsmen: "I wish you would, son."

On a windy day in mid-November, the cornerstone to the Franklin Delano Roosevelt Library and Museum was laid. Franklin and Sara were there for the ceremonies. Just a few days later Franklin was in Warm Springs to dedicate the Sara Delano Roosevelt Community Center. She had decided to remain in Manhattan but planned a trip to Georgia for the spring. Franklin told the patients at Warm Springs, "I know my Mother is going to be very, very happy when she sees this building. And I also hope you will let her dedicate it instead of my dedicating it This will be a *preliminary* dedication."

Sara spent the remainder of the year in the city, expanding the work she was doing for Chinese refugees. Before she left for her annual White House Christmas visit, she pinned a cross on the Red Cross Christmas Tree of Peace to symbolize a membership drive on behalf of the organization, whose aid was urgently needed in Europe. Mayor La Guardia introduced

Sara by saying that she was "the one person in our whole land who is qualified to speak for American motherhood." After Sara said a few words about
the Red Cross, the mayor read a message from Queen Wilhelmina of the
Netherlands: "May Christmas spread its light over a happier world, a world
of peace and goodwill toward men."

44

"The Truth Must Be Shown"

Eleanor was concerned about Sara's health and wanted her to have a companion. Franklin agreed. Sara complained about their idea to Rita Kleeman: "I know they are doing it because they feel I should have someone with me. But I shan't take her. Why, if [I] had someone nearby always to say, 'Let me do this,' or 'Let me get that for you,' I'd be an old lady in no time."

Another time, a younger friend told Sara that her mother had gone south for the winter. Sara, who spent every winter in New York, replied approvingly: "I'm so glad. New York is no place for old people in the winter."

The only relative older than Sara was her ninety-three-year-old sister, Dora, who had finally returned from Paris in November 1939, having waited until she could berth in a good-size stateroom. At her age, she could not be assigned to a cot, as many returning Americans had been. She was fortunate to get out before June 1940, when the Germans invaded France. After arriving in New York, Dora joined Frederick at Algonac. After this last voyage, Dora estimated that she had crossed the Pacific by ship ten times and the Atlantic at least fifty.

Sara's age did not keep her from promoting contemporary ideas, though. At the end of January 1940, she attended a luncheon of the Birth Control

Federation of America (later Planned Parenthood) and applauded loudly when its director said, "Theology must not oppose a thing that may be of immense physical, mental and spiritual value to the people." Sara also joined in the applause when Eleanor's name was mentioned as an important supporter of the movement.

Sara was also concerned about China. Japan had attacked the country yet still held "most-favored nation" trade status in early 1940. A group called the American Friends of the Chinese People formed to strip the aggressor nation of its preferred ranking. Sara was one of fifty prominent people to sign the letter to the president. Franklin also relied on Sara's history and used it at his convenience: when Treasury Secretary Morgenthau, who was also a Dutchess County neighbor, disagreed with Franklin about a China matter, Franklin responded, "Please remember that I have a background of a little over a century in Chinese affairs."

As the year began, speculation roiled about the possibility of a third term. In February, Sara went with John to see the satirical newsreel "Hellzapoppin." The filmmakers put authentic footage of FDR in the movie, with his voice dubbed to announce that he would be running in the next election. "What's this? What's this?" Sara said in the loud voice of someone whose hearing was going. "Why hadn't he told me?"

In April reporters asked Sara her thoughts on Franklin's running for a third term. "I cannot say whether I would want him to run again, unless he would do good by being president. Of course, I'd like to have him at home. He is very fond of our country place and I think he would enjoy being there." That same month Sara had five sittings for a portrait she would give to the new library under construction. (It now hangs there in the replica of Franklin's Oval Office.)

By spring 1940 *Life* magazine estimated that Eleanor had traveled more than a quarter of a million miles since her husband had become president and had visited every state except South Dakota. In addition to her travels, Eleanor's writings made her the country's most widely syndicated columnist. She ranked in the top ten of the most influential Washington leaders, which was a true first for a First Lady. "She was in action, in motion, it seems, 24 hours a day," noted Franklin's biographer Geoffrey Ward.

Sara, for her part, kept up the activities that meant the most to her. For the second year in a row, Sara went to the large mother-daughter Hadassah tea for the purpose of aiding Palestine projects, including the resettlement of Jews escaping from Germany and Poland. A Hadassah leader announced that seven hundred trees had been planted in the Sara Delano Roosevelt Grove from the previous year's Mother's Day proceeds. In addition, Hadassah had resettled a quarter of a million Jewish refugees and sponsored orphanages serving nine thousand children. Others attending the tea included Rita Kleeman, several members of the Warburg family, and the mother of the late George Gershwin.

Sara was moving more slowly, but she honored her husband's Dutch heritage and her own Delano Dutch nationality (albeit with French blood) when she accepted the honorary chairmanship of the Queen Wilhelmina Fund. The fund set a goal of $3 million for war relief in the Netherlands. The national chairman was the Dutch-American author Hendrik W. van Loon, who described Nazi soldiers as "young men who love cruelty for the sake of cruelty and death for the sake of death."

In June, Sara hosted Franklin at the simple ceremony to turn the actual FDR Library building over to the federal government. The collection to be transferred from Washington and other locations already numbered more than 6 million items—and Franklin's second term had not yet ended.

Franklin wanted to visit Hyde Park more frequently because of Sara's age and for a respite from world tensions. During 1940 he went to his Hudson Valley home on fifteen different occasions and stayed for a total of fifty-six days, more than any other previous White House year. In July he was in Hyde Park to rest before the upcoming Democratic convention and to consider whether to seek an unprecedented third term. Sara, consistent with her earlier views, wanted her son to be successful if he ran.

Jim Farley stopped by the house, intending to resign as postmaster general and take a private job. If he did, it would mean that he would not manage Franklin's next campaign. When he arrived, Sara greeted him. "You know, I would hate to think of Franklin running for the presidency if you were not around. I would like you to be sure to help my boy."

Sara's health prevented her from attending the Chicago convention, which she felt was no loss. "I shall 'listen in' to the Convention," she assured Franklin. "I hope it will be dignified & not too awful." Nor did Sara travel to Campobello, even though the summer air at Hyde Park made breathing difficult. "I can't bear heat," she wrote Kleeman, "and have called off everything."

Franklin had carefully crafted a Draft Roosevelt movement to "spontaneously" emerge at the convention, but he kept it from both Sara and Eleanor. They understood his real intentions only during the convention itself. Once again, he made a key political decision without consulting his wife or mother, just as he had done when he ran for governor.

Sara also did not want to be far from Dora. She visited her sister in mid-July and realized that the end might be near. She telegraphed Frederick, who was in San Francisco, to come to Algonac immediately. On July 21 Dora died, with Sara, Eleanor, and Frederick by her side. They traveled together to Riverside Cemetery in Fairhaven for the burial. She had been Sara's closest friend.

Sara responded to Kleeman's sympathy note in a spidery hand: "My dear sister was very precious & to me always my ideal. We shall miss her always but we must thank God for her long life. I try to think she did not suffer in those last four days & she knew my brother, Mrs. Roosevelt & I were with her to the end—Mrs. Roosevelt is en route for Campobello where I hope she will rest after the sad parting & a cool change will help to give her strength."

In September, Sara reached her eighty-sixth birthday. Family members at her private party included Eleanor, Franklin, and three of her grandsons. Sara posed for a special four-generation photo with Franklin, Franklin Jr., and Franklin III. Franklin Jr. had earlier made an announcement that he was applying for Army Air Corps training—James was already in the Marine Corps reserves—and Eleanor stated that her sons should be the first "summoned to active duty because their wives are financially independent."

In October, Sara was at a documentary titled *Pastor Hall* when scenes of concentration camp victims flashed on the screen. Several women ran out of the theater in horror, but Sara stayed and said afterward, "I did not consider 'Pastor Hall' brutal. I would be more inclined to call it realistic. Anti-Nazi movies have my approval because the truth must be shown now as never before.

"I hope to see it again soon and I think everyone should see it."

She backed up her beliefs with financial contributions, giving money to 132 separate organizations in 1940, including those for war relief in Czechoslovakia, France, Finland, the Netherlands, Britain, and China. She gave money to refugees fleeing Italy. She continued the contributions she had been making to Greenwich House since the turn of the century, as well as to dozens of other charities, including the Chrystie Street House of Hospitality, Florence Crittenden League, Gallaudet Home of Dutchess County, Jacob Riis Settlement House, and National Jewish Hospital. In fact, several of her organizations were "questionable," according to a list prepared by the FBI, and her name appeared on a "suspicious persons" list along with several of Franklin's cabinet members.

Sara was fatalistic about Franklin's quest for a third term. After his election, she admitted that she had not wanted him to run because "I thought it might not turn out so well. But as long as he did and it turned out well, I'm happy. Franklin's perfectly capable of getting through another four years." She said that she thought Franklin had "a lucky star."

She also had harsh words for the men who had thrown eggs and fruit at Wendell L. Willkie, who was the Republican contender for the presidency.

"Those attacks are disgusting. I can't believe that any real American would stoop to such a thing."

On election night Franklin was, of course, at Hyde Park, where he talked to the torchlit procession of neighbors from the portico. Franklin said of Hyde Park, "My heart has always been here. It always will be."

When the returns showed that Franklin had won a third term, Sara said that she was "a mother of history. Few mothers of Presidents ever lived to see their sons elected even to a first term. Why, when you read history it seems as if most of the Presidents didn't have mothers, the way they fail to appear in the accounts."

All that she would say about Wendell Willkie is that he did not have enough experience, but still she "didn't think Franklin would have such a walkover, especially after the great sums of money spent even by our friends and relatives in an effort to defeat him."

As the evening ended, Grace Tully, Franklin's private secretary, noticed Sara, exhausted, leaning against a sideboard in the hallway. Tully wrote that Sara was heavyhearted and told her, "A lot of my friends and some of my relatives are not going to like this at all tomorrow." Tully was touched: "My heart went out to her and by way of comfort, I reminded her of the millions throughout the country who would be rejoicing at the outcome. My remark evoked an assenting shake of the head and a forced smile. I know of her great devotion to her family and how deeply hurt she was when any one of them criticized her son's handling of government affairs."

As 1940 drew to a close, Sara was at the White House for Christmas and for a graver purpose. Franklin planned on addressing the nation to share his thoughts on national security, which he interpreted as assisting Western nations in their fight against Hitler. He had gathered a few cabinet members to join him. Also sitting at his side was Sara.

45

⤬

Brave Heart

Sara was concerned about Franklin's unprecedented third term and still saw her mother's role as looking after her son. At Hyde Park late one evening before the inauguration, Eleanor began to badger Franklin about how real estate interests were hurting the poor. Franklin was obviously too tired to talk about it, but Eleanor would not let up. Sara rang for her butler and told him that the president was ready to retire for the night. Franklin went up to bed, and Sara told Eleanor good night.

Sara traveled to Washington for Franklin's third inauguration. It would be her last trip to the capital city, capping the seventy-seven days she had spent at the White House since the 1933 inauguration. Sara shone at the festivities, and spontaneous applause rippled through crowds as she was recognized. She was still in mourning for Dora and wore a black velvet gown that set off her wavy silver hair, piled high. The next day on the inaugural platform, diplomats and cabinet members approached her one by one to pay their respects.

"Perhaps she moved a bit more slowly than she did in 1933," reported the *Washington Star*. "Perhaps she relied a little more on her polished cane as she passed from room to room in the White House. However, she'd had a grand time throughout the inaugural weekend, and hers was an honor that had come to no other American mother. Her 86 years rested lightly."

Some of the great-grandchildren were present, too, and the eldest printed a note after returning home. "Dear Granny, Mummy told me that you paid our expenses to Washington. I think it is very nice of you to do so. Thank you very much. Love and kisses, Sistie."

In March, Sara stepped up her role as good citizen. The president supported legislation that would lend goods to countries fighting Germany. Through his Lend-Lease program, Franklin would move the country slightly away from its isolationism. Sara put her name on a telegram that went to Vice President Henry Wallace, president of the Senate, protesting filibuster tactics on "the lease-lend bill or on any proposed amendments." The telegram was a bipartisan effort on behalf of thirty-one prominent women to support "intelligent debate." Another signatory was Mrs. William Taft, widow of the former Republican president.

In another effort to aid friends abroad, Sara autographed British stamps whose sale would assist the British American Ambulance Corps and the British War Relief Society. She also donated her French 1830 post-Empire sewing kit for auction by Bundles for Britain. Sara was the guest of honor at a dinner of Youth Aliyah, which supported the transport of Jewish children from Nazi-occupied countries to Palestine. Then she traveled to Ontario to address the Toronto Hadassah. "Isn't she amazing?" Eleanor remarked to Anna. (When Sara arrived in Canada, she left the train station so quickly that she did not realize that she had left in her wake an honor guard there to meet her. The Canadian officers followed her car to her hotel, where she inspected the guard in the lobby.)

Back in New York, she also appeared at a Mother's Day celebration to address her concern over "the great multitude—many millions—of homeless mothers, war-orphans, impoverished refugees. . . . This we shall do without neglecting the needy of our own land." She gave her traditional radio address on Mother's Day from Hyde Park. Eleanor remarked in her column: "There is no one I know who sets a greater value on the duties and pleasures of motherhood." That same month she attended a dinner in honor of columnist Dorothy Thompson (the wife of novelist Sinclair Lewis). Thompson urged the three thousand guests to "not make the mistake of every other nation, of waiting too long." After these remarks, Sara presented the columnist with a bust of Thompson herself.

Perhaps Sara had not spent enough time taking care of her own health. By June she was ill. The problem, as she put it, was "blood pressure." She was not allowed downstairs for weeks and complained of being "useless." She wrote Kleeman: "I read war news, & hear the radio & cannot get interested in novels or books with all the *war news*." Although she had to remain quiet and at home, the Jewish Section of the Interfaith Committee for Aid to Democracies established a children's hospital in England in Sara's honor.

Sara was worried that news of her failing health would enervate Franklin. "It would upset him," she said, "and he needs so much to be free of personal concern." Yet the European tragedies grieved her, and Dora's death left her with a sense of emptiness.

Sara decided to go to Campobello in the hope that its fresh air would be invigorating. Eleanor wrote Anna: "Granny was laid up nearly three weeks & narrowly missed a stroke so I'm going to take her to Campo this year so I'm glad to have the I.S.S. [International Student Service] group there to give me a little more incentive for going! I'm not staying just seeing her settled."

Eleanor and Franklin hired Kathleen Crawford as Sara's companion. This time Sara did not object. By July friends were sending Sara worried letters because they had not heard from her yet that summer. Crawford began to write on her behalf. "Mrs. R. went out today for the first time. Her headaches seem to be better but she has not regained her strength. She is kept very quiet and only comes downstairs twice a day." One note from Crawford was to Kleeman: "Dear Mrs. Roosevelt is back in bed again for a few days to rest her heart but she told me she has had a happy day." Then Crawford added a postscript: "I shall write you again soon. Please do not alarm anyone—you understand . . ."

A trained nurse came from Boston, resisted initially by Sara until Franklin told her that she was disturbing his "peace of mind." Then she capitulated. Perhaps Sara recognized that she was failing, as she suddenly increased her acts of generosity to her grandchildren. Sara received an enthusiastic note from Anna: "The enormous check from you came as a tremendous surprise. Did you strike oil on the front lawn?" Still, Elliott said of his brothers and sisters, "We dismissed the fancy that she was growing frail, because we could only think of her as ageless."

In August, after a lifetime of heavy correspondence and journal writing, Sara sent her last letter. It was to Franklin. "We have a lovely day & I am sitting in a sunny window, & writing one or two notes, nothing important—trying to plan my return home early in September. Here comes the doctor—I think laziness is *my* chief trouble—I think of *you* night and day. It is lovely having Aunt Kassie & she does not mind the *very* quiet life. The nurse is perfect & I shall keep her on at Hyde Park for a time anyway."

(Sara could not have known that Franklin was not too far away on the presidential yacht, sailing on the bright August waters off Cape Cod. Of course, he moved from that boat onto the USS *Augusta* to meet Winston Churchill farther up the coast for secret talks.)

Sara left Campobello for Hyde Park in early September. Her physician said that she should be carried down the steps. She refused. Halfway down, she stopped to rest. She noticed her rector, standing near the stairs to say good-bye, and smiled at him. "You've never seen the 'old lady' in this condition before, have you?"

Eleanor had noticed her mother-in-law's worsening health and wrote Anna that she must have had a stroke. Eleanor was at Hyde Park to greet Sara when she returned. Looking at her the next morning, Eleanor had a premonition and called Franklin on Friday evening, urging him to come home from Washington. He arrived at Hyde Park the next morning. Although Sara had wanted to greet him on the portico, she was incapable of going down the stairs. Instead, she put on her finest bed jacket and tied a blue ribbon in her braid before reclining on her chaise longue. When Franklin arrived, he and Sara chatted quietly. He had not seen her since before she had gone to Campobello, and was concerned.

That night Sara slipped into a coma. At midday Sunday she died peacefully in the same bed in which Franklin had been born fifty-nine years earlier. It was September 7; she was exactly two weeks from her eighty-seventh birthday.

A few minutes after her death, an enormous crash outside the house made the head of Franklin's Secret Service detail run out into the yard. The air was still and quiet, yet the tallest deciduous tree on Hyde Park's land, an ancient oak, had toppled. Although geologists would later say that it was not unheard of, that the Hudson Valley had only a shallow layer of earth to support heavy trees, no one at the estate that afternoon doubted that the tumbling of the old oak was a sign. Franklin left his mother's still body and went out to where the tree had fallen. He sat there staring at the roots torn from the earth and the thick trunk heavy on the ground.

The day she had returned from Campobello, Sara had insisted on talking to a Canadian news reporter who had stopped at the house. He didn't keep her long but asked her where the times were taking the world. "For the first time," he wrote, "Sara Delano Roosevelt didn't seem to hear because she said nothing for a full 10 seconds, and the big logs crackled in the fireplace and darkness was falling over the river. Then suddenly, thrusting her chin into the air, she answered:

"'There is nothing to fear on that score. We don't know where the times are taking us, but if we all did the sensible thing and have brave hearts, a better world is bound to come.'"

~

She had wanted a simple ceremony. On Wednesday, three days after Sara's death, vested choristers from St. James Episcopal Church opened the service in the library of her Hyde Park home. Reverend Frank R. Wilson read excerpts from the order for the burial of the dead from the Book of Common Prayer of the Episcopal Church. There was no eulogy, in accordance with the custom of the time for private citizens. The service ended with the choir's "Abide with Me," one of Sara's favorite hymns. Simultaneously a service with the same hymns and prayers was being held at St. Ann's Church on Campobello Island.

Then a group of her employees, including William Plog, the estate manager who had carried James's casket forty-one years earlier and was still in her service, lifted Sara's red mahogany coffin onto their shoulders and brought her to the hearse for burial at the St. James churchyard. The president had asked for privacy, and out of respect for his wishes, there was almost no one standing to see the funeral cortege make its way north to the cemetery. A hush seemed to fall over the Hudson Valley that afternoon. Condolence telegrams for Franklin had been patched into a Poughkeepsie hotel, but when the service began, the switchboard coincidentally fell silent for the length of the ceremony.

When the thirteen-car cortege reached the yard of the ivy-covered church, Franklin's vehicle stopped only a few feet from the open grave. Franklin got out and stood, supporting himself with one hand on the open car door. His face was solemn and his head was bowed. He wore a dark blue business suit with a black mourning band around his left arm and a black tie. Frederick was formally suited in a cutaway and striped trousers. Standing with the men were Eleanor, in a black silk crepe dress and a black hat, James, Elliott, and John. (Anna could not fly in from Seattle, and Franklin Jr. was in the service.) Betty was there, as was Kassie, who, like her brother, was more formally dressed, wearing a long black mourning veil.

On the other side of the grave were standing the invited villagers and staff from the estate. Franklin's bowed head was lit by the setting sun, and he looked up only twice: once when his Aunt Kassie coughed, and then again when one of Sara's employees fainted.

The group joined in the Lord's Prayer, and then Sara's casket was lowered into the grave. She was put at James's left, because his first wife, Rebecca, was to his right. Nearby was the tiny grave of Franklin's first namesake. Despite a plethora of flower arrangements that had already arrived at the churchyard, only one ample yet unostentatious bouquet of Sara's own autumn flowers and ferns adorned the coffin's wood. It included the orange Sara Delano Roosevelt gladioli, as well as her favorite roses, asters, and ferns. Franklin looked down as the coffin was lowered, glancing neither at it nor at Eleanor, who was watching him anxiously.

The news of Sara's death was on the front page, and was sometimes the lead headline, of newspapers throughout the country. Editorials mourned her passing and stated that she "was noted for her broad-mindedness and understanding, for generosity and never for snobbishness." One read: "Probably no woman has fitted more closely the public's conception of what a President's mother should be than she did."

Thousands of messages poured in—from Sara's friends, organizations she had assisted, and those who merely needed to send sympathy because she had been the president's mother. Among the tributes were ones from the Hadassah and B'rith Abraham. A spokeswoman from the Young Women's Zionist Organization of America said, "Her understanding of the problems of minority groups and her sympathies with their aims endeared her to Americans of all faiths."

The White House responded to the notes from friends by sending black-bordered acknowledgment cards that either Eleanor or Franklin would personalize. On one card, Eleanor wrote: "You must know only too well how deep this sorrow is."

The Queen Mother sent a telegram from Marlborough House, and her son King George VI from Buckingham Palace.

Franklin responded with personal messages to all of the telegrams from royalty and world leaders. There was only one exception. He received a radiogram of condolence from the Japanese emperor Hirohito, and to this message his secretary noted, "Respectfully referred to the Department of State for appropriate action."

Eleanor asked Franklin plaintively to redecorate the house at Hyde Park to suit her own tastes. "I want to buy some little upholstered chairs & some few little things to make the rooms more livable. May I?" After more than three decades of marriage, Franklin refused. In essence, the house was to remain frozen in time. The only change was that the staff called Eleanor, rather than Sara, "Madam."

Three days after the funeral, Eleanor wrote to Anna with calculations of how much money they could expect from Sara's estate. Then she added: "Pa sprang it on me today that I had better take Granny's room but I just can't & told him so. Of course, I know I've got to live there more, but only when he is there & I am afraid he hasn't realized that & isn't going to like it or understand."

Anna wrote her mother a letter that her eldest children interpret differently. Curtis Roosevelt believes that his mother wrote what his grandmother wanted to hear. Ellie Roosevelt Seagraves, on the other hand, remembers that her mother Anna grieved deeply for Sara and that underlying her sadness was "another case of family having to keep emotions in check."

Anna's letter reads:

> You, I know, realized that Pa would forget all of the disagreeable things when Granny died. In the first place, it would be part of his natural philosophy. In the second place, Pa has so organized his life that I wonder if there is anyone besides himself who ever really knows what he is really thinking or feeling. It's a lonely state of affairs, for my thinking, but it's of his own making. Granny was a part of his pattern of life—one of the few things that didn't ever shift—and for this reason alone he is bound to miss her.

Miss her he did. Franklin donned a black armband that he would not remove for more than a year. A few weeks after his mother's funeral, he went back to Hyde Park to organize the many boxes of memorabilia piled up in the FDR Library. Franklin and his private secretary came across a box labeled in Sara's hand. They opened it and found inside objects wrapped in paper tissue. The little bundles had notes attached, explaining what each object meant: Sara's gloves worn at her wedding to James, a lock of her hair and of Franklin's, his baby shoes, and so on. Tears sprang to Franklin's eyes, the eyes that were his mother's. He asked to be alone, and his secretary left him to his memories and his tears.

46

※

"Every Play Has to Have
Its Heavy"

A mourning nation revered Sara. Tributes to her continued through the
next decade. In 1943, for example, donors purchased the dual Roosevelt houses in Manhattan from the family and gave them to Hunter
College. The dwelling was to be renamed the Sara Delano Roosevelt Interfaith House and would be used to house different religious groups. Shortly
before the opening ceremony, Cardinal Spellman complained about the
word *interfaith* being part of its name and refused to attend the ceremonies if
it remained. The center was renamed the Sara Delano Roosevelt House.
Still, Franklin sent a letter to be read at the opening: "I feel that my dear
mother would be very happy . . . [that] the old home . . . is now to become
'Interfaith House.'" Eleanor, who was present, added to his comments and
acknowledged Sara's "many friends of all races and religions."

At the time of Sara's death, the public was respectful of Franklin's deep
love for her, and Eleanor acknowledged his affection, somewhat begrudg-
ingly, in the "My Day" column she wrote shortly after Sara's death. Privately, Eleanor wrote Anna that she was "appalled" at herself for not being
able to "feel any real grief." To her friend Joseph P. Lash, who would later be
her biographer, she wrote: "I looked at my mother-in-law's face after she
was dead & understood so many things I had never seen before. It is dread-

ful to have lived so close to someone for 36 years & to feel no deep affection or sense of loss."

Eleanor might have been numb because she had endured a series of blows. At the beginning of the year, she had been ambivalent about seeing Franklin inaugurated for a third term in January 1941. Then the death of her brother, Hall, came on the heels of her mother-in-law's. Their deaths were less than three weeks apart. The loss of Hall was expected, but Eleanor was dismayed at the repulsion she felt at his physical condition. Cirrhosis of the liver had swollen Hall, bloated him hard, and colored his skin an odd brown shade. Eleanor felt nothing but disgust for the brother she had loved so dearly for years, and again she could not grieve.

Eleanor's friend Marion Dickerman commented on Eleanor's absence of feelings in her oral history. "This seems to emphasize a side of Eleanor that is not known to many people," said Dickerman. "She was kind, she was compassionate, but when certain matters touched her personally she could be very hard, and sometimes cruel."

Geoffrey Ward, Franklin's biographer, thought Eleanor plagued by depression that began in childhood and deepened from adolescence on. He has suggested that Eleanor's constant whirlwind of activities served to mask her sadness. If so, her absence of feeling and numbness over the latest two losses in her life would be consistent with how a depressed person might react.

Eleanor did realize that Sara's death struck Franklin hard. James noted that Eleanor displayed to Franklin "more affection during those days than at any other time I can recall." Yet Eleanor was not capable of supplying Franklin with the emotional support he craved. Daisy Suckley wrote in her diary: "His wife is a wonderful person, but she lacks the ability to give him the things his mother gave him. She is away so much, and when she is here she has so many people around—the splendid people who are trying to do good and improve the world, 'uplifters,' the P. [president] calls them—that he cannot relax and really rest."

Suckley wrote her thoughts about Franklin a year after Sara's death. "He misses his mother. The house has no hostess most of the time, as his wife is here so rarely—always off on a speaking tour, etc."

Eleanor's adult children did not see their mother much, either. When they visited the White House, Eleanor "accorded them no special privileges because they were Roosevelts," said the chief usher. "Mrs. Roosevelt saw them briefly by appointment or at breakfast, treating them just like any other houseguest."

~

Just as Sara had acted as a mother to her grandchildren, she was also a grandmother to her great-grandchildren. Perhaps Eleanor resented the depth of her children's and grandchildren's feelings for Sara. Curtis Roosevelt said of her, "I felt totally confident in her company and with her discipline. The relationship was very easy. She loved you in an unreserved fashion.

"Yet you were expected to behave. If not, you were sent off with the nurse. You'd realize you would rather be in the main arena."

Eleanor, on the other hand, did not have the time or inclination to take her grandchildren into bed with her and read them the comics, for instance, as Sara had. Eleanor later admitted that she had not been the mother that her children should have had, but she did not compensate for that with her grandchildren until they were young adults. Then, she followed Sara's example by establishing a special relationship with each of her grandchildren and would accept speaking engagements in locations near them, remembered Ellie Roosevelt Seagraves.

Nor did Eleanor acknowledge Sara's financial support of her family, except with animosity. Eleanor may have harbored mixed feelings about a husband who could not, or would not, live within his own income. If she did, she suppressed her thoughts and laid the onus on Sara's shoulders. Eleanor's problems with Sara may have been owing to her own unresolved issues with Franklin. Still, if it had not been for Sara's constant infusion of cash, Franklin would never have been able to lead his life in the style he expected while in public office.

Franklin's former son-in-law Curtis B. Dall, who had been divorced by Anna, noted that "FDR was not forced to avail himself of such maternal advantages and facilities, so warmly offered, unless he decided it best suited his program to accept them. Therefore, in properly describing his mother, the words *generous, devoted, interested, thoughtful*, etc., should be properly used to replace some mischievous words used, such as *domineering, autocratic, snobbish* and the like."

Sara had enjoyed the equivalent of a $28 million inheritance from her father and a $2 million legacy from her husband (using today's valuation). Sara paid expenses that included the costs of her Hyde Park estate, the two Manhattan houses, and the two Campobello houses. After that, Sara picked up Franklin and Eleanor's bills and subsidized Franklin's two terms as governor of New York as well as his first two presidential terms. When she died, she left Franklin a fortune equivalent to $12–$13 million, before taxes. (There had been no federal death taxes when she received her inheritance.) With her large property added to his smaller one, Franklin became the largest landowner in the Dutchess County area.

Franklin, of course, died in 1945 when he was only sixty-three. His death was due to the effects of polio and the tremendous stress of both the Depression and the world war. This is what Sara had feared would happen when he reentered political office in 1928. Franklin's half-brother, Rosy, who was born in 1854, a generation before Franklin, lived to be seventy-three. Franklin's father, born more than a century earlier in 1828, lived to seventy-two. Franklin's own death was indeed premature.

Franklin was not left enough time even to settle Sara's estate. (He did, however, make sure that her overdue books were returned to the local library. Sara, who picked up the entire cost of running the library, never saw any need to get her books back before the due date.) At his death, Franklin left the value of his insurance policy to the Warm Springs Foundation and bequeathed to Eleanor the equivalent of $10 million from his own estate and $10 million from Sara's.

Franklin included a provision in his will for his friend Missy LeHand. She was to receive half the interest on his estate. LeHand had died in 1942, so James questioned his father: did he want to strike out the provision for LeHand? She was dead, James noted, and the press might make an issue of the bequest.

"If it embarrasses Mother," Franklin told James, "I'm sorry. It shouldn't, but it may." He left his will intact.

Eleanor became a wealthy woman in her own right when Franklin died. She continued her generous ways, not splurging on herself but doing for family and friends. "Mother had looked for money only for handing out to others," Elliott commented.

When Eleanor died in 1962, she left less than today's equivalent of a million dollars. She generously had gifted the federal government with more land and houses from the Hyde Park property for the memory of FDR and had sold the East Sixty-fifth Street houses for a modest sum. The five children, too, always seemed to be in need of money. It took only nineteen years from Sara's death to use up the vast Delano fortune.

Franklin had made several generous gestures, including turning over twelve acres of the Hyde Park estate to the National Park Service, which received the property in 1946. Elliott wrote of his mother: "She felt no more regret about giving up the place than in quitting the White House. It was a relief to be rid of a mansion she had not enjoyed as a home." Eleanor retained more than one thousand acres, much of it the land across Albany Post Road where her own Val-Kill was located. Although she continued to live at Val-Kill, it would revert to the government upon her death. She also gave acreage to her sons, who needed money and eventually sold their holdings. Now inexpensive taverns and motels have drifted onto the property across the road from Sara's house.

By the 1950s Sara's image started to erode. It was a decade when women, especially mothers, were blamed for emasculating men and raising troubled children. The memory of a strong woman, in the era of *Father Knows Best*, became an object of ridicule.

In 1952 *Time* published an article on Eleanor with an anonymous quote claiming that Sara had reprimanded her publicly, "Eleanor, don't act the fool." Sara's biographer Rita Kleeman wrote an indignant letter, published by the magazine: "The legend of her unkind treatment of her daughter-in-law grows and grows—now that she is gone, and her son is no longer here to deny it."

Kleeman continued: "I spent a great deal of time with Mrs. Roosevelt in her later years, and again and again, I heard people bait her in the hope of getting a reply that would bolster it [the animosity toward Eleanor] and make a good story. And again and again I noted their chagrin when, instead of the expected criticism, Mrs. Roosevelt replied with praise of her daughter-in-law." She went on to say that the tales of an overbearing Sara embodied "only the usual, and frequently unjust, criticism of mothers-in-law and grandmothers."

Kleeman, a widely published professional writer, wrote a profile of Sara on the centennial of her birth in 1954 and submitted it to many magazines, yet none accepted it for publication. Kleeman felt that worshipful myths surrounded Eleanor at the expense of her mother-in-law. Kleeman wrote: "The world was more interested in the unfortunate legend that had grown up since Mrs. Roosevelt and her son had gone—the legend that she was a selfish, domineering, jealous woman who had spoiled the grandchildren (yet the great-grandchildren were still being sent to her for the summer in her last years) and dominated her son and his wife . . . who never appeared cowed to those who knew them." Kleeman concluded that Eleanor was envious of Franklin's love for Sara. She paraphrased Mary Bass, editor of *Ladies' Home Journal*, saying that Bass "told me frankly that no magazine would dare publish [a respectful profile of Sara] in the face of the public idolatry of Eleanor!"

The shipwreck of Sara's memory, however, was caused by Dore Schary's 1956 drama, *Sunrise at Campobello*, which was a hit on Broadway and then a popular movie. The Broadway play starred Ralph Bellamy as FDR and Mary Fickett as Eleanor. (In the movie, it was Greer Garson.) Anne Seymour played Sara. It purportedly shows the impact of Franklin's polio attack on his family and career. Sara is in nine of the play's eleven scenes, always as the dark cloud, sourly commenting on politics, speaking nastily of politicians and politicos, and bossing Eleanor and Franklin while spoiling the grandchildren. "I think," said James Roosevelt, commenting on the negative image of his grandmother, "it all started with this portrayal."

Anna's daughter, Ellie Roosevelt Seagraves, was shocked at the traducing of her great-grandmother. "She was a real harridan in that thing, an ogre, shrew! And that was not the way she was at all. I mean, she never raised her voice. That would just be terribly out of character."

Another great-granddaughter, Nina Roosevelt Gibson, remarked, "It's a very harsh portrayal." She commented on the years when it was produced: "We did not want strong women then. We wanted June Cleaver—and we wanted to get rid of the aristocracy, we wanted to minimize them."

Eleanor finally said in 1958, "An excellent play . . . but I have no feeling of reality about it. It had no more to do with me than the man in the moon." Joseph Lash also said that Eleanor told him privately that the play was "unfair to the President's mother, who was a great personality, never petty."

However, the grandchildren protested the treatment of Sara at the time. Schary had gathered Eleanor and the four children (Anna was not present) to read the script aloud. When he ended, Franklin Jr. spoke up. "That's awfully rough on Granny. That's not an accurate picture."

Eleanor was quiet. Then Dore Schary laughed. "Well, Franklin, every play has to have its heavy."

Edna Gurewitsch, the widow of Eleanor's personal physician and close friend David Gurewitsch, noted of Eleanor that "her motivation for cooperating with the project became clear when she explained to David that her five children, seemingly always in need of money, would share in the royalties."

Eleanor's former son-in-law had a slightly different take. Dall said that "it was to make her [Sara] appear a snob, somewhat overbearing, creating an image whereby her daughter-in-law would attract some 'political sympathy.'"

EPILOGUE

At the end of the millennium, *Time* magazine published the names of the one hundred leaders who most influenced our world in the past century; both Eleanor and Franklin Roosevelt were at the top of the list. Their contribution—shaping the political and social fabric of our nation. Eleanor, still a revered figure today, was herself named by historians as "America's most influential First Lady."

There is no question that they belong on the list. Franklin was killed by the effects of polio and the stress of leading the nation, triumphant, through the Great Depression and World War II. For the last twenty-four years of his life he could not support his own body but managed to hold the entire world, Atlas-like, on his back.

Upon receiving word of Franklin's death, Eleanor stated simply, "The story is over," but she was wrong; it was far from over. Eleanor lived beyond Franklin for another seventeen years, fighting for the things she cared about: the rights of labor, blacks, and women; the World Court and international peace; and, of course, social equality.

As the scholar Allida M. Black has noted: "She wrote, without a ghost writer, four autobiographies, seven monographs, seven children's books, and more than 550 articles. She delivered more than fifty speeches a year for more than thirty years. In February 1933, she began a monthly column, which existed in a variety of forms until her death in November 1962. On December 30, 1935, she began "My Day," a five-hundred-word column published five days a week, which ran continuously until September 27, 1962."

Eleanor's granddaughter Ellie Roosevelt Seagraves has pointed out that Eleanor would have been amazed to know she has become iconic to several generations of women. Ellie often heard Eleanor say that she was certain she would be forgotten within a decade of her death. She was wrong. Eleanor Roosevelt's continued accomplishments are many, her influence remains great, and the work she began still goes on.

There was, however, another woman in FDR's life.

During Franklin's lifetime, his mother, Sara, symbolized stability and graciousness, even when the world was rocked by the war in Europe. Her estate, Hyde Park—during a decade of mortgage foreclosures and evictions—remained an anchor to the core values of home and hearth that Americans, no matter what their background, hoped to keep alive. She represented a safe harbor.

She herself knew what her life had been. "I have been an unusually fortunate woman," Sara wrote her son. "First I had the love and protection of your grandfather, then of your father, and in my old age you have made possible for me the interesting life that I am now leading." She could not know, of course, that the good she did would be interred with her bones.

After Franklin's death, Eleanor dutifully maintained the outward signs of respect for his mother. Each year before the anniversary of Sara's death, this busy woman would handwrite a note to a Hyde Park florist, asking for "my usual order of flowers in memory of Mrs. James Roosevelt." She placed a plaque to commemorate Sara on St. James Church. In 1951 Eleanor even named Sara as one of "the Seven People Who Shaped My Life."

However, as the decade wore on, Eleanor began to snipe at her mother-in-law and twist Sara's actions to suit herself. Eleanor has always been given a wide berth when it comes to her criticisms of her mother-in-law. Her statements have been used as a lens scrutinizing Sara's character—what did Sara do to make Eleanor feel this way?—rather than as a basis for an analysis of Eleanor—what was lacking in *Eleanor* that made her so unappreciative of the woman who did so much for her, her husband, and her children? After all, it was Eleanor who famously said, "No one can make you feel inferior without your consent."

Eleanor may have been envious of her children's respect and love for their grandmother. The boys, especially, had bleak memories of Eleanor as a mother. James wrote: "Mother let Sara guide the rearing of the children. Mother wrote Sara for advice when we misbehaved, and she seldom complained when Sara took charge. If mother ever hinted her displeasure, Sara simply said, 'Why, Eleanor, I didn't think you'd mind.' Most of the time mother pretended she didn't. It was easier than pretending she could take charge."

The servants in the White House noticed that Eleanor "was a little jealous of how much her children clung to their grandmother." One said, "Through the years, Eleanor grew to be more and more hostile toward her husband's mother."

Nina Roosevelt Gibson never knew Sara, but she has given the relationship much thought. She said, "It appalls me that Sara is dismissed as a difficult, arrogant snob who is mean to her daughter-in-law." Moreover, Gibson, a developmental psychologist, believes that Eleanor unconsciously used Sara as her role model. Eleanor, she has pointed out, came from a dysfunctional family with a weak mother and grandmother. Her mother-in-law, who was strong, "for the first time in Eleanor's life made her feel safe and secure. The life Sara offered her fit cognitively with how Eleanor was supposed to have been raised. But she could never connect to Sara's love."

Gibson has also pointed out that Sara allowed Eleanor to be herself, which enabled Eleanor to be a trailblazer for all women. "Sara gave her the perfect opportunity to get out of the house. Sara took care of the children and the household. Sara relieved Eleanor of this responsibility."

However, Eleanor would not acknowledge Sara's contributions. She got off one last shot at her mother-in-law in "I Remember Hyde Park," which was published in *McCall's* and then abridged for *Reader's Digest*. Eleanor elucidates her complaints in this memoir. "For over forty years, I was only a visitor there," she wrote of Hyde Park. "My mother-in-law did *all* the housekeeping there." She did not mention her own lack of interest in those duties, nor that the house was in fact Sara's.

She wrote, correctly, that Sara opposed her marriage because of Franklin's youth and then, incorrectly, "and because she thought he could have made a more worldly and social match." She wrote: "Then, when she knew it was going to happen anyway, she determined to bend the marriage the way she wanted it to be. . . . As it turned out, Franklin's children were more my mother-in-law's children than they were mine."

She admitted that "undoubtedly, this was partly my fault, since for a great, great many years, she completely dominated me, and I permitted her to keep me under her thumb." She added: "I was not allowed to take care of the children, nor had I any sense of how to do it."

She attacked Sara on other bases, too. "My mother-in-law judged people almost solely by their social position, and she continually tried to teach my children to do the same."

This mean-spirited story, not borne out by the record, was published after Eleanor's death and was her final legacy to her husband's beloved mother.

Eleanor's worldly accomplishments are not diminished by her failure in her family relationships. Eleanor herself reflected on her shortcomings as a wife when she wrote in her autobiography that Franklin "might have been happier with a wife who was completely uncritical."

It must have been difficult for her to realize that her children thought that "Sara was the source of all the good things in life when [they] were little." Elliott put it best when describing Eleanor: "I am convinced that she was motivated by a profound psychological hunger. None of us children in our grown-up years had turned to her for comfort, guidance or protection. We saw her as an austere, rather distant woman, who seldom could communicate with us. The warmth in our lives came from Father and Granny."

Sara's loving-kindness toward her family was bountiful. Earning adoration from a son, his children, and his grandchildren would be a substantial achievement for any woman, but this particular mother's contributions went well beyond her family. *Look*, for example, published a story in 1939, "Who Influences the President More—His Wife or His Mother?" However, Sara Delano Roosevelt would not have objected had her influence and her accomplishments in the public arena gone unrecognized.

Franklin Delano Roosevelt rightly remains a towering figure in the pantheon of America's leaders. Eleanor Roosevelt was an extraordinary woman whose work profoundly influenced the course of the twentieth century. However, for the sake of historical accuracy, it is only fair to add that their achievements would not have been possible without the strength, constancy, and generosity of Sara Delano Roosevelt. The intersecting lives of Sara and Eleanor produced two extraordinary women: one, a mother; the other, her daughter-in-law.

NOTES

PROLOGUE

Degregorio, William A. *The Complete Book of U.S. Presidents*. New York: Wing Books, 1996.

Kleeman, Rita S. Halle. *Gracious Lady: The Life of Sara Delano Roosevelt*. New York: D. Appleton-Century Co., 1935.

"Time 100 Polls, Leaders & Revolutionaries." *Time*, April 13, 1998.

Outer Island/Beloved Island. Video shown at Visitors Centre, Roosevelt Campobello International Park, New Brunswick, Canada.

Interviews

Curtis Roosevelt, Washington, D.C.

Eleanor (Ellie) Roosevelt Seagraves, Washington, D.C.

Nina Roosevelt Gibson, telephone

Ron Beckwith, Roosevelt Campobello International Park, New Brunswick, Canada

Note: All current (2002) dollar equivalencies throughout the text are calculated from the Web site of the Federal Reserve Bank of Minneapolis, www.mpls.frb.org.

CHAPTER 1: "FRENCH BY ANCESTRY, DUTCH BY BIRTH, AND ENGLISH BY ASSOCIATION"

Austin, Jane G. *Standish of Standish: A Story of the Pilgrims*. New York: Houghton, Mifflin & Co., 1895.

Cushing, Muriel Curtis. *Philip Delano of the Fortune 1621*. Plymouth, Mass.: General Society of Mayflower Descendants, 1999.

Longfellow, Henry Wadsworth. "The Courtship of Miles Standish."

Roberts, Gary Boyd. "Ancestor Fan Chart of Ulysses S. Grant." *Ancestors of American Presidents*. Santa Clarita, Calif.: Carl Boyer, 1995.

Interviews

Muriel Curtis Cushing, Punta Gorda Isles, Florida

> Ms. Cushing is a descendant of Philippe de Lannoy and published the most accurate genealogy of the Delano family (cited above). When facts were contradictory, her history was used as definitive. In addition, she corrected family myths that have been repeated in biographies of ER and FDR; for example, that Philippe had a brother, Jacques, and that they had both fallen in love with Priscilla Mullins Alden.

Peggy Baker, historical librarian, Pilgrim Society, Pilgrim Hall Museum, Plymouth, Massachusetts

CHAPTER 2: ON THE WEST BANK OF THE HUDSON RIVER LIVED THE DELANOS

All Souls History, Who We Are. New York: All Souls Church, 2001.

Darden, Genevieve M. *Unitarian Society of Fairhaven, 1832–1982*. Fairhaven, Mass., 1982.

Delano, Daniel W. *Franklin Roosevelt and the Delano Influence*. Pittsburgh, Pa.: James S. Nudi Publications, 1946.

Delano, Major Joel Andrew. *The Genealogy, History and Alliances of the American House of Delano, 1621–1899*. New York: n.p., 1899.

Johnson, Alvin Page. *Franklin D. Roosevelt's Colonial Ancestors: Their Part in the Making of American History*. Boston: Lothrop, Lee & Shepard Co., 1933.

Mosgrove, Mildred C. *America's Cathedral Beautiful: Memorial Church*. Fairhaven, Mass.: Associated Printers, 1986.

Mr. History Person (Christopher Richard). "The Delano Family of Fairhaven." *Navigator*, Jan. 2002.

Ward, Geoffrey C. *American Originals*. New York: HarperCollins, 1991.

Research Collections

Franklin Delano Roosevelt Library and Museum (FDR Library)

> Delano Family Papers
> Sara Delano Roosevelt Papers

Interviews

Cynthia McNaughten, Memorial Church, Fairhaven, Massachusetts

Christopher Richard, "Mr. History Person," Fairhaven Office of Tourism, Fairhaven, Massachusetts

Paul Beauchamp, current owner of original Delano Homestead, Fairhaven, Massachusetts

Debbie Charpentier, archivist/facility manager, Millicent Library, Fairhaven, Massachusetts

Chapter 3: "My Orderly Little Life"

Butow, R. J. C. "A Notable Passage to China; Myth and Memory in FDR's Family History. *Prologue: Quarterly of the National Archives and Records Administration*, Fall 1999.

————. "Delano Reactions to News of the War at Home." *Prologue*, Fall 1999.

Chesneaux, Jean, et al. *China: From the Opium Wars to the 1911 Revolution*. New York: Pantheon Books, 1976.

Churchill, Allen. *The Upper Crust: An Informal History of New York's Highest Society*. Englewood Cliffs, N.J.: Prentice-Hall, 1970.

————. *The Roosevelts: American Aristocrats*. New York: Harper & Row, 1965.

Davis Kenneth S. *F.D.R.: The Beckoning of Destiny, 1882–1928*. New York: G. P. Putnam's Sons, 1972.

"De Lano, Clayton Harris." *National Cyclopedia of American Biography, Being the History of the United States*, vol. 17. New York: James T. White & Co., 1920.

Delano, Major Joel Andrew Frederick A. *Algonac, 1851–1931*. Privately printed pamphlet, 1931.

"Delano, Frederick Adrian." *National Cyclopedia of American Biography*, vol. 40. New York: James T. White & Co., 1955.

"Delano-Hitch." *New York Home Journal*, Sept. 23, 1877.

Delano, Major Joel Andrew. *Genealogy, History and Alliances*.

"Delano, Warren." *National Cyclopedia*, vol. 34. New York: James T. White & Co., 1948.

"1845–1941." *The New Republic*, Sept. 15, 1941.

Fairhaven, Massachusetts: A Small Town. Fairhaven, Mass.: Office of Tourism, 2002.

Fairhaven, Massachusetts: The Gifts of Henry Huttleston Rogers. Fairhaven; Mass.: Office of Tourism, 2002.

Geckle, William F. *The Hacketts and the Roosevelts and Other River Families*. Poughkeepsie, N.Y.: Cunneen-Hackett Trust, 1984.

Gifford, Preston W., Jr. "The Delano Family Burial Plot at Riverside Cemetery in Fairhaven, Massachusetts." Unpublished, 1994.

Gunther, John. *Roosevelt in Retrospect: A Profile in History*. New York: Harper & Brothers, 1950.

Homberger, Eric. *Mrs. Astor's New York: Money and Social Power in a Gilded Age*. New Haven, Conn.: Yale University Press, 2002.

————. *The Historical Atlas of New York City: A Visual Celebration of Nearly 400 Years of New York City's History*. New York: Henry Holt and Co., 1994.

Kleeman. *Gracious Lady*.

Local History Arc—and Delano Gifts. Fairhaven, Mass.: Millicent Library, 2002.

Polachek, James M. *The Inner Opium War*. Cambridge, Mass.: Harvard University Press, 1992.

"Radcliffe and Harvard Announce Proposed Merger." *Radcliffe Quarterly*, Feb. 1999.

"Robbins, Warren Delano." *Encyclopedia of Biography*. New York: American Historical Society, 1934.

Roosevelt, Elliott. *A Rendezvous with Destiny: The Roosevelts of the White House*. New York: Dell Publishing Co., 1976.

Schriftgiesser, Karl. *The Amazing Roosevelt Family: 1613–1942*. New York: Wilfred Funk, Inc., 1942.

Visitors Guide, Fairhaven, Massachusetts: A Small Town with a Big History. Fairhaven, Mass.: Office of Tourism, 2002.

"Walking Through History in Fairhaven, MA." *Traveler*, May 2002.

Ward, Geoffrey C. *Before the Trumpet: Young Franklin Roosevelt*. New York: Harper & Row, 1985.

"Warren Delano." *Fairhaven Standard*, Jan. 22, 1898.

"West, William Edward." *Dictionary of American Biography*, vol. 10. New York: Scribner & Sons, 1936.

Research Collections

FDR Library

    Sara Delano Roosevelt Papers

    Delano Family Papers

    President's Personal Files, (PPF) 275, Macon, Georgia, April 20, 1940

    Oral history: Roland Redmond

National Park Service, "Springwood," Hyde Park, New York

    Interview with Norman Reid, conducted by Preston W. Gifford, Jr.

The New York Public Library

    Local History Archives

Chapter 4: The Contented Spinster

"All Souls History."

Burt, Nathaniel. *First Families: The Making of an American Aristocracy*. Boston: Little, Brown and Co., 1970.

Butterfield, Fox. "Not Quite Your Ancestors' Mayflower." *New York Times*, June 25, 2001.

Poe, Elizabeth E. "Half-Forgotten Romances of American History: James Roosevelt–Sara Delano." *Washington Post*, February 18, 1935.

Research Collections

FDR Library

    Sara Delano Roosevelt Papers

    Delano Family Papers

Chapter 5: On the East Bank of the Hudson River Lived the Roosevelts

Alsop, Joseph, and Robert Kintner. "The Roosevelt Family Album." *Life*, Sept. 9, 1940.

Bank of New York Company. *The Bank of New York History*. New York: Bank of New York Company, 2001.

Cushing, Muriel Curtis. "Ancestor Fan Chart of Franklin Delano Roosevelt." Unpublished, n.d.

Debates in New York Convention on Ratification of the Constitution, July 26, 1788. Austin, Tex.: Constitution Day, 2002.

Duffus, R. L. "Two Stems of the Roosevelt Family Tree." *New York Times*, July 31, 1932.

Evans, Dorinda. *The Genius of Gilbert Stuart*. Princeton, N.J.: Princeton University Press, 1999.

Hess, Stephen. *America's Political Dynasties*. New York: Doubleday & Co., 1966.

Holgate, Jerome B. *American Genealogy, Being a History of Some of the Early Settlers of North America and Their Descendants*. Albany, N.Y.: Joel Munsell, 1848.

Homberger. *Historical Atlas*.

"Jewish Origins of FDR." *American Freedom Magazine*, 1938.

Johnson. *Roosevelt's Colonial Ancestors*.

McLanathan, Richard. *Gilbert Stuart*. New York: Henry N. Abrams, 1986.

Patterson, Jerry. *The Best Families: The Town & Country Social Directory, 1846–1996*. New York: Henry N. Abrams, 1996.

Roberts. *"Ancestor Fan Chart* of Ulysses S. Grant."

———, "Franklin D. Roosevelt Ancestor Table," in *Ancestors of American Presidents*. Santa Clarita, Calif.: Carl Boyer, 1995.

Ward. *Before the Trumpet.*

Research Collections
FDR Library
    Sara Delano Roosevelt Papers
    Roosevelt Family Papers

CHAPTER 6: "A GENTLEMAN OF THE OLD SCHOOL"
"James Roosevelt." *National Cyclopedia of American Biography*. New York: James T. White & Co., 1935.

Partridge, Bellamy. *Imperial Saga: The Roosevelt Family in America*. New York: Hillman-Curl, 1936.

Whittelsey, C. B. *The Roosevelt Genealogy 1649–1902*. Hartford, Conn., n.p., 1912.

Research Collections
FDR Library
    Sara Delano Roosevelt Papers
    Roosevelt Family Papers
New-York Historical Society

CHAPTER 7: HYDE PARK
Anderson, Dennis R. *Art in the Home of Franklin D. Roosevelt*. National Park Service. U.S. Department of the Interior, Hyde Park, New York.

National Park Service, U.S. Department of the Interior. *Grounds: Home of Franklin D. Roosevelt National Historic Site*. Hyde Park, N.Y.: Roosevelt-Vanderbilt National Historical Association, 2002.

"A Notable Social Event: The Wedding of Miss Astor and Mr. Roosevelt." *New York Times*, Nov. 19, 1878.

Roosevelt, Eleanor. *FDR's Love for Stories About Hyde Park*. Hyde Park, N.Y.: Manuscript for National Park Service, 1999.

Ward. *Before the Trumpet.*

Research Collections
FDR Library
    Sara Delano Roosevelt Papers
    Rebecca Howland Roosevelt Papers
    Franklin Delano Roosevelt Papers
The Eleanor Roosevelt Papers, George Washington Universtiy, Washington, D.C.

Interviews
Eleanor Roosevelt Seagraves

CHAPTER 8: "A DEMOCRAT CAN BE A GENTLEMAN"

"Roosevelt–Delano." *New York World*, Oct. 8, 1880.

Steeholm, Clara and Hardy. *The House at Hyde Park*. New York: Viking Press, 1950.

Schriftgiesser. *Amazing Roosevelt Family*.

Research Collections

FDR Library

    Rebecca Howland Roosevelt Papers

    Sara Delano Roosevelt Papers

    Roosevelt Family Papers

    Rosedale Papers

Harvard University, Houghton Library

    Theodore Roosevelt Papers

New-York Historical Society

New York University Archives

Vassar College Library

CHAPTER 9: "SALLIE AND MR. ROOSEVELT"

"Dancing Patriarchs." *New York Herald*, Dec. 11, 1888.

"Guests of the Patriarchs." *New York Times*, Dec. 24, 1884.

National Park Service, U.S. Department of the Interior. *Grounds*.

"Patriarchs Who Dance." *New York World*, Dec. 8, 1883.

Sinclair, David. *Dynasty: The Astors and Their Times*. London: J. M. Dent, 1983.

Steeholm. *House at Hyde Park*.

"The Patriach's Dance." *New York Times*, Dec. 11, 1884.

"Third Patriarchs' Ball." *New York Daily Tribune*, Feb. 15, 1881.

Ward. *Before the Trumpet*.

Research Collections

FDR Library

    Sara Delano Roosevelt Papers

    Delano Family Papers

    Roosevelt Children Papers

CHAPTER 10: "WE THREE"

Cheek, Robert. *Springwood*. Hyde Park, N.Y.: Roosevelt-Vanderbilt Historical Association, 1993.

Delano, Frederic A. *Algonac*.

Dows, Olin. *Franklin Roosevelt at Hyde Park*. New York: American Artists Group, 1949.

Dwyer, Michael Middleton, ed. *Great Houses of the Hudson River*. Boston: Bulfinch Press, 2001.

Klein, Jonas. *Beloved Island: Franklin & Eleanor and the Legacy of Campobello*. Forest Dale, Vt.: Paul S. Eriksson, 2000.

Mr. History Person (Christopher Richard). "The Delano Family of Fairhaven."

Steckel, Richard H. *Health and Welfare during Industrialization*. Chicago: University of Chicago Press, 1997.

Ward, Geoffrey C. *Before the Trumpet.*

————. "Sally, Franklin & Babs." *House & Garden,* Jan. 1982.

Weshub, Leonard Paul. *One Hundred Years of Medical Progress: A History of the New York Medical College Flower and Fifth Avenue Hospitals.* Springfield, Ill.: Charles C. Thomas, 1967.

Research Collections
FDR Library
    Sara Delano Roosevelt Papers
    Frank R. Wilson Papers
    Frederick A. Delano Papers
    PPF 8
Campobello Public Library and Museum, New Brunswick, Canada

Interviews
Amy Hebert, community relations, Terrence Cardinal Cooke Health Care Center, New York, New York

Gwenn Klein, Campobello Public Library and Museum, New Brunswick, Canada
    Eleanor Roosevelt Seagraves

CHAPTER 11: THE OYSTER BAY CLAN
Bully! Colonel Theodore Roosevelt. Montauk, N.Y.: The Rough Riders & Camp Wikoff, 1898.

Collier, Peter, and David Horowitz. *The Roosevelts: An American Saga.* New York: Simon & Schuster, 1994.

Donn, Linda. *The Roosevelt Cousins: Growing Up Together, 1882–1924.* New York: Alfred A. Knopf, 2001.

Hagedorn, Hermann. *The Roosevelt Family of Sagamore Hill.* New York: Macmillan Company, 1954.

McCullough, David. *Mornings on Horseback.* New York: Simon & Schuster, 1981.

Morris, Edmund. *The Rise of Theodore Roosevelt.* New York: Ballantine, 1979.

Research Collections
FDR Library
    Sara Delano Roosevelt Papers
    PPF 8
Library of Congress
    Theodore Roosevelt Papers, Manuscript Division

CHAPTER 12: "A BEAUTIFUL FRAME"
Kleeman. *Gracious Lady.*

Klein. *Beloved Island.*

Miller, Lina D. *New York Charities.* New York: Charity Society of the City of New York, 1912.

Roosevelt, Sara Delano. *My Boy Franklin.* New York: Ray Long & Richard R. Smith, 1933.

Steeholm. *House at Hyde Park.*

Ward. *American Originals.*

————. *Before the Trumpet.*

Worth, Robert F. "The Race Was on Ice, the Champagne in a Cup." *New York Times,* Jan. 30, 2003.

Research Collections
FDR Library
>   Sara Delano Roosevelt Papers
>   Franklin Delano Roosevelt Papers
New-York Historical Society

CHAPTER 13: GROTON SCHOOL
Ashburn, Frank D. *Peabody of Groton: A Portrait.* Cambridge, Mass.: Riverside Press, 1967.
Hatch, Alden. *Franklin D. Roosevelt.* New York: Henry Holt and Co., 1947.
Nisenson & Vitelli, n.f.i. *Franklin Delano Roosevelt.* Cleveland: World Syndicate Publishing Co., 1934.
Roosevelt, Sara. *My Boy Franklin.*
Ward. *Before the Trumpet.*
Whipple, Wayne. *The Story of Young Franklin Roosevelt.* Chicago: Goldsmith Publishing Co., 1934.

Research Collections
FDR Library
>   Sara Delano Roosevelt Papers
>   Franklin Delano Roosevelt Papers
Groton School Archives, Groton, Massachusetts

Interviews
Peter H. Congleton, director of planned giving, Groton School, Groton, Massachusetts
Douglas Brown, archivist, Groton School

CHAPTER 14: ALLENSWOOD SCHOOL
Angelo, Bonnie. *First Mothers: The Women Who Shaped the Presidents.* New York: William Morrow, 2000.
Booknotes. Interview with Betty Boyd Caroli. C-SPAN.
Brough, James, *Princess Alice: A Biography of Alice Roosevelt Longworth.* Boston: Little, Brown, and Co., 1975.
Cook, Blanche Wiesen. *Eleanor Roosevelt,* vol. 1. New York: Penguin Books, 1992.
Lash, Joseph P. *Eleanor and Franklin.* New York: W. W. Norton & Co., 1971.
Rixey, Lilian. *Bamie: Theodore Roosevelt's Remarkable Sister.* New York: David McKay Co., 1963.
Roosevelt, Eleanor. *The Autobiography of Eleanor Roosevelt.* New York: Harper & Brothers, 1958.
Roosevelt, Elliott, ed. *F.D.R.: His Personal Letters: Early Years.* New York: Duell, Sloan and Pearce, 1947.
Teichmann, Howard. *Alice: The Life and Times of Alice Roosevelt Longworth.* Englewood Cliffs, N.J.: Prentice-Hall, 1979.
The American Experience. "Eleanor Roosevelt." PBS broadcast.

Research Collections
FDR Library
>   Sara Delano Roosevelt Papers
>   Eleanor Roosevelt Papers

Franklin Delano Roosevelt Papers
Library of Congress
Theodore Roosevelt Letters, Manuscript Division

CHAPTER 15: MOTHER AND GUARDIAN

Bethel, John T. "Frank Roosevelt at Harvard." *Harvard Magazine*, Nov.–Dec. 1996.

Burns, James MacGregor. *Roosevelt: The Lion and the Fox*. New York: Harcourt, Brace, Jovanovich, 1956.

Celebrate Life in Christ at St. James Church. Hyde Park, N.Y.: St. James Church, n.d.

Churchill. *The Upper Crust*.

History of Bard. Red Hook, N.Y.: Bard College, 2003.

Kopser, Arnold. *The 1811 Church: St. James Church at Hyde Park*. Hyde Park, N.Y.: St. James Church, 1997.

Research Collections

FDR Library
    Sara Delano Roosevelt Papers
    Franklin Delano Roosevelt Papers
    Eleanor Roosevelt Papers
    Oral history: Marion Dickerman
Library of Congress
    Theodore Roosevelt Collection, Manuscript Division
Harvard University, Widener Library
    Special Collections

CHAPTER 16: SPARKS AND SMOLDERS

Black, Ruby. *Eleanor Roosevelt: A Biography*. New York: Duell, Sloan and Pearce, 1940.

Blair, Karen J. *The Clubwoman as Feminist: True Womanhood Redefined, 1868–1914*. New York: Holmes & Meier Publishers, 1980.

Cook. *Eleanor Roosevelt*, vol. 1.

International Association of Labour History Institutions. *The Great Strike: A 100th Anniversary Commemoration of the Anthracite Coal Strike of 1902*.

"1902 Miners' Strike Symbolizes Northeast Penn. Heritage." *American Heritage*, Oct. 2002.

Riis, Jacob. *How the Other Half Lives*. New York: Charles Scribner's Sons, 1890.

Rixey. *Bamie*.

Roosevelt, Eleanor. *Autobiography*.

Research Collections

FDR Library
    Sara Delano Roosevelt Papers
    Eleanor Roosevelt Papers
    Franklin Delano Roosevelt Papers
Vassar College Library

Interviews

Eleanor Roosevelt II (Hall Roosevelt's daughter), Sacramento, California

Kenneth C. Wolensky, historian, Pennsylvania Historical and Museum Commission
Nina Roosevelt Gibson

CHAPTER 17: "FOR LIFE, FOR DEATH!"

Auchincloss, Louis. *A Woman in Her Time*. New York: Viking Press, 1971.

Browning, Elizabeth Barrett. "A Woman's Shortcomings," from Burton Egbert Stevenson, ed., *The Home Book of Verse*. New York: Henry Holt and Co., 1953.

Harlan, Louis R. *Booker T. Washington, The Making of a Black Leader, 1856–1901*. London: Oxford University Press, 1972.

Lash. *Eleanor and Franklin*.

Meier, Arthur. *Negro Thought in America, 1880–1915*. Ann Arbor: University of Michigan Press, 1963.

Patridge. *Imperial Saga*.

Roosevelt, Eleanor. *You Learn by Living*. New York: Harper & Brothers, 1960.

Schroeder, Alan. *Booker T. Washington: Educator and Racial Spokesman*. Philadelphia: Chelsea House Publishers, 1992.

Washington, Booker T. *Up from Slavery*. New York: Doubleday, Page & Co., 1901.

Youngs, J. William T. *Eleanor Roosevelt: A Personal and Public Life*. New York: HarperCollins, 1985.

Research Collections

FDR Library
>   Sara Delano Roosevelt Papers
>   Eleanor Roosevelt Papers
>   Franklin Delano Roosevelt Papers
>   Oral history: Roland Redmond

Interviews

Curtis Roosevelt
Eleanor Roosevelt Seagraves
Nina Roosevelt Gibson

CHAPTER 18: "KEEPING THE NAME IN THE FAMILY"

Ashburn. *Peabody of Groton*.

Brough. *Princess Alice*.

Donn. *Roosevelt Cousins*.

Felsenthal, Carol. *Alice Roosevelt Longworth*. New York: G. P. Putnam's Sons, 1988.

Gunther. *Roosevelt in Retrospect*.

Longworth, Alice Roosevelt. *Crowded Hours*. New York: Charles Scribner's Sons, 1933.

Rixey. *Bamie*.

Roosevelt, Eleanor. "I Tell My Life Story in Pictures." *Look*, Sept. 16, 1947.

Roosevelt, James, and Sidney Shalett. *Affectionately, F.D.R.: A Son's Story of a Lonely Man*. New York: Harcourt, Brace and Co., 1959.

Teague, Michael. *Conversations with Alice Roosevelt Longworth*. Garden City, N.Y.: Doubleday & Co., 1981.

Teichmann. *Alice*.

"The President Is Royally Greeted in New York City." *Poughkeepsie Daily Eagle*, Mar. 18, 1905.

Research Collections

FDR Library

Sara Delano Roosevelt Papers

Eleanor Roosevelt Papers

Harvard Law School Library

Special Collections, Class of 1907

Eleanor Roosevelt Papers, George Washington University

Museum of the City of New York

Library of Congress

Theodore Roosevelt Papers, Manuscript Division

CHAPTER 19: ROOSEVELT AND ROOSEVELT

Encyclopedia Judaica. New York: Macmillan, 1972.

Miller, Nathan. *F.D.R.: An Intimate History.* New York: New American Library, 1983.

Riis. *How the Other Half Lives.*

Rixey. *Bamie.*

Roosevelt, Eleanor. *Autobiography.*

———. *You Learn by Living.*

Roosevelt, Elliott, ed. *F.D.R.: His Personal Letters, 1905–1928.* New York: Duell, Sloan and Pearce, 1948.

Roosevelt, Elliott, and James Brough. *An Untold Story: The Roosevelts of Hyde Park.* New York: G. P. Putnam's Sons, 1973.

Schlesinger, Arthur Jr. *The Age of Roosevelt.* Boston: Houghton Mifflin, 1957.

Research Collections

FDR Library

FDR Childhood Collection

Sara Delano Roosevelt Papers

Rita Halle Kleeman Collection

Interviews

Christopher Richard, "Mr. History Person," Fairhaven, Massachusetts

Preston W. Gifford Jr., Volunteer Park Service Interpreter, Poughkeepsie, New York

Nina Roosevelt Gibson

CHAPTER 20: "DEAREST MAMA"

Cook. *Eleanor Roosevelt,* vol. 1.

Lash, Joseph P. *Eleanor and Franklin.*

———. *Love, Eleanor: Eleanor Roosevelt and Her Friends.* New York: McGraw-Hill, 1982.

Ward. *Before the Trumpet.*

Research Collections

FDR Library

Sara Delano Roosevelt Papers

Anna Roosevelt Papers

Franklin Delano Roosevelt Papers

Interviews
    Curtis Roosevelt
    Eleanor Roosevelt Seagraves
    Nina Roosevelt Gibson

CHAPTER 21: "MODERN IDEAS"

Encyclopedia Judaica.

Gunther. *Roosevelt in Retrospect.*

Harlan, Louis R., and Raymond W. Smock. *The Booker T. Washington Papers, 1903–1904*, vol. 7. Urbana: University of Illinois Press, 1972.

Hulbert, Ann. *Raising America: Experts, Parents and a Century of Advice about Children.* New York: Alfred A. Knopf, 2003.

Rixey. *Bamie.*

Roosevelt, Eleanor. "Insuring Democracy." *Collier's,* June 15, 1940.

Ward. *Before the Trumpet.*

Research Collections

FDR Library
    Sara Delano Roosevelt Papers
    Eleanor Roosevelt Papers
    Franklin Delano Roosevelt Papers
    Roosevelt Children Papers
Library of Congress
    Theodore Roosevelt Papers, Manuscript Division
Harvard University School of Law Archives
    Chronological List: Harvard Graduates, 1907

Interviews
    Nina Roosevelt Gibson

CHAPTER 22: "THE CHICKS"

Black. *Eleanor Roosevelt.*

Blair. *The Clubwoman as Feminist.*

Charles Adams Platt: 1861–1933. New York: Hunter College of the City University of New York, n.d.

Churchill, Allen. *The Roosevelts: American Aristocrats.* New York: Harper & Row, 1965.

Cook. *Eleanor Roosevelt,* vol. 1.

Cott, Nancy F. *The Grounding of Modern Feminism.* New Haven, Conn.: Yale University Press, 1987.

Davis. *F.D.R.*

Gray, Christopher. "For Eleanor and Franklin, a Built-In Mother-in-Law." *New York Times,* June 6, 1997.

———. "Streetcapes." *New York Times,* June 8, 1997.

———. "The Roosevelt Townhouse 47–49 East 65th Street," in Kips Bay Boys and Girls Club Decorator Show program, April–May 1994.

Homberger. *Mrs. Astor's New York.*

Hunter College. Office of Institutional Advancement. *Roosevelt House and Hunter College Time Line*. New York: Hunter College, 2001.

Hunter College. Office of the President. *Historic Roosevelt House to Become Conference Center for Hunter College: Curtis Roosevelt Joins with Hunter Foundation to Initiate $6 Million Campaign.* New York: Hunter College, 2001.

Miller. *FDR: An Intimate History.*

"Mr. Martin's Analysis of New York Society: Chaos, He Declares, Followed the Retirement of Mrs. Astor." *New York Times*, May 3, 1908.

National Park Service, U.S. Department of the Interior. *Grounds.*

"Preview Held of Ex-Roosevelt House at Hunter." *New York Herald Tribune*, Nov. 18, 1943.

"Preview Listing No. 51218: Franklin D. Roosevelt's Summer Home on Campobello Island, New Brunswick, Canada." Circa mid-1950s.

Roosevelt, Curtis. *The Proposed Renovation of the Sara Delano Roosevelt Memorial House.* Hunter College of the City University of New York: n.d.

Roosevelt, Eleanor. *This Is My Story*. New York: Harper & Bros., 1937.

Roosevelt, Elliott. *An Untold Story.*

Roosevelt, James. *Affectionately, F.D.R.*

Roosevelt, Sara. *My Boy Franklin.*

Rose, Beaton and Rose. "Study for the Rehabilitation of Roosevelt House, Hunter College, New York." New York: Rose, Beaton & Rose Architects & Engineers, n.d.

Stone, May N. "From Presidential Home to Campus Center and Now, a City Landmark." *News Hunter*, Dec. 1973.

Town Topics. Dec. 8, 1887.

Research Collections
FDR Library
    Sara Delano Roosevelt Papers
    Eleanor Roosevelt Papers
    Roosevelt Children Papers
    Anna Roosevelt Papers
    Hunter College Library
        Archives and Special Collection

Interviews
Deborah Gardner, Hunter College
Danielle Cylich, Hunter College
Curtis Roosevelt
Nina Roosevelt Gibson

Chapter 23: "A Really Fine and Dignified Position"
"Achievements in Public Health, 1900–1999: Family Planning." *Morbidity and Mortality Weekly Report*, Oct. 15, 1999.

American Child Health Association. "Scope and Content." *Papers*, 2002.

Lash. *Love, Eleanor.*

Myers, Gustavus. *The History of Tammany Hall*. New York: n.p., 1901, 2nd ed., New York: Boni & Liveright, 1917.

Rixey. *Bamie.*

Roosevelt, Elliott. *F.D.R.: His Personal Letters, 1905–1928.*

Tauxe, Robert V. "Food Safety and Irradiation: Protecting the Public from Foodborne Infections." Atlanta: Emerging Infectious Diseases Conference, 2002.

Research Collections

FDR Library

    Sara Delano Roosevelt Papers

    Eleanor Roosevelt Papers

    PPF 8

    Oral history: James Roosevelt

    Oral history: Elliott Roosevelt

Library of Congress

    Theodore Roosevelt Collection, Manuscript Division

Adriance Memorial Library, Poughkeepsie, New York

    John M. Hackett Papers

    Delano Papers

    Roosevelt Papers

    Helen W. Reynolds Correspondence

Interviews

Eleanor Roosevelt Seagraves

CHAPTER 24: "LAUNCHED IN YOUR WORK"

Adams, Henry. *The Education of Henry Adams.* Boston: Houghton Mifflin Co., 1918.

Anderson, Isabel. *Presidents and Pies: Life in Washington 1887–1919.* Boston: n.p., 1920.

Brock, H. I. "Five Decades in the Life of Roosevelt." *New York Times,* Jan. 27, 1935.

Brough. *Princess Alice.*

Churchill. *The Roosevelts.*

Delano. *Algonac.*

Felsenthal. *Alice Roosevelt Longworth.*

Freidel, Frank. *Franklin D. Roosevelt: The Apprenticeship.* Boston: Little, Brown and Co., 1952.

Morgan, Ted. *F.D.R.: A Biography.* New York: Simon & Schuster, 1985.

Myers. *History of Tammany Hall.*

Riordan, William. *Plunkett of Tammany Hall.* New York: E. P. Dutton, 1963.

Rixey. *Bamie.*

Roosevelt, Elliott. *F.D.R.: His Personal Letters, 1905–1928.*

"16th Amendment to the U.S. Constitution: Federal Income Tax, 1913." Transcript, Joint Resolution, Sixty-first U.S. Congress, Mar. 15, 1909.

Slayden, Ellen Maury. *Washington Wife: Journal of Ellen Maury Slayden, 1897–1919.* New York: Harper & Row, 1963.

Research Collections

FDR Library

    Sara Delano Roosevelt Papers

Eleanor Roosevelt Papers

Franklin Delano Roosevelt Papers

Roosevelt Children Papers

Oral history: Elliott Roosevelt

Oral history: James Roosevel

Martin Luther King Jr. Memorial Library, Washington, D.C.

Clippings and Photographs, Sara Delano Roosevelt, Washingtoniana Division

Interviews

Preston W. Gifford Jr.

Nina Roosevelt Gibson

Curtis Roosevelt

CHAPTER 25: "THE TRADITIONS SOME OF US LOVE BEST"

Delano. *Algonac*.

Geckle. *Hacketts and the Roosevelts*.

Historical Society of Washington Collections: "The Family." *Washington History*, Spring/Summer, 2001.

Kleeman. *Gracious Lady*.

Lash. *Eleanor and Franklin*.

Miller. *F.D.R.*

National Park Service, U.S. Department of the Interior. *Franklin D. Roosevelt and Hyde Park*. Hyde Park, New York.

———. *Grounds*.

Partridge. *Imperial Saga*.

Roosevelt, Eleanor. *The Wisdom of Eleanor Roosevelt*. New York: McCall Publication, 1963.

Roosevelt, Elliott. *F.D.R.: His Personal Letters, 1905–1928*.

———. *An Untold Story*.

"Save Roosevelt House." *New York Times*, Sept. 28, 1915.

Schlesinger, Arthur Jr. *The Crisis of the Old Order*. Boston: Houghton Mifflin Co., 1957.

Youngs. *Eleanor Roosevelt*.

Research Collections

FDR Library

    FDR Dispatches, Navy Department

    Eleanor Roosevelt Papers

    Sara Delano Roosevelt Papers

    Rita Halle Kleeman Papers

    Oral history: James Roosevelt

    Oral history: Elliott Roosevelt

National Park Service, Hyde Park

    Oral history: Norman Reid

Library of Congress

    Theodore Roosevelt Collection, Manuscript Division

Columbia University, Butler Library

Oral history: Marion Dickerman
Podesta Collection, Manuscripts

CHAPTER 26: "A KALEIDOSCOPE OF WORK"

Anderson. *Presidents and Pies.*
Auchincloss, Louis. *Edith Wharton: A Woman in Her Time.* New York: Viking Press, 1971.
Clarke, Ida Clyde. *American Women and the World War.* New York: D. Appleton and Co., 1918.
Papenfuse, Edward C., et al. *Archives of Maryland, Historical list. New series, vol. 1.* Annapolis, Md.:
    Maryland State Archives, 1990.
Randall, James Ryder. "Maryland, My Maryland." *Archives of Maryland, Historical List. New Series,*
    vol. 1, Annapolis, Md., Maryland State Archives, 1990.
Roosevelt, Elliott. *F.D.R.: His Personal Letters, 1905–1928.*
Scharf, Lois. *Eleanor Roosevelt: First Lady of American Liberalism.* Boston: Twayne, 1987.
Slayden. *Washington Wife.*

Research Collections
FDR Library
    Sara Delano Roosevelt Papers
    Eleanor Roosevelt Papers
    Roosevelt Children Papers
    Oral history: James Roosevelt
    Oral history: Elliott Roosevelt

CHAPTER 27: MISS MERCER

Browning. "A Woman's Shortcomings."
Daniels, Jonathan. *The Washington Quadrille: The Dance Beside the Documents.* New York: Double-
    day and Co., 1978.
Lash. *Love, Eleanor.*
Roosevelt, Eleanor. "Divorce." *Ladies' Home Journal,* Apr. 1938.
Roosevelt, Elliott. *F.D.R.: His Personal Letters, 1905–1928.*
Teichmann. *Alice.*
Ward. *Before the Trumpet.*

Research Collections
FDR Library
    Sara Delano Roosevelt Papers
    Eleanor Roosevelt Papers
    James Roosevelt Papers
    Oral history: James Roosevelt
    Oral history: Elliott Roosevelt

Interviews
Eleanor Roosevelt Seagraves
Curtis Roosevelt
Nina Roosevelt Gibson

Chapter 28: "Our Boy"

Cook. *Eleanor Roosevelt*, vol. 1.

Davis, Kenneth. *F.D.R.: The New York Years, 1928–1933*. New York: Random House, 1985.

Freidel, Frank. *Franklin D. Roosevelt: A Rendezvous with Destiny*. Boston: Little, Brown and Co., 1990.

Gallagher, Hugh. *F.D.R.'s Splendid Deception*. New York: Dodd, Mead and Co., 1985.

Hickok, Lorena. *The Road to the White House*. Philadelphia: Chilton Books, 1962.

Lash. *Franklin and Eleanor*.

Martin, Kati. *Hidden Power: Presidential Marriages That Shaped Our Recent History*. New York: Pantheon Books, 2001.

Miller. *F.D.R.*

Morgan. *F.D.R.*

Roosevelt, Elliott. *F.D.R.: His Personal Letters, 1905–1928*.

Schlesinger, Arthur Jr. *The Age of Roosevelt*. Boston: Houghton Mifflin, 1957.

Ward. *Before the Trumpet*.

Research Collections
FDR Library
    Sara Delano Roosevelt Papers
    Eleanor Roosevelt Papers
    Franklin Delano Roosevelt Papers
    James Roosevelt Papers
    Oral history: James Roosevelt
    Oral history: Elliott Roosevelt

Chapter 29: "Rainy Day"

Democratic National Committee. James M. Cox/Franklin D. Roosevelt contribution certificate #32202, Oct. 28, 1920.

Geckle. *Hacketts and the Roosevelts*.

Literary Digest, July 31, 1920.

"19th Amendment to the U.S. Constitution." Transcript, Joint Resolution, Sixty-sixth U.S. Congress, June 4, 1919.

Partridge. *Imperial Saga*.

Roosevelt, Elliott. *F.D.R.: His Personal Letters, 1905–1928*.

Roosevelt, Hall. *Odyssey of an American Family: An Account of the Roosevelts*. New York: Harper & Brothers, 1939.

Research Collections
FDR Library
    Sara Delano Roosevelt Papers
    Eleanor Roosevelt Papers
    Franklin Delano Roosevelt Papers
    James Roosevelt Papers
    Roosevelt Children Papers

CHAPTER 30: "SOLIDLY IMPORTANT INDIVIDUAL"
Hershan, Stella K. *A Woman of Quality*. New York: Crown Publishers, 1970.
Hulbert. *Raising America*.
"Mrs. Roosevelt Goes on Tour of Former Home, Now a Center." *New York Herald Tribune*, Nov.
    13, 1942.
Roosevelt, Eleanor. *Wisdom of Eleanor Roosevelt*.
Roosevelt, Elliott. *F.D.R.: His Personal Letters, 1905–1928*.

Research Collections
FDR Library
    James Roosevelt Papers
    Marion Dickerman Papers
Columbia University, Butler Library
    Jacob J. Podell Collection of Franklin Delano Roosevelt Letters and Manuscripts

Interviews
Nina Roosevelt Gibson

CHAPTER 31: "I GOT UP THIS PARTY FOR YOU"
Gallagher. *Splendid Deception*.
Goldberg, Richard Thayer. *The Making of Franklin D. Roosevelt: Triumph Over Disability*. Cam-
    bridge, Mass.: Abt Books, 1981.
Klein. *Beloved Island*.
Roosevelt, Elliott. *F.D.R.: His Personal Letters, 1905–1928*.

Research Collections
FDR Library
    Sara Delano Roosevelt Papers
    Eleanor Roosevelt Papers
    Franklin Delano Roosevelt Papers
    James Roosevelt Papers
    Oral history: James Roosevelt
    Oral history: Elliott Roosevelt

CHAPTER 32: GRIT AND GRACE
Black, Allida M. *Courage in a Dangerous World: The Political Writings of Eleanor Roosevelt*. New York:
    Columbia University Press, 1999.
Booknotes. Doris Kearns Goodwin, C-SPAN, January 1, 1995.
Roosevelt, Eleanor. *Wisdom of Eleanor Roosevelt*.
Roosevelt, Elliott. *Eleanor Roosevelt, with Love*. New York: E. P. Dutton, 1984.
——. *F.D.R., His Personal Letters, 1928–1945*. New York: Duell, Sloan and Pearce, 1950.
Ward, Geoffrey C. "The House at Hyde Park." *American Heritage*, Apr. 1987.

Research Collections
FDR Library
    Sara Delano Roosevelt Papers
    Eleanor Roosevelt Papers
    Anna Roosevelt Collection
    James Roosevelt Papers
Columbia University, Butler Library
    Podesta Collection, Manuscripts

Interviews
Nina Roosevelt Gibson

CHAPTER 33: "ELEANOR'S WORK AMONG THE WOMEN"

Bethune, Mary McLeod. "My Secret Talks with F.D.R." *Ebony*, Nov. 1949.
Halasa, Malu. *Mary McLeod Bethune*. Philadelphia: Chelsea House Publishers, 1998.
Holt, Rackham. *Mary McLeod Bethune: A Biography*. New York: Doubleday & Co., 1964.
Peare, Catherine Owens. *Mary McLeod Bethune*. New York: Vanguard Press, 1951.
Roosevelt, Elliott. *F.D.R.: His Personal Letters, 1928–1945*.
Roosevelt, James, and Sidney Shalett. *Affectionately, FDR*.

Research Collections
FDR Library
    Sara Delano Roosevelt Papers
    Eleanor Roosevelt Papers
    Oral History: Marion Dickerman
National Archives for Black Women's History, Bethune Council House, Washington, D.C.
    Mary McLeod Bethune Papers

CHAPTER 34: SPLINTERED

Beasley, Maureen H. *Eleanor Roosevelt and the Media: A Public Quest for Self-Fulfillment*. Urbana: University of Illinois Press, 1987.
Black, Allida M. *Casting Her Own Shadow: Eleanor Roosevelt and the Shaping of Postwar Liberties*. New York: Columbia University Press, 1996.
Churchill. *The Roosevelts*.
Donn. *Roosevelt Cousins*.
Roosevelt, Elliott. *F.D.R.: His Personal Letters, 1928–1945*.
———. *Rendezvous with Destiny*.
Roosevelt, Elliott, and James Brough. *Mother R: Eleanor Roosevelt's Untold Story*. New York: G. P. Putnam's Sons, 1977.
Ward, Geoffrey C. *First-Class Temperament: The Emergence of Franklin Roosevelt*. New York: Harper & Row, 1989.

Research Collections
FDR Library
    Sara Delano Roosevelt Papers

Eleanor Roosevelt Papers
Roosevelt Children Papers
Oral history: Marion Dickerman
Oral history: Florence Kerr

Interviews
Eleanor Roosevelt Seagraves

CHAPTER 35: "IF HE DOES, I HOPE HE WINS"

Brough. *Princess Alice.*
Cook. *Eleanor Roosevelt,* vol. 1.
Dows. *Franklin Roosevelt at Hyde Park.*
Felsenthal. *Alice Roosevelt Longworth.*
Flynn, John T. *Country Squire in the White House.* New York: Doubleday Doran, 1955.
Freidel. *Franklin D. Roosevelt: A Rendezvous with Destiny.*
Gallagher. *Splendid Deception.*
Greene, Marian Schomer. "Lonely (First) Lady." *American Heritage,* Oct. 2000.
Lash. *Love, Eleanor.*
"Mrs. Franklin D. Roosevelt Answers a Big Question." *Good Housekeeping,* Aug. 1930.
Perkins, Frances. *The Roosevelt I Knew.* New York: Viking, 1946.
"Roosevelt Decides on Harvey Charges." *New York Times,* May 4, 1931.
Roosevelt, Elliott. *F.D.R.: His Personal Letters, 1928–1945.*
"Roosevelt Makes Plans to Sail on Wednesday, But Has Not Yet Decided on Trip to Mother."
     New York Times, May 31, 1931.
"Roosevelt's Mother Is Stricken in Paris; He Delays Departure on Vacation Trip." *New York
     Times,* May 1, 1931.
"Roosevelt Weighs Trip to See Mother." *New York Times,* May 2, 1931.
"Roosevelt Will Go to Mother in Paris." *New York Times,* May 5, 1931.
Teichmann. *Alice.*
Wisehart, M. K. "What Is a Wife's Job Today?" *Good Housekeeping,* Aug. 1930.

Research Collections
FDR Library
     Sara Delano Roosevelt Papers
     Eleanor Roosevelt Papers
     Roosevelt Children Papers
     Rita Halle Kleeman Papers
Columbia University, Butler Library
     Oral history: Frances Perkins
     Oral history: Marion Dickerman
     Oral history: Eddie Dowling

CHAPTER 36: HAPPY DAYS

Alsop, Joseph. *FDR: A Centenary Remembrance.* New York: Viking, 1982.
"Brief Reviews: My Boy Franklin." *New York Times Book Review,* Feb. 26, 1933.

Brinkley, Alan. *Voices of Protest: Huey Long, Father Coughlin and the Great Depression.* New York: Vintage Books, 1982.

Caroli, Betty Boyd. *The Roosevelt Women.* New York: Basic Books, 1998.

Cook. *Eleanor Roosevelt,* vol. 1.

Coup, Jeannine. "Honoring Mothers." *The Political Bandwagon.* May 2002.

Felsenthal. *Alice.*

Fried, Albert. *FDR and His Enemies.* New York: St. Martin's Press, 1999.

Freidel, Frank. *FDR: Launching the New Deal.* Boston: Little, Brown and Co., 1973.

"Governor Roosevelt Off on Aquitania Today." *New York Times,* May 6, 1931.

"Governor's Wife Rides with Red Devil Pilot," *Lake Placid* (New York) *News,* Feb. 12, 1932.

Hair, William Ivy. *The Kingfish and His Realm.* Baton Rouge, La.: Louisiana State University Press, 1991.

Halle, Rita S. "That First Lady of Ours." *Good Housekeeping,* Dec. 1933.

"Honors Mother of the President." *New York Times,* May 4, 1933.

Ilsley, Henry R. "Killearn Magician Horse Show Victor." *New York Times,* Sept. 1, 1933.

Kurtz, Michael L., and Morgan D. Peoples. *Earl K. Long: The Saga of Uncle Earl and Louisiana Politics.* Baton Rouge, La.: Louisiana State University Press, 1990.

Lash. *Franklin and Eleanor.*

Leighton, Isabel. "Eleanor Roosevelt—A Recent Portrait." *Ladies' Home Journal,* Mar. 1933.

LeVert, Suzanne. *Huey Long: The Kingfish of Louisiana.* New York: Facts on File, 1995.

Miller. *FDR.*

"Mother Always Could Find Time to Laugh; Shaft at a Dinner Silenced Even Huey Long." *New York Times,* Sept. 8, 1941.

"Mother and Aunt Sign President's Agreement." *New York Times,* Aug. 16, 1933.

"Mother Describes Roosevelt as Boy." *New York Times,* Feb. 25, 1933.

"Mother Welcomes Roosevelt Home." *New York Times,* July 30, 1933.

"Mrs. J. Roosevelt Aids Nurse Drive." *New York Times,* Nov. 3, 1933.

"Mrs. Roosevelt Sr. at Sale." *New York Times,* Nov. 30, 1932.

"My Boy Franklin." *Time,* Mar. 6, 1933.

"Not Very Much Surprised." *New York Times,* July 8, 1932.

"Nursing Service Is Facing a Crisis." *New York Times,* Nov. 27, 1933.

"President Motors to Leesburg, VA." *New York Times,* Oct. 13, 1933.

"President's Mother Goes to White House." *New York Times,* Mar. 18, 1933.

"President's Mother Heard." *New York Times,* May 15, 1933.

"President's Mother, 79, to Tour Virginia in Auto." *New York Times,* Oct. 10, 1933.

"President's Mother to Be Honored." *New York Times,* Aug. 12, 1933.

Roosevelt, Elliott. *F.D.R.: His Personal Letters, 1928–1945.*

Roosevelt, Sara. *My Boy Franklin.*

"Roosevelt in Paris to See Ill Mother." *New York Times,* May 14, 1931.

"Roosevelt in Radio Talk." *New York Times,* May 16, 1931.

"Roosevelt On Way Home." *New York Times,* May 23, 1931.

"Roosevelt Reflects Greatness." *New York American,* Sept. 11, 1932.

"Roosevelt to Return from Paris Next Week." *New York Times,* May 19, 1931.

"Roosevelt Visits French Exposition." *New York Times,* May 15, 1931.

"Roosevelts Mark 28th Anniversary." *New York Times,* Mar. 18, 1933.

"Roosevelt's Mother at New York Rally." *New York Times*, Nov. 7, 1932.

"Roosevelt's Mother Returns from France." *New York Times*, June 10, 1931.

"Sara Delano Roosevelt, Only Member of Family," *New York Times*, Oct. 4, 1933.

Teichmann. *Alice*.

The Golden Rule Foundation. "The Golden Rule Mother's Day Program." May 14, 1933.

"The President and His Family Leaving the White House for Church." *New York Times*, Mar. 6, 1933.

"The President's Mother: 'I Am the Child of My Son.'" *News-Week*, July 10, 1933.

CHAPTER 37: FIRST MOTHER

Roosevelt, Elliott. *An Untold Story*.

Geckle. *Hacketts and the Roosevelts*.

Graff, Robert, et al. *F.D.R.* New York: Harper & Row, 1963.

"Mrs. Roosevelt Was Victorian." *New York Times*, Sept. 9, 1941.

Perkins. *The Roosevelt I Knew*.

"President Is Overruled by Mother on Krum Elbow." *New York Times*, Aug. 3, 1933.

Roosevelt, Elliott. *F.D.R.: His Personal Letters, 1928–1945*.

West, J. B. *Upstairs at the White House*. New York: Warner Books, 1973.

Research Collections

FDR Library
    Sara Delano Roosevelt Papers
    Eleanor Roosevelt Papers
    Roosevelt Children Papers
    PPF 8
Columbia University, Butler Library
    Oral history: Marion Dickerman
    Oral history: Frances Perkins

CHAPTER 38: "THE DUCHESS"

"Acts to Name Street for President's Mother." *New York Times*, Mar. 9, 1934.

"Aldermen Name Park for Roosevelt's Mother." *New York Times*, Mar. 14, 1934.

Angelo. *First Mothers*.

"Asks Aid for Cancer Hospital." *New York Times*, Sept. 13, 1934.

"Backs Anti-Litter Drive." *New York Times*, Mar. 8, 1934.

Bottome, Phyllis. *From the Life*. London: Faber and Faber, 1949.

"British May Cut Navy Demands." *New York Times*, June 26, 1934.

Cook. *Eleanor Roosevelt*, vol. 2.

Culbertson, Mary Haeseler. "Our Hospitable and Home-loving First Family and Favorite White House Recipes." *Better Homes and Gardens*, May 1934.

"Democrats Honor Mrs. J. Roosevelt." *New York Times*, Feb. 18, 1934.

"80th Birthday Starts Early for Mrs. Roosevelt." *New York Daily News*, Sept. 24, 1934.

"F.D.R.'s Mother Hears Battle in Her Name." *New York Daily News*, Mar. 9. 1934.

Ferguson, Edna. "Mother of F.D.R. A Movie Censor: Surprise to Her." *New York Daily News*, Mar. 13, 1934.

"Film Drive Opened by Mrs. Belmont." *New York Times*, Mar. 22, 1934.

"5 Widows of Presidents Honor U.S. 'First Mother,'" *New York Daily News*, May 14, 1934.

"Fund Drive Opened for Historic Church." *New York Times*, Dec. 5, 1934.

Geckle. *Hacketts and the Roosevelts*.

Goodwin, Doris Kearns. *No Ordinary Time: The Home Front in World War II*. New York: Simon & Schuster, 1994.

Homberger. *Historical Atlas of New York City*.

"Honor to Mothers to Be Paid Today." *New York Times*, May 13, 1934.

Marks, Frederick W. III. *Wind over Sand*. Athens, Ga.: University of Georgia Press, 1988.

"Mayor Urges Gifts to Nursing Services." *New York Times*, Oct. 10, 1934.

Morgan. *F.D.R.*

"Mother Buys Suit for the President." *New York Times*, Aug. 17, 1934.

"Mother Roosevelt Home with Suiting for Franklin." *New York Daily News*, Aug. 17, 1934.

"Mothers Honored by Homage of City." *New York Times*, May 14, 1934.

"Mothers Laud Nurses." *New York Times*, July 18, 1934.

"Mrs. James Roosevelt Calms Ruffled Babydom." *New York Daily News*, Mar. 13, 1934.

"Mrs. J. Roosevelt Delights French." *New York Times*, August 10, 1934.

"Mrs. J. Roosevelt Feted." *New York Times*, July 14, 1934.

"Mrs. J. Roosevelt Feted." *New York Times*, July 20, 1934.

"Mrs. J. Roosevelt Will Be 80 Today." *New York Times*, Sept. 21, 1934.

"Mrs. Roosevelt and Queen Chat at Scottish Fete." *New York Times*, July 11, 1934.

"Mrs. Roosevelt in Paris." *New York Times*, July 19, 1934.

"Mrs. Roosevelt on Radio." *New York Times*, July 27, 1934.

"Mrs. Roosevelt's Trip." *New York Times*, July 10, 1934.

"Navy Ball Group Meets at Luncheon." *New York Times*, May 11, 1934.

"Notables on List for O'Day Dinner." *New York Times*, Oct. 24, 1934.

"Opening Day Ceremonies." *New York Times*, Sept. 11, 1934.

Orrick, Phyllis. "Lost Acres: The Forgotten Park of the Lower East Side." *New York Press*, May 27–June 2, 1992.

"Our Merchant Mariner." *New York Times*, June 22, 1934.

"Park Name Unsettled." *New York Times*, Mar. 13, 1934.

Parks, Lillian Rogers. *The Roosevelts: A Family in Turmoil*. Englewood Cliffs, N.J.: Prentice-Hall, 1981.

"Play Area Finally Finished." *New York Times*, July 28, 1934.

"President Painted Without His Smile." *New York Times*, Apr. 10, 1934.

"President's Mother Attends Church Fete." *New York Times*, Nov. 12, 1934.

"President's Mother Departs for Europe." *New York Times*, June 19, 1934.

"President's Mother Honored." *New York Times*, July 25, 1934.

"President's Mother Inspects a Famous Painting." *New York Times*, May 16, 1934.

"President's Mother Lands in England." *New York Times*, July 4, 1934.

"President's Mother Lives 'American Life,' Finding Stay Abroad a 'Round of Visits.'" *New York Times*, July 16, 1934.

"President's Mother Opens Benefit Sale." *New York Times*, Nov. 27, 1934.

"President's Mother Quits France for U.S." *New York Times*, Aug. 11, 1934.

"President's Mother Spends Hours at Palace in a Chat with the British King and Queen." *New York Times*, June 27, 1934.

"President's Mother Urges Better Films." *New York Times*, Mar. 19, 1934.

"Roosevelt and Mother Speak, Cross Seas Today." *New York Times*, July 26, 1934.

Roosevelt, Elliott. *F.D.R.: His Personal Letters, 1928–1945*.

———. *An Untold Story*.

———. *Rendezvous with Destiny*.

"Roosevelt Justice Lauded by Mother." *New York Times*, Feb. 10, 1934.

"Roosevelt's Mother Arrives in England." *New York Times*, June 25, 1934.

"Roosevelt's Mother, 80 Today, Gets Flowers from Admirer." *New York American*, Sept. 21, 1934.

"Roosevelt's Mother Gossips with Queen over Cup of Tea." *New York Evening News*, June 26, 1934.

"Roosevelts: Happy Birthday for the President's Mother." *News-Week*, Sept. 29, 1934.

"Roosevelts: President Hopes Home State Bill Will Pass." *News-Week*, Mar. 24, 1934.

"Roosevelt Toasts His Mother at Party on Her 80th Birthday." *New York Times*, Sept. 22, 1934.

"Sketch 2247, Sara Delano Roosevelt, in the Event of Her Death." AP Newswire, May 1, 1934. (Files of *Washington Star*.)

"Sky Isn't Falling. Earth Is Sinking, and Residents Are Worried." *New York Times*, Sept. 2, 2001.

"Society: F.D.'s Mother in Cap, Gown to Get Degree." *New York Daily News*, June 8, 1934.

"Society: F.D.'s Mother Keeps Pace with Tireless Roosevelts." *New York Daily News*, Jan. 27, 1934.

"Society: Mother of President, 80, Feted by Roosevelt Clan." *New York Daily News*, Sept. 12, 1934.

"Society: President's Mother Attends Baby Musical." *New York Daily News*, Dec. 4, 1934.

"Souvenirs Needn't Be Useful." *New York Times*, Aug. 18, 1934.

"Speeches Delivered at Opening of Roosevelt Park." *New York Times*, Sept. 14, 1934.

"The President Goes to Church." *New York Times*, Nov. 5, 1934.

"Trees Dedicated by Mrs. Roosevelt." *New York Times*, Apr. 22, 1934.

"U.S. 'Shocked' by John Bull's Big Navy Talk." *New York Daily News*, June 20, 1934.

"Visits Roosevelt's Nurse." *New York Times*, Feb. 13, 1934.

"Visits Speech Hospital." *New York Times*, May 19, 1934.

"Will Get Moravian Degree." *New York Times*, May 24, 1934.

"Will Visit the Astors." *New York Times*, June 30, 1934.

Woolf, S. J. "His Mother Tells About the Press." *New York Times Magazine*, Feb. 18, 1934.

"World's Most Wonderful Woman." *Southampton* (England) *News Chronicle*, June 25, 1934.

Research Collections

FDR Library

    Sara Delano Roosevelt Papers

    SDR Trips to White House

    Eleanor Roosevelt Papers

    Roosevelt Children Papers

    Anna Roosevelt Papers

    PPF 8

    Rita Halle Kleeman Papers

    Lizzie McDuffie unpublished manuscript

Adriance Library, Poughkeepsie, New York.

    Helen W. Reynolds Correspondence, 1932–1940

Stanford University Libraries

    Sara Delano Roosevelt Papers, Special Collections

Columbia University, Butler Library
     Jacob J. Podell Collection, Manuscript Division
     Oral history: Marion Dickerman
     Oral history: Jacob Viner
New York City Department of Parks and Recreation Archives
     "Memorandum, Sara D. Roosevelt File," Sept. 3, 1996
     "Press Release," New York City Parks Department, Feb. 28, 1934
New York City Department of Parks and Recreation Photo Archives
     Sara Delano Roosevelt Park
Library of Congress
     White House Scrapbooks of ER's Social Secretary, Edith Helm, Manuscript Division
Martin Luther King Jr. Memorial Library, Washington, D.C.
Clippings and Photographs, Sara Delano Roosevelt, Washingtoniana Division

CHAPTER 39: GRACIOUS LADY, MODERN WOMAN

"Again Aids Blind Sale." *New York Times*, Dec. 18, 1935.

"Aides for Birthday Ball." *New York Times*, Jan. 18, 1935.

"Biography." *New York Herald* (Paris), Aug. 8, 1935.

"Biography: The Life Story of U.S.'s Gracious 'Queen Mother.'" *News-Week*, Sept. 29, 1935.

Black. *Casting Her Own Shadow*.

"Brilliant Throng at Opera's Opening." *New York Times*, Dec. 17, 1935.

Burns, James MacGregor, and Susan Dunn. *The Three Roosevelts: Patrician Leaders Who Transformed America*. New York: Atlantic Monthly Press, 2001.

"Celebration." *New York Times*, Feb. 3, 1935.

"Child Gardeners Receive Awards." *New York Times*, Sept. 28, 1935.

"Child Held Aided by Responsibility." *New York Times*, Feb. 10, 1935.

"Concert Attended by More than 3,000." *New York Times*, Aug. 11, 1935.

Cook. *Eleanor Roosevelt*, vol. 2.

"Cripples Greet Mrs. Roosevelt." *New York Times*, Mar. 28, 1935.

Dray, Philip. *At the Hands of Persons Unknown: The Lynching of Black America*. New York: Random House, 2002.

"European Dahlias Win Show Honors." *New York Times*, Sept. 28, 1935.

"F.D.R.'s Dad Built Her Son, Says President's Mother." *New York Daily News*, Jan. 18, 1935.

Felsenthal. *Alice Roosevelt Longworth*.

"Gay Pageant Here Honors President." *New York Times*, Jan. 31, 1935.

"Gould Farm Group Honored at a Tea." *New York Times*, Feb. 14, 1935.

"Gracious Lady." *New York Herald Tribune*, Nov. 24, 1935.

"Honor Is Accepted by Mrs. Roosevelt." *Washington Star*, Apr. 8, 1935.

Hughes, Alice. "Mother of President to Talk." *New York American*, May 5, 1936.

"Hyde Park Is Host to Madame Lebrun." *New York Times*, June 7, 1935.

"Inspecting Post for President's Birthday Celebrations." *New York Times*, Jan. 18, 1935.

Kelly, Florence Finch. "Sara Roosevelt, Mother of the President." *New York Times Book Review*, Oct. 20, 1935.

"Leaders Dedicate Fairy Doll House." *New York Times*, Apr. 6, 1935.

Love, Cornelia Spencer. *Famous Women of Yesterday and Today*. Chapel Hill: University of North Carolina Library Extension Publication, Jan. 1936.

Mathews, Edith L. "Author Visiting St. Louis Tells How She Wrote Biography of Mr. Roosevelt's Mother." *St. Louis Star-Times*, Dec. 19, 1936.

"Mother's Day Proclamation." U.S. House Joint Resolution 263, 1935.

"Mother Unveils Roosevelt Canvas." *New York Times*, Mar. 27, 1935.

"Mrs. James Roosevelt Guest of Macy's for Mother's Day." *Sparks* (Macy's in-house publication), June 1935.

"Mrs. James Roosevelt to Speak." *New York Times*, Jan. 20, 1935.

"Mrs. Roosevelt at Delano Home." *New York Times*, Apr. 11, 1935.

"Mrs. Roosevelt Hostess Today." *New York Times*, Feb. 6, 1935.

"Mrs. Roosevelt to Hear Concert." *New York Times*, Aug. 8, 1935.

"Mrs. Roosevelt Views Benefit Art Exhibit." *New York Times*, Mar. 12, 1935.

Myers, Helen. "Hyde Park Playhouse." *New York Times*, Dec. 8, 1935.

National Park Service, U.S. Department of the Interior. *Eleanor Roosevelt*. Hyde Park, N.Y., 1999.

"New Painting Shows President's Mother." *New York Times*, Apr. 24, 1935.

"Niche in History Awaits Mother of the President." *Detroit Free Press*, Dec. 8, 1935.

"Plans Completed for Birthday Ball." *New York Times*, Jan. 26, 1935.

Portrait Collection 2. The New York Genealogical & Biographical Society, New York, 2001.

"President and Members of His Family at Their Church." *New York Times*, Sept. 23, 1935.

"President's Mother Aids." *New York Times*, Apr. 25, 1935.

"President's Mother Drops in on Neighbor." *New York Times*, Mar. 26, 1935.

"President's Mother, 81, Shares Birthday Party." *New York Times*, Sept. 21, 1935.

"President's Mother Guest." *New York Times*, July 11, 1935.

"President's Mother Is 81." *New York Times*, Sept. 22, 1935.

"President's Mother Plans Family Breakfast Sunday." *Atlanta Journal*, June 28, 1935.

Randolph, Nancy. "Society: Darlingtons Present a Bride and a Debbie." *New York Daily News*, Dec. 27, 1935.

"Ready-Made Home Sold in a Package." *New York Times*, Apr. 2, 1935.

"Rita Halle Kleeman Is Guest in City." *Fort Worth Press*, Mar. 21, 1936.

"Rita Halle to Speak." *New York Times*, Nov. 24, 1935.

Robinson, Grace. "F.D.R.'s Wife and Mother Receive Ovation in Rain." *New York Daily News*, Nov. 4, 1935.

Roosevelt, Eleanor. *Wisdom of Eleanor Roosevelt*.

———. *This I Remember*. New York: Harper & Brothers, 1949.

Roosevelt, Elliott. *F.D.R.: His Personal Letters, 1928–1945*.

"Roosevelt Backs Parents' Campaign." *New York Times*, Jan. 18, 1935.

"Roosevelt Family Marks Day Simply." *New York Times*, Dec. 26, 1935.

Roosevelt-Vanderbilt Historical Association. *The Grounds of Val-Kill*. Hyde Park, N.Y., 1998.

"Servants' School Reports Success." *New York Times*, Mar. 28, 1935.

"Society: All-American Ball to Fete Roosevelt." *New York Daily News*, Jan. 14, 1935.

Teichmann. *Alice*.

"The President's Mother: 'I Am the Child of My Son,'" *News-Week*, July 10, 1933.

"To Carry Roosevelt Daisies." *New York Times*, May 30, 1935.

"To Honor President's Mother." *New York Times*, Mar. 27, 1935.

"To Speak at Wellesley Club." *New York Herald Tribune*, Nov. 24, 1935.

"Typical Mother' Broadcasts Plea." *New York Times*, May 1, 1935.

"Wellesley Club Honors Opening of New Quarters." *New York Sun*, Oct. 15, 1935.

"Who Influences Roosevelt More: Wife or Mother?" *Look*, Mar. 14, 1939.

Within the Fairy Castle. Chicago: Museum of Science and Industry, 2002.

Research Collections

FDR Library

    Sara Delano Roosevelt Papers

    SDR Trips to White House

    Eleanor Roosevelt Papers

    PPF 8

    FDR Trips to Hyde Park

    Rita Halle Kleeman Papers

    Anna Roosevelt Papers

    FDR Year by Year, Pare Lorentz Chronology

Library of Congress

    Harold Ickes Diaries, Manuscript Division

    White House Scrapbooks of ER's Social Secretary, Edith Helm

Adriance Library, Poughkeepsie, New York

    Helene W. Reynolds Correspondence

Martin Luther King Jr. Memorial Library, Washington, D.C.

    Clippings and Photographs, Sara Delano Roosevelt, Washingtoniana Division

Stanford University Libraries

    Motion Picture Research Council Collections

Columbia University, Butler Library

    Oral history: Clarence Francis

    Oral history: Anna Roosevelt Halsted

CHAPTER 40: "YOU ARE MY LIFE"

"Birthday at Hyde Park." *New York Times*, Sept. 27, 1936.

Catlege, Turner. "Salvos of Cheers Greet President." *New York Times*, June 28, 1936.

"Child Gardeners Receive Awards." *New York Times*, Sept. 30, 1936.

Clark, Delbert. "Rise in the Roosevelt Vote over the 1932 Total." *New York Times*, Nov. 4, 1936.

Cook. *Eleanor Roosevelt*, vol. 2.

"Dahlia Show Thursday." *New York Times*, Sept. 6, 1936.

"Dall to Visit Hyde Park." *New York Times*, Apr. 10, 1936.

"Elated by the People's Endorsement of His Administration." *New York Times*, Nov. 5, 1936.

"500 Attend Dinner for Gen. Nolan." *New York Times*, Apr. 16, 1936.

"Flower Show Visit Delights Hoovers." *New York Times*, Mar. 21, 1936.

"French Musicians Aid School Here." *New York Times*, Feb. 17, 1936.

"Good Progress Made by Mrs. Roosevelt." *New York Times*, Sept. 20, 1936.

"Happenings." *Junior League Newsletter*, Dec. 1936.

Hurd, Charles W. "Roosevelt Finds Mother Improved." *New York Times*, May 24, 1936.

———. "Roosevelt Lands at Summer Home." *New York Times*, July 29, 1936.

————. "Roosevelt Leaves for Quebec Parley after Quoddy Visit." *New York Times*, July 31, 1936.

"Landslide." *New York Times*, Nov. 8, 1936.

"Leaders of Clubs Begin Garden Tour." *New York Times*, May 21, 1936.

"Lycee Fund to Gain by Concert Feb. 16." *New York Times*, Feb. 2, 1936.

McLaughlin, Kathleen. "Lunch for Guests Stirs First Lady." *New York Times*, Nov. 4, 1936.

————. "Visitors Greeted at Convention Tea." *New York Times*, June 22, 1936.

"Mother of President Enigmatic on Election." *New York Times*, July 9, 1935.

"Mother Visits President." *New York Times*, Mar. 12, 1936.

"Mrs. James Roosevelt Talks on Mother's Day." *New York Herald Tribune*, May 11, 1936.

"Mrs. Roosevelt, 82, Suffers Hip Injury." *New York Times*, May 21, 1936.

"Mrs. Roosevelt Happy." *New York Times*, Nov. 4, 1936.

"Mrs. Roosevelt Sr. Starts Home." *New York Times*, Sept. 18, 1936.

"Musician's Wives Luncheon Guests." *New York Times*, Dec. 16, 1936.

"Negro Drive Aided by Mrs. Roosevelt." *New York Times*, Dec. 17, 1936.

"Pageant Feature of Birthday Ball." *New York Times*, Jan. 5, 1936.

"Peach Color Favored for President's Ball." *New York Times*, Jan. 29, 1936.

"President at Hyde Park Church Today." *New York Times*, Nov. 2, 1936.

"President's Family Honor His Mother." *New York Times*, Sept. 22, 1936.

"President's Mother Aids." *New York Times*, Apr. 29, 1936.

"President's Mother Better." *New York Times*, May 22, 1936.

"President's Mother, Injured in Fall, Confined to Home." *Washington Star*, May 20, 1936.

"President's Mother on Trip." *New York Times*, Aug. 22, 1936.

"President's Mother Stops Over Here to See Elliott." *St. Louis Daily Globe-Democrat*, Apr. 30. 1936.

"President's Mother to Aid Charity Drive." *New York Times*, Apr. 28, 1936.

"President's Wife and Mother to Be Dance Patronesses Here." *New York Times*, Mar. 22, 1936.

"President's Wife at Sale for Blind." *New York Times*, Dec. 8, 1936.

Roosevelt, Alice. "The Ideal Qualifications for a President's Wife." *Ladies' Home Journal*, Feb. 1936.

"Roosevelt, Assured That Wife Is Better, Leaves Capital to Visit Mother, 82 Today." *New York Times*, Sept. 21, 1936.

"Roosevelt Ends Hyde Park Visit." *New York Times*, Feb. 25, 1936.

Roosevelt, Elliott. *F.D.R.: His Personal Letters, 1928–1945.*

————. *Rendezvous with Destiny.*

————. *Mother R.*

"Roosevelt Votes with His Family." *New York Times*, Nov. 4, 1936.

"Roosevelts & Recriminations." *Time*, May 11, 1936.

"Seal Sale Opened by Mrs. Roosevelt." *New York Times*, Nov. 27, 1936.

"Sick List: Mrs. James Roosevelt." *News-Week*, May 30, 1936.

"Tea for Tete Group." *New York Times*, June 13, 1936.

"Tea Service Brings $650." *New York Times*, June 13, 1936.

"The President and His Family Gather for Christmas." *New York Times*, Dec. 25, 1936.

"Tributes Are Paid to 'First Mother.'" *New York Times*, May 7, 1936.

"Two Roosevelt Women Try to Fill Will Rogers's Shoes." *News-Week*, Jan. 4, 1936.

"Visits Doll Exhibition." *New York Times*, Jan. 3, 1936.

"Will Attend Notification." *New York Times*, June 25, 1936.

Worden, Helen. "Mrs. James Roosevelt Gives Tea Party for Women of Press." *New York World Telegram*, Jan. 30, 1936.

Research Collections

FDR Library
    Sara Delano Roosevelt Papers
    SDR Trips to White House
    Eleanor Roosevelt Papers
    PPF 8
    FDR Trips to Hyde Park
    Rita Halle Kleeman Papers
    Anna Roosevelt Papers
    FDR Year by Year, Pare Lorentz Chronology
Library of Congress
    Harold Ickes Diaries, Manuscript Division
    White House Scrapbooks of ER's Social Secretary, Edith Helm
Adriance Library, Poughkeepsie, New York
    Helen W. Reynolds Correspondence
Martin Luther King Jr. Memorial Library, Washington, D.C.
    Clippings and Photographs, Sara Delano Roosevelt, Washingtoniana Division

Interviews

Preston W. Gifford Jr.

CHAPTER 41: "HYDE PARK AND ME"

"Aids Nurses' Campaign." *New York Times*, Jan. 30, 1937.
Angelo. *First Mothers*.
"Birthday Party Held by People's Chorus." *New York Times*, Apr. 20, 1937.
Black. *Casting Her Own Shadow*.
"Bullitt Host to Mrs. J. Roosevelt." *New York Times*, Sept. 21, 1937.
Bullitt, Orville, ed. *For the President*. Boston: Houghton Mifflin Co., 1972.
Cook. *Eleanor Roosevelt*, vol. 2.
"Cornerstone Laid for First Fair Unit." *New York Times*, Apr. 28, 1937.
"Duce Meets a Roosevelt." *New York Times*, July 13, 1937.
"Du Pont Guests Put Political Enmity Aside." *New York Herald*, July 1, 1937.
"Gay Throng Sees Roosevelts Sail." *New York Times*, July 4, 1937.
"Headliner: Sara Roosevelt, Matriarch of an American Clan." *News-Week*, July 10, 1937.
"Hit by Roosevelt Car, Wins $21,000 Verdict." *New York Times*, Dec. 21, 1937.
"Home Arts Viewed by Mrs. Roosevelt." *New York Times*, Apr. 2, 1937.
"Honors Hampton Institute Head." *New York Times*, Jan. 13, 1937.
"Housing Leaders Hail Small-Home Project." *New York Times*, July 10, 1937.
Hull, Cordell. *The Memoirs of Cordell Hull*. New York: Macmillan Co., 1948.
"Hyde Park Traveler." *New York Times*, July 17, 1937.
"Jury Gets Roosevelt Case." *New York Times*, Dec. 18, 1937.
Kleeman, Rita Halle. "7 Proud Women." *Good Housekeeping*, May 1937.
"Lebrun Host to Mrs. J. Roosevelt." *New York Times*, Sept. 16, 1937.

"Medal as Mother to Mrs. Roosevelt." *New York Times*, Apr. 23, 1937.

"Medal to Mrs. Roosevelt." *New York Daily News*, Apr. 8, 1937.

"Mother of President Visits East Side Park." *New York Times*, Mar. 23, 1937.

"Mothers Honored Over the Nation." *New York Times*, May 10, 1937.

"Mrs. James Roosevelt." *New York Times*, July 24, 1937.

"Mrs. James Roosevelt Honored." *New York Times*, Aug. 29, 1937.

"Mrs. J. Roosevelt Lucky." *New York Times*, Aug. 24, 1937.

"Mrs. Roosevelt at Genoa." *New York Times*, July 12, 1937.

"Mrs. Roosevelt Busy." *New York Times*, Dec. 24, 1937.

"Mrs. Roosevelt Lands." *New York Times*, July 11, 1937.

"Nine Fetes Here Honor Roosevelt." *New York Times*, Jan. 31, 1937.

"Notables Acclaim Miss Wald at 70." *New York Times*, Mar. 11, 1937.

"Our Distinguished Visitor." *George V Bulletin*, Oct. 1937 (hotel publication), Paris, France.

"Pageant to Honor President at Ball." *New York Times*, Jan. 24, 1937.

"Plants Coronation Trees." *New York Times*, May 4, 1937.

"President Leaves for Warm Springs." *New York Times*, Mar. 12, 1937.

"President on Picnic, His Mother in Party. *New York Times*, Oct. 17, 1937.

"President's Mother Back from Europe." *New York Times*, Oct. 6, 1937.

"President's Mother Guest." *New York Times*, Feb. 17, 1937.

"President's Mother Is Honored." *New York Times*, Sept. 21, 1937.

"President's Mother Off to Venice." *New York Times*, July 20, 1937.

"President's Mother Opens Housing Drive." *New York Times*, Feb. 19, 1937.

"President's Mother Reception Hostess." *New York Times*, Jan. 19, 1937.

"President's Mother Sails for U.S." *New York Times*, Sept. 30, 1937.

"President's Mother Sightseeing at Pompeii." *New York Times*, July 21, 1937.

"President's Mother to Entertain Today." *New York Times*, Jan. 18, 1937.

"President's Mother Loses $21,000 Suit." *Washington Star*, Dec. 20, 1937.

"President Roosevelt." *Life*, Jan. 4, 1937.

"President Upholds Debate on Religion." *New York Times*, Oct. 17, 1937.

"Reception to Honor President's Mother." *New York Times*, Feb. 14, 1937.

"Roosevelt, at Hyde Park, Rests and Swims; Visits with Mother and Meets Vestrymen." *New York Times*, May 31, 1937.

"Roosevelt-du Pont Wedding." *New York Times*, July 8, 1937.

Roosevelt, Elliott, ed. *F.D.R.: His Personal Letters, 1928–1945*.

"Roosevelt Auto Suit One." *New York Times*, Dec. 14, 1937.

"Roosevelt Goes West to Say 'Howdy' and 'Meet the Wife.'" *News-Week*, Oct. 4, 1937.

"Roosevelt Helps to Open Stockings." *New York Times*, Dec. 26, 1937.

"Roosevelt Serves as Gold Handicap." *New York Times*, Mar. 13, 1937.

"Roosevelt Talks to His Neighbors." *New York Times*, Oct. 14, 1937.

Roosevelt, James. *Affectionately, F.D.R.*

"Roosevelts & Recrimination." *Time*, May 11, 1936.

Roosevelt, Sara. *My Boy Franklin*.

"Roosevelts End Family Reunion." *New York Times*, July 3, 1937.

"Salzburg Stay Extended." *New York Times*, July 27, 1937.

"Society: President's Mother at N.Y. Birthday Ball." *New York Daily News*, Jan. 31, 1937.

Streitmatter, Rodger, ed. *Empty Without You: The Intimate Letters of Eleanor Roosevelt and Lorena Hickok.* New York: The Free Press, 1998.

"Sues President's Mother." *New York Times,* Oct. 14, 1937.

"The Met's 53d Season Gets Under Way." *New York Times,* Nov. 30, 1937.

"The President's Mother Sees Him Off to Washington." *New York Times,* June 3, 1937.

"Toscanini Directs Salzburg Opening." *New York Times,* July 25, 1937.

"2,000 Children Cheer Mother of President." *New York Daily News,* Mar. 23, 1937.

"Visits War Poster Show." *New York Times,* Mar. 17, 1937.

"Will Meet Roosevelts." *New York Times,* July 10, 1937.

Research Collections

FDR Library
    Sara Delano Roosevelt Papers
    SDR Trips to White House
    Eleanor Roosevelt Papers
    PPF 8
    FDR Trips to Hyde Park
    Rita Halle Kleeman Papers
    Anna Roosevelt Papers
    FDR Year by Year, Pare Lorentz Chronology
Library of Congress
    Harold Ickes Diaries, Manuscript Division
    White House Scrapbooks of ER's Social Secretary, Edith Helm
Adriance Library, Poughkeepsie, New York
    Helen W. Reynolds Correspondence
Martin Luther King Jr. Memorial Library, Washington, D.C.
    Clippings and Photographs, Sara Delano Roosevelt, Washingtoniana Division
Columbia University, Butler Library
    Oral history: Anna Roosevelt Halsted

Interviews

Preston W. Gifford Jr.

CHAPTER 42: "THE DOWAGER MRS. ROOSEVELT"

"Colonies to Receive 20,000 Jewish Exiles." *New York Times,* Nov. 26, 1938.

"Einstein Medal for Humanitarianism Is Awarded to Mother of the President." *New York Times,* Apr. 4, 1938.

Fleeson, Doris. "F.D.R. and Mother Write—and Get Paid." *New York Daily News,* Feb. 6, 1938.

"Logan Hits Third Term." *New York Times,* July 14, 1938.

"Mrs. J. Roosevelt Cited." *New York Times,* Mar. 21, 1938.

"Nahant in Gala Mood for Wedding; Roosevelts Join in Final Rehearsal." *New York Times,* June 18, 1938.

"President's Son Weds at Nahant." *New York Times,* June 19, 1938.

"Return to Campobello." *The New Yorker,* Apr. 21, 1945.

"Society: Back Bay Yawns as John, Anne Wed." *New York Daily News,* June 19, 1938.

"Tribute and Concert Honoring Sara Delano Roosevelt." Program, The Waldorf-Astoria, Apr. 3, 1938.

"Troubled Doubles Present Pageant." *New York Times*, Jan. 20, 1938.

Ward, Geoffrey C., ed. *Closest Companion: The Unknown Story of the Intimate Friendship between Franklin Roosevelt and Margaret Suckley*. Boston: Houghton Mifflin Co., 1995.

"Will Get Medal Today." *New York Times*, Apr. 3, 1938.

Research Collections

FDR Library
    Sara Delano Roosevelt Papers
    SDR Trips to White House
    Eleanor Roosevelt Papers
    PPF 8
    FDR Trips to Hyde Park
    Rita Halle Kleeman Papers
    Anna Roosevelt Papers
    FDR Year by Year, Pare Lorentz Chronology
Library of Congress
    Harold Ickes Diaries, Manuscript Division
    White House Scrapbooks of ER's Social Secretary
Adriance Library, Poughkeepsie, New York
    Helen W. Reynolds Correspondence
Martin Luther King Jr. Memorial Library, Washington, D.C.
    Clippings and Photographs, Sara Delano Roosevelt, Washingtoniana Division

Interviews

Preston W. Gifford Jr.

CHAPTER 43: "A WORLD OF PEACE"

"Aids China Refugee Fund." *New York Times*, May 22, 1939.

"Americans to Guard Safety, Says Hull." *New York Times*, Sept. 23, 1939.

Asbell, Bernard, ed. *Mother and Daughter: The Letters of Eleanor and Anna Roosevelt*. New York: Coward, McCann and Geoghegan, 1982.

"Assisting China Relief." *New York Times*, Oct. 23, 1939.

Belair, Felix. "Cheering New Yorkers Greet King and Queen." *New York Times*, June 11, 1939.

Bullitt. *For the President*.

"Capitol Speculates on 'Charming Dozen.'" *New York Times*, July 13, 1939.

Caroli. *Roosevelt Women*.

"Close Family Ties, Mother's Day Plea." *New York Times*, May 12, 1939.

Davis, Kenneth. *F.D.R.: Into the Story*. New York: Warner Books, 1993.

"Discussed Peril with Press." *New York Times*, Aug. 25, 1939.

"FDR Can Take It—Mother." *New York Daily News*, July 13, 1939.

"F.D.R.'s Mother Sails for Home." *New York Daily News*, Aug. 25, 1939.

Geckle. *Hacketts and the Roosevelts*.

Lash. *Love, Eleanor*.

McLaughlin, Kathleen. "King Departs for Canada: Attends Roosevelt Church and Eats Hot Dogs at Picnic." *New York Times*, June 12, 1939.

———. "Many Feminine Touches Revealed as Women Analyze Attractions." *New York Times*, May 1, 1939

O'Donnell, John, and Doris Fleeson. "F.D.R. Home Life Sampled by Royal Pair." *New York Daily News*, June 11, 1939.

———. "F.D.R. Host to Royal Couple at Hyde Park." *New York Daily News*, May 29, 1938.

———. "Royal Pair Entrain for Canada; F.D.R. Swims with King." *New York Daily News*, June 12, 1939.

"Oracle: Anna Eleanor Roosevelt." *Time*, Apr. 17, 1939.

Parks, Lillian. *My Thirty Years Backstairs at the White House*. New York: Fleet Publishing, 1961.

"President's Mother Aide." *New York Times*, June 7, 1939.

"President's Mother Sails." *New York Times*, Aug. 25, 1939.

"President's Mother Sails to Visit Her Sister in Paris." *New York Times*, July 7, 1939.

President Roosevelt's Remarks on the Dedication of the Sara Delano Roosevelt Community Center. November 24, 1939. Warm Springs, Ga.: Warm Springs Foundation.

"President's Mother Unveils Head of Her Son at the Fair." *New York Times*, Apr. 27, 1939.

"President Opens Fair as Symbol of Peace." *New York Times*, May 1, 1939.

"Queen's Hostess." *Life*, May 29, 1939.

Richards, Guy. "U.S. Lists Ship to Bring Home Citizens; Liner Back from Reich." *New York Daily News*, Sept. 1, 1939.

Roosevelt, Eleanor. "Hostess at Hyde Park." *Saturday Evening Post*, June 18, 1939.

———. *This Is My Story*.

Roosevelt, Elliott. *An Untold Story*.

"Roosevelt Party Back from Europe." *New York Times*, Sept. 1, 1939.

"Roosevelt's Reply to Landon on 3d Term Just a Smile." *New York Daily News*, Sept. 24, 1949.

"Third Term Idea Scouted by Roosevelt's Mother." *New York Times*, Sept. 22, 1939.

"Third Term Scouted by Roosevelt's Mother." *New York Daily News*, Sept. 22, 1939.

"Yule Peace Tree Is Dedicated Here." *New York Times*, Nov. 28, 1939.

Research Collections

FDR Library
    Sara Delano Roosevelt Papers
    SDR Trips to White House
    Eleanor Roosevelt Papers
    PPF 8
    FDR Trips to Hyde Park
    Rita Halle Kleeman Papers
    Anna Roosevelt Papers
    Roosevelt Children Papers
    FDR Year by Year, Pare Lorentz Chronology
Library of Congress
    Harold Ickes Diaries, Manuscript Division
    White House Scrapbooks of ER's Social Secretary
Adriance Library, Poughkeepsie, New York
    Helen W. Reynolds Correspondence
Martin Luther King Jr. Memorial Library, Washington, D.C.
    Clippings and Photographs, Sara Delano Roosevelt, Washingtoniana Division

Columbia University, Butler Library
      Oral history: Marion Dickerman
Letter of Sara Delano Roosevelt, author's collection

Interviews
Eleanor Roosevelt Seagraves

CHAPTER 44: "THE TRUTH MUST BE SHOWN"
Black. *Courage in a Dangerous World.*
Brinkley, David. *David Brinkley: A Memoir.* New York: Alfred A. Knopf, 1995.
Brock, H. I. "Hyde Park: A New Shrine." *New York Times Magazine*, Nov. 11, 1945.
Burns, James MacGregor. *Roosevelt: The Soldier of Freedom 1940–1945.* New York: Harcourt, Brace, Jovanovich, 1970.
"Christmas in the White House." *Life*, Jan. 8, 1940.
"Curb on Japan Is Asked." *New York Times*, Feb. 12, 1940.
"F.D.R. Mother Loses Her Fears." *New York Daily News*, Nov. 6, 1940.
"F.D.R.'s Mother Attends Birth Control Forum." *New York Times*, Jan. 25, 1940.
"F.D.R. Toils on Holiday." *New York Daily News*, Sept. 22, 1940.
"Film Fools Mrs. R." *New York Daily News*, Feb. 4, 1940.
Flynn, John T. *The Roosevelt Myth.* New York: Devin-Adair, 1948.
"Hadassah Tea Aids Palestine Project." *New York Times*, May 8, 1940.
Hellman, Geoffrey T. "Mrs. Roosevelt." *Life*, Feb. 5, 1940.
"Hyde Park Library Is Given to Public." *New York Times*, June 5, 1940.
"Mother Didn't Want President to Run Again." *New York Daily News*, Nov. 6, 1940.
"Mrs. Dora Forbes, Roosevelt's Aunt." *New York Times*, July 22, 1940.
"Picture of the Week." *Life*, Apr. 29, 1940.
"President's Mother Backs Anti-Nazi Film; Brands Attacks on Willkie as Disgusting." *New York Times*, Oct. 3, 1940.
Roosevelt, Eleanor. *This Is My Story.*
"Roosevelt's Mother Uncertain of 3d Term Unless Son 'Would Do Good as President.'" *New York Times*, Apr. 5, 1940.
"$3,000,000 Sought for Dutch Relief." *New York Times*, May 29, 1940.
Tully, Grace. *F.D.R., My Boss.* New York: Charles Scribner's Sons, 1949.
Ward. *First-Class Temperament.*

Research Collections
FDR Library
      Sara Delano Roosevelt Papers
      SDR Trips to White House
      Eleanor Roosevelt Papers
      PPF 8
      FDR Trips to Hyde Park
      Rita Halle Kleeman Papers
      Anna Roosevelt Papers
      Roosevelt Children Papers
      FDR Year by Year, Pare Lorentz Chronology

Library of Congress
     Harold Ickes Diaries, Manuscript Division
     White House Scrapbooks of ER's Social Secretary, Edith Helm
Adriance Library, Poughkeepsie, New York
     Helen W. Reynolds Correspondence
Martin Luther King Jr. Memorial Library, Washington, D.C.
     Clippings and Photographs, Sara Delano Roosevelt, Washingtoniana Division

Interviews
Preston W. Gifford Jr.

CHAPTER 45: BRAVE HEART

"A Challenge from the American Mother for 1941." The Golden Rule Society Program, May 1941.

Alden, John. "Sara Delano Roosevelt." *Boston Daily Globe*, Sept. 9, 1941.

"An Aristocrat: Sara Delano Roosevelt." *Charlotte* (N.C.) *News*, Sept. 8, 1941.

Angelo. *First Mothers*.

Asbell. *Mother and Daughter*.

Boettiger, Anna Roosevelt. "President's Mother Lived Up to Her Code." *Seattle Post Intelligencer*, Sept. 12, 1941.

Bressler. "From a Devoted Son" (editorial drawing). *Bergen County* (N.J.) *Record*, Sept. 9, 1941.

"British Aided by Gift." *New York Times*, May 14, 1941.

Columbia Broadcasting System. "Mrs.Sara Delano Roosevelt Died. . . . ," Sept. 7, 1941.

Davis, Kenneth. *F.D.R.: The War President 1940–1943*. New York: Warner Books, 2000.

"Dorothy Thompson Asks a New Society." *New York Times*, May 7, 1941.

Dows. *Franklin Roosevelt at Hyde Park*.

"Gets Pledge to Canada." *New York Times*, Aug. 7, 1941.

"G. Hall Roosevelt Dies in Capital; White House Rites First in 5 Years." *New York Times*, Sept. 26, 1941.

Goodwin. *No Ordinary Time*.

Haugh, Tom. "May She Rest in Peace" (editorial drawing). *Monticello Bulletin*, New York, Sept. 9, 1941.

"Highlights in Life of President's Mother." *Chicago Herald American*, Sept. 8, 1941.

"Hirohito Cables Condolences." *New York Times*, Sept. 18, 1941.

"Inaugural Crowds Demonstrate Affection for President's Mother." *Washington Star*, Jan. 21, 1941.

Lash. *Love, Eleanor*.

McKernan, Maureen. "'I Felt I Must See Her at Once.'" *New York Evening Post*, Sept. 8, 1941.

McLaughlin, Kathleen. "President Shuts Self from World." *New York Times*, Sept. 9, 1941.

————. "Sara D. Roosevelt Has Simple Burial." *New York Times*, Sept. 10, 1941.

"Misses Guard of Honor." *New York Times*, May 13, 1941.

"Mother of Chief Executive Buried." *Springfield* (Ohio) *Sun*, Sept. 10, 1941.

"Mother of President Dies at Her Home in Hyde Park." *New York Times*, Sept. 8, 1941.

"Mrs. Sara Delano Roosevelt." *Hartford Courant*, Sept. 8, 1941.

"Mrs. Sara D. Roosevelt." *Indianapolis News*, Sept. 8, 1941.

Murphy, William C. Jr. "Buried at Hyde Park in Simple Ceremony." *Philadelphia Inquirer*, Sept. 8, 1941.

"President's Mother Buried with Simple Episcopal Rites." *Washington Star*, Sept. 8, 1941.

"President Masters Grief at Mother's Graveside." *Providence Journal*, Sept. 10, 1941.

"President's Mother Is Guest." *New York Times*, Apr. 22, 1941.

"President's Mother Is Honored in Congress." *New York Times*, Sept. 9, 1941.

"Protest Filibuster on Lease-Lend Bill." *New York Times*, Mar. 6, 1941.

Roosevelt, Eleanor. *Autobiography*.

———. *This Is My Story*.

———. *You Learn by Living*.

Roosevelt, Elliott. *An Untold Story*.

———. *Mother R*.

———. *Rendezvous with Destiny*.

Roosevelt, James. *Affectionately, F.D.R.*

"Sara Delano Roosevelt." *Wall Street Journal*, Sept. 9, 1941.

"Sara Delano Roosevelt's Final Wish for Her Son." *Boston Daily Globe*, Sept. 8, 1941.

"Stamp Sale Aids British." *New York Times*, Apr. 20, 1941.

"To Aid British Children." *New York Times*, June 19, 1941.

Tully. *F.D.R., My Boss*.

Research Collections

FDR Library
> Sara Delano Roosevelt Papers
> SDR Trips to White House
> Eleanor Roosevelt Papers
> PPF 8
> FDR Trips to Hyde Park
> Rita Halle Kleeman Papers
> Anna Roosevelt Papers
> Roosevelt Children Papers
> FDR Year by Year, Pare Lorentz Chronology

Library of Congress
> Harold Ickes Diaries, Manuscript Division
> White House Scrapbooks of ER's Social Secretary, Edith Helm

Adriance Library, Poughkeepsie, New York
> Helen W. Reynolds Correspondence

Martin Luther King Jr. Memorial Library, Washington, D.C.
> Clippings and Photographs, Sara Delano Roosevelt, Washingtoniana Division

Columbia University, Butler Library
> Oral history: Marion Dickerman

Interviews

Curtis Roosevelt

Eleanor Roosevelt. Seagraves

CHAPTER 46: "EVERY PLAY HAS TO HAVE ITS HEAVY"

Asbell. *Mother and Daughter.*

"Estate of President's Mother $1,089,872: Nine-tenths Left to the Chief Executive." *New York Times*, Apr. 24, 1942.

Gurewitsch, Edna P. *Kindred Souls: The Friendship of Eleanor Roosevelt and David Gurewitsch.* New York: St. Martin's Press, 2002.

"Home of President and Mother to Be Hunter Community House." *New York Times*, June 25, 1942.

Kleeman, Rita Halle. Letters to the Editor, "On a Roosevelt Centennial." *New York Herald Tribune*, Oct. 4, 1954.

Lash, Joseph P. *A World of Love: Eleanor Roosevelt and Her Friends, 1943–1962.* New York: Doubleday and Co., 1984.

"Mrs. Sara Roosevelt Had $1,412,263 Estate." *New York Times*, Mar. 16, 1946.

"President Gets Hyde Park Home and Bulk of Mother's Estate." *New York Herald Tribune*, Sept. 11, 1941.

"President Lauds Sara Roosevelt House Project." *New York Times*, Nov. 18, 1943.

"President's Home to Be Sold." *New York Times*, Sept. 16, 1941.

Roosevelt, Eleanor. "My Day," syndicated newspaper column, September 9, 1941.

"Roosevelt Home to Be Dedicated." *New York Times*, Oct. 17, 1943.

"Sunrise at Campobello." *Look*, Apr. 1, 1956.

"Sunrise at Campobello." *Theatre Arts*, Feb. 1958.

"Unto My Beloved Son." *Time*, Sept. 22, 1941.

Ward. *A First-Class Temperament.*

West. *Upstairs at the White House.*

Research Collections

FDR Library
    Sara Delano Roosevelt Papers
    SDR Trips to White House
    Eleanor Roosevelt Papers
    PPF 8
    FDR Trips to Hyde Park
    Rita Halle Kleeman Papers
    Anna Roosevelt Papers
    Roosevelt Children Papers
    FDR Year by Year, Pare Lorentz Chronology
Library of Congress
    Harold Ickes Diaries, Manuscript Division
    White House Scrapbooks of ER's Social Secretary, Edith Helm
Adriance Library, Poughkeepsie, New York
    Helen W. Reynolds Correspondence
State Library, Albany, New York
    Franklin D. Roosevelt Collection
Martin Luther King Jr. Memorial Library, Washington, D.C.
    Clippings and Photographs, Sara Delano Roosevelt, Washingtoniana Division

Interviews

Nina Roosevelt Gibson

Curtis Roosevelt

Eleanor Roosevelt Seagraves

EPILOGUE

Black. *Courage in a Dangerous World*.

Caroli, Betty Boyd. *First Ladies*. New York: Oxford University Press, 1987.

Churchill. *The Roosevelts*.

"Eleanor Roosevelt." *The American Experience*. PBS Transcript.

Gurko, Leo. *The Angry Decade*. New York: Dodd, Mead and Company, 1947.

Hennefrund, Bill. "The Last Campobello Survivor." *Yankee*, Sept. 1982.

Lash, Joseph P. *Eleanor: The Years Alone*. New York: W. W. Norton, 1972.

Parks. *The Roosevelts*.

Roosevelt, Eleanor. *If You Ask Me*. New York: D. Appleton-Century, 1946.

————. "I Remember Hyde Park." *McCall's*, Feb. 1963.

————. "The Seven People Who Shaped My Life." *Look*, June 19, 1951.

Roosevelt, Elliott. *Mother R*.

————. *Rendezvous with Destiny*.

————. *An Untold Story*.

"Sara Roosevelt." *News-Week*, Sept. 15, 1941.

Schary, Dore. *Sunrise at Campobello*. New York: Random House, 1956.

Siena Research Institute. "Top First Ladies Poll." Siena Research Institute, Sienna College, Loudonville, New York, 1993.

"Sunrise at Campobello: The Story of Two Comebacks." *Life*, Nov. 4, 1956.

Ward. *First-Class Temperament*.

————. "Sally, Franklin & Babs."

"Who's More Influential, Wife or Mother?" *Look*, Mar. 14, 1939.

Research Collections

FDR Library

    Dore Schary Papers (*Sunrise at Campobello*)

    Sara Delano Roosevelt Papers

    Eleanor Roosevelt Papers

    PPF 8

    FDR Trips to Hyde Park

    Rita Halle Kleeman Papers

    Anna Roosevelt Papers

    O'Connor and Farber Papers

    Last Will and Testament, Sara Delano Roosevelt

    FDR Year by Year, Pare Lorentz Chronology

    Oral history: Eleanor Roosevelt Seagraves

Library of Congress

    Harold Ickes Diaries, Manuscript Division

    White House Scrapbooks of ER's Social Secretary, Edith Helm

    Dore Schary, *Sunrise at Campobello* Photographs, Photograph Division

Adriance Library, Poughkeepsie, New York
    Helen W. Reynolds Correspondence
Martin Luther King Jr. Memorial Library, Washington, D.C.
    Clippings and Photographs, Sara Delano Roosevelt, Washingtoniana Division
Columbia University, Butler Hall
    Oral history: Marion Dickerman
Hunter College Library
    Sara Delano Roosevelt House Archives
New York City Department of Records and Information Services
    Muncipal Archives, 67–69 East Sixty-fifth Street
Eleanor Roosevelt letter, author's collection

Interviews
Nina Roosevelt Gibson
Eleanor Roosevelt Seagraves

ACKNOWLEDGMENTS

Researching and writing the story of Sara Delano Roosevelt and Eleanor Roosevelt has been sheer pleasure. Historians, archivists, and family members alike were eager for me to tell the tale of these remarkable women, examine their lives, and reveal the authentic influence of Sara on Eleanor.

I would like to start with the Roosevelt family. Eleanor (Ellie) Roosevelt Seagraves is the first-born grandchild of Eleanor and Franklin Delano Roosevelt. She and her brother, Curtis, are the only grandchildren with strong memories of Sara, their great-grandmother. Ellie, who lives near me in the Washington, D.C., area, was generous with her stories of her great-grandmother and grandmother. Her interpretations of other Roosevelt biographies gave me a head start in my research and were especially helpful. Ellie has made herself available in whatever way possible. My deep gratitude goes to her.

Both Ellie and Curtis are the children of Eleanor and Franklin's only daughter, Anna. Curtis lives in France, but we met or talked when he was in the United States. (Curtis dropped his father's name, Dall, and instead uses his mother's maiden name.) He, too, shared memories of his grandmother and great-grandmother, and his perception of their interaction. Curtis's keen ability to place Sara and Eleanor within the context of their time and class was crucial to understanding these women. Curtis's efforts to assist me went beyond merely granting an interview—for example, he spoke with Diana Hopkins Halsted on my behalf. She is the daughter of Harry Hopkins, who lived at the White House and stayed at Hyde Park under Sara's watchful eye. I remain grateful to him for his kindnesses.

Nina Roosevelt Gibson, Ph.D., is the daughter of Franklin and Eleanor's youngest child, John. Because she is a psychologist, her analysis of the relationship between Sara and Eleanor—especially about their roles as daughters, wives, and mothers—was unique. I appreciate her sharing with me the many insights she has developed through the years about Eleanor and Sara. Her enthusiastic support encouraged me during some of the more exhausting workdays.

Eleanor Roosevelt II, as she is known, is the daughter of Eleanor's beloved younger brother, Hall (the only brother who lived beyond childhood). She adored her aunt Eleanor and treasured their relationship, memories of which she liberally shared with me.

I would also like to thank the Delano clan. Not all of them use the name Delano: some are de la Noyes, DeLanos, and Delanoys, along with other variations. A special thank-you goes to Muriel Curtis Cushing, a Delano descendant who wrote *Philip Delano of the "Fortune" 1621*, published by the General Society of Mayflower Descendants. Mrs. Curtis is a descendant of eighteen *Mayflower* families with sixty-two lines, and is the Delano Kindred genealogist. When information about the Delano family conflicted, Mrs. Curtis was the expert on whom I relied. My thanks also go to the Delano Kindred Society and especially to its president, George DeLano; the society has maintained the family's Riverside Cemetery in Fairhaven, Massachusetts, and has been instrumental in ensuring that the Delano family history remains available and accessible.

I am grateful for the assistance given me by Peggy Baker, historical librarian, Pilgrim Society, Plymouth, Massachusetts. She had a quick answer for every factual question about the early colonial days. For information about the coal industry in the 1800s, I relied on Kenneth C. Wolensky, historian of the Pennsylvania Historical Museum Commission.

The Franklin Delano Roosevelt Library in Hyde Park is the ultimate collection of Eleanor Roosevelt and Sara Delano Roosevelt documents. During her lifetime, Sara donated her Hyde Park land to the nation for the library and museum building, so her Delano siblings gave their family papers to the library. The Delano files contain such fascinating pieces as a sketch of a sailboat drawn by a young Sara on the back of her father's logbook of Chinese opium imports. I would like to thank Cynthia M. Koch, Ph.D., director of the library and museum, who took the time to talk with me about Sara. Thanks also go to the deputy director of the museum, Mark A. Hunt, for arranging for me to see the newly acquired portrait of Sara's mother, Catherine Lyman Delano. Raymond J. Teichman, Ph.D., is the supervisory archivist of the library and museum; he always had a friendly hello and a good thought about research ideas.

The archivists and archivist technicians of the FDR Library and Museum are unsung heroes and heroines. Robert W. Clark was thoughtful, informative, and helpful, and he kept his warm sense of humor no matter how many overworked researchers made unreasonable document requests. I would also like to thank Robert H. Parks and Karen P. Anson. I was lucky to find them on duty during the many days I spent in the archives room. Thank you to Mark A. Revovitch, the library's audio-visual specialist, who patiently helped arrange photographs for this book.

I appreciate the work of the National Park Service in preserving Hyde Park's treasures, including the Roosevelt house, Val-Kill, and the Vanderbilt house. As this book indicates, I disagree that Sara Delano Roosevelt's house should be called by the name the Park Service uses—Springwood—and hope that at some point this nomenclature might be revisited so that the house reverts to the name that Sara, Franklin, and Eleanor (and the rest of the nation) called it—simply, Hyde Park. The National Park Service interpreters, of course, make the history of the house and its inhabitants informative and interesting. As a woman and a wife, I think it was unkind of Franklin to refuse Eleanor her requested redecoration of the house after Sara's death, but as a biographer I appreciate the house's having remained frozen in time.

Diane Boyce is both a Delano descendant and a Park Ranger at the Roosevelt house. I was fortunate that she was the Delano Kindred's featured speaker at their 2003 meeting, and their guide and interpreter of the house in Hyde Park. In particular, I appreciate her insight on the Sara-Eleanor relationship and her creative work as a playwright that assists in ensuring Sara's good memory.

Special thanks go to a seasonal Park Ranger volunteer at the FDR house, Preston W. Gifford Jr. He has a unique perspective on the family, having grown up in Fairhaven a block or so from the Delano house and having retired to Poughkeepsie, a few miles from Hyde Park. In fact, Pres remembers seeing as a young boy from the vantage point of his father's shoulders FDR's last visit to the Delano house. He shared his knowledge and checked my layout of the house at Hyde Park. Pres also sent me copies of a number of things he had authored, including articles about the Delanos and Roosevelts in the in-house organ *VIP Focus* and notes on the Delano family tomb at Riverside Cemetery in Fairhaven, which he visited, lighting matches inside the crypt so as to see the gold-leaf inscriptions of names and dates. Perhaps most valuable was an interview Pres conducted for the Park Service at Riverside Cemetery with Norman Reid. Mr. Reid, who is at this writing ninety-five years old, lived at Algonac, the Delano family home on the Hudson, at the age of seven. His father, Hay Bruce Reid, was superintendent of the grounds, after having undergone seven rigorous years of training in Scotland to become a master groundskeeper. Norman Reid played with the children of Eleanor and Franklin and was treated kindly by Sara and her Delano siblings. In 1931 Frederick Adrian Delano, Sara's brother, asked Hay Reid to take over the management of Riverside Cemetery, so the Reids moved to Fairhaven.

I would also like to acknowledge the staff at the Franklin Delano House on Campobello Island, New Brunswick, Canada. Ron Beckwith of the Roosevelt Campobello International Park was particularly helpful. This Campobello site is the world's only international park, and is run cooperatively by Canada and the United States. In addition, thanks go to the Campobello Public Library and Museum, especially to librarian Gwenna Klein for her assistance.

The staff of the City of New York Parks and Recreation Department was very useful in helping me learn the history of the Sara Delano Roosevelt Park, located in Manhattan's Lower East Side. Special thanks go to historian Scott Sendrow and photo archivist Sachiko Onishi.

Hunter College, City University of New York, owns the house at 47–49 East Sixty-fifth Street, built by Sara as a dual dwelling for herself and her son and daughter-in-law. I would like to thank development officer Danielle Cylich for escorting me through the Sara Delano Roosevelt House while it was being refurbished. Thanks also go to Deborah Gardner of the president's office for helping arrange this special tour. I would like to thank Julio L. Hernandez-Delgado and his staff at the Hunter College Archives for helping me research the dozens of boxes of archival material on the Roosevelt House, as well as showing me the Roosevelt portraits that are now in storage.

Of course, Columbia University's Oral History Research Office in Butler Library was essential to my research. Thanks go to its archivists and in particular to Associate Director Jessica Widerhorn. The librarians of the Local History Room at the New York Public Library, the New-York Historical Society, and the Museum of the City of New York also provided vital assistance. I am grateful to Amy Hebert, public relations officer of the Terence Cardinal Cooke Health Care Center, for checking the presence of the Laura Franklin Delano bas-relief.

In Dutchess County, New York, thanks go to the Vassar College Library staff and to the local history librarian Terry Sparks of the Adriance Memorial Library in Poughkeepsie. I am also grateful to the James Roosevelt Memorial Library of Hyde Park, which Sara funded throughout her lifetime in memory of her husband. Amy Rajczi of St. James Episcopal Church provided material on the church where the Roosevelts worshipped, and John Seagren provided access to its graveyard, where Sara and James Roosevelt are buried, along with the infant son of Eleanor and Franklin and other family members.

I would like to thank Debbie Charpentier, archivist and facility manager of the Millicent Library in Fairhaven, which acquired many gifts of art from the Delano family. I appreciate the assistance of Christopher Richard of the Fairhaven Office of Tourism. He has certainly earned his title, "Mr. History Person." Thank you to Cynthia McNaughten, a volunteer at Fairhaven's Memorial Church, which still displays a stained-glass window in honor of the Delano family. Thanks go to the current owner of the Delano Homestead, Paul Beauchamp, for information about his house, which is now being operated as the Delano Homestead Bed and Breakfast. (It was a pleasant surprise to learn that it was less than an hour's drive to Fairhaven from Newport, Rhode Island, where I had researched my previous dual biography, *Janet and Jackie: The Story of a Mother and Her Daughter, Jacqueline Kennedy Onassis.*)

I appreciate the assistance of Marianne Hansen, special collections librarian of Bryn Mawr College Library, as I do that of Steven Mandevill-Gamble, assistant head of Special Collections, and Polly Armstrong, public service specialist of Stanford University. I would like to thank the staff of the Albert and Shirley Small Special Collections Library of the University of Virginia. I was also assisted in my research on the friendship among Sara, Eleanor, and Mary McLeod Bethune by staff of the Florida State Archives, the Amistad Research Center in New Orleans, Louisiana, and the National Archives for Black Women's History, Bethune Council House, Washington, D.C.

I would like to thank the staff at the Library of Congress in the Manuscript Division, the Fine Arts Division, the Periodical and Newspaper Division, the Photography Division, and the Main Reading Room. A number of such valuable Roosevelt manuscripts as the diaries and correspondence of Harold Ickes are held at the LOC rather than the FDR Library. I was also able to use the Theodore Roosevelt correspondence at the LOC. The playwright Dore Schary (*Sunrise at Campobello*) divided his papers; some relevant materials are available at the FDR Library, and others are at the LOC.

I would also like to thank Susan L. Malbin, Ph.D., former chief of the Washingtoniana Division, Martin Luther King Jr. Memorial Library, Washington, D.C., and her staffers Margaret Goodbody, Margaret H. Appleman, Faye Haskins, Muhammad Jaleel, Maria Perry, and Jerry McCoy for providing me with the valuable clip and photography files. I serve as president of the Friends of the Library, Washingtoniana Division, and am delighted whenever my research leads me here. I also appreciate the assistance of the Biography Division librarians.

Thanks again to Groton School in Massachusetts for providing alumni information, this time on the Roosevelt family. Special thanks to Douglas Brown, archivist, and to Peter H. Congleton, director of planned giving. I appreciate the willingness of Dean Harry R. Lewis of Harvard University to provide some clues regarding the Porcellian Club. Anne Lozier of Harvard's Law School Library provided me with important records about graduates of the law school class of 1907, which I could then compare with Columbia's Law School alumni. I am also grateful to the staff of the Schlesinger Library of Radcliffe College.

I am grateful to Allida M. Black, assistant professorial lecturer in history and director of the Eleanor Roosevelt and Human Rights Project History at George Washington University, for talking to me about Sara and giving me some leads. Thanks also to Michael Weeks, assistant editor and grants coordinator of the Eleanor Roosevelt Papers at G.W.U., for his able assistance.

I am especially indebted to the late Rita Halle Kleeman, who in 1935 wrote the first biography of Sara Delano Roosevelt. Kleeman believed that after both Sara and FDR died, Sara's memory became tarnished by those who wished to sully her memory and that firsthand recollections of that "gracious lady" evaporated over time. Decades after Sara's death, Kleeman was not able to recover Sara's authentic story; I hope that this book would have given Mrs. Kleeman some sense of satisfaction.

It has been my joy to write *Sara and Eleanor* under the guidance of a skilled and thoughtful senior editor, Hope Dellon. In our work together, Hope carefully constructed queries that enhanced this dual biography. I am so very grateful to have worked with Hope for this book and for *Janet and Jackie*. Editorial assistant Kris T. Kamikawa always went the extra mile to give me any support I needed and remained always pleasant under the stress of deadlines, both mine and those of her office. Kris's friendship is one I value. John J. Murphy, director of publicity for St. Martin's Press, knows everyone and has good ideas on everything. Thanks go to Joan Higgins for her publicity work, and to Meg Drislane, whose production staff turned this manuscript into a handsome book.

Pam Bernstein is the agent who brought this book to Hope Dellon. Pam is a wonderful woman, and I feel that she gave me my career back after what was a particularly difficult decade. Pam, to my regret, closed up shop before *Sara and Eleanor* was completed, but she put me in the capable hands of Mel Berger of William Morris Agency, who has given me only the best advice.

I would also like to thank my family: husband Andrew S. Fishel and daughters Tracy and Carrie Pottker-Fishel. They have supported me in every way possible. The excellent eye and substantive comments of my sister, Mary Helene Pottker Rosenbaum, are always invaluable to me as I write. Her husband, Professor Stanley N. Rosenbaum, carefully corrected my faulty memory of the French language so that I could accurately translate all Delano correspondence.

Other relatives and friends that deserve thanks are Olga S. Pottker, Scott Bernstein, Roni and Jay Bernstein, and Diane F. Bialick. The many friends who encouraged me throughout this project include Eleanor Baker, Doreen Conrad, Judith D. Pomeranz, Catherine O'Donnell, Susan Schmidt, M Kathleen McCulloch, Steven Brady, Chris Klepac, Dave Cutler, Kristina Arriaga de Bucholz, Randy Bekerman, Cynthia Vartan, Rhoda Hyde, Aremita and Rudy Watson, Meir Wolf, Pamela L. Weller, Ari Brooks, Esther Simmonds, Mary Kay Ricks, Barbara K. Rew, Mary Ann Elliott, David Hochberg, Fiona Houston, C. David Heymann, Carol Haddad, Pam and Ron Kessler, Diane Leatherman, Deborah Hudson, Judith Deshotels, Jo Ann Schram, Moira Sullivan and Lance Kuehne, Edna Szymanski, Robin Roland and Gene Meiger, Rodger Murphey, Marilyn J. McDermett, Cheryle Rosen, Rosemary Reed, Bob Speziale and Jack Weiser, Roger Simmons, Van Seagraves, Janet Saihar, Kajsa Seals, Alysa and John Simms, Rikke Andersen, Mark Woodland and David Blum.

I am indebted to each one of you.

INDEX